LIFE AND TIMES

OF

GIROLAMO SAVONAROLA.

SAVONAROLA.

(*From a Painting by Frà Bartolommeo.*)

𝕷𝖎𝖋𝖊 𝖆𝖓𝖉 𝕿𝖎𝖒𝖊𝖘

OF

𝕲𝖎𝖗𝖔𝖑𝖆𝖒𝖔 𝕾𝖆𝖛𝖔𝖓𝖆𝖗𝖔𝖑𝖆

BY

PROFESSOR PASQUALE VILLARI

TRANSLATED BY

LINDA VILLARI

WITH

PORTRAITS AND ILLUSTRATIONS.

VOLUME I.

HASKELL HOUSE PUBLISHERS LTD.
Publishers of Scarce Scholarly Books
NEW YORK, N. Y. 10012
1969

First Published 1888

HASKELL HOUSE PUBLISHERS LTD.
Publishers of Scarce Scholarly Books
280 LAFAYETTE STREET
NEW YORK, N. Y. 10012

Library of Congress Catalog Card Number: 68-25276

Standard Book Number 8383-0174-6

Printed in the United States of America

To the

RIGHT HON. WILLIAM EWART GLADSTONE,

CHAMPION OF ITALIAN FREEDOM,

MASTER OF ITALIAN LEARNING,

AUTHOR AND TRANSLATOR

Dedicate this Book

IN TOKEN OF FRIENDSHIP AND RESPECT.

Florence, 1888.

CONTENTS.

BOOK I.

LIST OF ILLUSTRATIONS.

TRANSLATOR'S FOREWORD.

HILE translating this "Life of Frà Girolamo Savonarola" as faithfully as possible, the author has sanctioned occasional liberties with the text and arrangement of sentences, in order to meet the requirements of English historical prose. Other slight variations have been introduced as the fruit of fresh researches undertaken by the author ; while the publication of new documents in the second edition of Signor Gherardi's "Nuovi Documenti e Studi intorno a G. Savonarola" (Florence, 1888) has enabled me to give some additional notes. Several notes unlikely to interest the general reader have been abridged under the author's direction. The documents given in Appendix to the original work are purposely excluded, since all students capable of reading old Italian must, necessarily, be too well versed in modern Tuscan to consult the book in its English dress.

The well-known translation by the late Mr. Leonard Horner of the first edition of "Savonarola and his Times" has been long out of print, and the present edition being so greatly altered and enlarged as to form almost a new work, an entirely fresh version was found to be required.

LINDA VILLARI.

FLORENCE, *September*, 1888.

PREFACE TO THE NEW EDITION.

MANY reprints of this work have appeared since its first publication more than twenty-five years ago. During this period much fresh light has been thrown on the history of the Italian Renaissance, and many of my own ideas concerning it have been changed. Were I now studying Savonarola's life for the first time, my work would be undoubtedly different in kind, although my views as to the Friar's character and historic value have remained substantially unchanged. But I have no intention of offering the reader a new book; I merely reproduce an old one, and while adding necessary corrections and supplements have preserved its original form and physiognomy.

During this long interval I have naturally detected errors which demanded revision. Also, many fresh documents have been discovered and made known to the world. The late Count Carlo Capponi, a devoted and reverent admirer of Savonarola's memory, continued to publish the results of his protracted

research.   The Archivio Storico Italiano, and other
societies in Florence, Ferrara, Modena, and elsewhere, have likewise brought out many new documents.   It is needless to enumerate them here, as
they are all quoted in the notes, and my valued
pupil, Professor A. Cosci, has given a most minute
and accurate account of them.[1]   I will only mention
two publications of very special importance, namely:
" The Despatches of the Modenese Ambassador in
Florence," comprising new letters of Savonarola and
his friend Duke Ercole I., collected at Modena by
Signor A. Cappelli in 1869,[2] and furnished with a
learned introduction; and the noteworthy collection
of " Nuovi Documenti," published in 1876, at the
request of Father Ceslao Bayonne, of the Dominican
Friars, by Cavaliere A. Gherardi of the Florence
Archives.   In both these works the value of the
documents is enhanced by their editors' critical skill
and unerring judgment.[3]   And, although, as Professor
Cosci has justly remarked, these new documents
make no essential change in our previous conception of Savonarola's life and character, they furnish
fresh details requiring consideration, and modify
others which were hitherto imperfectly understood.

[1] "Archivio Storico Italiano," series iv. vol. iv. 1879.

[2] " Frà Girolamo Savonarola e notizie intorno il suo tempo," by A.
Cappelli, Modena, 1869.   This work is extracted from vol. iv. of the
"Atti e Memorie della R. Deputazione di Storia Patria per le pro-
vincie Modenesi e Parmensi."

[3] "Nuovi Documenti e Studi intorno a Girolamo Savonarola."
Florence : Carnesecchi, 1876.

Meanwhile I too had collected a considerable stock of fresh documents and of Savonarola's inedited writings. I had caused an exact copy to be made of his marginal notes in the Bible in the Florence National Library, and on the sheets he had added to it, and these were found to comprise several unpublished tractates and sermons. A precious autograph codex, now in the Museum of St. Mark in Florence, supplied me with several summaries of other unknown discourses, throwing much light on Savonarola's first years in Florence, during the reign of Lorenzo the Magnificent. Numerous unpublished ambassadorial despatches add to our knowledge of the iniquitous plots organized against him in various quarters. In a similar way much was gleaned from other unpublished documents and compositions of Savonarola which will be quoted in due course.

But during this quarter of a century few works have appeared on Savonarola of any real historic merit. The most celebrated of these has been a novel, George Eliot's "Romola"; but although admirable as a work of art, it has contributed no new facts to history, since, as was only natural, its illustrious author accepted established conclusions without dispute.

A biography of Savonarola, by Mr. W. R. Clarke, published some years ago, is, as the author allows, a mere compilation.[1] Father Bayonne, on the con-

[1] Rev. William R. Clarke, "Savonarola and his Life and Times." London: S.P.C.K., 1878.

trary, undertook a new biography, based on long
preliminary studies. He collected, translated, and
edited three volumes of Savonarola's religious works.[1]
But, with the fixed idea of writing the life of a
saint and prophet, he accorded so much time and
attention to the miracles and prophecies, that his
" Studio su G. Savonarola " is of scanty historic
value. He even failed to extract any real profit from
the "Nuovi Documenti," [2] and died without writing
the complete biography on which his thoughts had
so long been engaged.

The biographical essay, published in 1877, by
the illustrious Professor Ranke of Berlin, calls for a
very different verdict. The writer's keenly critical
spirit was swift to grasp and define the historic,
moral and religious importance of Savonarola. His
terse, clear and rapid narrative is based on previous
works, published documents, and some of the old
chronicles, and cannot be said to comprise any element of novelty, save that naturally imparted to it
by the noble intellect of its writer. It is an historical essay, rather than a biography, for not one of
Savonarola's works is passed in review.[3]   Yet, after

[1] " Oeuvres Spirituelles Choisies de Jèrôme Savonarola, Collation-
nées et Traduites," par le Rev. P. Emmanuel.   Ceslao Bayonne du
même ordre.   3 vols.   Paris: Librarie Poussièlgue Frères, 1879.
[2] " Étude sur Jèrôme Savonarola d'après de nouveaux documents,"
par le Rev. P. Emmanuel. Ceslao Bayonne, Paris: Librarie Poussièlgue
Frères, 1879.
[3] L. von Ranke, "Savonarola und die Florentinische Republik
gegen Ende des fünfzehnten Jahrhunderts," in the volume of " His-
torisch-Biogratische Studien," pp. 181–357.   Leipzig : Duncker und
Humblot, 1877.

the fashion of all great men, Professor Ranke contrived, even within these brief limits, to moot a new
point, and one of high importance to any biographer
of Savonarola. Having treated the question in
detail elsewhere,[1] it is only requisite to briefly allude
to it here.

Long ago, it was suggested by an Italian writer
that the two ancient biographies attributed to Burlamacchi and Pico were both forgeries. No one
echoed the doubt at the time, but Professor Ranke
has given it serious attention. In his opinion the
biography undoubtedly written by Giovan Francesco
Pico was composed in 1530, the date of the preface,
and during the siege of Florence, of which mention
is made in chapter xxiv. At that period, he
remarks, the Piagnoni were again ascendant in
Florence, had revived the memory of Savonarola,
and certain heated imaginations had invented new
legends about him. These Pico had collected,
and accordingly his book, written so long after
Savonarola's time, and in the midst of popular enthusiasm, can have no genuine historic value. On the
other hand, the biography attributed to Burlamacchi
cannot possibly have proceeded from his pen. Burlamacchi died in 1519, and his chronicle not only
records posterior events, but makes two allusions to
the year 1566.[2] Hence Professor Ranke holds it
to be a compilation of Pico's work, which is not

---

[1] " Rivista Storica Italiana," Fasc. i. Turin : Fratelli Bocca, 1884.
[2] *Vide* pp. 165 and 209 in the Lucca edition of 1764.

only quoted in it, but from which certain passages are literally translated. Thus the two chief sources of the life-history of Savonarola are reduced to one that has neither a critical nor historical basis. The illustrious German accordingly relied almost exclusively upon printed documents and the old chronicles, giving great and, perhaps, undue importance to the unpublished records of Cerretani and Parenti, and turning to account certain fragments from those writers which he had copied in his youth. But although this course was allowable in an historical essay, it would have been highly detrimental to a work on a larger scale. How could he have written a Life without referring to the works of previous biographers? Nor would the well-known chronicles of Cerretani and Parenti have sufficed to fill the gap. Their numerous details concerning Savonarola are merely scattered through a vaster narrative, and are not altogether impartial. Neither are they more valuable, historically, than many of our printed chronicles. We made frequent reference to them in the first edition of this work; but, treating of times when political passions were fierce, and party spirit ran high, we could only arrive at the truth by constantly collating them with other authorities. In any case, exclusive reliance on the chroniclers and printed documents would deprive us of numerous particulars and anecdotes, serving to give colour and vitality to the person and character of Savonarola, his kindred, companions, and friends. A dry and unattractive string of facts would be all that we could achieve. Consequently the question raised by Professor Ranke was of capital importance to every biographer of the Friar.

We hold that had Ranke written his work in Florence, with the numerous MSS. of the period before his eyes, he would have arrived at a very different conclusion concerning the two biographers, and would have been less prompt to reject them. Pico states in his proem that having been Savonarola's friend for six years, it was immediately after the Friar's martyrdom that he resolved to write his life ; and Pico's letters prove that the task was certainly completed in 1520. He afterwards corrected, improved, and amplified it, and consequently delayed its publication to 1530, as he mentions in the proem, *ad hoc usque tempus distuli editionem.*[1]

The Italian biography conventionally attributed to Frà Pacifico Burlamacchi was certainly written by another, for although he died in 1519, posterior dates and events are recorded in the work. First published in 1761 in Baluzio's "Addizioni alla Miscellanea," it was transcribed from a codex incorrectly copied from another of older date. In fact many older and more trustworthy codices are to be found in the Florence libraries. Nearly all these are of the sixteenth century, and mostly anonymous, excepting where Burlamacchi's name has been added by a later hand. This name first

[1] *Vide* our before quoted essay in the " Rivista Storica Italiana."

appears, no one knows why, towards the close of
that century.[1] Both the older codices, as well as
the later, which are still more numerous, show
many points of difference, and are essentially diver-
gent as regards the prophecies and miracles, which
were increased and modified by devout copyists,
according to existing traditions in St. Mark's and
other convents of the Order. But the biographical
narrative remains substantially the same, with certain
slight variations in form and arrangement.

All these different patchworks of the so-called
Burlamacchi are derived, and more or less freely
translated, from a Latin biography, in the collection
of MSS. from suppressed convents, in the National
Library of Florence.[2] The calligraphy of this
MS. is of the first half of the sixteenth century;
its numerous alterations and corrections make us
believe it an autograph; while the frequent repetitions and a greater disorder than in other compilations serve to prove that this biography is the
original source from which later writers derived or
rather translated their materials. It is anonymous,

[1] In the Casanatense Library in Rome we recently found a seven-
teenth century codex attributing this biography to P. Frà Vincenzo
di Bernardo dell' Ordine de' Predicatori, who in the " Annali di San
Marco" (a. c. 174) is mentioned as the Superior of the Convent in
1566. At c. 125 there is his signature dated 1569. A later hand
than that of the copyist of the biography attributes it, as usual, to
Burlamacchi, with the remark that it is already printed; another
hand adds, " Revised by P. Maestro Frà Timoteo Bottonio," and this
was also inscribed on the printed version.

[2] It is marked I. vii. 28. We referred to it in our first edition,
and refer to it still more frequently in the present one.

but the author was certainly a brother of St.
Mark's, a contemporary of Savonarola, and his
faithful follower. This we know by his own words,
and he also tells us that in 1524 he continued
writing his book, and that he only narrates facts
which he had witnessed himself, or learnt from
other trustworthy eyewitnesses. He had made use
of Placido Cinozzi's biographical epistle, Pico's
biography, which he styles admirable, and other
works. Of his great diligence we have a striking
proof in the fact that he continually refers his
readers to a volume now in the Riccardian Library
(cod. 2053), written in the same hand, and which,
together with the works of Cinozzi and Pico,
contains a most precious series of authentic documents. This Latin Life, or Biography, as we will
call it to distinguish it from the others, is therefore
not only the real source of the so-called Burlamacchi, but the work of an eyewitness, founded
on the writings of other contemporaries, and upon
important documents collected by the author and
copied in his own hand. Also, while praising
and often referring to Pico's biography, he is by
no means content to give an imitation, reproduction,
or summary of it. His own is a work of greater
extent, contains many more facts, and has an
independent historical value. Indeed it is not
improbable that Pico himself may have referred to
this Latin Biography, for the corrections and
additions he mentions in his proem. Certainly

the manuscript copy of the first compilation of his
work, in the Riccardi Codex, 2053, contains few
of the facts posterior to 1520, which are comprised
in the Latin Biography, and were added to its
printed version of 1530.

All this plainly proves that the two old biographies cannot be reduced, as Professor Ranke
thought, to one alone, since, in spite of the connection between them, each has an independent
and indisputable historic value of its own. As to
Burlamacchi, or the Latin Biography on which his
work is founded, we can assure the reader that we
have documentary proof of its historical accuracy.
We shall therefore continue to quote from it under
the conventional title (which in default of a better is
even accepted by Professor Ranke), always, however,
verifying it by the original Latin and by Pico,
whose authority has been less often disputed.

Besides, it may be clearly seen from what we have
said that even were Pico and Burlamacchi put aside,
it would be quite possible to dispense with their aid.
Nearly all the facts they narrate might be gleaned,
not only from other documents, chronicles, and the
works of Savonarola, but from the contemporary
writings, chiefly in manuscript, of Frà Benedetto,
Lorenzo Violi, Domenico, and Girolamo Benivieni,
and Placido Cinozzi, whose " Epistola," frequently
quoted by us, is perhaps the oldest source of the
various biographies.   It was impossible for Professor
Ranke to know this in Berlin, where he could not

consult the numerous codices contained in the Florentine libraries, and thus ascertain on how solid a basis
the two ancient biographies are grounded.

It is natural that the doubts of the modern reader
should be aroused by the strange prophecies and
miracles so minutely described by Pico and Burlamacchi, in which we can have no belief. But at
that time every follower of Savonarola spoke of and
believed in these things, and chroniclers as well as
biographers deemed them deserving of record. It
would be a mistake, however, to accept this as a
reason for doubting all that contemporary writers
relate of the Friar of St. Mark's. We have not to
deal here with the myths and legends of a primitive and uncultured society incapable of analysis,
criticism, or historical accuracy. On the contrary,
these Savonarola-legends were the natural outcome
of an age often lapsing into the ultra-credulity
consequent upon exaggerated scepticism. Without
miracles there could be no belief in the supernatural;
accordingly miracles were imagined. Thus, men
who jeered at all things, denied all things, ended by
having the blindest faith in the occult sciences, in
prodigies, prophecies, and spirits of the air. And
even such men as Guicciardini and Machiavelli
shared the latter belief. This is one of the problems
that the historian of Savonarola must specially keep
in view and specially try to solve. By examining it
we may learn not only the explanation of the catastrophe that led him to the scaffold, but the nascent

germ of the malady still afflicting our countrymen, and by which they are incapacitated from giving due importance to religious questions whether in abstract studies or in the realities of life.

This conviction first stirred us, more than twenty-five years ago, to write Savonarola's life; this conviction gave us strength and patience to re-explore original sources, seek out fresh authorities, and revise and correct our first work with unwearying care. We now re-publish the book, holding the same opinions with which we originally began it, and confirmed in our previous judgment on the Friar of St. Mark's and his executioners. The protests of those who would reduce the Italian Renaissance to a mere revival of Paganism leave us totally unmoved. From their point of view Christianity would have then almost disappeared, whereas, on the contrary, it gained new force with Luther's Reformation and the counter-reformation of the Roman Church. In our opinion Savonarola's historic grandeur consists in his having dared to believe amid general doubt, in having upheld, against the scandals of the Borgia and the sceptical cynicism of the philosophers, the forgotten and derided rights of Christianity, liberty, and reason. He devoted his energies to the moral renovation of mankind, when others thought solely of man's intellectual renovation; he held virtue to be the assured basis of religion, and the source of true liberty, when all seemed convinced that political and Christian virtue,

patriotism, and religion were unavoidably and irre-
concilably opposed. It was this that won him the
admiration of the very scholars whose excesses he
so sternly combated, for although apparently satisfied
with Paganism, these men felt that it left a painful
void in their souls. For the same reason he was
admired by many cold and keen-witted politicians,
who, while recognizing the fact that there was no
room for conscience as States were then guided,
admitted that this fact bewildered their judgment,
and seriously disturbed their minds. Thus, in attacking philosophers and statesmen, the Friar of St.
Mark's seemed to reveal to both their most secret
thoughts, and to restore their lost peace. Hence
the great admiration and devotion felt for him by
many.

Only those without any intimate knowledge of
Savonarola can regard him as one who desired to revive
the Middle Ages, and again sacrifice earth to heaven,
the world to the Church. To all familiar with his
life and writings, he appears, on the contrary, in his
true light, as a soul yearning for the Christian ideal
he proclaimed to his contemporaries; *i.e.*, that
without virtue, self-sacrifice, and moral grandeur,
both mankind and society must fall to ruin. Surrounded by scholars, philosophers, poets, and artists,
who were among the most ardent of his followers,
he was no enemy to the Italian Renaissance, but he
saw and felt the inherent defects which were leading to its decay. With the eloquence and ardour

of inspiration he proclaimed this from the pulpit, and was a true precursor and prophet of the future. To his faith in virtue—virtue sanctified by religion— and sanctifying freedom, he dedicated his whole life and died in its cause. Superstitions, blunders, hallucinations, and weaknesses notwithstanding, he therefore stands out from the Italian Renaissance, of which he is an essential part, in heroic proportions and irradiated with the halo of martyrdom. And so long as men have faith in virtue, so long will their admiration for him endure.

PREFACE TO THE FIRST EDITION.

URING the lifetime of Frà Girolamo Savonarola all Europe rang with his fame, and for more than two centuries afterwards he engaged the attention of our greatest writers. But in the eighteenth century his name was either completely forgotten, or mentioned with quasi-contempt. Such was the common fate, in that age, of all religious men, all religious works. Bayle, in his dictionary, merely expressed the general opinion in making the poor Friar the butt of keen, biting sarcasm, and designating him as a base and ridiculous impostor who had well merited the martyrdom inflicted on him.

In 1782 an anonymous life of Savonarola appeared,[1] written in Italian, and falsely dated from Geneva. It was the work of a Florentine, one Modesto Rastrelli, an historian of some note in his day. He shared Bayle's ideas in the main, but repeated in wrathful earnest all that the former had said in jest. The venomous sneers of Bayle were penned with the coldness of a sceptic, those of Rastrelli with exaggerated fury and zeal. This too evident animus robbed the book of its merit, for otherwise it gave proof of careful research, and possessed a certain incorrect and lawless charm often to be noted in our last century writers.

[1] "Vita del Padre Girolamo Savonarola." Geneva, 1781.

A year after the publication of this work a new
" Storia di P. G. Savonarola " [1] appeared at Leghorn, also
without the author's name. It was written by the Dominican, Vincenzo Barsanti, who, in answer to the other
anonymous biographer, warmly defended his brother in
the faith. Barsanti stood alone, in that century, as an admirer of Savonarola's sermons ; he had studied the old
biographies, and the precious manuscripts, afterwards
long believed to have perished, of Lorenzo Violi's
" Giornate," and amassed much minute information on
a subject that, however disregarded by his contemporaries, was very dear to his heart. Uninfluenced by
the current of the age, he adopted the tone of more
primitive times, and seemed destined to rank with the
ancient biographers. For the spirit of the old chroniclers
is revived in his work : it is stamped by the same devotion, the same errors, the same fanaticism, although
devoid of the ingenuous originality which in their pages
so vividly reproduces the colour of the times. Besides,
Barsanti is so lavish of quotation, so minute in confuting
all Rastrelli's assertions, that his book is difficult to read,
and unlikely to tempt any one to closer knowledge of
Savonarola. In fact, for fifty years after its appearance
none followed up the theme, and the name of the Friar
of St. Mark's seemed completely forgotten.

The nineteenth century inaugurated a very different
order of ideas, and gave a new direction to historical
studies. The Middle Ages, so despised in Voltaire's day,
were again raised to honour ; the examination of religious
questions was no longer deemed beneath the notice of
serious minds, and it was now possible to praise a monk
without exciting universal scorn. Germany turned to
these new researches with an almost feverish zeal, and

---

[1] " Della Storia del Padre Girolamo Savonarola : libri quattro, dedicati
e S. A. Pietro Leopoldo." Leghorn, 1782.

that country has the honour of being the first to call the real attention of the literary world to the character and doctrines of Savonarola.

In 1835 Rudelbach brought out a biography [1] in which, without dwelling much on Savonarola's character, without giving new facts, or fresh explanations of those already known, he chiefly sought to analyze and determine the value of his hero's doctrines. He was certainly the first to deduce a system of theology from Savonarola's works, the first who had the courage to assure modern Europe that those works, upon which such violent abuse had been poured, deserved the attention of the learned, and were the product of a lofty, speculative intellect. He declared his views with the genuine enthusiasm of a discoverer of new truths, and his book met with great success in Germany. This perhaps was less owing to its intrinsic merit than to the author's purpose, inasmuch as he accepted Savonarola as a precursor of the Reformation. Luther himself had canonized the Friar as a Protestant martyr, but in the eighteenth century this verdict had been entirely forgotten. Now, however, it was again revived by the efforts of Rudelbach, supported and fortified by his thorough examination of all Savonarola's works. Hence the great applause accorded to his book in Germany and England, and the steadfast sympathy subsequently evinced by writers of those countries for the Friar of St. Mark's.

Nevertheless, on impartial review, many grave errors are to be detected in Rudelbach's work. As a life history of the man it tells us nothing new, and as an examination of his doctrines it is very imperfect. With much wrest-

---

[1] "Hieronymus Savonarola und seine Zeit. Aus den quellen dargestellt," von A. G. Rudelbach. Hamburgh, 1835. The reader will find several of these quotations repeated in the notes, but it seemed indispensable to collect here all necessary information on the biographers.

ling and labour the author stretches these doctrines on a
Procrustean couch, changing and distorting them in such
wise that we should often be tempted to doubt his good
faith did we not know to what extent a man may be blinded
by party spirit ; and he leaves unmentioned such of the
writings as are too plainly opposed to his ideas. An instance of this may be seen in his minute exposition of the
" Triumph of the Cross." This work was actually reprinted by the press of the Propaganda Fide, and its
first three books treat of those articles of the Christian
faith on which Protestants and Catholics are almost
agreed. These Rudelbach carefully expounds, for the
sole purpose of discovering in them some hidden Protestant meaning. But on reaching the fourth book, where
Savonarola speaks of the Sacraments in a manner that puts
his Catholicism beyond doubt, his German biographer
abandons all attempt at analysis and hastens to quit the
subject. And he recurs to this method again and again.

The analysis of " Savonarola's prophetic character," as
the author calls it, should have been by rights the best
part of this biography. It was a new and important
theme, for no one had really studied it before. Nevertheless, instead of carefully collecting all facts, and impartially
determining their value, Rudelbach set to work to explain
theories solely evolved from his own imagination. First
of all he defines what we are to understand by *evangelical
prophecy*, and then marshals before us in an unbroken line
all the prophets of the Reformation, inclusive of the Abbot
Joachim, St. Bridget, and Savonarola. Plainly this is
neither history nor criticism, but a mere flight of fancy in
search of support to a foregone conclusion.

In 1836 a second German biography appeared in Berlin,[1]
from the pen of Karl Meier, who has chiefly studied the

---

[1] " Girolamo Savonarola, aus grossen Theils handschriftlichen Quellen
dargestellt," von Karl Meier. Berlin, 1836.

part of the subject most neglected by Rudelbach— namely,
—the life and character of Girolamo Savonarola. By long
and persevering researches in the libraries and archives of
Florence and Venice he had gleaned a precious harvest of
documents, and armed with these returned to Germany to
write his book. Nearly every codex declared by later
writers to have been unearthed by themselves, nearly all
the documents afterwards published as *new*, had been
already discovered by Meier, and either quoted or reproduced in his pages.[1] But, incredible as it may seem,
the author was incapable of turning his materials to
account. His work shows the strangest mixture of marvellous patience and industry with unpardonable negligence and inexactitude. He sometimes deplores the loss
of certain documents, which are actually contained in the
very codices discovered and frequently quoted by him. In
collating the documents he has published we often meet
with errors and gaps such as would be unpardonable in the
most negligent of writers, and are inexplicable in one who,
at other times, is really careful and scrupulous. Meier
writes the biography of an illustrious man, and enriches it
with many new and most interesting particulars ; but, without ceaseless reference to the notes, the reader would never
perceive that the book was the fruit of original research.
Throughout the work Savonarola remains a lifeless puppet,
or rather an empty abstraction ; the new details of his life
neither diminish nor add to the vague and confused conception of him afforded us by previous biographers.
Meier's book is a clear and eloquent proof of the worth-
lessness of the most precious documents in the hands of
one who is unable to deal with them.

Almost the same verdict must be passed on the portion
of the work devoted to Savonarola's doctrines. It is true

---

[1] Proofs of this will be adduced in the course of this book and in the
Appendix to the Italian edition.

that Meier tries to modify the exaggerated conclusions of Rudelbach, and fails to find in the writings so complete and absolute a system of Protestant theology ; nevertheless he strives to include him, at all costs, among the martyrs of the Reformation.   Nor are his arguments to this effect very different from those of Rudelbach.   The latter had, at least, the excuse of being led astray by the force of his unbridled imagination, whereas Meier, who is all moderation, and picks his way with timid steps, is altogether inexcusable.   What, too, can be said, when we find him pausing to remark that Savonarola hardly ever mentioned Purgatory, and that his enemies accused him of seldom alluding to the Virgin Mary ?   Meier would deduce from this that the Friar already shadowed forth the ideas of the Reformation, but apparently lacks courage to rely on such feeble arguments, since he is frequently obliged to record sermons full of almost superstitious utterances concerning the Virgin, and others in which the faithful are openly exhorted to pray for the dead.

Another serious blunder is to be noted in Meier's work. While moving cautiously forward, and minutely explaining such of the Friar's doctrines as are merely copied from St. Thomas and the scholiasts, he fails to observe all that is special to Savonarola, and serving to prove the originality of his mind.   He pauses now and then to dwell on passages which seem to him to contain germs of the Reformation, but appears so slenderly convinced by his own words that he naturally fails to convince his readers.   And when he treats of the prophecies it is very difficult to ascertain his meaning.   He is disposed to condemn Rudelbach's verdict, to demonstrate that, if Savonarola were no prophet, neither did he believe himself to be one, nor desire to be esteemed as such by others.   But then again he shrinks from roundly pronouncing a judgment that is so manifestly contradicted by facts, and, as usual, halts half-way, in a state of puzzled uncertainty.

On comparing the two German biographies with each other, we are bound to conclude that Rudelbach's fantastic dissertation, in spite of its numerous errors, gives a truer idea of what may be called Savonarola's uncouth originality than that to be gained from the researches, documents, and pretended accuracy of Karl Meier's work. Rudelbach's mistakes were too lightly condoned, the merits of Meier too unjustly forgotten; but in either case the public verdict was really more just than it seemed at first sight.

These German works, and more especially the weight of Luther's authority, served to diffuse the notion that Savonarola was really a precursor of the Reformation ; hence increased sympathy was aroused for him in England and Germany, and the attention of Europe directed, with a somewhat anxious curiosity, to the history of his life. It was then that an eloquent voice was heard from the Convent of St. Mark's, claiming Savonarola as the champion of Catholicism and liberty. Father Vincenzo Marchese, of the Preaching Order, was already known in Italy by his " Storia dei Pittori Domenicani." An elegant writer, a sincere Catholic, and an ardent lover of truth and liberty, his residence in St. Mark's had fired him with a passionate admiration for Savonarola. With a respect and reverence almost amounting to worship, he collected every memorial of the Friar to be found in the convent, ransacked the Florentine libraries and archives, and on several occasions produced the results of his studies in the pages of the " Archivio Storico Italiano " in the shape of unpublished letters of Savonarola or writings illustrative of his life. And although these documents were not always of much intrinsic worth, the care and acumen with which they were edited and brought to bear upon history gave them a certain importance. The author's name, and the nature of his subject, won them a kind reception, and at last Padre Marchese, encouraged by the public favour, published his " Storia del Convento di San Marco." [1] The principal and most noteworthy part of the work was almost a complete biography of Savonarola. The author represented him as a reformer of morals, politics, and religion ; described his life and manners, and commented on his writings and discourses. By dwelling upon a part of the Friar's history that had been hitherto neglected, he made us understand the intensity of Savonarola's love of liberty, and how this had first led to his persecution, and then to his death. Admiration for this martyred brother of his Order wrought Padre Marchese to genuine eloquence, and endued his book with a vivid force and reality which are totally wanting in the German biographies. It met with deserved success, and the public mind in Italy was roused to an ardent and enthusiastic interest in the republican Friar who had so daringly defied the Borgia and the Medici, had sought to strengthen the old bond between liberty and religion by re-establishing both on their true basis, and who had suffered martyrdom for his country and his God.

But Padre Marchese's work, although admirably fitted to arouse public curiosity, could not entirely satisfy it. His researches were too partial and fragmentary to enable him to write a complete biography. Only acquainted with a portion of the Friar's works and sermons, he could contribute an eloquent chapter to the history of his convent, but no finished study of Savonarola. This, indeed, was forbidden by the nature of his work. Besides, he was too great an admirer of the hero, whom he venerated almost as a saint, to be his truly impartial historian. Consequently fresh studies and researches were needed for the task.

---

[1] First published in the " San Marco Illustrato " (Prato, Passigli, 1850–53). and afterwards in the " Scritti Varii " of Padre Vincenzo Marchese. Florence : Le Monnier, 1855.

But in 1853 a biography of Savonarola appeared in France.[1] Its author, M. Perrens, had made accurate researches in Florence ; he had procured in Piedmont, from the learned Abbé Bernardi, copies of many documents contained in the Marcian Library of Venice, several of which, although made known to Germany by Meier's work, were quite ignored in Italy and France. Enriched by these precious materials, his book, although here and there bearing too evident marks of haste, was nevertheless the most complete work that had appeared on Savonarola, and obtained great and deserved success.

The first volume, giving a narrative of facts, is delightful reading. The author has little eloquence, but he was the first to give us a clear, well-ordered, and ample account of all the events of Savonarola's life. The stirring, tumultuous drama of this life has a certain fascination and eloquence of its own which keep the reader's attention on the alert, and compensate for the author's defects. But unfortunately there is a radical fault in the book. Mons. Perrens has no clear grasp of his theme, no definite view of the personage he tries to describe, and this serves to keep the reader's mind in a very painful state of uncertainty, which the author seems almost wishful to increase. When we are on the point of admiring Savonarola's courage, he hastens to assure us that the Friar sometimes showed exaggerated timidity ; when about to express our admiration for his steadfast opposition to the Medici, we find him accused of being their eulogist. It would almost appear as though Mons. Perrens feared to commit himself to any decided opinion of his hero, since no sooner does one escape him than he endeavours to attenuate its force. In the last and most terrible hours of Savonarola's life he turns from the persecuted man with words of condemna-

---

[1] " Jérôme Savonarole, sa vie, ses prédications, ses écrits," par F. T Perrens. Two Vols. Paris, 1853.

tion, not only without having discovered any proofs to justify the harshness of his verdict, but even without any real examination of already known documents.   Thus the reader is left discouraged, confused and uncertain whether Savonarola or his biographer be most deserving of blame.

A somewhat serious defect is also to be found in the second volume.   This treats of the Friar's works, but only gives mere summaries of them, and occasional extracts, without any decided verdict or criticism.   Mons. Perrens frequently alleges his incapacity to judge religious doctrines, but falls into errors, for which even his modesty is no sufficient excuse.   After having invariably represented Savonarola as a sincere Catholic, he refers us to an authority he considers weightier than his own, and gives in his Appendix a long chapter from Rudelbach, in which the German biographer has endeavoured to prove that Savonarola was a precursor of Luther.   In this way the French author demolishes his own edifice.   It is true that he entrusted the translation of this chapter to another hand, and we may therefore suppose that he was too hurried even to read it with attention, but how can such negligence be excused in so earnest a writer as Mons. Perrens?   Nevertheless, this French biography ' being the most complete to which the Italian public had access at the time, its author has a distinct claim on our gratitude.

Other works had appeared and were appearing on the same theme, but all of far slighter merit.   In France Rio's "Art Chretien" [1] comprised some very eloquent pages upon Savonarola.   In Germany Hase published a short popular biographical sketch of the Friar, and Lenau a little poem full of force and imagination.[2]   In England

[1] "Art Chretien," par Rio.   Paris, 1836.

[2] "Neue Propheten, Drei historisch-politische Kirchenbilder," von D. Karl Hase.   Leipzig, 1851.   These are three essays on Joan of Arc, Savonarola, and the Anabaptists.   "Savonarola, ein Gedicht," von Nicolaus Lenau.   Vierte Auflage : Stuttgart and Tubingen, 1853.

many biographies of Savonarola have appeared, but are all mere compilations, written without any real knowledge of the facts, and with the sole purpose of claiming the Prior of St. Mark's as one of the martyrs of the Reformation. The last English work, published in 1853, in two stout volumes, has somewhat more merit.[1] The author, Mr. Madden, professes moderate Catholic opinions, but is over-anxious to attribute his own views to Savonarola, and while assuring us that he has most carefully studied the subject, shows so slight an acquaintance with its time and place, that his book is brimful of mistakes. To cite one of many instances, he tells us, as a proof of Savonarola's great and untiring activity, that, after preaching in Santa Maria del Fiore, he also preached in the Duomo (the identical church) on the same day! Thus the book is quite useless to Italians, and conveys most inexact ideas to foreigners. England, the country of great historians, has produced no work on Savonarola worthy of its fame.[2]

Having been engaged for many years upon a biography of Savonarola, the appearance of the above-mentioned works by no means discouraged me from the task, but rather served as an incitement to higher efforts, by reminding me of the duty of carrying it out with unsparing labour and research.[3] For the accomplishment of my purpose, I made it a rule to read all modern works upon the subject, but to rely upon no authority but that of contemporary writers, Savonarola's own works, and

[1] "The Life and Martyrdom of Girolamo Savonarola, illustrative of the History of Church and State Connexion," by R. R. Madden. London, 1854.

[2] The works of Perrens and Madden were reviewed by me at greater length in the "Archivio Storico Italiano," N.S., vol. iii. 1856.

[3] Among more recent works, we must mention the "Vita di Frà Jeronimo Savonarola," by Bartolommeo Aquarone. Two Vols. Alessandria, 1857 and 1858. As the work of a friend, and published almost simultaneously with my own, I refrain from passing any judgment upon it.

original documents ; and, warned by frequent experience of
the danger of quoting second-hand, to read and verify
everything with my own eyes.

The earlier biographies had, of course, to be studied as
well as the modern, and among the former the best were
those of Father Pacifico Burlamacchi and Count Giovan
Francesco Pico della Mirandola. Burlamacchi, a Lucchese
of high birth, had been one of the most constant of
Savonarola's hearers, and was moved by his discourses to
assume the Dominican frock. He entered the monastery
of San Romano in Lucca in 1499—*i.e.*, the year after
Savonarola's martyrdom, and died in 1519 in the odour of
sanctity. He had enjoyed intercourse with Savonarola
and known his most intimate friends ; he had discoursed
with eyewitnesses of the chief events of the Friar's life,
and had seen many of them himself. His work, without
being that of a trained historian, has much of the simple
force of an old chronicle, is carefully written, and shows
an intimate knowledge of facts. After remaining long
unknown, the Manuscript began to circulate in monasteries, and served as a model for numerous other biographies of no special value, compiled by devout fanatics. It
was finally published in 1761 among Mansi's "Addizioni alla
Miscellanea del Baluzio,"[1] and besides the miracles narrated
by Burlamacchi, others were added in the words of
Father Timoteo Bottonio, who cannot be regarded as a
trustworthy authority.

Count Giovan Francesco Pico della Mirandola, nephew
of the famous Giovanni Pico, had personally known
Savonarola and conceived the deepest admiration for him.
He had lived in Florence during the most eventful years
of the career he sought to describe ; he had witnessed the

---

[1] It was afterwards published separately, and reprinted later with the
addition of a " Lettera Apologetica ; Vita del P. F. Girolamo Savonarola,"
by P. F. Pacifico Burlamacchi, of Lucca. New Edition. Lucca, 1764.

martyrdom of his hero, and devoutly cherished his relics. He was a philosopher, an elegant Latinist, and one of the most learned and purest men of his time; he collected facts with incredible diligence ; wrote and rewrote his book many times, and made numerous changes in its construction; submitted it to the judgment of numerous friends of Savonarola, and finally gave it to the world in 1530.[1]

The great resemblance between these two biographies gave rise to the idea that the one was copied or modelled from the other. But the evidence of contemporary writers and the examination of ancient codices prove that, in the main, each is independent of the other. And in the course of my studies I acquired great confidence in both authors, and found them far more deserving of belief than might be supposed from the fanatic and superstitious tone so often to be noted in their pages.

It would be a superfluous task to cite all the un-edited biographies of which I made use. I need only mention those of Frà Marco della Casa,[2] Frà Placido Cinozzi,[3] and a third and more important one, of unknown authorship[4] in the Magliabecchiana Library of Florence. All three are by contemporaries and fellow-brethren of Savonarola. There is another and better known biography by P. Serafino Razzi, also a Friar of St. Mark. His work is only a compilation from Pico and Burlamacchi ; for he was not a contemporary of Savonarola, and had little aptitude for original research. But he had conversed with certain old Florentines who had

---

[1] " Vita R. P. Fr. Hieronymi Savonarolæ," auctore Ill. D. Joan. Franc. Pico. Parisiis, 1674. This edition, revived by Quétif, is in two volumes ; the second and half of the first contain additions by Quétif, who also published a third volume, containing Savonarola's letters.

[2] In the Monastery of St. Mark.

[3] Written in the form of letters, and contained in Codex 2053, of the Riccardian Library.

[4] Convent MSS., I., VII., 28.

known the Friar, including the octogenarian, Lorenzo
Violi, of whose manuscript diaries "Giornate," he made
an abridgment. He also collected and transcribed a large
number of Apologies and other works on the life and
doctrines of his hero.[1]

After studying the biographies I began to search for
new documents, particularly for all relating to the trial,
which had always excited my keen curiosity. The
printed report of the trial was generally known; but
Savonarola underwent three examinations, and I succeeded
in finding the manuscript records of the second and third,
and also of the trial of his fellow-martyrs, Frà Silvestro and
Frà Domenico. Although containing important information,
tion, these documents need very cautious examination, for
they were much changed and falsified by the notary of the
Florence Signory. The examinations or depositions of
many other persons, either implicated in Savonarola's case,
or simply interrogated as witnesses, are in a codex of the
Florence archives, first discovered, but only cursorily
examined, by Meier. This codex was extremely useful
on account of the light thrown by it on Savonarola's last
days; and help was also derived from other documents
found, but not studied by Meier.

Fresh research brought to light a copy of Frà
Domenico's genuine and unaltered statements written in
his own hand. But, as to Savonarola's avowals, there
was no hope of obtaining them. He had not been
allowed to write his own confession; his replies had been
falsified by the notary who transcribed them, and, with
added alterations, had been used for the printed report of
the first examination and the manuscript version of the
two others. The first notes taken by the scribe might
have contained some germ of truth; but these documents

---

[1] Razzi's works exist, in manuscript, in the Magliabecchian, Riccardian,
and Laurentian Libraries.

had been kept hidden for some time and then destroyed. Nevertheless I discovered the manuscripts of two writers who had seen the original notes, and, comparing them with the falsified reports, had pointed out their essential divergences.[1]

One of these two MSS. consisted of the third part of the "Vulnera Diligentis" of Frà Benedetto, the devoted friend and follower of Savonarola. I shall have occasion elsewhere to speak of this work and its author, and need only say here that the third part, relating almost exclusively to the trial, was unknown to all. The other manuscript was the "Apologia" or "Giornate" of Lorenzo Violi, long believed to be lost, and which I had the good luck to disinter. Violi had taken down nearly all Savonarola's sermons as they fell from his lips; in this work he recorded everything that he had seen or heard of the Friar's life, in the form of a long "Apologia," and continued his task until loss of sight at the age of eighty compelled him to relinquish his pen. From these documents I gleaned the fullest account of Savonarola's trial down to the minutest particulars. Even the obscure and much contested

---

[1] So much curiosity was roused by my discovery of these documents, particularly of the reports of the trials, that others hastened to profit by it and to forestall me in the publication of some of the papers. I was powerless to prevent this, much time being still needed for the due completion of my work. Meanwhile Professor Paolo Emiliani-Giudici published in the Appendix to his "Storia dei Comuni Italiani" not only the printed report of Savonarola's first trial, but the MSS. of the two others discovered by myself. The learned compilers of the "Giornale Storico degli Archivi Toscani" (vol. ii.) published the trials of Frà Domenico and Frà Silvestro, also unearthed by me; together with the examinations of other prisoners and witnesses. The latter documents had been first mentioned by Herr Meier, and, as Father Marchese had announced in 1855 ("Scritti Vari," p. 246, note 2), I had collected them for my work. I accordingly reproduced all these documents, not only because, in a literary sense, they were mine, but because they had been hastily and not always correctly printed, without notes or comments of any kind. All this, however, is a story of the past. Since then I have received much courtesy and assistance from the Florence archives, and owe special thanks to Comm. Guasti, Professor Paoli, and Cav. Gherardi.

incident of the Ordeal by Fire was now seen in its true light.

Having arrived at a precise and accurate knowledge of the main facts of Savonarola's life, I next undertook an accurate study of his writings. This soon taught me to marvel at the incredible and unpardonable negligence of his biographers; for I found that they could not have read the works they so frequently quoted. No other explanation can account for their blundering statements, their imperfect acquaintance with Savonarola's doctrines, and their absolute ignorance of his philosophical system. They never discovered that they were dealing with a great thinker; for while dwelling upon some utterly insignificant composition, they pass without notice all those revealing the originality of the author's mind. Although professedly eager to ascertain the nature of Savonarola's meditations in prison, and the state of his mind, they barely glance at the writings composed during his confinement. Consequently I resolved to leave no line of his works unread, and devoted years of patient study to this arduous but indispensable task. Without it no authentic biography could have been achieved.[1]

Without limiting my inquiries to Savonarola's printed works, I also searched for his letters and unpublished writings, and succeeded in finding a few. In order to penetrate, as it were, to the inmost recesses of his mind, I

---

[1] It is a duty to record that it was chiefly by the kindness of Count Carlo Capponi that I was enabled to thoroughly carry out this investigation. His collection of the works, pamphlets, and letters of Savonarola, and of all materials for the Friar's life, is so complete and well arranged, that no other private collection in Italy or elsewhere can, I think, be compared with it. The kindness with which Count Capponi placed his treasures at my disposal calls for a public expression of gratitude. I would also tender my thanks to many others for their generous assistance, and above all to Father Marchese, who has always encouraged me with paternal affection. Dr. Danzi, of Milan, was another true friend, for, without being a personal acquaintance, he entrusted me with all the documents in his collection.

examined his marginal notes to his own copies of the Bible, written in his microscopic and almost undecipherable hand. I was the first, and perhaps the only student of these notes, and they enable me to state that Savonarola was always true to himself; that in the solitude of his cell, in his most private manuscripts, he repeated exactly what he preached from the pulpit to the mass of his hearers. His letters chiefly serve to show us on what terms he stood with friends and kinsmen, and throw light on his dispute with Rome, which is further illustrated by some Borgian Briefs that were hitherto unknown.

Savonarola's political career and the vicissitudes of the Florentine Republic also demanded fresh examination. For this purpose neither the splendid narratives of Nardi, Machiavelli, and Guicciardini, nor the more recent researches of Meier and Marchese, could suffice. By means of the decrees (*provvisioni*), or rather laws of the Republic, I was enabled to form an accurate idea of its constitution ; by means of the deliberations (*pratiche*), or, as they may be called, drafts of the speeches delivered in the Councils, I gained intimacy with the men and passions that had re-moulded and breathed new life into the Republic. I am not aware that any other modern writer has made use of these Florentine *pratiche*, but I believe them to contain unexplored treasures of the wisdom and eloquence of Italian politicians of the past. Finally, by collating all these documents with Savonarola's sermons I ascertained that the Friar of St. Mark was beyond all doubt the leading spirit of the great political drama before me.

It will now be easily understood why it was impossible in this biography to keep the narrative portion separate from the examination of my hero's works, and why I should be so frequently obliged to quote his own words. The books, precepts, and sermons of Savonarola are not to be solely judged from a literary point of view ; they were his

chief and almost only mode of action, the instruments
he used for the reconstitution of the Republic, and by
which he paved the way for the moral and religious regeneration of the whole nation. Accordingly his written and
spoken words are one with his actions, and often constitute
in themselves some of the most important events of his
life. Besides, in these eighteen or twenty volumes of sermons and ascetic works, in these numerous letters and
pamphlets, flashes of lofty genius and marvellous bursts of
eloquence are frequently hidden in a thicket of scholastic
and even puerile conceits. Thus, without a biographer to
act as pioneer, and clear the way by hard strokes, there was
great danger that the genius of Savonarola might still
remain partially buried and unknown.[1]

It is needless to enumerate all the other chronicles and
manuscripts I have collated or read. The unpublished
letters of private individuals, secret reports of the ambassadors and spies of Italian governments, a large number
of religious and political pamphlets, popular poems, both
manuscript and in print—all were ransacked. Nothing, in
short, was neglected that might aid to the production of a
faithful portrait of the men and the passions of the time.

In bringing this too lengthy preface to an end, I must
first confess that, although assisted by research and docu-

[1] I may repeat here what was mentioned elsewhere in the first
edition. Extracts from documents and printed works are frequently
given in our text. Wherever a faithful and extended summary is given
the extracts have quotation marks at the beginning and end ; but verbatim extracts are indicated by continued quotation marks in the
margin. In quoting from Savonarola's works, I have generally moder-
nized the orthography and corrected the more glaring grammatical
mistakes. This was necessary to avoid too sudden changes of form
and language in the text. But in the Appendix, to the Italian edition,
I give the original words, blunders and all. I should add that Count
Capponi's collection of Savonarola's works has been recently purchased
by the Italian Government, and, together with a no less precious store
presented by Count Guicciardini, is now in the National Library of
Florence.

mentary evidence, my best aid in the accomplishment of my work was the fact of having undertaken it unhampered by preconceived ideas. The subject was chosen because it seemed to me that the part played by Savonarola in the events of the century closing the Middle Ages and initiating the dawn of modern civilization was as great as it was unrecognized. And precisely for that reason I saw that this fifteenth century Friar must not be converted into an advocate of the ideas and passions of the present age. This history of Savonarola is free from all political bias, and aims at neither the attack nor the defence of Rome. Had I found any proof that he was a heretic or an unbeliever I should have certainly represented him as such. But, on the contrary, I have found him to be essentially Catholic, and therefore presented him to the reader in that light. To use history as an engine of party feelings and opinions—no matter of how pure and noble a kind—is to go on a false system. For whoever undertakes a narrative of past events stands on sacred and inviolable ground. There is no need for the author to come forward as the advocate of virtue and freedom ; on the contrary, he should feel convinced that the history of mankind is a living drama in itself, leading man on to liberty, elevating his moral tone, and developing his civilization. Therefore, in venturing on even the slightest change, he attempts to correct the ways of Providence, and only succeeds in destroying their sublime harmony.

In writing the history of Girolamo Savonarola and his times, I have adhered to these rules, and should I succeed in proving that his name is one of the most glorious on Italy's noble list of thinkers, heroes, and martyrs, my end will be achieved and my labour abundantly rewarded.

BOOK I.

CHAPTERS I.—X.

(1452–1494.)

CHAPTER I.

FROM THE BIRTH OF SAVONAROLA TO HIS BECOMING A MONK.

(1452–1475.)

HE Savonarola were originally of Paduan descent. The first of the family mentioned by the chroniclers was Antonio Savonarola, a valiant warrior, who, about the year 1256, defended the city against the tyrant, Ezzelino. In memory of this event one of the gates of Padua was named Porta Savonarola, and still bears the same designation. In the middle of the fifteenth century a branch of the family removed to Ferrara at the request of its lord, one of the then sovereign House of Este. Nicholas III. was a lover of letters and the arts, a patron of learning, and, taking pride in attracting distinguished men to his Court, invited Michele Savonarola to attend on his person. This Savonarola was a physician of high repute in the Paduan school, was very learned, fervently pious, and extremely charitable in bestowing his services on the poor.[1] His name has been transmitted to posterity not only by numerous

[1] "Vita R. P. F. Hieronymi Savonarolæ," auctore J. F. Pico, p. 4 ; Cappelli, " Frà Girolamo Savonarola," &c., p. 6, and fol. Several notices of the Savonarola family are to be found in a codex of the eighteenth century, in the Landau Library in Florence, compiled from original documents preserved in the same library. Antonio Savonarola's merits are also mentioned in the chronicles of the period.

valuable works,[1] but also by his affection for his grandson, Girolamo Savonarola, who was afterwards to achieve a worldwide celebrity.

Settling in Ferrara in 1440, he taught with success in the University, and won much honour and rich reward in his capacity of physician to the Court. Pope Nicholas made him a Knight of Jerusalem, and the successors of Marquis Nicholas III. added to his lands and revenues, and even invested him with a small fief.[2] Lionello, the immediate successor of Nicholas, retained him as medical attendant, increased his salary, and exempted him from all other duties, in order to leave him leisure to write.[3]

Of Michele's son Niccolò little is known. It appears that he studied medicine and school lore; but no writings remain to record his name. He dawdled through life as a hanger-on at the Court, and squandered the fortune gained by his father's talents and industry.

His wife Elena, one of the illustrious Mantuan family of Bonacossi, seems to have been a woman of lofty temper and almost masculine firmness. The chroniclers[4] have little

---

[1] Some of his printed works passed through many editions, namely : " Practica de ægritudinibus," Papiæ, 1486 ; " Practica canonica de febribus," Venetiis, 1498 ; " De Balneis omnibus Italiæ sive totius orbis, proprietatibusque eorum," Venetiis, 1592 ; " De arte conficiendi aquam vitæ," &c., Hagenoæ, 1532 ; " In Medicinam practicam Introductio," &c., Argentinæ, 1533. There are also many unpublished works, several of which are on religious and moral topics. Among these a " Confessionale " and a " Dialogus moralis " (*vide* I. I. Mangeti, " Bibliotecha scriptorum medicorum veterum et recentiorum ; " Cappelli, " Frà Girolamo Savonarola," &c., at the beginning ; L. N. Cittadella, " La nobile famiglia Savonarola in Padova ed in Ferrara," Ferrara, 1867).

[2] The original patents are in the Landau Library.

[3] This is recorded in a very remarkable patent, also preserved in the Landau Library. *Vide* Appendix to the Italian edition, doc. i.

[4] *Vide*, among others, Frà Benedetto of Florence, " Vulnera Diligentis." This work gives several important and authentic details on Savonarola, and there are two manuscript copies of it in the National Library of Florence, Class xxxiv., Cod. 7, and Class xxxvii., Cod. 318. Concerning Frà Benedetto, the disciple of Savonarola, and who wrote other works on his master, we shall have frequent occasion to speak.

to say of her, but that little testifies to the nobility of her character. Certainly, the letters of her son Girolamo, who in the worst and most painful moments of his life seems to have turned to her as his best and surest confidante, not only confirm the report of her virtues, but serve to enforce the repeated observation that one of the most constant and unchanging affections of great minds is a love, almost amounting to worship, for their maternal parent.

Girolamo Savonarola, the subject of this biography, came into the world on September 21, 1452,[1] third of the seven children to whom Niccolò and Elena gave birth. His biographers tell marvellous tales of him even in his earliest infancy ; but every one knows how little faith can be lent to similar accounts. It is easier to believe that he was by no means an attractive child ; for he was neither pretty nor playful, but already serious and subdued. Probably no one foresaw the destiny that awaited him. Nevertheless, the eldest son, Ognibene, having adopted a military career, and the second, who was probably a youth of scanty parts, devoting himself to the care of the paternal estate, all the hopes of the family were concentrated on Girolamo, even in his boyhood ; and it was their dream to see him become a great physician. The Savonarola naturally held the medical profession in the highest esteem,

---

[1] According to the biographers these children were : Ognibene, afterwards a soldier ; Bartolommeo, of unknown profession ; Girolamo ; Marco, who, as Frà Maurelio, received the monastic robe in St. Mark's from his brother's hands in 1497 ; and Alberto, who took his Doctor's degree April 20, 1491, and became a distinguished physician ; Beatrice, who remained at home unmarried, and Chiara, who, on becoming a widow, returned to live at home with her brother Alberto. But Signor L. N. Cittadella, in his work " La nobile famiglia Savonarola in Padova ed in Ferrara," places the children in the following order : Chiara, Alberto, Bartolommeo, Ognibene, Girolamo, Marco, Beatrice. This gentleman is known to be a careful writer, but as he does not give the source of this information, we prefer to rely on the authority of the old chroniclers and biographers.

as the source of the dignity and honour of their house. Accordingly the grandfather, Michele, gave his tenderest care to Girolamo. With the patience and simple directness gained by long years and experience, this wise old scientist devoted himself to the development of his grandson's intellect, the careful unfolding of its budding thoughts and ideas. Such a training was undoubtedly the best of schools, and the boy soon rewarded his grandsire's devotion by showing a true passion for study. So great was his ardour for books that even those beyond his comprehension were eagerly seized upon and ransacked for hidden treasures.

Unfortunately the grandfather soon died,[1] and the boy was left to the sole guidance of his father, who began to instruct him in philosophy. In those days natural science was merely regarded as one of the chief branches of philosophy, and the latter, although used as a preliminary to the study of medicine, was, as we all know, purely scholastic. It is true that in some parts of Italy, and even in Ferrara, a faint glimmer of the dawning Platonic philosophy was beginning to appear, together with some faithful translations of Aristotle from the original Greek ; but these things were considered to be daring innovations ; and the young Savonarola had to study the works of St. Thomas Aquinas, and the Arabic commentaries on Aristotle. These were given to him as indispensable guides and introductions to the study of medicine ; and it was strange to behold so young a boy plunged in this sea, or rather

---

[1] The exact year of his death is unknown. Fossi, in his well-known "Catalogo Magliabecchiano," tells us : " Eius obitus contigisse videtur circa finem, anni 1461, vel tardius." Capelli gives the same date, 1461, in his " Frà Girolamo Savonarola," &c., p. 10 ; but Cittadella, in " La Casa di Frà Girolamo Savonarola in Ferrara " (Ferrara, 1873), states that there are documents proving that Michele died between 1466 and 1468. A diploma of Duke Borso, dated 20th October, 1461, conferring fresh rewards upon Michele Savonarola, " phisico nostro precarissimo," in the Landau Library, proves that Michele still lived at that date.

labyrinth, of confused syllogisms, and finding so much pleasure in the task as soon to become a very skilful disputant.[1] The works of St. Thomas fascinated him to an almost inconceivable extent ; he would be absorbed in meditating on them for whole days at a time, and could hardly be persuaded to turn his attention to studies better adapted to his medical training. Thus, while the natural tendency of his mind drew him in one direction, his parents urged him in another ; and, though no one could foresee it, this was the beginning of the struggle that was afterwards to decide his future and crush the hopes of his kindred. Enamoured of truth, and as yet unconscious of his own powers, he was still filled with the joyous intoxication felt by the young when all nature seems to gaily beckon them across the threshold of life. He devoured the ancient writers, composed verses, and studied drawing and music.[2]

All particulars, however, of Savonarola's boyhood are unfortunately wanting. History seems to have purposely concealed from us by what process his nature was developed or his mind trained. We have no details of the progress of his studies, nor of the difficulties he had to encounter ; no means of tracing the mental and spiritual growth of this man who was to play so prominent a part in the world's affairs. It may, perhaps, be taken for granted that his early days were marked by no facts sufficiently remarkable to be transmitted to posterity. Probably the true history of his youth consisted of private thoughts and secret impressions, such as could not be generally known. Therefore, to understand the state of his mind, we must study his material surround-

---

[1] J. F. Pico, "Vita," &c., chap. ii. p. 9.

[2] Frà Benedetto, "Vulnera Diligentis," bk. i. chap. vii. ; Burlamacchi, "Vita del P. F. Girolamo Savonarola," p. 4, new edition, Lucca, Giusti, 1784.

ings, inasmuch as he was at no time wholly absorbed in solitary meditation, but always felt drawn towards humanity and the people; always, indeed, preferring to share the life of his fellow-men, save when repelled by invincible disgust for their vices.

The deserted aspect of modern Ferrara, with its lonely, grass-grown streets, makes it difficult for us to realize the former splendour of the capital of the House of Este. Then it was a city of 100,000 inhabitants,[1] and its Court one of the most famous in Italy, was continually visited by princes, emperors, and popes, and the scene of interminable festivities. This was the Ferrara of Savonarola's childhood and youth. His family being attached to the Court, he must have heard continual mention of all these pageants and revellings, and received his earliest impressions from them. Accordingly it will be no digression from our subject to devote a few words to the Court of Ferrara.

In 1402 Niccolò III. was the reigning Marquess of Ferrara, and of the rich and fertile province of Modena, still annexed to that State. After sixteen years of continuous warfare with the lords of the neighbouring strongholds, he had at last subdued them by force of arms, cunning, and treachery; he was now an absolute sovereign, and devoted his peaceful reign to enhancing the glory of his Court. He began the erection of the cathedral tower, and the palace of Belriguardo; he built the church of Santa Maria di Belfiore and other splendid edifices. We have seen how Michele Savonarola came from Padua at his bidding, and he summoned many others in the same way, among them the celebrated scholar Guarino of Verona, to whom he entrusted the education of his two natural sons, Lionello and Borso. These boys were afterwards legitimized, and, by their father's express desire, named his successors,

[1] Such, at least, is the census given by historians.

in preference to Ercole, his legitimate son, who was then an infant. Accordingly Lionello ascended the throne on Niccolò's decease, in 1441, and Borso succeeded Lionello in 1450. They reigned during difficult times. The extinction of the House of Visconti, the revolt of Milan, and the jealousy of Venice and the neighbouring States, had kindled war on all sides, so that it seemed impossible for the Este to avoid being embroiled with one or the other of the contending parties. Yet they not only contrived to remain neutral, but so often mediated successfully between hostile princes and States as to gain for Ferrara the title of "the land of peace." But the Este were chiefly renowned for the magnificence of their Court and as the first Italian potentates who were noted patrons of learning. Lionello, in fact, befriended many scholars ; he was the protector of Guarino, Valla, Trapezunzio, and others : he composed Latin orations, Italian sonnets, founded the famous Este museums, caused the University to flourish, built the Hospital of St. Anna, and many public edifices. His Court was maintained with dazzling luxury, and the festivities held there at the time of his marriage were the talk of the whole country. But, after reigning only nine years, he died in 1450, and was succeeded by his brother Borso, who soon threw his munificence and splendour into the shade. The Marquis Borso was a man of the Medicean stamp, and, although not devoid of good qualities, even these were born of vanity and personal ambition. He loved justice, and caused it to be strictly observed whenever it did not clash with his interests ; but better than justice itself he loved his title of "The Just," which was universally conferred upon him. He taxed all the citizens in equal proportions, supported the university at his own expense, introduced in Ferrara the new-born art of printing, founded the Carthusian monastery, fortified the city bastions on the banks of the Pò, and succeeded in extending his territories. The quarrels which had burst forth in Italy during Lionello's reign grew fiercer in his own, and he lived in more difficult times; nevertheless he preserved his neutrality, and was the chosen arbiter in nearly all disputes among the other Italian States. So widespread was his fame, that Indian princes sent him rich gifts in the belief that he was the king of all Italy.

It may seem hazardous to assert that his great reputation was mainly acquired by the luxury of his Court and the perpetual festivities with which he entertained his people, yet this was undoubtedly the case. Borso's reputed justice never withstood any serious test; nor was his life free from grave reproach. The vaunted prudence enabling him to remain at peace while surrounded by fighting neighbours, really consisted in cautiously refusing to espouse any man's cause, and being always ready to join the stronger side. But as lord of Ferrara he was lavish of hospitality to all, had a rare collection of manuscripts and antiquities, was always seen dressed in gold brocade, and the richest stuffs in Italy were worn at his Court. He had the finest falcons, horses, and dogs that had ever been seen; he was even famous for the excellence of his buffoons, while descriptions of his State entertainments were printed and circulated throughout the whole of Italy.

In 1452 the Emperor Frederic III., with two thousand followers in his train, halted at Ferrara on his way to assume the imperial crown in Rome. Borso rode forth to meet him, attended by all his nobles and clergy, received him under a State canopy, and for ten successive days gave tournaments, banquets, concerts, and balls in his honour. The emperor having decided, on his return from Rome, to confer a ducal title upon Borso, all these festivities were then renewed on a still grander scale. A sumptuous platform was erected in the Piazza, and there the emperor sat enthroned, wearing his mantle and an imperial crown adorned with precious stones to the value of 150,000 florins. Borso, attired in cloth of gold and likewise loaded with jewels, issued from his palace attended by all the nobles of Ferrara, amidst the applause of the people and loud cries of "The Duke, the Duke! Long live Duke Borso!" Then, mounting the platform, Borso knelt at the emperor's feet, and received the coveted title.

But the festivities which Savonarola must have witnessed as a child were still more magnificent and given on a far more remarkable occasion. The fall of Constantinople in 1453, the increasing power of the Turks, and the consequent danger to Christendom, were continual subjects of interest; all yearned for a fresh crusade, but the general indifference and indolence were too great for any one to set it afoot. At last, in 1458, Enea Silvio Piccolomini, recently elected to the pontificate as Pope Pius II., summoned a council at Mantua under his own presidency, for the purpose of inciting the Christian Powers to war with the infidel. He set forth on his progress in 1459 with a *cortége* of incredible pomp, and with ten cardinals, sixty bishops, and many secular princes in his train. The cities through which he passed strove to outshine one another in the luxury and splendour of his reception. The Pontiff entered Florence borne on the shoulders of Galeazzo Maria Sforza and of the lords Malatesta, Manfredi, and Ordelaffi; and the festivals ordained him by the Republic were such as were generally accorded to no one but the emperor or some other great temporal potentate. At Ferrara the Pope made his entrance under a canopy of gold brocade; the streets through which he passed were carpeted with cloth and sprinkled with flowers; rich tapestries hung from the windows, and the city echoed with music and song. On reaching the cathedral, Guarino read him a long Latin oration, crammed with learned allusions and praise of the Holy Father. For a whole week Pius II. was detained in Ferrara by a succession of festivities. Continuing his journey under the same circumstances, he at last reached Mantua on May 27, 1459. There he made a marvellous display of eloquence in the Latin tongue, and moved his hearers to tears by his description of the woful sufferings of the Christians in Constantinople. Other Latin speeches were delivered by Francesco Filelfo and Ippolita, daughter of Francesco Sforza; and, lastly, the Greek ambassadors aroused the deepest and truest emotion by recounting the miseries of their country and the ferocious cruelty of the Turks. All the princes offered help in money and men, and Duke Borso promised the (for him) enormous sum of 300,000 florins. But it was soon seen that he had been more crafty than generous. For these grand preliminaries all ended in talk, and the foolhardy attempt of René of Anjou to conquer the Neapolitan kingdom with a handful of French sufficed to put an end to the proposed expedition to the East.

In 1460 the Pope returned to Ferrara without having achieved anything; nevertheless, his reception was even more splendid than before. The Duke went up the Pò to meet him in a magnificent barge, surrounded by a swarm of boats gaily decked with banners and musical instruments, spreading across the river from bank to bank. A multitude of youths dressed in white, and bearing wreaths in their hands, stood arrayed on the flower-strewn shores, and at the spot where the Head of the Church was to land, statues of the Pagan divinities were set up in his honour !

Savonarola must have certainly witnessed this pageant, and heard it long discussed. But it is not easy to say what depth of impression it made on his childish mind. His religious zeal would seem to have been severely shocked by similar profanities, and even in earliest youth his heart was torn by passions driving him to open war with the world around him.

Borso continued to lead this kind of existence, and the people of Ferrara to revel in these entertainments. Throughout Italy the same state of things unfortunately prevailed. Carelessness and corruption everywhere! From all sides Paganism invaded the land, and its inhabitants were absorbed in wanton and thoughtless enjoyment.

On the 9th of August, 1471, the Duke passed away, and was scarcely cold in his grave before Lionello's son, Niccolò, and Ercole I. (the legitimate son of Niccolò III.), who was now of age, fiercely disputed the succession by force of arms. Ercole proved the victor, and, entering Ferrara in triumph, was proclaimed sovereign by the people. At the same moment Niccolò's followers were slaughtered in the streets, and those who succeeded in escaping were condemned to death in contumacy. On the morrow feasting and dancing went on as usual, and the people seemed to forget the bloodshed of the previous day.[1] Such was the famous, splendid, jovial Court of the Este; such were the rulers courted, and probably praised to the skies, by Savonarola's kindred.

There is nothing to be gleaned from the biographers as to the effect of these facts on our hero's mind, nor of his judgment concerning them. They do not allude to the subject. But they describe his sad and lonely mode of life, his humble and dejected demeanour, his wasted form, his increasingly fervent devotion, the long hours he passed in church, and the frequency of his fasts. *Heu fuge crudeles terras, fuge litus avarum*, was the cry that often and, as it were, unconsciously issued from his lips.[2]

---

[1] Muratori, " Antichità Estensi ; " Sismondi, " Histoire des Républiques Italiennes," chap. lxxviii. (Bruxelles, 1839); Litta, " Famiglie Italiane ; " Tiraboschi, " Storia della Letteratura," tom. vii. chap. ii. ; Frizzi. " Memorie per la Storia di Ferrara," 2nd edition, vol. iv.

[2] *Vide* a letter to his father, of which we shall speak later on.

During this period he was entirely absorbed in studying the Scriptures and St. Thomas Aquinas, allowing himself no recreation save that of playing sad music on his lute, or writing verses expressing with a certain simple force the griefs that weighed upon his heart. As a specimen of these poetical efforts we may cite the " Canzone De ruina Mundi," composed in 1472, and clearly descriptive of his state of mind, and the dreariness of his thoughts :—

> " Vedendo sotto sopra tutto il mondo,
>   Ed esser spenta al fondo
>   Ogni virtude ed ogni bel costume,
>   Non trovo un vivo lume
>   Nè pur chi di suoi vizii si' vergogni.
>
> *   *   *   *
>
>   Felice ormai chi vive di rapina
>   E chi dell' altrui sangue più si pasce ;
>   Chi vedoe spoglia e i suoi pupilli in fasce,
>   E chi di povri corre alla ruina.
>   Quell' anima è gentile a peregrina
>   Che per fraude e per forza fa più acquisto ;
>   Chi sprezza il ciel con Cristo,
>   E sempre pensa altrui cacciare al fondo,
>   Colui onora il mondo." [1]

[1] Seeing the whole world overset ; all virtue and goodness disappeared ; nowhere a shining light ; no one taking shame for his sins. . . . Happy now is he that lives by rapine, and feeds on others' blood. Who despoils widows and infants trusted to his care, who hastens the ruin of the poor ! Gentle and beautiful of soul is he who wins most by fraud and violence : he who scorns Heaven and Christ, and ever seeks to trample on his fellows. He shall win honour in the world. . . . (*Vide* " Poesie di Geronimo Savonarola," p. 31 fol. Florence : Baracchi, 1847.)

Some of these verses were published in the fifteenth century, either during the author's life or soon after, being included among his other works. Frà Benedetto afterwards made a collection of them from a "*copia fidelissima*," and his MS. is in a Magliabecchian codex of the Florence National Library, cl. xxxv., cod. 90. Herr Meier was the first to make use of this codex in the Appendix to his valuable biography of Savonarola. Afterwards Signor Audin di Riano used the same MS. for his edition of the poems (1847) quoted above. Lastly, Count Carlo Capponi and Comm. Cesare Guasti published the " Poesie di Girolamo Savonarola, tratta dall' autografo" (Florence : Cecchi, 1862). The auto-

Savonarola was so strongly moved by these feelings that, as his biographers tell us, having been once taken by his parents to the ducal palace, he refused, with a firmness highly remarkable in so young a lad, ever to cross its threshold again.[1]

Certainly, that grim quadrangular building, with its four massive towers, guarded by moats and drawbridges, must then have seemed typical of the tyranny entrenched amidst the people of Ferrara. Its walls were as yet unhallowed by memories of Tasso and Eleonora, whose immortal spirits still seem to haunt its splendid halls, and dispel all gloomy associations. On the contrary, the castle had recently been the scene of Parisina's love-tragedy. In those times no one thought of visiting for amusement the subterranean dungeons guarded by seven gratings from the light of day. They were full of immured victims, and the clanking of chains and groans of human beings in pain could be heard from their depths, mingling with the strains of music and ceaseless revelry going on above, the ringing of silver plate, the clatter of majolica dishes, and clinking of Venetian glass. The young Savonarola, with his ardent mind and impassioned heart, must have been forcibly impressed by these contrasts, and throughout his life he preserved a painful remembrance of the scenes of those early days, when, almost delirious with grief, he could find no refuge save in church. Prayer,

graph MS. of which they made use does not appear to have been revised by the author. It would rather seem to have been the first rough sketch. The copy used by Frà Benedetto is less faulty, and certain of the corrections contained in it are to be found in the few poems published during Savonarola's life, in works revised by his own hand. For these reasons, and also to avoid reproducing old and incorrect spelling, we quote from the better known edition of 1847, only referring to the original autograph for the poems which remained unprinted until 1862, and were not included in Frà Benedetto's copy. We have written at length on this subject in the " Civiltà Italiana," issue of the 1st of January, 1865.

[1] Burlamacchi, " Vita," &c., p. 5 ; J. F. Pico, "Vita," &c., p. 9.

indeed, was his continual solace, and his tears would bedew
the altar steps, where, stretched prostrate for hours at a
time, he besought aid from heaven against the evils of this
vile, corrupt, and dissolute age.

There dwelt at that time, close to his home, a Florentine
exile of the illustrious name of Strozzi, who had an
illegitimate daughter. An exiled citizen from Dante's
native town must have had a special attraction for the
young Savonarola. In fact, the latter regarded him as a
victim of unjust persecution, a sufferer in the cause of
patriotism and freedom. The exile's family seemed of
altogether a different stamp from his Ferrarese acquaintances. When his eyes met the glance of the young
Florentine maiden, he felt that first inward stirring of the
heart by which men win belief in earthly happiness. The
world lay before him irradiated by a new light ; tumultuous
hopes kindled his fancy, he dreamed of blissful days to
come, and finally, full of ardour and confidence, he revealed his feelings to the object of his passion. What was
not his grief on receiving a haughty reply to the effect that
no Strozzi might stoop to alliance with a Savonarola ! He
met the insult with words of burning indignation,[1] but his
heart was none the less crushed by it. His dream-world
of long cherished hopes lay suddenly shattered before him ;
the happiness of his life had fled, and he was once more

---

[1] This love episode of Savonarola's youth, after long remaining un-
known, was found recorded in Frà Benedetto's "Vulnera Diligentis,"
MS. *cit.*, bk. i. chap. ix.   On this point also justice must be done to
Herr Meier, who was the first to recur to Frà Benedetto's writings, and to
appreciate their importance.   Rediscovered at a much later date by
Italians unacquainted with Meier's work, they were announced as a novelty.
The researches of Cittadella in his pamphlet, "La Casa di Savonarola,"
prove that Savonarola's home was next to that of the Strozzi.   And Cav.
A. Gherardi has shown ("Nuovi Documenti," p. 7) that one Laodamia,
the natural daughter of Roberto Strozzi, lived in Ferrara at that period,
and was probably the object of Savonarola's passion.   It should be remembered that Frà Benedetto learnt many of the particulars narrated in
his life of Savonarola from his master's own lips.

alone in the midst of the uncongenial herd. He was not
yet twenty years of age; the recent occurrences on the
succession of Ercole I. had led him to despair of his
country, and the love on which his whole happiness
depended had ended in a cruel delusion. Where now was
his weary, heavy-laden soul to find rest? Thereupon his
thoughts turned spontaneously to his Maker.

> " Se non che una speranza
> Pur al tutto non lascia for partita,
> Ch'io so che in l'altra vita
> Ben si vedrà qual alma fu gentile,
> E chi alzò l'ale a più leggiadro stile." [1]

Religious feelings took complete possession of his soul, and,
by creating a new source of comfort for his heart, opened a
way of safety before him. His supplications were uttered
with daily increasing fervour, and nearly always ended with
these words: " Lord, make known to me the path my soul
should tread ! " [2] Worldly life became more and more
irksome to him. All Ferrara was absorbed in the festivities of which the Duke was so crazily fond. The
carnival of 1472 had been celebrated with greater splendour than usual, and Lent was devoted to the preparation
of still grander pageants to welcome the arrival from
Naples of the Duke's bride, Eleonora of Aragon. Increasingly angered and irritated by this state of things,
Savonarola shunned all contact with his fellow-men. The
plan of forsaking the world and seeking refuge in religion
was already pressing on his mind, and his admiration for
St. Thomas Aquinas inclined him to adopt the Dominican
robe. At Faenza, in 1474, a sermon preached by an

---

[1] *Vide* the same poem, " De ruina Mundi." It may be roughly translated thus : Yet one hope at least remains, for know I not that in the
other life, 'twill well be seen whose was the fairest soul, whose wings were
spread to noblest flight.

[2] *Vide* the letter to his father, before quoted.

Augustinian friar made so.deep an impression on him that, the same day, he formed the irrevocable decision of devoting himself to the monastic life.[1]

He was full of cheerfulness on his way back to Ferrara, but no sooner was he beneath the paternal roof, than he realized how hard a struggle he would have to endure. It was necessary to hide his resolve from his parents, but his mother, as though already divining it, regarded him with a glance that pierced his heart ; and he no longer dared to meet her eyes. This struggle went on for a whole year, and in after life Savonarola often recalled the intense anguish it had cost him. " Had I made my mind known to them," he would say, " verily my heart would have broken, and I should have renounced my purpose." [2] One day, towards the end of that period, April 23, 1475, he sat down, and, taking his lute in hand, sang so sad an air to its accompaniment that his mother was inspired with a foreboding of the truth, and, turning suddenly to him, piteously exclaimed : " Oh, my son, this is a token of separation ! " [3]   But he, making an effort, continued to touch the strings with trembling fingers, without once raising his eyes to hers.

The following day, the 24th of April, was the great festival of St. George, and Savonarola's parents went with all the rest of Ferrara to attend the celebration. This was the moment he had fixed upon to fly from his home, and directly he was left alone he set forth on his journey to Bologna.   On reaching that city he hurried to the Monastery of St. Dominic, announced his intention of

[1] Savonarola refers to this incident in his sermons, saying that *one word* remained so strongly impressed on his heart, that he never forgot it, and that by the next year he was a monk.   But as to this *one word* he always preserved a mysterious silence, refusing to reveal it even to his closest friends.   *Vide* also Pico, Burlamacchi, Frà Benedetto, &c.

[2] *Vide* the already quoted letter to his father.

[3] Frà Benedetto, " Vulnera Diligentis," bk. i. chap. x.

taking the vows, and asked to be employed in the humblest services.   He craved to become the convent drudge, since he came, as he said, to do penance for his sins, and not, according to the general custom of the day, to *merely change from an Aristotle in the world to an Aristotle of the cloister.*   He received instant admittance and began to prepare for his noviciate.

But hardly was he alone in his cell, than his thoughts flew to his kindred, and without loss of time he wrote a most affectionate letter to his father on the 25th of April, in order to comfort him and justify his own flight. He was chiefly impelled to this step, he said, by the impossibility of any longer tolerating the gross corruption of the world, and by seeing vice exalted and virtue degraded throughout Italy. His decision had not been formed in childish haste, but after prolonged meditation and suffering. He had not had the courage to reveal his purpose beforehand, fearing lest his heart should fail him at the moment of putting it into execution.   " Dearest father," he said in conclusion, " my sorrow is already so great, do not, I pray you, add to it by yours !   Be strong, seek to comfort my mother, and join with her in granting me your blessing." [1]

Such was the tenour of his letter, and he also added that he had left some papers by his window descriptive of the state of his mind.   The father lost no time in searching for them among his son's books, and found in the spot indicated a treatise entitled " Contempt of the World." This repeats the sentiments expressed in the letter, describes the manners of the period, and compares them with

[1] This letter, so often quoted by us already, is given by all the biographers, but always incorrectly.   Count Carlo Capponi, having discovered the original autograph, restored the true reading of it in a pamphlet (of which eighty copies only were printed) entitled " Alcune Lettere di Frà Girolamo Savonarola," Florence, 1858. This authentic reading being very rare, we subjoin a copy of it in Appendix to the Italian edition, doc. ii.

those of Sodom and Gomorrah. "Not one, not a single righteous man is left; it behoves us to learn from babes and women of low estate, for in these only doth there yet linger any shadow of innocence. The good are oppressed, and the people of Italy become like unto the Egyptians who held God's people in bondage. But already famine, flood, pestilence, and many other signs betoken future ills, and herald the wrath of God. Divide, O Lord, divide once again the waters of the Red Sea, and let the impious perish in the flood of Thy wrath!" [1]

This short composition was believed by all the biographers to be lost, but was finally unearthed among the records of a Florentine family, to whom it had been confidentially entrusted by Marco Savonarola in 1604.

It has great interest as an evident proof that, even before becoming a monk, Savonarola foresaw the woes Italy was to suffer; and also that he already believed himself endowed with a special mission from God. He supplicates the Lord to divide the waves of the Red Sea for the passage of the righteous and to overwhelm the wicked, but at the same time he cannot conceal his expectation of one day wielding the rod that would

[1] *Vide* Appendix to the Italian edition, doc. iii. Signor Bartolommeo Aquarone, in his "Vita di Frà Jeronimo Savonarola" (vol. i. p. 19, and doc. iii.), states that the little composition, "Dispregio del Mondo," was only a set of verses contained in the Magliabecchiana Library, cl. vii. cod. 365. But the old manuscript of it, formerly belonging to the Gondi family, removes all doubt, inasmuch as it contains these words: "I remember how, on the 24th April, which was the Feast of St. George, in 1475, Geronimo, my son, student of the Art (*i.e.*, of medicine), left his home and went to Bologna, and entered the brotherhood of St. Dominic, in order to become a monk; and left to me Niccolò della Savonarola, his father, the consolations herein written for my comfort." This brief composition and the letter sent by Savonarola to his father were discovered by Count Carlo Capponi among the archives of the Gondi family. When publishing the letter in 1858, the Count alluded to the existence of the pamphlet, "Dispregio del Mondo," and finally brought out an edition of it of eighty copies only. (Florence: Bencini, 1862.) This, too, being a very rare work, is reproduced in the Appendix to the Italian edition.

command the waves. He vainly endeavoured to conceal
this hope from himself, vainly sought humiliation by
undertaking the lowest drudgery of the convent. Extraordinary hopes and designs were already stirring in his
soul.

We are ignorant of the effect produced by these writings
on his parents; but it may be readily conceived that
they were bitterly afflicted by their son's unexpected
resolve, inasmuch as in his second letter Savonarola, somewhat impatiently, reproves their immoderate complaints.
" If," said he, alluding to his elder brother's profession,
" some temporal lord had girt me with a sword, and
welcomed me among his followers, you would have regarded it as an honour to your house, and rejoiced ; yet, now
that the Lord Jesus Christ has girt me with His sword
and dubbed me His knight, ye shed tears of mourning."[1]
After this the parents were reduced to resignation, and
Savonarola threw himself heart and soul into his new
duties.

He was of middle height, of dark complexion, of a
sanguineo-bilious temperament, and a most highly-strung
nervous system. His dark grey eyes were very bright,[2]
and often flashed fire beneath his black brows ; he had
an aquiline nose and a large mouth. His thick lips were
compressed in a manner denoting a stubborn firmness of
purpose ; his forehead, already marked with deep furrows,
indicated a mind continually absorbed in meditation of
serious things. But although his countenance had no
beauty of line, it expressed a severe nobility of character,
while a certain melancholy smile endued his harsh features
with so benevolent a charm as to inspire confidence at first

[1] This unpublished letter is in the Riccardi Library, cod. 2053. *Vide*
Appendix to the Italian edition, doc. iv.

[2] Sometimes giving forth red flashes, says Frà Benedetto in his
" Vulnera Diligentis."

sight. His manners were simple, if uncultured ; his language rough and unadorned. But on occasion his homely words were animated by a potent fervour that convinced and subdued all his hearers.[1]

While in the Monastery of St. Dominic he led a silent life, and became increasingly absorbed in spiritual contemplation. He was so worn by fasting and penance that, when pacing the cloisters, he seemed more like a spectre than a living man. The hardest tests of the noviciate seemed light to him, and his superiors were frequently obliged to curb his zeal. Even on days not appointed for abstinence he scarcely ate enough to support life. His bed was a grating with a sack of straw on it and one blanket ; his clothing of the coarsest kind, but strictly clean ; in modesty, humility, and obedience he surpassed all the rest of the brethren. The fervour of his devotion

---

[1] Besides the accounts of Pico and Burlamacchi, minute descriptions of Savonarola's appearance are to be found in Frà Benedetto's " Vulnera Diligentis," and the little poem, " Cedrus Libani," written in his master's honour, and first quoted by Meier. This poem was afterwards published by Father Marchese in the "Archivio Storico Italiano " (Appendix, vol. vii.). There are also three portraits of Savonarola of some artistic merit. One, in the gallery of the Uffizii, is an admirable *intaglio* in cornelian, by Giovanni della Corniola ; another is a painting by Frà Bartolommeo della Porta, representing him as St. Peter Martyr—probably, therefore, finished after Savonarola's death—in the Academy of Fine Arts in Florence. The third, also attributed by some authorities to Frà Bartolommeo, belonged to Signor Ermolao Rubieri, and was left by him to his Florentine heirs.

These portraits represent Savonarola under three different aspects. In the intaglio we see the daring preacher vituperating the vices of Italy and prophesying her fall : he has an excited air, and his eyes seem to flash fire. The second depicts the martyr's goodness and benevolence. The third, a saint in rapt contemplation. Many other portraits exist, but they are not by contemporary artists, and their authenticity is doubtful. In all, Savonarola is represented with his cowl drawn over his head, save that in the Academy. In this a certain flatness of the upper part of the cranium may be observed : according to some writers this was why he always covered his head. The modern terra-cotta bust by Bastianini is also an excellent portrait. Cittadella's pamphlet, " La nobile Famiglia Savonarola," contains a list of all the Savonarola portraits and medals.

excited the wonder of the superiors, and his brother monks often believed him to be rapt in a holy trance. The cloister walls seemed to have had the effect of restoring his peace of mind by separating him from the world, and to have purified him of all desires save for prayer and obedience.

CHAPTER II.

(1475–1481.)

SAVONAROLA passed seven years in the Dominican monastery of Bologna. In those lonely cloisters, and the majestic church where Niccolò Pisano's noble monument enshrines the remains of the founder of the Order, he spent his time in prayer and penance. But his learning and extraordinary mental gifts had quickly attracted the notice of his superiors, and instead of being employed in the menial work he had craved, he was charged with the instruction of the novices. At first it was grievous to him to be prevented from giving his whole time to prayer and religious exercises; but then, remembering that obedience was his first duty, he willingly devoted himself to the novel task.

Nevertheless, it would be a mistake to suppose that Savonarola's whole mind and heart were absorbed in the duties of obedience and humility. His spirit, though full of faith, was equally full of daring and ardour. The corruption of the age had driven him to the cloister, and prayer and solitude seemed to have brought him peace. But whenever he reflected on the miserable state of the Church he was roused to fury, and in the heat of his indignation formed venturous projects which the bonds of religious discipline and the utmost efforts of his will were alike impotent to restrain.

During the same year of exalted fervour, in which he had fled from the world, he wrote a canzone entitled "De ruina Ecclesiæ," exhaling the most secret thoughts of his soul. In this poem he asks the Church—represented in the likeness of a chaste virgin—" Where are the ancient doctors of the law; the ancient saints; where the learning, love, and purity of olden times?" And the virgin, taking him by the hand, leads him into a cavern, and replies—" When I beheld proud ambition invade Rome, and contaminate all things, I fled here for refuge."

> *" Ove io conduco la mia vita in pianto."*
> (" Where I spend my life in tears.")

She then shows him the wounds disfiguring her beautiful body; and thereupon Savonarola turns in his grief to the saints in heaven and bids them mourn this dire misfortune:

> *" Prostrato è il tempio e lo edifizio casto."*
> (" Cast down is the temple, and the edifice of chastity.")

" But who has brought things to this pass?" he resumes. And the Church, alluding to Rome, replies, " Una fallace, superba meretrice" (a false, proud harlot). Then the devout young novice, the humble, solitary monk, reveals his whole soul in the following words :—

> *" Deh! per Dio, Dona,*[1]
> *Se romper si potria quelle grandi ali!"*
> (" O God, Lady, that I might break those spreading wings!")

To which the Church replies, almost in a tone of reproof:—

> *" Tu piangi e taci; e questo meglio parme."*[2]
> (" Weep and keep peace; so seemeth best to me.")

[1] Donna—Lady.
[2] " Poesie del Savonarola," Canzone ii., with the author's comments. A few of these poems bear the date of the year in which they were written.

Such, then, was Savonarola's convent life : while finding comfort in fasting and prayer, and recreation in teaching the novices, his heart was overwhelmed with grief, and stirred to irrepressible indignation by beholding the debasement and corruption of the Christian Church. He weeps and keeps silence, it is true, but again and again he is moved by the thought, " O God ! that those spreading wings could be crushed, those wings of perdition ! " If we realize what an effect the events daily happening throughout Italy must have made on so excited a mind, the dreadful pictures he must have conjured up of the obscenities of the Roman Court, we shall understand the burning indignation of his naturally inflammable spirit.

The scandalous corruption of the papacy, dating from the death of Pius II. in 1464, had already begun, and was to reach its climax under Alexander VI. The bad faith and unbounded avarice of Paul II. were soon patent to all the world ; and when this pontiff was succeeded in 1471 by Francesco della Rovere as Pope Sixtus IV., a still sadder time was foreseen to await the Church. It was publicly asserted that the election of the new Pope had been carried by simony ; and Rome echoed with the names of those who had sold their votes and obtained preferments in exchange. The scandalous lust of Sixtus was literally unbounded ; the lavishness of his expenditure only equalled by his unquenchable thirst for gold ; and so greatly was he blinded by his passions, that he shrank from no infamy to accomplish his wicked aims, and no act was too scandalous for him to commit.

The treasures accumulated by the grasping avarice of Paul II. disappeared almost instantaneously ; and the dazzling splendour of the nephews of Sixtus soon proved into whose hands they had been poured. There were four of these nephews. One was made Prefect of Rome; another a cardinal, afterwards Pope Julius II. ; the third pur-

chased the city of Imola for the sum of 40,000 gold
ducats, and married the daughter of Galeazzo Sforza; but
the worst of the four, and the Pope's favourite, was Pietro
Riario. The strong affection of Sixtus for this youth,
aged twenty-six, caused many infamous rumours in Rome.
From a simple friar he was suddenly raised to the dignity
of cardinal-prelate, with the title of San Sisto ; he was
named Patriarch of Constantinople and Archbishop of
Florence. He had unbounded influence at Court, and
whenever he went there the streets overflowed with the
followers in his train, while his receptions were even more
crowded than those of the Pope. As a contemporary
writer informs us,[1] his luxury surpassed all that was displayed by our forefathers, or can even be imagined by our
descendants. On receiving the ambassadors of France he
gave them a banquet, to which nearly all the arts known
at the period were called to contribute. The land was
ransacked for all that was most rare and precious; no
means was spared to achieve results such as no future age
should be able to reproduce ; and the rhymed descriptions
of this festival were not only circulated throughout Italy,
but across the Alps and all over Europe. When Eleonora
of Aragon, daughter of the Neapolitan king, halted in
Rome on the way to her nuptials at Ferrara (1473), the
reception accorded to her was of unparalleled magnificence.
The bride was met by a procession of cardinals and
ambassadors, who led her to the Pope's presence through
streets draped with rich stuffs and tapestries ; she was
then conducted to a palace the young Riario had erected
expressly for her use, next to his own dwelling. Its walls
were of precious woods; its interior brilliant with gilding
and shining silks; the plates, beakers, and other table
utensils were all of silver and gold.[2]

[1] Jacopo Ammanati, Cardinal of Pavia, "Papiensis Cardinalis
Epistola 548. Ad Franciscum Gonzagam Cardinalem."

[2] Sismondi, "Histoire des Républiques Italiennes," vol. vi. chap. i. ;
Muratori, "Antichità Estensi," in "The Life of Duke Ercole I."

Thus Cardinal Riario, in less than a year, had squandered the sum of 200,000 florins, and notwithstanding his numerous and very lucrative appointments, incurred a debt of 60,000 florins. But this did not have the effect of checking his excesses; on the contrary, he went to Milan the same year, and rivalled the luxury of Duke Galeazzo, one of the most dissolute of Italian princes. He afterwards went to Venice, and there plunged into such depths of debauchery, that at last his strength failed, and, returning to Rome, he died on January 5, 1474. In this way that scandal of the papacy, known to history by the name of nepotism, continued to spread and flourish ; and Sixtus IV. went on reigning in the same fashion to his death, in 1484. Notwithstanding the great corruption of the age, general uneasiness was excited by the degraded condition of the Church, general abhorrence felt for the scandalous lives of the Pope's nephews, and even for the Pope himself, who, in his greed for power, his avarice, and lust, blindly gave vent to all his passions.[1]

But wretched as was the aspect of the States of the Church, that of the rest of Italy was equally disheartening. Those were truly miserable times. Men not only mourned their long-lost liberty, but the absence in the ruling tyrants of the energy and political gifts by which their predecessors had risen to power. All strength of character, all ardour of ambition had vanished ; everywhere the race of princes seemed fallen into decay. In the kingdom of Naples Alphonso the Magnanimous had been succeeded (1458) by Ferdinand I. of Aragon, who might have been fitly surnamed " the Cruel," for he overcame his

---

[1] *Vide* Sismondi, Leo, Gregerovius, &c. ; Steph. Infessuræ, "Diarium Curiæ Romæ," in Yo. Ge. Eccardi, " Corpus historicorum medii ævi," tom. ii., Lipsiæ, 1723 ; Platina, " De Vitis Pontificum," Basiliæ, 1523. Rudelbach, " H. Savonarola, und seine Zeit, aus den Quellen dargestellt. Erste Abtheilung : die Signatur des funfzehnten Jahrhunderts," pp. 4-16. Hamburg, 1835.

enemies solely by cunning, deceit, and treason, and pushed his meanness and avarice to the extent of meddling in trade, to his own advantage and the injury of his subjects. In Florence, the sagacious, keen-witted Cosimo de' Medici had been succeeded in 1465 by the incapable Piero, who so endangered the supremacy of his house during his brief reign that, had he lived longer, it would have been impossible for his son Lorenzo to grasp the reins of government. In Milan, the valiant general and astute politician, Francesco Sforza, had been succeeded in 1466 by the feeble Galeazzo; and lastly, in Venice, the able and ambitious rule of Francesco Foscari had been followed in 1457 by that of Pasquale Malipiero, whose chief enterprises consisted of festivals in the Square of St. Mark. So general a degradation had almost the air of a strange freak of destiny, but is easily accounted for by the fact that, whereas the former rulers had fought their way to power over the heads of their enemies, and through innumerable obstacles and dangers, their sons, born in peace and reared in Courts, were only trained to luxurious ease.

As though Italy were not sufficiently crushed by all these evils, others, equally serious, combined to assail her. By a reaction against the feeble tyranny of her rulers, daring spirits arose among her people, ready to resort to the most desperate deeds, rather than submit to the actual state of things. Conspiracy was rampant throughout those years. In 1476 three plots were hatched. Girolamo Gentile tried to deliver Genoa from the Milanese yoke; Olgiati, Visconti, and Lampugnani assassinated Duke Galeazzo in church, and were themselves torn to pieces by the enraged populace in the streets of Milan; Niccolò d'Este, with a band of six hundred men, tried to gain possession of Ferrara and overthrow his brother, Duke Ercole, but, together with most of his followers, perished in the attempt. Thus, all these plots ended in the destruction of their authors, and only increased the misery of the people by consolidating the power and rousing the cruelty of their oppressors.

Nevertheless, undismayed by danger, men were rather urged by it to more desperate ventures, and no year passed without fresh attempts. ' The most terrible conspiracy of all was that of the Pazzi in Florence. On April 26, 1478, while Mass was being celebrated in the cathedral, and at the moment of the elevation of the Host, Giuliano de' Medici was stabbed by the Pazzi. Lorenzo escaped the blows aimed at himself, and, having time to draw his sword, was able to fight his way into the sacristy. Angelo Poliziano, who helped to save him by promptly closing the door, tells us that the noise and confusion was so great at the moment that it seemed as though the church itself were falling down.[1]

This conspiracy was certainly extraordinary in all its details ; remarkable for the sagacity and daring of its plan; the moment chosen for its execution; the high rank of those engaged in it ; and the number of victims slain, both at the time and afterwards. Most astonishing of all was the number and rank of the ecclesiastics implicated in the plot. The dagger that was to despatch Lorenzo de' Medici was entrusted to a priest ; Archbishop Salviati was the leader of the conspiracy in Florence and Rome ; and, according to public rumour, the Holy Father, Sixtus IV., himself was one of the hottest and most determined of its promoters. He had hoped to increase his nephews' power by this means, and infuriated by the failure of the plot, threw all other considerations to the winds and made open war upon the Florentines as their declared enemy.

It was in these times and amid these events that the

[1] A. Politiani, " De Pactiana conjuratione, Historia sive commentarium."

MEDAL IN COMMEMORATION OF THE PAZZI CONSPIRACY.

mind of Savonarola grew into shape. The state of the world and the Church filled him with a horror-stricken grief, only to be relieved by prayer and study. Owing to the increasing esteem felt for him by his superiors, he was promoted from his office of instructor to that of preacher. He undertook the task with great ardour; for his original intention of remaining in silence and solitude was beginning to yield to an imperious need of moral and intellectual activity, and he therefore rejoiced to find a new field for his young and abounding energies.

In his first sermons he seems to have adopted the same style as in his lectures, although giving more space to practical remarks and moral precepts. Then, gradually discarding Aristotelian rules, he drew nearer and nearer to the Bible, which was soon to become his sole and inseparable guide. Nothing more is known of these sermons; and they cannot have had much success, since no writer of the time has mentioned them, nor any record of them survived. We only know that a certain Giovanni Garzoni, Professor of Philosophy at the University of Bologna, reproved Savonarola for having abandoned the rhetorical rules he had taught him, and denied Priscian in favour of the Bible.[1]

In the year 1481 he was sent by his superiors to preach in Ferrara. He lived there as one dead to the world, seeing none of his acquaintances, and very little of his family, for fear of awaking his dormant affections. The streets, houses, and churches of his native town spoke to him of a past that he sought to banish from his mind. Apparently his fellow-citizens cared little for his preaching, since we afterwards hear him complain that he had proved the truth of the old saying: *Nemo propheta in*

[1] " Cognovi te Prisciano grammatico bellum indixisse." Apparently Savonarola had at first sought the advice of this Professor Garzoni. *Vide* some of his letters in Gherardi's " Nuovi Documenti," &c., pp. 8–10.

patria sua.[1]   In the absence of any report of these sermons it is impossible to ascertain why they made no effect upon their hearers. We may, however, conjecture that Savonarola adhered to his purpose of disregarding the example of other preachers who floundered in the mazes of scholastic sophistry, or indulged in a coarseness of speech such as, in our time, would barely be tolerated in the lowest public resorts.[2]   Besides, Savonarola had not yet learnt to wield his own special gifts of oratory, and was too uncertain of himself to dominate his hearers and carry them with him by a new path.   Nevertheless there must already have been flashes of power and eloquence in his speech, as, indeed, may be inferred from many anecdotes given by the biographers.   One day, for instance, he was journeying up the Pò from Ferrara to Mantua by boat.   There were eighteen soldiers on board who were noisily gambling and swearing without any respect for his monastic robe or position.   Suddenly Savonarola addressed them in terms of indignation ; and straightway eleven of the men fell on their knees before him and asked pardon for their sins.[3]   But of course it is easier to impress a few ignorant troopers and persuade them to listen to the voice of conscience, than to preach

---

[1] Letter to his mother, from Pavia, dated the day of the Conversion of St. Paul, 1490.   It was published by Father Marchese, in the "Archivio Storico Italiano," Appendix of vol. iii. : "Lettere e documenti inediti di Frà Girolamo Savonarola." The same complaint was frequently repeated in Savonarola's sermons.

[2] *Vide* Tiraboschi, "Storia Della Letteratura," concerning the sacred oratory of the fifteenth century. See also the sermons of Frà Paolo Attavanti, compared by Ficino with Orpheus, and those of Frà Roberto da Lecce, the most famous disciple of Frà Bernardino. The latter's style, however, was marked by a great simplicity, almost childish ingenuousness of which all traces had disappeared towards the close of the century. In the "Archivio Storico per le Provincie Napolitane" (1882, No. 1, pp. 140–165) there is a learned study on Frà Roberto da Lecce, by Professor F. Torraca. The author does not seem to me to have proved that the Friar had any oratorical power.

[3] Burlamacchi, p. 12 ; Pico, p. 150.

a forcible sermon from the pulpit to a large congregation. In the first case natural eloquence is enough, and with that Savonarola was abundantly endowed; in the second, oratorical art is required, and in this he seems to have been as yet unversed .

In the same year 1481, serious alarms of war were threatening Ferrara from all sides. Already many of the inhabitants had fled, and before long the University, in which the Dominicans taught theology, was closed. Thereupon, either from economy or as a measure of precaution, the Superior of the Order despatched the greater part of his monks elsewhere. Savonarola was directed to go to Florence. He thus bade a last farewell to his family, friends, and native town, for he was destined never to see them again.[1]

This war, solely directed, at first, against the Duke of Ferrara, gradually spread on all sides, until nearly the whole of Italy was split into two camps. The true motives of it were, on the one hand, the rising ambition of the Venetians to extend their power on the mainland; on the other, the covetous desire of the Pope to increase his nephew's dominions. These reasons, however, were kept concealed. The Pope pretended that he sought revenge on the Duke for having served under the Venetians when they were forced into war with him, after the failure of the Pazzi plot; while the Venetians found pretexts for hostility in certain frontier disputes and the usual quarrels concerning their salt trade. In vain, the Duke of Ferrara offered to yield on all these points : the two powers were now determined on war, and drew into it not only the

---

[1] The early biographers all assign Savonarola's departure from Ferrara to the year 1481. In the first edition we adopted the date given by Father Marchese, of 1482, when the war really burst out. But it is most probable that tumults, anxieties, and preparations had gone on for some time before. To fix his departure in 1482 would necessitate the displacement of many other dates.

Genoese Republic, but a number of petty potentates in
Romagna and the Marches. On the other hand, the
Florentine Republic, the King of Naples, Duke
of Milan, Marquis of Mantua, Bentivoglio, lord of
Bologna and the powerful House of Colonna, all
sided with the Duke of Ferrara. Thus the whole of
Italy was in arms, and although the Florentines took
only a verbal part in the contest, the rest of the allies
were already in the field. The Duke of Calabria
encountered the papal forces commanded by Roberto
Malatesta; the Colonna issued from their strongholds
and ravaged the Roman Campagna, while the Genoese
attacked the western frontier of the Duchy of Milan.
But the chief part in the campaign was played by the
Venetians. Investing Ferrara with two of their armies,
they marched a third against the Duke of Milan ; and
urged on hostilities with so much vigour that Ferrara was
already reduced to famine and could hold out no longer.
It was plainly evident that all the profits of the war would
be reaped by the Venetians.

But directly Sixtus IV. realized that his coveted prey
was about to escape him, he hastened, in the blindness of
his fury, to change sides. Concluding a treaty with the
Neapolitan king, he granted the Duke of Calabria free
passage through his states ; excommunicated the Venetians,
whom he branded as foes of Christ, and incited all the
powers of Italy to make war upon them. This sudden
transformation was only amazing to those unacquainted
with the impetuous nature of Sixtus IV., and the excesses
he was prepared to commit in order to fill his treasury and
widen his frontiers. And although the Venetians remained
undismayed, the Pope's desertion changed the whole
aspect of the campaign. The Duke of Calabria had
already conveyed supplies to Ferrara and disturbed the
progress of the siege : thus all decisive operations were

again deferred. The hostile forces remained facing each other, without coming to open battle; the neighbouring country was continually ravaged ; numbers died of hunger, none by the sword. The campaign dragged on in this incredibly feeble manner to the year 1482, when all wearied of a war that was equally hurtful to either side. Then the Venetian general accepted proposals of peace ; all the combatants withdrew, and to the universal satisfaction hostilities were suddenly at an end.

The Pope, however, was implacable. He had never ceased to fan the blaze he had kindled, and could not resign himself to the loss of all he had hoped to obtain by the war. On the 12th of August, 1484, when the ambassadors appeared before him, and read the terms of the peace, he was wild with rage, and, starting to his feet, exclaimed, " The peace you announce is humiliating and shameful ! " The following day his chronic malady, gout, flew to his chest, and thus the Holy Father died of grief because peace was concluded.[1]

This, then, was the war that drove Savonarola from Ferrara to Florence. In crossing the Apennines by lonely mountain paths, on his way to a new city, an unknown people, his mind was harassed with sad thoughts. That a Pope, for the sake of aggrandizing two or three dissolute youths, should throw all Italy in confusion, when the infidels were almost at her gates, and when less than two years had passed since the Turks' descent on Otranto ! The wind whistling among the beeches and pines seemed almost to hurl maledictions against the wicked who were rending the robe of the Lord's spouse, and perhaps sounded like an echo to his own daring words :

" *Se romper si potria quelle grandi ali !* "
" Oh, that I might break those spreading wings ! "

[1] " Sismondi," vol. vi. chap. 6 ; Leo, bk. v., § vii. ; Steph. Jufessurae, " Diarium," &c.

On this, his first arrival in Florence, in 1481, he entered
the Monastery of St. Mark, where the brightest and also
the saddest years of his life were to be passed.   And
inasmuch as the name of Savonarola is always associated
with that of St. Mark, it will be well to say a few words
on the convent's history.

At the beginning of the fifteenth century it was a poor,
half-ruined building, inhabited by a few monks of the
order of St. Sylvester, whose scandalous life occasioned
numerous complaints to be laid before the Court of Rome.
Finally, Cosimo the Elder obtained the papal permission
to remove these monks elsewhere, and granted the house
to the reformed Dominicans of the Lombard congregation.
Then, deciding to rebuild it, he charged the celebrated
architect, Michelozzo Michelozzi, with the work ; and six
years later, in 1443, the monastery was finished at a cost
of 36,000 florins.   Cosimo was never sparing of expense
for churches, monasteries, and other public works fitted to
spread the fame of his munificence and increase his popularity.   While the convent was in course of erection, he
had been very generous in helping the Dominicans, and
now that the work was so successfully completed, he was
not satisfied until he could endow them with a valuable
library.   This, however, was a difficult undertaking and
one of considerable expense, since it was a question of
collecting manuscripts, which, just then, commanded exorbitant prices.   But the opportune decease of Niccolò
Niccoli, the greatest manuscript collector in Europe,
enabled Cosimo to fulfil his purpose.   Niccoli had been
one of the most learned men of his day, and spent his
whole life and fortune in acquiring a store of codices that
was the admiration of all Italy.   He had bequeathed this
treasure to Florence, but having also left many debts behind
him, his testamentary dispositions had not been carried out.
Accordingly Cosimo paid off the debts, and reserving a

ST. MARK'S CONVENT.

few of the more precious codices for himself, entrusted the rest of the collection to the Monastery of St. Mark. This was the first public library established in Italy, and the monks kept it in such excellent order as to prove themselves worthy of the charge. St. Mark's became almost a centre of erudition, and being joined to the congregation of the Lombard Dominicans, the more learned brothers of the Order resorted to Florence, and increased the new convent's renown. The most distinguished men of the time frequently came to St. Mark's to enjoy conversation with the friars. It was during these years that Frà Giovanni da Fiesole, better known as Frà Beato Angelico, was employed in covering the convent walls with his incomparable works. But above all their treasures of art and learning, the brethren chiefly gloried in their spiritual father and founder St. Antonine, one of those characters who are true glories of the human race.

History might be ransacked almost in vain for an example of more constant self-abnegation, active charity, and evangelical neighbourly love than that of St. Antonine. He was the founder or reviver of nearly every benevolent institution in Florence. His was the noble idea of converting to charitable uses the Society of the Bigallo, founded by St. Peter Martyr for the extermination of heretics, and that had so often stained the streets and walls of Florence with blood.[1] Thenceforward the Captains of the Bigallo, instead of burning and slaying their fellow-men, rescued and succoured forsaken orphans. St. Antonine was the founder of "St. Martin's Good Men" (Buoni Uomini di San Martino), a society that fulfils to this day the Christian work of collecting offerings for distribution among the *poveri vergognosi*—*i.e.*, the honest poor who are ashamed to beg. It would be quite impossible to relate all that he did for the public benefit ; but, at the period of which we

[1] Previously styled "Captains of the Faith."

write, many were still living who remembered having often
seen him going about the city and its environs, leading a
donkey loaded with bread, clothing, &c., for sufferers
from plague or pestilence.   His death in 1459 was
mourned in Florence as a public calamity ; and when
Savonarola came to St. Mark's in 1481, the memory of
St. Antonine was still cherished with so lively a veneration,
that the cloister still seemed to be pervaded by his spirit.
None mentioned his name save in accents of the deepest
respect; his sayings were continually recalled and carried
the greatest weight, and when the friars sought to describe
a model of Christian virtue, the only name that rose to
their lips was that of St. Antonine.[1]

During his first days in Florence, Savonarola was
accordingly half intoxicated with delight.   He was
charmed by the smiling landscape, the soft lines of the
Tuscan hills, the elegance of the Tuscan speech.   Even
before reaching the town, the gentle manner of the
countryfolk he met on the way had predisposed him to
expect happiness in this fairest of Italian cities, where art
and nature contend for the palm of beauty.   To his
deeply religious mind, Florentine art seemed the expression
of a divine harmony, a proof of the omnipotence of
genius when inspired by faith.   The paintings of Frà
Angelico appeared to have filled the cloisters of St. Mark

[1] Padre Vicenzo Marchese, " Storia di San Marco," bk. i. Florence :
Le Monnier, 1855. This work, written with much elegance of style,
care, and precision, contains many interesting particulars concerning
St. Antonine as well as the convent. For still minuter details the reader
may be referred to the " Summa Historialis," or " Chronicon " of the
Saint, with additions by the Jesuit Father, Pietro Maturo, "Lugduni,"
&c., ap. "Junctas," 1585 and 1586, vol. iii. ; Castiglioni, " Vita B.
Antonini," Verona, 1740. For minuter details of the charitable institu-
tions, *vide* Passerini, " Storia degli Istituti di beneficenza in Firenze,"
Florence, 1853. *Vide* also Richa, " Notizie storiche delle Chiese di
Firenze ; " " Annales Conventus S. Marci," Cod. 112 of the Library of
St. Mark, Florence, now comprised in the Laurentian Library ; Fabroni,
" Vita Magni Cosmi Medicei."

with a company of angels ; and as he gazed upon them, the Friar felt transported into a blessed sphere like unto the world of his dreams. The sacred memories of Antonine ; the Saint's deeds of charity still enduring and still venerated by the brotherhood ; the friars themselves so superior in culture and refinement to any that he had yet known—all combined to make him believe his lot cast among real brethren of the soul. His heart expanded with ingenuous hopes, he forgot all past disappointments, and did not anticipate the still sadder trials awaiting him when he should have been long enough in Florence to better understand the nature of its inhabitants.

CHAPTER III.

T the time of Savonarola's coming, Lorenzo the Magnificent had reigned in Florence for many years, and was then at the height of his power and fame. Under his rule all things wore an air of prosperity and well-being. The factions which had so frequently distracted the city had long been extinguished; all refusing to bend beneath the

---

[1] He was born in 1448, and ruled from 1469 to 1492. It is unnecessary to fill this chapter with quotations. The historians of Lorenzo di Medici are so well known that it would be superfluous to repeat their names. We need only say that Roscoe's " Life of Lorenzo de' Medici " is by no means an infallible guide. It is safer to refer to Fabroni (" Vita Laurentii Medicis Magnifici "), from whom Roscoe has borrowed wholesale both in the text and appendix of his book. But Lorenzo may be studied to most profit in his own writings : " Poesie di Lorenzo de' Medici," Florence, 1825, four vols. in quarto ; " Canti Carnascialeschi," Florentine edition of 1750 ; in his letters, many of which are still unpublished ; and also in numerous works by contemporaries who wrote freely upon him, and with no intention of courting his favour. Guicciardini's " Opere Inedite," recently published by the Counts Guicciardini, with annotations by Giuseppe Canestrini, also throws much light on the lives of Cosimo and Lorenzo. Particular reference may be made to the dialogue on the " Reggimento di Firenze " in vol. ii., and on the " Storia Fiorentina " in vol. iii. of the " Opere." Some of the " Discorsi " of Jacopo Nardi also serve to confirm our views of the Medicean rule. Long after the first appearance of our book, Baron von Reumont published his work on " Lorenzo de' Medici," two vols., Leipsic, 1875, which ran to a second edition in 1883.

Medicean yoke were either imprisoned, exiled, or dead; and general tranquillity reigned. Continually occupied with festivities, dances, and tournaments, the Florentines, once so jealous of their rights, seemed now to have forgotten the very name of freedom.

Lorenzo took an active part in all these diversions, and was perpetually seeking out or originating others. His most famous invention was that of the " Canti Carnascia-leschi." These were ballads of his own composition, to be sung in carnival masquerades of the triumph of death, troops of devils, or other whimsicalities of the same kind. The performers were the young nobles of Florence, who paraded the streets in disguises suited to their parts. Perusal of these songs brings the corruption of the time far more clearly before us than could any description. Nowadays they would excite the disgust not merely of cultured aristocrats, but of the lowest rabble; and to sing them in the streets would be an offence against public decorum not to be committed with impunity. Then, on the contrary, their composition was the favourite pastime of a ruler praised by the whole world, held up as a model to all other sovereigns, and proclaimed a prodigy of wisdom and of literary and political genius.

Such was the general opinion on Lorenzo in his own day, and even now many concur in the verdict. They are willing to pardon the bloodshed by which he maintained the power usurped by himself and his kin; the disorders he wrought in the Republic; his embezzlement of the funds of the State for his private extravagance;[1] the shameless profligacy, to which, despite his weak health, he was completely abandoned; and even his diabolical method of corrupting the popular mind by every means in his power! And all these sins are to be condoned in virtue of his patronage of letters and art!

[1] *Vide* Machiavelli, " Istorie Fiorentine."

The social conditions of Florence in Lorenzo's day bristled with sharp contrasts. Culture was generally diffused; every one knew Latin and Greek; every one admired the classics; many women were accomplished writers of Greek and Latin verse. Painting and the other fine arts, which had declined since Giotto's day, were now awakened to new life; stately churches, palaces, and elegant buildings were rising on all sides. But artists, men of letters, statesmen, nobles, and people, were all equally corrupt in mind, devoid of public or private virtue, devoid of all moral sense. Their religion was either an engine of government or a base hypocrisy: they were without faith of any kind, whether civil or religious, moral or philosophical; they were not earnest even in scepticism. Their dominant feeling was utter indifference to principle. These clever, keen-witted, intellectual men were incapable of real elevation of thought, and, despising all enthusiasm for noble and generous ideas, showed their contempt by coldly compassionate smiles. Unlike the sceptic philosophers, they neither combated nor threw doubt on such ideas; they simply regarded them with pity. And this *vis inertiæ* was more hurtful to virtue than a declared and active hostility. It was only in country places and among the lowest classes removed from all contact with politics and letters, that any germ of the old virtues was still to be found. And even this was not visible on the surface.

This state of morals could not fail to have a powerful effect upon mental culture. In fact, philosophy had shrunk to mere erudition; scholastic lore—which, although so much derided, possessed a youthful spirit and energy absent from fifteenth-century writings—had also decayed. Literature consisted of learned essays or of imitations of Virgil, Cicero, Homer, Pindar, and so on. Even at the time of Boccaccio's death, Franco Sacchetti mourned the decay of literature in his pure and simple verses. What chiefly afflicted him was not, he said, the loss of the great dead ; but the hopelessness of seeing their like again, the lack of souls able, at least, to comprehend them.[1] Had he lived in the times of which we write, he would have had still graver cause for lament; he would have heard the Italian tongue declared unsuited to the utterance of lofty ideas ; and Dante's " Divina Commedia " pronounced inferior to the " Ballate " and " Canti Carnascialeschi "[2] of Lorenzo de' Medici ! Even the fine arts, necessarily the last to suffer from the nation's moral and political calamities, were no longer inspired by the daring and all-embracing conceptions with which Giotto, Orcagna, and so many of their compeers had adorned Italian buildings. Most assuredly this age could have produced no edifice infused with the spirit of freedom discernible in Arnolfo's Cathedral and the Palazzo Vecchio.

Nevertheless, although causing so many ills, the loss of liberty had been of positive advantage to literature and the fine arts. All ways being barred to political action and ambition, to the exercise of any public virtue, and in the decline of all those branches of trade and commerce in which such enormous fortunes had been reaped, what active energy still survived was applied to artistic and literary ends. And although there were now no men of trans-cendent genius equal to those who had flourished during the Republic, there was a general atmosphere of intellectual activity, a general yearning for the study of new languages, the production of new books and pictures. This yearning was all the stronger because students were ignorant how to make their knowledge available for loftier aims. In

---

[1] Franco Sacchetti, "Opere," Canzoni IV., in the ." Lirici Italiani." Florence, 1839.

[2] The famous Pico della Mirandola was one of those maintaining this view.

fact the city bore the air of a vast school; there was a
general craze for the collection of manuscripts and ancient
statuary, and the only subjects discussed were points of
grammar, philology, or erudition.   The Greek sages,
driven by the fall of Constantinople to seek refuge in the
West, were enthusiastically welcomed in Florence, and their
doctrines and teaching gave additional impetus to the rage
for antiquity and the desire to visit Greece and ransack its
soil, monasteries, and temples in search of old remains.
Journeys to the East were undertaken by travellers willing
to face all discomforts and dangers and expend considerable
fortunes for the sake of acquiring literary treasures of more
or less value.   Some of these expeditions have been
recorded in history.   We know the successful researches
made by Poggio Bracciolini in almost all the cities of
Europe; the eastern travels of Guarino of Verona, whose
hair suddenly turned white, it was said, from grief at the
loss by shipwreck of the treasures of learning he had
laboured so hard to collect; the wanderings of Giovanni
Aurispa, who, returning to Venice with more than two
hundred manuscripts, which had cost him his whole
fortune, found himself in extreme old age as rich in fame
as he was poor in substance.   We also know the travels of
Francesco Filelfo and of many other visitors to the classic
land of Greece.   Throughout Italy, and especially in
Florence, the return of one of these pilgrims was an occasion of public festivity and triumph.   The leading men of
the place went forth to meet him; the ruler of the city
gave him a most honourable reception; laudatory reports
of his discoveries were drawn up, and private letters were
filled with the same theme.   Then came discussions on the
authenticity and interpretation of the manuscripts; there
were hot disputes on philological or grammatical details,
and the strife overleaping the limits of debate, these learned
scholars tore one another to pieces in violent onslaughts on

their respective honour and reputation. Liberty to quarrel
in this fashion was in fact the only freedom retained by
the Florentines, although nominally their government was
still a republic, and their gentle-mannered tyrant a mere
private citizen.

The fine arts .fared better, although their practitioners
indulged more freely than any other class in the frivolous enjoyments of the time, revelling and working
with equal absence of care. In those days of universal
art-patronage, painters and sculptors were everywhere
welcome guests, and throughout Italy all rich men and
nobles, all churches and convents, demanded their works.
Thus their lives were pleasantly divided between work and
amusement, and while forsaking their former lofty ideals,
they made infinite advance in truthful representation of
nature, delicacy of expression, and management of colour.
It was then, too, that the discovery of oil-painting marked
a new period in the history of art. Sculpture and architecture, in which, unlike painting, so much depends on the
materials employed, also made great progress, partly by
the influence of classic remains, partly through the numerous
difficulties which practice taught them to overcome. The
names of Donatello, Ghiberti, Brunelleschi and many others
have won immortality. Certainly at that period the arts
attained an unprecedented elegance and refinement of
execution that was destined to perish in the succeeding
century.

Nevertheless most of the facts we have just related had
their origin before the power of the Medici was established,
and consequently owed nothing to the latter's aid. The rage
for classical studies had begun to spread even in Petrarch's
and Boccaccio's time, had gone on increasing ever since,
and private citizens had willingly consumed their substance
in the travels and researches mentioned above, content to
reap glory as their sole reward. As to the artists, the

majority of them flourished at the beginning of the century; thus, Brunelleschi was born in 1379, and died in 1446; Ghiberti, 1378–1455; Donatello, 1386–1466; Masaccio 1402–1428: and their noblest works were produced without either the patronage or advice of the Medici.[1] The construction of the cupola afterwards executed by Brunelleschi, had been already decided upon in 1407 by the Cathedral workmen, and the Medici had nothing to do with its completion. Ghiberti began his bronze doors in 1403, at the instance of the Merchants or Calimala Guild, and received for the first of them the, then, enormous price of 22,000 florins. The frescoes by Masaccio and other famous artists in the Carmine chapel were executed at the expense of private individuals; and Beato Angelico, whose paintings were entirely inspired by love of art and religious enthusiasm, frequently refused all payment for his work.

The Medici therefore cannot be said to have created a state of things that, indeed, no human power could have called into existence. It was the necessary outcome of the vicissitudes of the Republic during many centuries, of the national culture, and of the general decay of freedom then going on throughout the whole of Italy. The Medici found it already in existence and fostered by the citizens at large; but they had the rare sagacity to make use of it and turn it, by their favour, to their own profit. And certainly Lorenzo de' Medici was the man of all others best adapted for the purpose. Gifted by nature with a brilliant intellect, he had inherited from Cosimo a subtle astuteness, rendering him,—although by no means a statesman of the first order,—very swift of resource, full of prudence and acumen, dexterous in his negotiations with other powers, still more dexterous in ridding himself of his enemies, and equally capable of daring and cruelty whenever emergencies

---

[1] Cosimo returned from exile in 1434; Lorenzo, as we have already noted, began his rule in 1469.

LORENZO THE MAGNIFICENT.

called for bold strokes. He was alike regardless of honesty and honour ; respected no condition of men ; went straight to his ends, trampling over all considerations, whether human or Divine. The cruel sack of unfortunate Volterra; the robbery of the funds of the Monte delle Fanciulle,[1] in consequence of which many dowerless girls fell into bad courses ; and his rapacious appropriation of public property, are all stains that even his blindest worshippers are unable to ignore.[2] His countenance was a true index to his character. It was a dark-skinned, sinister, unpleasing face, with a flattened, irregular nose, and a wide, thin-lipped, crooked mouth, suited to the accents of his nasal voice. But his eyes were lively and penetrating, his forehead lofty, and his manners marked by the most perfect finish of that cultured and elegant age; his conversation was full of vivacity, wit, and learning ; and he won the genuine affection of all who were admitted to his intimacy. He encouraged all the worst tendencies of the age, and multiplied its corruptions. Abandoned to pleasure himself, he urged the people to lower depths of abandonment, in order to plunge them in the lethargy of intoxication. In fact, during his reign Florence was a continuous scene of revelry and dissipation. It is true, that in the midst of this corrupt, pleasure-loving society, a mighty transformation of the human mind was already in progress. But it seemed to grow spontaneously by the natural force of things, uncared for and unnoticed. What was most visible at the time was the general passion for pleasure, the pride of pagan learning, the increasingly sensual turn, both of art and literature, under the fostering hand of the man who was master of all in Florence.

Lorenzo had a genuine poetic gift and a fine taste for

[1] A charitable institution for providing respectable girls with marriage portions.

[2] *Vide* Guicciardini, " Del Reggimento di Firenze e Storia Fiorentina," in the " Opere Inedite."

art. Leaving the commercial business of his House to
fall to ruin by his neglect, he devoted his leisure to the
literary studies in which he had been trained by the most
learned men of the time. He had learnt the art of poetry
from Landino, had studied the Aristotelian philosophy with
Argiropulus, and the Platonic system under Ficino. Even
as a child he had given proofs of intellectual gifts worthy
of dedication to the Muses : great quickness of comprehension, singular accuracy of expression, and a very lively
fancy. Afterwards, as the patron of scholars and artists,
his mansion became the resort of the finest minds of the
day. All literary men of any note in Florence gathered
round Lorenzo ; many came from other parts of Italy in
order to join his distinguished circle. And both at the
meetings held in his own house and those of the renowned
Platonic Academy, his genius shone amidst this chosen
band, while his literary culture gained no little nourish-
ment from their intercourse.

Accordingly, contemporary writers were eloquent in
their praise of Lorenzo, and some of the works they
lauded to the skies are still held in admiration. All his
poems in the vulgar tongue, and particularly his fable of
" Ambra," have a freedom of movement, a spontaneous
grace, and an observant feeling for nature by no means
common in his time. For although his verse is too frequently imitated from Poliziano's " Ottave," it is impossible to deny that he was possessed of rare intellectual
endowments. He was the typical man of his age— all his
qualities were confined to his intellect ; his courteous
manners were the result of mental refinement, not of
kindness of heart ; his patronage of the learned was born
of his passion for culture, and also because he found it a
pleasant pastime, and one useful to his influence as a ruler.

Lorenzo's life was strangely complex ! After hours of
strenuous labour over some new law framed to crush any

lingering remains of liberty, or after passing some new decree of confiscation or sentence of death,[1] he would repair to the Platonic Academy and take part in heated discussions on virtue and the immortality of the soul ; then go about the town to sing his "Canti Carnascialeschi" in the company of dissolute youths and indulge in the lowest debauchery. After this he would return home, receive Pulci and Poliziano at his table, and vie with them in reciting verses and discoursing on the poetic art. And whatever was the occupation of the moment, he threw himself into it as heartily as though it were the sole purpose of his life. Strangest of all, in no aspects of this multiform life do we find a single instance of genuine kindness either towards his people, his intimates, or his kindred. Had he performed any good deed, his indefatigable flatterers would certainly not have failed to record it. This is not only a proof of his depravity, but of the still worse depravity of the times ; for had justice and virtue been then rightly valued, Lorenzo would certainly have assumed their championship—at least in appearance.

Among Lorenzo's constant companions were two men of European reputation, and whose names have come down to posterity. One of these was Angelo Poliziano, the most learned man of letters of that learned age, and almost the only writer of his time with a vein of true poetry in his soul. He began a translation of Homer's " Iliad " when only fifteen years of age, and at eighteen composed Greek epigrams and a Latin elegy of incomparable beauty on the death of Albiera degli Albizzi. He was little more than twenty-one years old when his magnificent octaves on the "Tournament" of Giuliano de'

---

[1] Sismondi gives a list of the numerous citizens—chiefly nobles—put to death by Lorenzo for political reasons. See also the marvellous portrait of Lorenzo given by Guicciardini in his " Storia Fiorentina " and his remarks on the Medici at p. 43 and fol. of his " Del Reggimento di Firenze."

Medici established his fame as the first poet of the age and his right to immortality. Winning Lorenzo's favour by these works, he was appointed his private secretary, librarian, and preceptor to his children, and became a permanent member of his household. But in these new and luxurious conditions the sacred fire of poetry gradually waned, although his store of erudition waxed greater and greater until it was truly prodigious. Lorenzo naturally derived much benefit from the service and conversation of a man of such vast acquirements, but Poliziano's position was injurious to his fame. The pertinacity with which later ages have insulted his memory by accusations of unmentionable vice, is probably to be attributed to his excessive intimacy with Lorenzo, whom he sincerely loved and admired.

The prince's other intimate was Messer Luigi Pulci, a youth of noble birth and the brother of two poets whose renown has been almost eclipsed by the superior merit of his own poem the "Morgante Maggiore," a spirited, graceful medley of strange and sparkling fancies, in which an invocation to the Virgin is followed by another to Venus, and this again by a satire on the immortality of the soul. And as the poem, so was the man. He was the most fantastic and light-hearted of mortals : a sceptic brimming over with irony ; a lover of pleasure and sensual excess ; devoted body and soul to Lorenzo, and a sharer in his midnight revels and in all lawful and unlawful amusements. His work was composed at the instance of Lucrezia Tornabuoni, the mother of Lorenzo, and he recited it at the Medici table, where wine flowed as freely as verse.

Besides the company of his friends, Lorenzo also gave much time to the society of artists, taking part in their pleasures and showing a singular interest in their strange adventures and characteristics. He was not able to patronize them so efficiently as Cosimo, who had lavished treasures on the building and decoration of churches and palaces; but he always welcomed them with smiles, and helped and encouraged them by every means at the command of so powerful a prince. Had he done nothing else for the arts, the founding of the garden of St. Mark was in itself a most praiseworthy act. This enclosure contained all the ancient statues and fragments of sculpture he had been able to collect, together with the designs of the best masters, and he opened its gates to all students of any promise. Here Michelangiolo Buonarotti, then a poor and almost unknown youth, made his first essays with the chisel and enjoyed the hospitality that forms one of Lorenzo's best titles of merit.[1]

As yet we have made no mention of the man who, more than all the rest, may be designated as a creature of the Medici. This was Marsilio Ficino, the friend and instructor of Lorenzo, and head of the famous Platonic Academy, whose doctrines were then universally diffused, and modified, to some extent, even those of Savonarola. Of this Academy and its founder we shall speak at length in the ensuing chapter.

---

[1] *Apropos* to this, we may quote an English book: "The Life of Michael Angelo Buonarotti, also Memoirs of Savonarola, Raphael, and Vittoria Colonna," by John S. Harford, 2 vols. London, 1857. This work contains many particulars of Savonarola's times ; but although the author professes different political views from those of Roscoe, he adopts the latter's literary judgments, which are often exaggerated and occasionally false. Since the first edition of our biography, many valuable works on Michelangiolo have appeared. We need only quote that of Springer, " Raffael und Michelangiolo." Leipzig : Seemann, 1877–78.

CHAPTER IV.

HE Council held at Florence in 1439, to promote the union of the Greek and Latin Churches, while rendering no service to religion proved very beneficial to letters. For the representative of the Eastern Church, the Emperor John Paleologus, arrived from Constantinople with many profoundly learned men in his train. These scholars, speaking the tongue of Plato and Aristotle, at that time so generally studied and admired, were accordingly welcomed everywhere with enthusiasm and treated with a respect almost amounting to worship.

Giorgio Scolari [1] and Bessarion, afterwards a convert to Catholicism and ultimately a cardinal, were included in the band, but the most renowned of all the number was Gemistos Pletho, who, although somewhat unjustly neglected by posterity, was then esteemed the first of Greek philosophers. He might have been a contemporary of the sages of old, for so admirable were his writings that it was difficult for the best philologists to distinguish them from those of the brightest period of Grecian

---

[1] Also known as Gennadius.

literature.[1] It was in token of reverence for Plato and profound knowledge of his doctrines that he assumed the name of Georgios Gemistos Pletho. So great, indeed, was his passion for antiquity, that, in his frequent discourses on the approach of a religious reform when a single preacher would teach a single doctrine to the whole world and all differences of creed be swept away, it was easy to see by his words that he hoped for the restoration of the Pagan religion, though with certain modifications in accordance with his own Neo-Platonic beliefs. His principal work "On Laws," in which these ideas were enounced, was burnt by his enemies, after his death, and only a few fragments of it survive.[2] Here, as in all his other writings, the religious hopes of Gemistos are very clearly expressed. Yet—such were the times—he was chosen to represent the interests of the Greek Church, and willingly accepted the charge, believing this Church to be less hostile than the Catholic to his special ideas which were already finding favour in Greece. And even in Italy he was cordially welcomed. The gravity of his manners, his vast learning and advanced age, the elegance of his writings and his almost Platonic diction, endued

[1] On this point there can be no better judge than Giacomo Leopardi, who, in his "Discorso in proposito di una orazione Greca di G. G. Pletone, e traduzioni della medesima" ("Opere," vol. ii. p. 335. Florence: Le Monnier, 1865), deplores the oblivion into which this author has fallen, adding that his writings are dictated "with such abundance and weight of authority, with so much sobriety, power, and elevation of style, purity and refinement of language, that the reader is tempted to pronounce Gemistos the equal, in all save antiquity, of the great Grecian writers of old. And this was the verdict of the learned of his own land in his own age."

[2] Plèthon, "Traité des Lois ou recueil des fragments, en partie inédits, de cet ouvrage." Paris: Didot, 1858. The Greek text was collected by A. Alexandre, translated by A. Pellisier. See also F. Schultze, "Geschichte der Philosophie der Renaissance," vol. i. Jena, 1874. This volume—the only one, we believe, as yet published—is entirely devoted to Gemistos Pletho.

him with an authority that none could contest. But his Platonic convictions must have reaped little satisfaction in Florence, where at that time men read Aristotle and Plato with equal avidity, without noting, almost without perceiving, any difference between the two. After having so long studied the Aristotelian philosophy with the help of its Arabian commentators, the Italians of the fifteenth century at last possessed the original works both of Aristotle and Plato. But, as yet, they passed from one to the other without making any distinction between them. Learned students were then wholly absorbed in struggling with the difficulties of the language and its interpretation; all discussion turned upon points of grammar or philology; and philosophic learning had not yet come into existence. But it was about to arise, and could not fail to turn in favour of Plato, on account of the greater ease with which his doctrines could be brought into harmony with the Christian creed.[1]

It was Gemistos who suddenly started the question in the field of philosophy by his pamphlet " De Platonicæ atque Aristoteliæ philosophiæ differentia."[2] Here, after marshalling the respective claims of the two philosophers with much keenness and penetration, he decided all points in favour of Plato. This caused a mighty quarrel among the Greeks, in which the Italians took part; and thus arose the two parties of Aristotelians and Platonists who disputed with a fierceness that is well-nigh incredible at the present day. Giorgio Scolari and Teodoro Gaza, both Greeks of the Aristotelian camp, were the first to contradict Gemistos, the one with irony, the other with violence.

[1] Tiraboschi, "Storia della Letteratura"; Bruckeri, "Historia Philosophiæ." Leipzig, 1743.

[2] Basileæ, 1574. There is a copy of it in the Marucellian Library of Florence.

Thereupon Bessarion, their adversary's disciple, took up the pen, defending his master in an anonymous letter, in which he sought to reduce the dispute to a more peaceful footing. But, unfortunately, he let it be known that he considered Teodoro Gaza superior in learning to Trapezuntios,[1] another Greek, then in Florence. The latter was a violent, presumptuous man, rough-mannered, and exceedingly touchy. He immediately took up the gauntlet with a fierceness that was surprising to all. In spite of being an Aristotelian, he assailed both camps with equal violence ; styled them *non philosophos sed philotenebras*, and added all sorts of scurrilous abuse ; and then, not content with outraging the living, finally heaped insults on the dead.[2] According to him, Plato had been addicted to every vice—to gluttony, lust, and all kinds of excesses ; was devoid of truth, dignity, or sense of honour, and so on. This unseemly, indecent, and untruthful language naturally roused the disgust of honest men, and Trapezuntios found himself censured and forsaken by all. But this had no effect upon him ; and, persisting in the same course, he passed his closing years in an unhappiness that roused compassion in none.

Meanwhile Bessarion had been engaged on a great work, entitled " In Calumniatorem Platonis," [3] and brought it out when the strife was at the hottest. After triumphantly vindicating the great philosopher's good fame, he proceeded to show that the divergences between his doctrines and those

[1] Likewise known by the name of George of Trebizonde, the birthplace of his parents. He was a native of Crete.

[2] " Comparationes philosophorum Aristotelis et Platonis." Venetiis, 1523.

[3] He brought out two treatises, one of which (" De Natura et arte, adversus Georgium Trapezuntium cretensem ") recounted the whole history of the quarrel ; while the other (" In Calumniatorem Platonis ") treated at length the philosophic part of the question. In the folio edition of this work (Venetiis : in ædibus Aldi et Andreæ Soceri, MDXVI.) the first treatise is added to the second and incorporated in the same book.

of Aristotle, were neither so wide nor so deep as many
had sought to prove.[1]   The Hellenic Aristotle,[2] he concluded, might and could be brought into accord with
Plato: this had been accomplished by the Alexandrians,
therefore might also be accomplished by the Italians of the
fifteenth century.   Thus the discussion was resumed on a
more orderly and courteous basis ; and the philosophy
always known as the Platonic—although in reality Neo-
Platonic or Alexandrian—finally triumphed in Florence.
The tradition of it had always been kept alive in Greece,
and was now transplanted to Italy by its latest supporters.

But the most noteworthy fact in this philosophic strife
was the point on which the whole dispute hinged.   Gemistos maintained that both Plato and Aristotle are agreed
that the operations of Nature have a definite aim ; but,
whereas Plato insists that Nature works with a purpose
(*consulto agit*)—*i.e.*, that there is a spirit or *essence* in
Nature conscious of the aim she has in view—Aristotle
compares Nature to a labourer, who, having once learnt
his trade, continues to work mechanically (*non consulto*),
though always for a definite end.   And according to
Gemistos, the great superiority of the Platonic idea consisted in this : that Nature being the art of God, is vastly
superior to the art of man ; in Nature the hand and spirit
of God are ever present, and although man may sometimes
act by habit, God always acts by supreme reason alone.
The question, however drily and confusedly expressed, was
one of the deepest gravity.   It sought to decide whether
Nature works by reason or by chance ; whether, in short,
Nature be the manifestation of the Divine and universal
spirit, informing and ruling the world, or merely the blind

[1] For information concerning Bessarion, the reader may refer to Henri
Vast, " Le Cardinal Bessarion " (1403–1472) ; " Etude sur la Chrétienté et
la Renaissance." Paris : Hachette, 1878.

[2] Aristotle in the original Greek was always so called, in contradis-
tinction to the versions of the commentators and bad translations.

effect of the laws of matter.   That Gemistos Pletho, in the
fifteenth century, should not only have been able to suddenly
transport Italian scholarship into the field of philosophy,
but also to concentrate it upon a question of vital importance, proved him to be possessed of great philosophic
insight.   Nor was it less remarkable that his learned
contemporaries should have so quickly appreciated the
importance of the question and contested its grounds with
so much zeal.[1]

When Gemistos witnessed the ardour, tempered by
sobriety, with which Bessarion and his former pupil in
Greece championed the Platonic ideas, and saw that these
were triumphing in Florence, he entirely withdrew from
the discussion and sought some more effective way of dif-
fusing and making them permanent.   Having a singular
gift of inspiring others with his own reverence for Plato,
he accordingly sought the acquaintance of Cosimo de'
Medici, plied him with many arguments, gained his attention, and finally succeeded in rousing the enthusiasm of
that powerful ruler.   Then, when he saw that he had
kindled a passion for the new ideas, he went a step farther
and communicated to Cosimo his cherished plan of establishing in Florence a revival of the ancient Academy that
had won so much glory for Greece and been of so much
service in the propagation of the Platonic method.
Cosimo was enchanted with the plan, took it up warmly
and set to work to carry it into effect.   Such was the
origin of the famous Platonic Academy that throughout
the century had so much influence on the progress of
philosophy.[2]

[1] Gemisti Pletonis, "De Platonicæ atque Aristoteliæ philosophiæ
differentia"; Bessarionis, "In Calumniatorem Platonis"; Trapezuntii,
"Comparationes philosophorum Aristotelis et Platonis."

[2] The origin of this Academy is narrated by Ficino in the dedicatory
letter affixed to his Latin translation of Plotinus.   *Vide* Ficini, "Opera."
Basileæ, 1576.   Two vols. in folio.

The triumph of his doctrines being thus assured, Gemistos returned to Peloponnesus in order to pass his few remaining years in tranquillity. But his enemies gave him no peace, and forced him to continue the strife; for the same Scolarius who had been among the first to oppose him in Florence, and was now made Patriarch of Constantinople, carried on the warfare more fiercely than ever. With the zeal of a fanatic, he harassed Gemistos, during his life, by charges of heresy and unbelief; after the philosopher's death, tried to blacken his fame in every way, and finally cast into the flames his manuscript work " On Laws," which was thus irretrievably lost to the world. Nevertheless the name of Gemistos Pletho was greatly renowned in Italy, and so much love and veneration felt for him personally, that in 1465, fifteen years after his death, Sigismund Malatesta carried off his remains during the war in Morea, and brought them to Rimini as sacred relics. They lie buried in that city in a marble sarcophagus, inscribed to the memory of the " Prince of philosophers and learned men,"[1] outside the church of San Francesco, that, thanks to the gold of Malatesta and the genius of Leon Battista Alberti, is one of the noblest gems of the Italian Renaissance.

At that time Savonarola had not yet completed his fourteenth year. But what must he have thought on hearing of the funeral honours paid, at the gates of a church dedicated to St. Francis, to one who had hoped in the revival of Paganism? What, too, must he have felt on learning that the most splendid chapel in the church itself enshrined the monument (Divæ Isottæ Sacrum) erected to her who, before being the wife, was long the

---

[1] "Temisthii Bizantii, philosophor (um) sua temp. (estate) principis reliquum Sig. (ismundus) Pan. (dulfus) Mal. (atesta) Pan. (dulfi) F. (ilius) belli Pelop. (onnesiaci) adversus. Turcor. (um) regem. Imp. (erator) ob. ingentem. eruditorum. quo flagrat. amorem. huc. offerendum. introque. mittendum. curavit. MCCCCLXV."

CHURCH OF SAN FRANCESCO, RIMINI.

TOMB OF GEMISTOS PLETHO, RIMINI.

concubine of that bloodthirsty, sacrilegious adulterer, Sigismondo Malatesta? The whole temple, indeed, would seem to be dedicated to him, to his Isotta, and the deity of the Gentiles, rather than to the Virgin or the God of the Christians. This was certainly in accordance with the Renaissance spirit, and the elegant architecture of the building was deemed all the more worthy of praise. But although the world might laud the name of the blood-

LEON BATTISTA ALBERTI.

stained, sceptical Mecænas, whom a passion for ancient art had urged to this profanation of a Christian church, these were the views, these the men, whereby the fire of Savonarola's wrath was kindled.

But to return to Gemistos. It is an undoubted fact that, owing to the decline of Greek studies among us, his name has been unjustly consigned to oblivion. All students of the history of his times will recognize him as the first to introduce the Platonic philosophy in Italy, and consequently not only justifying the esteem of his contemporaries, but deserving of honour as one of the greatest benefactors of Italian culture.[1]

No sooner had Gemistos left Florence, than Cosimo perceived that the Platonic Academy could not possibly flourish without some ruling spirit at its head. He therefore fixed upon the son of his own medical attendant, a youth of marvellous promise, born in 1433, and named Marsilio Ficino. In his ardour for knowledge, the young Ficino had already devoured Plato's philosophy, and written voluminous works upon it, while still in his teens.[2] Now, spurred by Cosimo, he applied himself to the study of Greek, diligently reading the great philosopher in the original, making commentaries on his works, and preparing for their complete translation. And to this day, notwithstanding the progress achieved in Hellenic philology, Ficino's excellent version still keeps its place in the public esteem.

The young student's veneration for the philosopher reached so idolatrous a pitch that it was publicly asserted that, although a Canon of St. Lorenzo and the champion of Christian philosophy, he kept a lamp burning before

---

[1] Giacomo Leopardi makes an effort to vindicate the fame of Gemistos in the same " Discorso " from which we have before quoted. " If the fame of Georgios Gemistos Pletho, of Constantinople, has passed away simply for this reason, that human celebrity, as indeed may be said of all human things, depends rather on fortune than merit, . . . it is certain that Gemistos had one of the greatest and most beautiful minds of his time, *i.e.*, of the fifteenth century. He lived in honour in his native land ; and then as a survivor of his country and of his Grecian (or, as he said, Roman) name, was welcomed and held dear in Italy, . . . gained a splendid reputation in his new country, and likewise in all other parts of Europe where literary studies were then diffused." G. G. Pletho was born in Constantinople (1355), and died in the Peloponnesus (1450), aged about 95 years. Constantinople had not then fallen into the hands of the Turks ; therefore Leopardi was inaccurate in saying that Pletho "survived his own country and his Greek (he said Roman) name." *Vide* Schultze, op. cit., p. 106.

[2] In riper years he condemned these works to the flames.

Plato's bust. Soon extending his studies over the entire field of ancient literature, he eagerly devoured the works of every sage of old. Aristotelians, Platonists, Alexandrians, he read them all with untiring zeal. He sought out the remains of Confucius and Zoroaster; he studied the Book of Genesis; he leapt from one age to another, from this system to that, almost unconsciously: in his overflowing enthusiasm for ancient lore, all was grist to his mill. At one time the learned world had sworn by Aristotle alone, but now extended its faith to all the ancients. This was undoubtedly a token of advance; and the controversy between the Platonists and Aristotelians was in itself an indication of the approaching triumph of reason.[1] But the day of victory had not yet arrived. Philosophy had first to range the whole field of antiquity, and assimilate results, before becoming conscious of its own independence.

Ficino was so completely absorbed by his feverish passion for study, that he became a species of living dictionary of ancient philosophy, and his works are practically an encyclopædia of all the philosophic doctrines of his time. He was also versed in natural science, and had received some training in medicine from his father. Nevertheless these studies failed to give him habits of judgment and independent observation. Neither his own reason, the whole of nature, nor the consciousness of humanity, sufficed to guide him to the discovery of truth.

[1] In Gibbon's "Decline and Fall of the Roman Empire" we find the following just remark: "So equal, yet so opposite, are the merits of Plato and Aristotle, that they may be balanced in endless controversy; but some spark of freedom may be produced by the collision of adverse servitude." The closing pages of chapter lxvi. of this work are full of important details and remarks on the character and learning of the Greeks who emigrated to Italy. Recently, however, the works of Burckhardt ("Die Renaissance in Italien") and Voigt ("Die Wiederbelebung des classischen Alterthums") have thrown new light on the classic revival in Italy.

He was never content until he could verify results by
reference to Plato, or even to some ancient sceptic or
materialist.

There is a little work by Ficino on the Christian
religion, that, although of small intrinsic importance,
serves to give us the best notion of the strange jumble of
ideas in his brain.[1]   In order to demonstrate the truth of
Christ's teachings and His Divine mission, we find him
beginning with these words:

" The coming of Christ was frequently prophesied by
the Sybils ; the verses in which Virgil foretold it are known
to all.   Plato, on being asked how long the precepts of his
philosophy would endure, replied : Until the coming of
him by whom the source of all truth will be unsealed.
Porphyry says in his responses :—The Gods declared Christ
to be highly pious and religious, and affirmed that he was
immortal, *testifying of him very benignantly.*" Nearly the
whole of the work is based upon similar arguments.
Therefore, according to him, the testimony of the Sybils,
of Virgil, and of Plato, was needed to prove the truth of
the Christian religion ; together with Porphyry's assurance
that the Gods had kindly born testimony to Jesus Christ !
Such was the mind of Marsilio Ficino, such were his
studies ! He was the incarnation of the general spirit of
gladness aroused throughout Europe by the discovery of
the treasures of antiquity, and his mind was so thoroughly
saturated with learning as to become incapable of independent thought. We find him naïvely confessing to his
friends, that in composing his great work on " Platonic
Theology," he had at first intended to write it from a
purely pagan point of view, and only decided after mature
consideration on making it accord with Christianity.[2]

---

[1] " Della Religione Cristiana." Florence : The Giunti Press, 1568.

[2] Bruckeri, " Hist." &c. ; " Marsilii Ficini Vita," auctore Johanne
Corsio, published by Ang. Mar. Bandini.

This was Ficino's principal work,[1] in which he sought to marshal all his doctrines, in a certain logical and systematic form. But no one must expect to find in it any genuine philosophical unity. None existed in the author's mind, and all his writings take the shape of lengthy dissertations, here and there interrupted and confused by a crowd of secondary ideas gleaned from a host of different writers, Neither scientific unity nor logical sequence of thought is to be found in his works. We do not even find the elegance of style that might well be expected from an author who spent his whole life in the study of Greek literature. So true is it that genuine elegance is only born of clear and precise ideas, and by a spontaneous development of thought that had been stifled in the mind of Ficino.

Nevertheless, in the history of science, more especially in that of philosophy, there is a special unity to be found, a vitality appertaining rather to science itself than to its followers, that makes steady progress and cleaves its way through all difficulties opposed to it by the incapacity of its exponents. The quarrel of the Platonists with the Aristotelians had already concentrated philosophy upon a vital point, and thus Ficino was obliged to collect his ideas and arrange them, almost unconsciously to himself, in some sort of unity and system. In what manner does Nature operate ? This was the question then asked by all philosophers ; rather perhaps because it was the theme of the great controversy, than from any real appreciation of its importance. Ficino, although a Platonist, would have preferred either to agree with both parties, or keep silence altogether. This, however, was impossible ; he was forced, on the contrary, to reason out the subject and discuss it in detail. Thus, even his " Theologia Platonica " contained one fundamental problem, around which all secondary questions were necessarily grouped.

[1] V. Marsilii Ficini, " Opera." Basileæ, 1576.

Nature—so he tells us—is animated by a countless number of souls : water, earth, plants, stars, and light, have each a *third essence* or soul of its own. These souls are all rational and immortal, but inseparable from their outer form : they compel Nature to eternal motion by passing through successive transformations ; by them water spontaneously generates animals, the earth vegetation, the stars move in perfect order, and all nature is guided by the Eternal Reason. But do these souls correspond with the idea of Plato, or the form of Aristotle ? With both, said Ficino. According to Plato, matter exists in so far as it corresponds with an idea ; according to Aristotle, in so far as it is possessed of a form. But the latter recognizes in all things one primary form that also predominates in individual things. This form is not substantially different from the idea of Plato, and both are one with the rational soul or *third essence*. It was in this way that Ficino sought to bring Plato and Aristotle into agreement.

This infinite host of souls or *third essences* is divided into twelve orders, according to the twelve signs of the zodiac ; they have a mutual correspondence, and are all mirrored in the soul of man, who is almost the microcosm of all creation. Hence, all the souls of nature can act upon the soul of man, inasmuch as an intercorrespondence exists, and this consequently explains to us the influence of the stars. If the planet Mars, in a certain position, can exercise influence over a man, it is because the martial spirits, into which vigour is infused by the planet, are already existent in him. If some stone or herb excites one passion in us and extinguishes another, this is because the *third essence* of such stone or herb finds in our soul the correspondent or opposite passion. Thus the philosophy of Ficino confirmed all the prejudices of his age, from the which prejudices he was by no means exempt. In fact he ascribed his habitual melancholy to the influence of Saturn.[1]

[1] This we learn from his Epistolæ, particularly from those in Book III.

He always wore a great number of amulets, continually changing them to suit the condition of his mind, and in his tractate " De vita cœlitus comparanda,"[1] he gave a complete account of the influences of stars, stones, and beasts, and descanted on the occult virtues of the agate and topaz, of vipers' fangs, lions' claws, and so on.

Nor were these ideas peculiar to Ficino. They were characteristic of an age in which, as we have said, similar beliefs were gaining fresh strength and daily becoming more diffused. Whether the Greeks had imported them from the East, or because, in the general absence of assured

MARSILIO FICINIO.

faith and genuine science, men's minds were peculiarly disposed to superstition, it is certain that the most earnest thinkers of the day were entirely under their influence. Without strength or courage to think for themselves, they greedily pursued these vain imaginations. Alchemy, judicial astrology, and every other occult science, were again propagated at the Universities, the Courts, and in the public squares. All nature appeared to teem with hidden forces, and mysterious spirits holding converse with mortals. All men, and Italians in particular, were oppressed by presentiments of strange events, mighty changes, and

[1] Lugduni, 1567. It forms the principal part of his work " De Vita."

overwhelming misfortunes. There were many rumours, too, of the alterations and reforms about to take place in religion. We have seen how Pletho looked forward to the triumph of the Gods of Olympus ; and we find the grave and learned Landino drawing the horoscope of religion, and arguing from the conjuction of Jupiter and Saturn that the 25th November, 1484, would be the date of a mighty reform in the Christian faith.[1]   It was an age of doubt and superstition, of icy indifference and strange exaltation. Italians incapable of drawing sword in defence of their country willingly braved a thousand dangers in search of a manuscript ; and believed in spirits, while doubting the existence of a God.   In fact Niccolò Machiavelli said that he thought " the air to be full of spirits, who, in compassion to mortals, gave warning by means of evil omens of the ills about to befall them." [2]   And Francesco Guicciardini likewise affirmed the existence of " aerial spirits, namely those holding familiar converse with men, inasmuch as I have witnessed such an experience of this as to make it appear most certain." [3]   Accordingly Marsilio Ficino merely referred to antiquity in support of the strange beliefs of his age ; and the Neo-Platonic philosophy was marvellously suited to that end.

According to Ficino, we have to recognize two souls in man—namely, first, the sensitive soul or *third essence*, inseparable from the body and subjecting the body, after death, to the eternal transformations of matter ; and, secondly, the mind, or intellectual soul, which is the Divine breath of life, imparted to man by his Creator. This soul is our spiritual and universal nature, is a micro-

[1] Niccolò della Magna, " Commento Alla Divina Commedia." Florence, 1481.   See in particular the passage interpreting the " Veltro allegorico." It has been noticed *à propos* to this date, that Martin Luther was born in the month of November, 1483, or, according to some authorities, 1484.

[2] " Discorsi," bk. i. chap. xvi.

[3] " Ricordi politici e civili," Ricordo ccxi.

cosm of all creation, and in contact with all other souls. Consequently, while drawn to earthly cares, subject to the passions, and full of sorrow and misery, it can rise to the contemplation of celestial things; can see beyond the present, prophesy the future, and, rapt in ecstasy, can behold the blessed vision of Deity. This vision, granted to Plotinus and Porphyry, constitutes the highest felicity attainable on earth; it is the image of the beatitude awaiting us on High. But, what is the Supreme Being according to Ficino? It is Unity. To him, as to all the Neo-Platonists, perfection consists in The One; therefore the Deity is essentially *One,* or indeed *Unity* itself. It might also be said that God is Mind; only that would entail the conclusion that in Him mind is soul and body at the same time. But as the Creator could not deign to come into contact with Nature, He has surrounded His throne with angels, immortal and rational beings, by whose means the creation has been effected of all the *third essences* confided to their charge. Thus from the Supreme Being is emanated an infinite series of souls, of whom one-half is created and governed by the other. The Lord infused His Divine breath into man alone, willing him to be the work of His own hands, and made in His own likeness. For this reason, concludes Ficino, the centre point of the human mind is the point of sublime contact between the Creator and the created.[1]

Such was the substance of Ficino's doctrines: namely, an imitation of Neo-Platonic theories; an amalgamation, as it were, of all antiquity with the Alexandrian school, fusing these doctrines with Christianity by means of fantastic allegory and puerile device. Platonic ideas, Aristotelian forms, third essences, stars, heathen gods, and the angels of the Old and New Testaments, were to be united

[1] This exposition of Ficino's doctrines is entirely derived from his "Theologia Platonica."

in a single conception of a loftier kind. But this new
conception was beyond the powers of Marsilio Ficino.
He had only a confused feeling that the Pagan and
Christian philosophies might be brought into harmony
and cease to contradict each other. This was a need
strongly felt by his age, and consequently his doctrines,
although void of all intrinsic philosophic worth, all
originality and all organic unity, have an historic value
as an expression of the general sentiment by one who
shared it. And notwithstanding the defects of his works,
Ficino undoubtedly promoted the cause of science, aiding
its advance almost unconsciously, and, as it were, against
his will. When he said : The sea has a *third essence* of its
own, rivers another, stones again another, and so forth ;
but there is a *third essence* still more general, constituting
the soul of our whole planet ; even as in all things there is
one form dominating the form of individual things ;—he
was then, unknown to himself, clearing the way for the first
independent and original philosopher that Italy possessed.
For what did Giordano Bruno achieve, when, on the wings
of novel speculation, he took the sublime and daring flight
that led to his tragic end ? He merely united in a single
soul the numerous souls of Ficino. This, he said, is the
soul of the world—mind, body, and soul in one ; God and
nature at the same time, manifested in infinite ways and
infinite worlds ; unrestricted by any limits of time or of
space : in this soul all opposed terms are brought into
accordance. Having once attained to the conception of
this new and supreme Unity, Bruno gave free vent to his
imagination ; the vivid force of his speculative genius
broke through the servile traditions of the Platonic school,
and, full of " heroic fury," he soared into the free heaven
of science, where his star will shine for ever with a special
light of its own.

Bruno, however, was only born in the following century,

and Ficino never dreamt that he was hewing a path for a mind audacious enough to declare war against the adored antiquity in whose cause his whole life had been spent.

Besides his two great works—the translation of Plato and the "Theologia Platonica"—Marsilio Ficino produced innumerable translations from the Alexandrian writers, tractates, epistles, and orations. He gave public lectures in the Florentine school (studio); was the instructor of three generations of the Medici House, *i.e.*, of Cosimo, Piero, and Lorenzo; and was the leading spirit of the new Academy, which, under his rule, at last began to flourish, to the great contentment of its patrons and approbation of the public. When, later, Lorenzo de' Medici honoured its sittings by his presence and took an animated part in its debates, an infinite number of learned men hastened to solicit the privilege of joining the Academy. They used to read Plato's Dialogues, some of the members taking the parts of the various inter- locutors, commenting and supporting their arguments in order to prove that Christianity was taught in them by means of strange and subtle allegories. The Academicians also delivered lengthy Latin orations, and in these the vastness of Ficino's learning was always triumphantly displayed, and Lorenzo's fluent versatility gained hearty applause. The 27th November, the supposed anniversary of Plato's birth and death, and that had always been cele- brated with solemn rites by the Neo-Platonists of antiquity, was observed almost as a religious festival by the Floren- tine Academicians. Crowning the bust of the immortal philosopher with laurel, they enshrined it in a place of honour and hailed it with praises and hymns. By some, fanaticism even went to the extent of proposing that the Pope should be asked to canonize Plato as a saint.[1]

[1] Many authors have written on the Platonic Academy. Ficino fre- quently refers to it, both in his works and his letters. *Vide* also Corsi,

It is difficult to realize the immense importance then attached to this learned assemblage, and the distinction it conferred on Ficino, the Medici, and Florence itself. The city became the resort of scholars from all parts of Italy, and the studious youth of Germany, France, and Spain came there on purpose to attend the lectures of Ficino; for his works were eagerly read throughout Europe, and their merits and defects, truths and errors, alike contributed to swell his popularity. As the discoverer of a system of philosophy reconciling Christianity and Paganism, he was regarded with universal enthusiasm. Even Savonarola was greatly influenced by this Neo-Platonic mysticism, and Ficino praised and admired the Friar in the days of his prosperity, and then—after the fashion of the other learned men—basely forsook and betrayed him in his time of peril.

Meanwhile, however, these same learned men were the undoubted inaugurators of a new epoch of civilization, not only in Florence but throughout Italy. Everywhere professors lectured to attentive crowds, academies and universities flourished, erudite themes were continually discussed; there was an incredible ardour for study. The almost general habit of writing and speaking the Latin tongue, the introduction of printing, by which books were now multiplied and ideas rapidly diffused through the world; the continual effort to bring past, present, and future into harmony—all contributed to draw men closer together, rouse the human species to a consciousness of its

"Ficini Vita." It is mentioned in nearly all histories of Italian philosophy and literature, in those, for instance, of Fabroni, Roscoe, and Gibbon. In Mr. Harford's "Life of Mich. Ang. Buonarotti," &c., there are some pages on the Platonic Academy, which, although containing little fresh information, have the merit of not being mere repetitions of Roscoe and Tiraboschi. But the best account of the Academy is given by Sieveking, "Die Geschichte der Platonischen Akademie zu Florenz," as an appendix to his short history of Florence, published anonymously at Hamburg in 1844.

unity, and spread the sentiment of universal brotherhood that may some day prove the crowning triumph of Christianity. This was, in fact, the inauguration of modern culture, and, as the leader of the great movement, Italy was the school of the world, the civilizer and teacher of all the European nations, by whom her benefits were afterwards so cruelly repaid. Scholars and erudites, servile plagiarists of antiquity, even Lorenzo de' Medici himself, were all involuntary instruments of this great work, and unconscious contributors to the establishment of modern civilization and the triumph of free thought.

CHAPTER V.

*HIS FIRST RESIDENCE IN TUSCANY, TRAVELS
IN LOMBARDY, AND RETURN TO FLORENCE.*

(1481—1490.)

FTER the first few days in Florence, Savonarola was again oppressed by a feeling of isolation. Intimacy with the inhabitants quickly betrayed the confirmed scepticism and flippancy hidden beneath their great intellectual culture. The general absence of principle and faith once more threw him back upon himself, and his disgust was all the greater in consequence of the lofty hopes with which he had entered Florence. Even among the brethren of St. Mark's there was no real religious feeling, for although the name of St. Antonine was so often on their lips, it was uttered in a vainglorious rather than a loving spirit. But, above all, his indignation was aroused by the much-vaunted studies of the Florentines. It was a new and horrible experience to him to hear them wrangling over the precepts of Plato and Aristotle, without caring or even perceiving that from party spirit and in the heat of discussion they were denying the most essential principles of the Christian faith. Accordingly he began, from that moment, to regard all these men of letters, erudites, and philosophers, with a sort of angry contempt, and this

feeling increased in strength to the point of often leading
him to disparage the very philosophy in which, by many
years of strenuous labour, he was himself so thoroughly
versed.

But in no case would it have been possible for him
to have long retained the sympathy of the Florentines,
inasmuch as they were held apart from the newly arrived
Friar by an irreconcilable diversity of temperament.
Everything in Savonarola came from the heart, even
his intellect was ruled by its generous impulse, but his
manners and speech were rough and unadorned.   He
spoke with a harsh accent, expressed himself in a homely
way, and made use of lively and almost violent gesticulations.   Now the Florentines preferred preachers of
scholarly refinement of gesture, expression, and style, able
to give an unmistakable imitation of some ancient writer,
and copious quotations from others : as to the gist of the
sermon, they cared little about it ; often, indeed, conferring
most praise on the speaker who allowed them to see that
he had little belief in religion.   Savonarola, on the contrary, thundered forth furious diatribes against the vices
of mankind, and the scanty faith of clergy and laity ;
he spoke disparagingly of poets and philosophers, condemned the strange craze for ancient authors, and, quoting from no book save the Bible, based all his sermons on
its texts.   Now there were few Florentines who read the
Bible at all, since finding its Latin incorrect, they were
afraid of corrupting their style.

Having entered the Convent of St. Mark towards the
end of 1481, the following year Savonarola was charged
by the friar with the instruction of the novices, and
applied himself to the task with his accustomed zeal.
Continually dominated by the same mystic enthusiasm,
he constantly exhorted his pupils to study the Scriptures,
and often appeared among them with tear-swollen eyes,

and wrought almost to ecstasy by prolonged vigils and fervid meditation.[1]

His inspired oratory soon exercised a potent fascination over his youthful hearers, who listened most reverently to his words, and accordingly he was invited to preach the Lenten sermons in St. Lorenzo. But here, in the presence of a coldly critical public accustomed to another style of preaching, and preferring eloquence and doctrines of a very different sort, his words could make no effect. His congregation went on diminishing, until at last, towards the end of Lent, it was reduced to twenty-five persons, women and children included.[2]

Savonarola quickly understood the cause of his failure. He knew what kind of men were most successful in Florence, and the devices employed by them to attract

---

[1] Burlamacchi, p. 13 and fol. ; Cinozzi, "Epistola," Codex 2053. Riccardi Library, Florence.

[2] This is mentioned in Burlamacchi's " Biografia Latina," and Cinozzi, in his biographic " Epistle," states that he attended Savonarola's Lenten sermons in St. Lorenzo the year after the Friar's arrival in Florence, in 1481. Cav. Gherardi is inclined to doubt this (" Nuovi Documenti," p. 246 and fol.), inasmuch as the result of his researches (p. 11 and fol.) was that neither in the latter part of 1482, nor at any period in 1483, had Savonarola preached in St. Lorenzo. If we accept Father Marchese's opinion that Savonarola could not have come to Florence before May, 1482, the time when the war with Ferrara first broke out, it was certainly impossible that he could have preached in St. Lorenzo during the Lenten season of 1482. But we have already shown that, according to the evidence of all the biographers, he may have come to Florence at an earlier date. It is true that we find it recorded in the " Annals of St. Mark's Convent " (c. 219[t]) that " Savonarola erudiendis fratribus Florentiam missus est anno 1482 ;" but this is not enough to overthrow the testimony of the biographers, nor, above all, that of Cinozzi. All these writers were Savonarola's contemporaries and monks of the same convent. Consequently their evidence is at least as good as that of Ubaldini, who first began the compilation of the "Annals" in 1505, with the aid of an older volume (V.a.c.1[v]), giving fewer particulars regarding Savonarola. It is also quite possible that his vague, inexact phraseology was merely intended to express that Savonarola was charged with the instruction of the novices in 1482, not that he had only just then arrived in Florence.

the attention of a public almost deaf to the precepts of Christianity, and only delighting in Pagan quotations and elegant turns of speech, with an occasional dash of sceptical or indecent allusion. Accordingly there was no reason to be much disheartened by his want of success. But all who have any experience of the troubles always besetting the first steps of any man's career in life, and the doubts and uncertainties to be overcome, before he can attain to a sure appreciation of his own value, will easily see how painfully Savonarola must have been impressed by the coldness of his reception. He found himself checked at the very beginning of his path, for the way now closed to him was necessary to his existence. He was burning with an irresistible desire to address the world, in order to convert it to virtue and faith; and day by day his desire burnt more hotly within him. But how was he to move and gain power over hearers such as these? How could he rise to eloquence, when he could elicit no spark of sympathy? The cynical smiles with which his words were received had the effect of a cold douche on his head, paralyzed his heart, and checked his enthusiasm. Accordingly he determined to follow the advice given him by others, and return to teaching and interpreting the Scriptures. The decision cost him much pain, but he saw its necessity, and therefore announced it from the pulpit to his scanty congregation.[1]

Fortunately for him, he was just then sent by his superiors to Reggio d'Emilia, to attend a Chapter of the Dominicans held in that town. He set out on the journey much troubled and oppressed by his mishaps in Florence. His sadness was increased on the road by the news of the war that was then breaking out against his native Ferrara. Reflecting that these ills were solely caused by the insatiable ambition of a Pope, who shame-

[1] Burlamacchi, p. 14; Cinozzi, " Epistola."

fully plunged all Italy in confusion for the aggrandise-
ment of his so-called nephews, Savonarola became more
and more excited, and arrived at Reggio in a white
heat of indignation.   He came as the representative of St.
Mark's Convent, and the Chapter was attended not only
by a great number of ecclesiastics, but also by several
laymen of distinguished repute in letters and science.[1]

Of all these visitors, the personage who attracted most
attention was the celebrated Giovanni Pico, Count of
Mirandola.[2]   Although not yet twenty years of age,
he was already famed in Italy as a prodigy of science,
and the name of Phœnix of Genius, by which he was
afterwards known to all, was already bestowed on him
by many.   Even in childhood his precocious intelligence and marvellous memory had excited astonishment.
Making rapid progress in all his studies, he frequented
the principal universities of Italy and France, showing
a feverish ardour for work.   Not content with writing
Latin and Greek with even greater ease than his native
idiom, he was the first to devote himself to the study
of Oriental languages and of all other tongues for which
teachers and grammars could be found ; and was said
to be acquainted with no less than twenty-two.   In
science as well as languages he aspired to universal
knowledge, hoping to grasp the *omne scibile* of his time.

[1] Cav. Gherardi (" Nuovi Documenti," p. 250 and fol.) proves that the
Chapter of Reggio could not have been held in 1486, as was supposed,
but only in 1482. Hence the necessity of accepting the fact of Savonarola's brief journey to that place, of which the old biographers made no
mention. Nevertheless they all state that Savonarola attended the
Chapter, without fixing its date, and furthermore add that at the end of
the first Lenten season after his arrival in Florence, he immediately
set out towards Lombardy. This would seem to prove that we have
placed events in their due order, although the biographers have confused this short journey with the other, and much longer one, afterwards
made by Savonarola to the same part of Italy.

[2] Uncle to the Giovanni Francesco Pico who wrote the life of
Savonarola.

Being well versed in theology and philosophy, he sought
to bring them into agreement, and even to reconcile
Paganism with Christianity. Overwhelmed with praise
from all quarters, he conceived so lofty an opinion of
himself that, on going to Rome in 1486, he proposed
a philosophical tournament of a new and singular kind.
Issuing nine hundred propositions embracing, as he
declared, the whole range of science, he announced
himself ready to reply to all comers on every one of
these points, sent invitations to the learned world in
his own name, and promised to pay the expenses of all
combatants unable to afford the journey. His propositions were but poor stuff in the main, and of no special
significance ; but as some of them touched on judicial
astrology and serious philosophico-religious questions, all
the nine hundred were condemned by Pope Innocent
VIII., and his challenge fell to the ground.

Pico then wrote an Apology, and tendered his submission to the Court of Rome ; but it was long before he
was pardoned. Nevertheless, and perhaps in consequence
of all this, his fame continued to spread. Certainly no
other name, Lorenzo de' Medici's alone excepted, became
so rapidly and generally celebrated as that of Pico della
Mirandola. Posterity, however, has shown him little
indulgence, and his reputation has gradually died out.
His vast erudition was on the whole very superficial ;
he was inferior to Poliziano in letters, to Ficino in
philosophy.[1] As to his vaunted knowledge of twenty-
two languages and their respective literatures, it was so
slight that a Jew was able to palm upon him sixty
manuscripts as books written by the command of

[1] Io. Pici " Opera omnia." Basileæ, ex officina Henricpetrina. Two
folio volumes, the second of which contains the works of his nephew
Giov. Franc. Pico. Pico's philosophy was merely a feeble copy of
that of Ficino.

Esdrus, whereas in reality they were only the well-known " Cabbala." And it is certain that his acquaintance with some of the twenty-two tongues went little further than their alphabets. He wrote very inelegant Italian, and his literary judgment was so faulty, that he was one of the critics who rated the poems of Lorenzo de' Medici above those of Petrarch and Dante.[1] Nevertheless he had undoubted merits in other things. He was the first to extend the learning of his age to the Oriental tongues, previously unstudied by all; he was an example of unflagging industry in the cultivation of letters, and of a prince who renounced the privileges of rank to live on an equality with the learned world. His quickness of mind; his wonderful memory; the varied brilliancy of his conversation; his nobility and grace ; his youthful beauty ; the fair hair falling in thick curls on his shoulders; everything about him, in short, attracted sympathy, and helped to advance his reputation.[2] Such was the man who was the centre of attraction to all the distinguished scholars attending the Chapter at Reggio, and to whom homage was paid by the highest dignitaries of the Church. At that moment, fresh from the Universities of Bologna and Ferrara, where he had completed his studies in theology and philosophy, he was at the height of his youthful beauty, and already renowned for his eloquence.

[1] " Lettera " addressed to Lorenzo de' Medici, 15th July, 1484. There were many at that time who held Dante's poetry to be of very little account.

[2] A host of authors have written on G. Pico della Mirandola ; but a true appreciation of his powers can only be gained by perusal of his numerous works. These treat of the most varied topics, and although frequently very superficial, are always informed with a genuine and ardent love of truth. Among the many volumes devoted to Poliziano, we must not fail to mention a little known collection of historical essays by the Rev. W. Pair Creswell, published at Manchester, 1805. It contains much useful information on Poliziano and other men of learning.

PICO DELLA MIRANDOLA.

Meanwhile our hero, Savonarola, sat among the other monks, absorbed in his own thoughts, his cowl drawn over his head. His pale and haggard face, the fixed yet sparkling glance of his deep-set eyes, the heavy lines seaming his forehead—his whole appearance, in short, indicated a profoundly thoughtful mind. Any one comparing him with Pico, the one full of charm, courteous, sociable, and buoyant; the other full of gravity, lonely, severe and almost harsh, might have judged the two characters to be thoroughly antagonistic and incapable of coming to an understanding. Yet from that day each felt drawn to the other, and their sympathy went on increasing. Neither fame, flattery, nor self-conceit succeeded in spoiling Pico's heart. His nature, unlike that of the other learned men of the day, was essentially good, and readily receptive of the holy inspirations of truth and goodness. Thus, despite all real and apparent dissimilarities existing between them, these two men became united in an enduring friendship.

That same day Savonarola was suddenly stirred to action. So long as the discussion turned upon dogma he remained motionless and silent, not caring to take part in a merely scholastic dispute. But when a question of discipline was mooted, he started to his feet, and his powerful accents had the effect of a thunder-clap upon his hearers and transfixed them with amazement. Inveighing against the corruptions of the Church and the clergy, he was so carried away by the impetus of his own words, that he found it difficult to cease speaking. This harangue revealed him to his audience as an extraordinary man, of superior mental endowment.[1] Many sought his acquaintance; several entered into correspondence with him; but the person most transported by his eloquence was the youthful Pico, who from that day became his

---

[1] Burlamacchi, p. 15 ; " Biografia Latina," et c. 4ᵗ.

sincere admirer, although their reciprocal friendship only
grew up at a later date. He began to speak of him as a
wonderful man, gifted with a mysterious moral force, and
who, once known, could never be forgotten. At that
moment, however, Pico's classical studies were leading
him in a different groove and with other ideals in view.

On going back to Florence, Savonarola resumed his
special studies and his labours as a teacher; but he found
it impossible to adhere to his former decision of never
again attempting to preach. His first sermons, however,
were very modest, and only addressed to a small audience
in the little church of the Murate convent. The Florentine public still remained unimpressed by his words, for
erudition and Paganism were more triumphant in the
pulpit than ever.

Frà Mariano de Genazzano, a monk of the Augustinian
Order, was then preaching in Santo Spirito, and the great
church proved too small for the crowds flocking to hear
him. This Frà Mariano was in high favour with the
Medici, who had erected a convent for him outside the
Porta San Gallo, to which Lorenzo the Magnificent—in
his desire to prove the universality of his knowledge—
often repaired to discuss theology with him. He had
a great reputation in Florence, and especially among the
literary men of the Court, who all flocked to hear him
and praised him to the skies. Poliziano gives an eloquent
description of the orator's merits, in a very beautiful
letter, but, unconsciously to himself, his praises betray
the faults of preacher and congregation alike.

"I went," writes Poliziano to his friend, Tristano
Calco, "feeling badly disposed, and mistrustful of the
great praises I had heard of him. But no sooner did
I enter the church than the preacher's appearance, his
habit and his face, wrought a revulsion in my feelings,
and I at once desired and expected great things. I

confess to thee, that he frequently seemed to soar to a gigantic height in the pulpit, far beyond all human proportions. And now, behold, he begins to speak! *I am all ears to the musical voice, the chosen words, the grand sentences. Then I note the clauses, recognize the periods, am swayed by their harmonious cadence, &c.*" [1]

Thus, even a man of Poliziano's great taste and learning, was principally struck by the preacher's choice of words and harmonious periods. The friar's name has indeed been forgotten by posterity; but contemporaries extolled him to the sky, and so far, Savonarola was completely overshadowed by this rival. Even Girolamo Benivieni, already his faithful follower, said to him: " Father, one cannot deny that your doctrine is true, useful, and necessary; but your manner of delivering it lacks grace, especially as it is daily compared with that of Frà Mariano." To which Savonarola made reply, almost in anger : " These verbal elegancies and ornaments will have to give way to sound doctrine simply preached." [2] But that was still in the future, and meanwhile Frà Mariano's popularity daily increased. His words, phrases, and gestures were all studied; his lines from the Latin poets were declaimed with much elegance; and he was lavish of quotations from Plato and Aristotle. His sermons were copied from the orations of Ficino to the Platonic Academy, which were then considered models of the highest eloquence; he

[1] "Politiani Opera," two vols. Lugduni, 1533. *Vide* vol. ii. p. 116, the letter to Tristano Calco with the date *xi kal. Aprilis* 1489. Niccolò Valori, " Vita Laurentii Medicei." Florentiæ, 1749. In Quetif's additions to Pico's "Vita di Savonarola " there are some particulars regarding Frà Mariano da Genazzano. Vol ii. p. 22.

[2] " Epistola " of Girolamo Benivieni to Pope Clement VII., in defence of Savonarola's doctrines and prophecies. It is in the Codex 2022 of the Riccardi Library, and was published by Signor G. Milanesi at the conclusion of Benedetto Varchi's " Storia Fiorentina." Florence : Le Monnier, 1857–58.

frequently recounted laughable anecdotes, and used every device to swell the number of his hearers.[1]

The success of a rival of this kind was no humiliation to Savonarola. Nevertheless it irritated him to see a whole city running after polished niceties of form even in church, and, careless of Holy Writ, preferring a preacher who followed Cicero, rather than the Bible, the Fathers, or the martyrs of the Faith.[2] Instead of disheartening him, however, this irritation spurred his indignation and made him increasingly pertinacious of his own ideas. The popular indifference merely proved the necessity of his efforts and convinced him that he had a mission from above. He recalled the history of the prophets of old, and how they had been obliged to fight against the ingratitude of the Jews. The comparison heightened his wrath and strengthened his resolve to war to the death against the vices of the age and the scandals of Rome. In prayer, contemplation, and ecstasy he awaited some direct revelation from God. According to Ficino's philosophy, such revelation was not only possible, but could be scientifically explained, and the Friar, in his religious earnestness and mysticism, so ardently yearned for it, that he at last believed it vouchsafed to him.

In this strangely excited state of mind, further increased by prolonged watching and abstinence, it is not surprising that Savonarola should have seen many visions. On one occasion, while conversing with a nun, he suddenly, as he thought, beheld the heavens open: all the future calami-

[1] Burlamacchi, p. 24.

[2] All this is proved by Poliziano's letter, quoted above, and the letters of other contemporaries. One of these is given in the Appendix to the Italian edition. Frà Mariano's sermons have never, we think, been published. We have only two of his Orations : one addressed to Innocent VIII., the other to Alexander VI., published during the fifteenth century, and mentioned in Cappelli's " Frà Girolamo Savonarola," &c., p. 12. The second is only to be found in the Public Library of Modena, and neither serves to give us any idea of his sermons.

ties of the Church passed before his eyes, and he heard a
voice charging him to announce them to the people.[1]
From that moment he was convinced of his Divine mission,
held it to be the main duty of his life, and thought of
nothing but how best to fulfil it.   He longed to be able to
make his voice resound over the whole earth, and cry to
all nations : " Repent ye, and return to the Lord."   The
visions of the Old Testament and the Apocalypse stood
arrayed in his fancy as living realities, representing the
calamities of Italy and the Church, and symbolical of their
future regeneration by his efforts.   On all sides he heard
voices urging him to persist in his undertaking, without
yielding to weariness and without being cast down by the
indifference of the Florentines.

In the same year (1484) the death of Pope Sixtus IV.
occurred, and while many hoped that a successor would be
chosen able to put an end to the woes of the Church, it
was rumoured that there was some fear of a schism owing
to the serious dissensions going on in the conclave.   It was
then that Savonarola composed a laud, addressed to Jesus
Christ, containing these words : —

> " Deh ! mira con pietate in che procella,
>   Si trova la tua sposa,
> E quanto sangue, oimé ! tra noi s'aspetta,
>   Se la tua man pietosa,
> Che di perdonar sempre si diletta
>   Non la riduce a quella
> Pace che fu, quando era povereila." [2]

---

[1] This fact was mentioned in the Trial of Savonarola, printed in the
fifteenth century, and given, together with the other documents we discovered, in the Appendix to the Italian edition.   It is also mentioned
by Father Marchese, " Storia di San Marco," p. 118 ; and Frà Benedetto alludes to it in his writings.

[2] " Lauda composta l'anno," 1484 : Poem viii. in the Florence edition
of 1847.

Translation.—Ah, look with pity on thy storm-beaten bride ! Look on
the blood that must, alas, be shed, Unless Thy merciful hand, The hand
ever ready to pardon, Will not restore her to the peace of past days of
poverty.

The result of the election shattered the hopes of honest men. All Italy echoed with the details of the scandalous traffic carried on in the conclave ; every one knew the names of those who had sold their votes and the prices paid for them. And no sooner had Innocent VIII. ascended the Papal throne, than his conduct of affairs, incredible though it seem, made men look back with regret to the days of Sixtus ! For the present Pope no longer disguised his children under the title of nephews, but called them princes, and openly acknowledged them as his sons. He was not only a parent, and a dissolute parent, but so lenient to all descriptions of vice, that the Roman Court became the head-quarters of sensuality and scandalous living. All men were revolted by actions, equally threatening to religion and dishonouring to humanity ; nor was it possible to foresee to what fate Italy might be doomed, under the deepening misrule of the Papacy. It had seemed impossible that the successor of Sixtus should not be better than his predecessor, but now all hope and faith in the future were lost. And if this state of things roused even a corrupt people to wrath, what must have been its effect on the mind of Savonarola ? Certainly, the storm of emotion stirred in his soul can be more readily imagined than described.

Fortunately for him, in the years 1484-85,[1] he was sent as Lenten preacher to the little republic of San Gimignano among the Sienese hills. It was then very unlike the poor, deserted little town of the present day. Even now its lofty coronal of towers, visible from a great distance, its churches lined with the fairest works of Domenico Ghirlandaio, and Benozzo Gozzoli, and its municipal buildings remain to prove that San Gimignano was once a flourishing centre of artistic and political life. For although its inhabitants may have lacked the exquisite refinement of

[1] *Vide* the " Trial," before quoted.

the Florentines, at least their simplicity was uncorrupted by over-study and sophistry. Their religious ideas were not drowned in a sea of classic phraseology, nor were they, like Poliziano, content to hear nothing from their preachers save skilful syntax and a musical flow of words. Among those hills and valleys the land wears an eternal smile, spring is a season of almost heavenly beauty, and the broad, tranquil horizon seen from the heights reconciles man with nature, and draws him nearer to God.

Therefore, among the towers of San Gimignano, Savonarola could raise his voice more freely and with greater effect. It was here that he first expounded the ideas which had so long filled his soul, and pronounced the words which were to become his war-cry and the standard of his whole life : namely, first, that the Church will be scourged ; secondly, that it will be speedily regenerated ; thirdly, that all this will come to pass quickly. We have his own words to prove that he refrained at the time from announcing these utterances as revelations from Heaven, inasmuch as the people did not seem to him ripe for such things, and he supported them on natural reason and the authority of the Bible.[1]

The history of the Hebrew people, indeed, consists of an unceasing series of transgressions and punishments, and it accordingly furnished Savonarola with numberless arguments to the effect that the universal corruption of the Church must inevitably draw down the scourge of God's wrath.[2] And he expounded these arguments all the more forcibly since they had first convinced him that

---

[1] In Savonarola's " Compendium Revelationum," and in his sermons of 97 and 98, we find the history of his preachings frequently repeated. See, too, the " Processo," Benivieni's "Epistola," Burlamacchi, Frà Benedetto, &c.

[2] To Franc. Pico, " Vita," &c. In chap. v. it is minutely explained how Savonarola discovered in the Bible the first grounds of his belief in the necessity of the chastisements he foretold to Italy and the Church.

he was divinely inspired, even before his religious excitement was heightened by the heavenly visions of which he believed himself the recipient. Besides, his courage always rose whenever he inveighed against the corruption of manners, or predicted the scourges to come; his words flowed more freely, were more eloquent and effective; the public attention was roused, his audience moved almost to ecstasy. Accordingly, at San Gimignano he at last found his true vocation; discovered that his own gloomy presentiments were also lurking in the hearts of the multitude, and that by his daring announcement of the scourges at hand he almost revealed the Italians to themselves, and found a general echo to his own thoughts. He therefore returned to Florence in a calmer mood and with greater confidence in himself; but while strengthened in his principles, he had also learnt caution from experience, and was more reticent in his addresses to the indifferent public.

He retained his modest post of lecturer to the novices to the Lent of 1486, when he was sent to preach in various cities of Lombardy, and especially in Brescia. Here, with the Book of Revelations for his theme, he found it easier to stir the sympathies of his hearers. His words were fervent, his tone commanding, and he spoke with a voice of thunder; reproving the people for their sins, denouncing the whole of Italy, and threatening all with the terrors of God's wrath. He described the forms of the twenty-four elders and represented one of them as rising to announce the future calamities of the Brescians. Their city, he declared, would fall a prey to raging foes; they would see rivers of blood in the streets; wives would be torn from their husbands, virgins ravished, children murdered before their mothers' eyes; all would be terror, and fire, and bloodshed. His sermon ended with a general exhortation to repentance, inasmuch as the Lord would have mercy on the just. The mystic image of the elder made a deep impression upon the people. The preacher's voice seemed really to resound from the other world; and his threatening predictions awakened much alarm. During the sack of Brescia, in 1512, by the ferocious soldiery of Gaston de Foix, when, it is said, that about six thousand persons were put to the sword, the inhabitants remembered the elder of the Apocalypse and the Ferrarese preacher's words.[1]

The great success of these Lenten sermons at last made the name of Savonarola known to all Italy, and decided the course of his life, for henceforward he no longer doubted his mission. Yet, such was the goodness and candour of his nature, that self-confidence only made him more modest and humble. His ardour for prayer, his faith and devout exultation rose to so great a height, that, as his companion, Frà Sebastiano of Brescia, says, Savonarola, when engaged in prayer, frequently fell into a trance; after celebrating mass was so transported with holy fervour as to be obliged to retire to some solitary place; and a halo of light was often seen to encircle his head.[2]

Savonarola remained in Lombardy until the January of 1489, and during that period wrote to his mother from Pavia a long and most affectionate letter. In this he begs her to forgive him if he has nothing but prayers to offer to his family, since his religious profession precludes him from helping them in other ways; but he adds that in his heart he still shares their sorrows and their joys. " I have renounced this world, and have become a labourer in my Master's vineyard in many cities, not only to save my own soul, but the souls of other men. If the Lord have entrusted the talent to me, I must needs use it as He wills;

[1] Burlamacchi, pp. 13–14 ; Frà Benedetto, " Vulnera Diligentis," bk. i. chap. xvii. ; Pico, chap. v. See also Barsanti, " Della Storia del Padre Girolamo Savonarola da Ferrara." Leghorn, 1782.

[2] Burlamacchi, p. 13 and fol. ; Barsanti, &c.

and seeing that He hath chosen me for this sacred office, rest ye content that I fulfil it far from my native place, for I bear better fruit than I could have borne at Ferrara. There it would be with me as it was with Christ, when His countryman said : ' *Is not this man a carpenter, and the son of a carpenter ?* ' [1] But out of my own place this has never been said to me; rather, when I have to depart, men and women shed tears, and hold my words in much esteem. I thought to have written only a few lines; but love hath caused my pen to run on, and I have opened my heart to you far more than was my purpose. Know, then, that this heart of mine is more than ever bent on devoting soul and body, and all the knowledge granted to me by God, to His service and my neighbours' salvation ; and since this work was not to be done in my own land, I am fain to perform it elsewhere. Encourage all to righteous living. I depart for Genoa this day." [2]

Of Savonarola's preachings in Genoa nothing is known to us. But we know that in the summer of 1489 he was suddenly recalled by his superiors to Florence, and, strangely enough, at the express desire of Lorenzo de' Medici. The prince made the request in order to gratify his favourite friend, Pico della Mirandola, who had earnestly pressed him to do so. At this moment Pico

[1] Savonarola used the term *smith* (fabbro) instead of "carpenter," but we have preferred to give the usual reading.—TRANSLATOR'S NOTE.

[2] Padre Marchese, "Lettere inedite di Frà Girolamo Savonarola," Letter I. (Appendix of the "Archivio Storico Italiano,' vol. viii.). This letter to his mother is published from a sixteenth century copy, preserved in the Library of St. Mark and dated : *Scripta in Pavia, in pressia, el dì de la conversione di San Paolo Apostolo*, 1490, the which date signifies the 25th of January 1490, since the Lombards did not reckon by the Florentine calendar, according to which the year would have really been 1489. It is our belief that the letter was certainly written in 1489, and that the copyist either made a mistake or reckoned by the Florentine calendar. Otherwise Savonarola could not have returned to Florence in 1489, although we have his own words to prove that he really returned in that year.

was in a very difficult position. His nine hundred propositions, published at the end of 1486, had been recently
censured in Rome. He had instantly declared his submission to the authority of the Church, and even published an
"Apology"; but this only inflamed the anger of the Pope,
who threatened the author with excommunication unless he
retracted all that he had said. Pico resolutely refused to
do this, denying that he had asserted any heretical doctrine,
and faithfully adhering to his own theories on philosophy
and religion. The matter began to look serious, for Pico
was so furious that Lorenzo de' Medici, who had assumed
the part of mediator, wrote to Rome to warn the Pope not
to go too far, unless he was prepared for a great scandal
and wished to drive a devout believer from the fold of the
Church.[1] Meanwhile Pico remained very uneasy and disturbed in his mind, and felt the need of advice from some
one of real independence of character as well as of lively
faith in religion. In these circumstances he remembered the
zealous Friar, worn with watching and prayer, whose voice
had thundered so grandly at Reggio against the corruption
of the Church and the clergy. He accordingly entreated
Lorenzo to recall this Friar to Florence, assuring him that
the man would be a source of renown both to himself and
the city. Lorenzo readily granted his friend's wish, and,
making him write the order of recall, affixed his own seal
to it and despatched it to the superiors of the Order.

Thus the future foe of the Medici, and the destroyer
of their power, was summoned back to St. Mark's at the
instance of their chief. Pico was as yet slightly acquainted
with the man of whom he was afterwards to become so

---

[1] He wrote many letters, some of which are dated 1489. Part of
them were published by Fabroni among the documents appended to
his "Vita Laurentii Medicis Magnifici;" others were given by Prof.
D. Berti in his essay, "Intorno a G. Pico della Mirandola, cenni e
documenti," first published in the "Rivista Contemporanea" of Turin
(1859). Pico had been to Paris, and was then in Florence.

fervent a disciple; and Lorenzo, with all his keen sagacity,
neither foresaw the evils he was bringing on his house,
nor the flame his own hands were kindling in the convent
that his grandfather had built.[1]

[1] Burlamacchi, p. 15, tells us that Savonarola's recall to Florence was
effected by Pico's entreaties to Lorenzo and the orders given by Lorenzo
to the superiors of the convent. The same statement is repeated in Burlamacchi's " Biografia Latina," C. 4*t*. Mons. Perrens (" Jérome Savonarola, sa vie, ses prédications et ses écrits," vol. i. p. 35. Paris, 1853)
expresses doubt as to the interference of Pico and Lorenzo, and, relying
on a Codex in the Marcian Library of Venice, says that he was merely
recalled by his superiors. This, however, does not preclude the intervention of Lorenzo in the affair. Further particulars are given in certain
sixteenth century manuscripts containing an older and more extended compilation of Burlamacchi than the printed version, and one in closer accordance with that author's " Biografia Latina." In fact, we find it stated in
the Magliabecchian Codex, I. viii. 43, dating from the sixteenth century,
that Pico warmly entreated Lorenzo, and that the latter, " to gratify the
Count, for whom he had a singular affection, sent for Ser Piero da Bibbiena, his secretary and counsellor, and bade him write his commands to
the Lombard Fathers of the Order of St. Dominic. And then he turned
to the Count and said : Since you know that I will faithfully serve you
with good will and good ink, your Excellency shall compose the letter
after your own fashion, and my secretary shall write it out, and having
written it, shall seal it with my seal. And thus was it done. And it befell
Lorenzo, as it befell Pharaoh, whose daughter saved Moses and fostered
him, by whose means her father was doomed to be drowned." Professor
Ranke, in his recent essay on Savonarola, also refuses to credit this fact.
But,-like Mons. Perrens, he is unacquainted with the Italian Codex from
which we quote, and also with the " Biografia Italiana." He observes,
however, that the fact must have been known to Pico's nephew, who
merely says in his biography of Savonarola, that the friar *ab præposito
accersitus, qui Joanni Pico patruo meo hac in re morem gerebat, Florentiam appulit* (*vide* Ranke, op. cit. p. 349). Pico really says : " *Post
hæc, et angelicis colloquiis monitus, et ab eius præpositis accersitus,
qui Ioanni, Pico patruo meo hac in re morem gerebant, Florentiam
appulit* " (chap. vi.). That is to say, he was recalled by his superiors, who in so doing obeyed the will of my uncle, Giovanni Pico. And,
according to the Italian codex before quoted, the latter had dictated the
letter that was sealed with Lorenzo's seal. Therefore Pico's statement
agrees in the main with that in the printed version of Burlamacchi, with
the Italian codex and the " Biografia Latina," or at least does not contradict them. But the crowning proof is contained in Lorenzo's "Memoranda " of his daily correspondence, preserved in the " Archivio Medicio
avanti il principato " (Cod. No. 63), in which, at sheet 94*t*, we find the
following. record : " April, 1489, 29th day.—To the General of the
Preaching Friars for the recall of Frà Hieronymo of Ferrara." We are
indebted for this detail to the kindness of Cav. Gherardi.

Savonarola obediently responded to the summons, but throughout the journey felt a presentiment of coming change. At Brescia strange prophecies had been vouchsafed to him of what should befall him in Florence, and he was therefore convinced that he was bidden to go thither by the Lord's command.[1] Passing by Bologna, he crossed the Apennines on foot. It was the same road he had traversed before ; he was returning to the city that had received him so coldly ; he felt himself drawn by an irresistible force towards some new and mysterious fate. It was a hot season, and he became exhausted by the fatigues of the journey and great mental excitement. At Pianoro, about eight miles from Bologna, his strength suddenly failed, and he was unable to continue his road, or to take any sustenance. All at once a mysterious stranger appeared before him, restored his courage and strength, led him to a hospice, forced him to take food, and then bore him company to Florence. On reaching the San Gallo Gate the stranger said to him : "Remember to do that for which God hath sent thee," and then disappeared.[2]

It is not very wonderful that, when overwrought by fatigue, Savonarola should have seen a vision of this kind, and it may well be that he mistook for an angelic messenger some mortal companion who succoured him by the way. The reader can furnish his own interpretation to the tale. We recount it, with other legends, as part of the history of the times when even great minds had faith in similar visions.[3] Of Savonarola's special belief in them we have

[1] Burlamacchi, G. F. Pico, and the other biographers all repeat this on several occasions.

[2] Burlamacchi, p. 15 ; "Biografia Latina," sheet 4*t*.

[3] We might quote innumerable examples of this belief, but will only refer to the famous letter of Christopher Columbus (also quoted in Libri's "Histoire des sciences mathematiques") describing a similar hallucination that occurred to him in America, when, at the moment that he was for-

already seen something, and better proofs will be found
further on.   But, notwithstanding his new fears and excited imagination, the sight of the walls of Florence
must have recalled painful memories of his failure to stir
the hearts of its citizens.   He decided, therefore, to feel
his way very cautiously, in order not to incur fresh disappointments, and, resuming his philosophical lectures
to the novices, made them the principal objects of his
care and hope.   While endeavouring to imbue these young
men with his own thoughts and feelings, and make
them his true disciples, he was content to wait quietly for
better times.   But the rumour of how he had been called
back to Florence at Lorenzo's desire, and how much
anxiety Pico had shown to consult him, soon attracted the
public attention, and all became anxious to hear his voice.
At first his lessons were attended only by the Friars; then
a few laymen sought admittance, and he was obliged to
consent to their request.   In the convent garden of St.
Mark's, beneath a damask rose tree that, owing to the
veneration of the brotherhood, has been re-grafted down
to our own times, he began to expound the Apocalypse
to a large and enthusiastic congregation.[1]   Then, almost
without his being aware of it, his lectures were gradually
transformed into sermons.   The audience increased daily;
the orator spoke in a higher tone, and he was urged by
the general entreaty to again mount the pulpit and preach

saken by all, he heard a heavenly voice encouraging him to persevere in
his enterprise.   And Libri justly considers that this letter is one of the
finest examples of eloquence in our literature.   It gives us a faithful picture of the character of Columbus and his times.

[1] Of Savonarola's lectures on the Apocalypse and other subjects in St.
Mark's, as well as of many of his unpublished sermons during these
years, nothing remains to us excepting the rough and incorrect notes
contained in several autographs, and a few apocryphal manuscripts, of
which further details will be given in a special note.   Many of these
rough notes are included in the Appendix of the Italian edition of this
work, doc. v., in order to give the reader some idea of discourses which
were probably never written out *in extenso.*

to the people in church. When no longer able to refuse the request, he begged his hearers first to beseech the Lord to enlighten his mind, and finally, one Saturday, issues the following announcement : " To-morrow we will speak in church, and give a lecture and a sermon."

It was the 1st of August, 1489; the church of St. Mark was thronged with people, some sitting, some standing,[1] others clinging to the iron gratings, in order to see and hear the preacher, who, after remaining unnoticed in Florence, had gained so great a reputation in Upper Italy. At last Savonarola appeared in the pulpit; he continued his exposition of the Apocalypse, and the walls of St. Mark echoed for the first time with his three, already well-known, conclusions. At one moment the audience was raised to a transport of ecstasy by his intellectual might and enthusiasm, and his voice resounded with an almost supernatural effect. He had achieved a signal success ; all Florence spoke of him, and even the learned men forsook Plato to discuss the merits of the new Christian preacher.

Nevertheless, owing to his continued predictions of calamity, the general wonder and admiration began to be exchanged in many instances for feelings of doubt and even irritation. Opinions began to be divided, and some already regarded the Friar as an ignorant, visionary fanatic, who made an effect rather by dint of loud words and fantastic imagery, than by any real logic or eloquence. But Savonarola was quite prepared for these charges, and having once taken the plunge into rough waters, refused to draw back. He felt that the moment for conflict had arrived. First of all, however, he determined to publish some of his writings, in order to instruct the people and refute the learned men who accused him of ignorance.

[1] Burlamacchi, p. 19 ; " Biografia Latina," sheet 5 and fol.

We must now turn to these writings for a better appreciation of his intellectual endowments.   Hitherto there was
little to be said on this point, his earlier sermons and
writings having nearly all perished, or only survived in
the shape of well-nigh unintelligible notes.

CHAPTER VI.

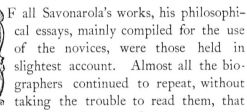F all Savonarola's works, his philosophi-
cal essays, mainly compiled for the use
of the novices, were those held in
slightest account. Almost all the biographers continued to repeat, without
taking the trouble to read them, that
they were poor and servile imitations of Aristotle and St.
Thomas Aquinas. To us this appears a most erroneous
judgment, but many circumstances helped to diffuse it.
In the first place, the scanty bulk of these essays, and the
slight estimation in which they were held by their author ;
and secondly, in consequence of the numerous charges the
Friar brought against philosophy and philosophers, and
the vanity of such studies. It seemed improbable that he
could have written anything of value on a science of
which he spoke with so much contempt ; and as parts of
the essays were really translations and compendiums
of Aristotle and St. Thomas, the prevailing opinion was
apparently justified.

Nevertheless, in our anxiety to ascertain the grounds of
this verdict, we determined to examine these writings with
the utmost care. We knew in how dense a darkness the
first glimmer of modern philosophy was veiled, and the
difficulty experienced by historians in tracing the source

of that dawning light ; we knew that in Savonarola's day all writers felt bound to take Plato, Aristotle, or some other ancient authority as their model ; but we also knew that when the hour of its regeneration had struck, the new philosophy forced its way through Aristotelians, Platonists, and all the labyrinths of the schools. And thereupon imitators, translators, and commentators began gradually to pulsate with a new life, and follow a new path; but hardly one of these early innovators had the courage to set forth without the support of some ancient sage. Therefore the true value of a philosopher of the Renaissance must not be determined by the fact of his being or not a follower of Aristotle, or having copied him or not in many respects ; but rather by his recognition or neglect of the authority of his own reason and his own conscience. Is he really informed by the new spirit? That is the chief question. Thus, in examining Savonarola's philosophical writings, we have not cared to ascertain to what extent he translated from Aristotle, imitated from Boethius, or copied from Aquinas, but rather sought to discover if he had anywhere said : We must rely on our own experience, our own reason ; we must believe in the voice of our own conscience and the conscience of mankind.

And another consideration withheld us from accepting the verdict of the earlier biographers : namely, the remembrance of the tremendous vigour with which Savonarola always inveighed from the pulpit against the ancient world in general, and its heathen influences on his own times. On numberless occasions he had accused of materialism the Aristotelian philosophy, of which he has been supposed to be so blind a disciple. " Your Aristotle," he repeatedly said, " does not even succeed in proving the immortality of the soul ; is uncertain upon so many capital points, that in truth I fail to comprehend why you should waste so much labour on his writings." But what was still more convincing to us was the freedom and independence of judgment manifested in all Savonarola's compositions, whether on politics, theology, or morals ; his subtlety of analysis, his keenness of induction. In order to accept the general verdict we should have been forced to allow—that Savonarola had two opposite systems of philosophy : that in the one he was the slave of Aristotle, a follower of the scholastic method already forsaken by many, and that this was the system he taught in his philosophical writings and imparted to the novices ; while in the other, he was free, independent, full of boldness and daring, proclaimed its doctrines in a countless number of theological, political, and moral writings ; preached them from the pulpit, and bore witness to them by his whole life. It was to avoid this contradiction that we diligently studied Savonarola's works and philosophical principles, and, the task ended, all contradiction had disappeared.

At that time there were two reigning schools of philosophy in Italy, the Platonist and the Aristotelian. The former, inaugurated by the Florentine Academy, spread in the south, and pushed its theories further and further, until, as we have seen, they were finally merged in the transcendental idealism of Giordano Bruno.[1] The latter, first flourishing under Pomponaccio and many others, spread to the north, in the Universities of Bologna, Padua, Pavia, and throughout Upper Italy ; it promoted the experimental method, gave a powerful impulse to physical science, and attained its highest glory in Galileo Galilei. Thus, not only in the ancient, but also in the modern world, Aristotle was the true founder of experimental philosophy, and his fame was unjustly slighted by

---

[1] Chap. iv.

those incapable of distinguishing between the real Aristotle and the Aristotle of the scholiasts.

From these two schools a third was afterwards evolved. This may be said to have been initiated by Bernardino Telesio, and established by Tommaso Campanella, both natives of Calabria. Telesio studied at Padua, where he was trained in experimental philosophy and physics. He tried to combat Aristotle and promote the experimental method, but in reality he was rather a follower of Parmenides, and composed his book, "De Rerum Natura," under the influence of that writer's ideas. On returning to his native Cosenza, he founded the famous Cosentine Academy, in which Tommaso Campanella was trained. The latter was a thinker of idealistic tendencies, and in deviating to some extent from the path traced by Telesio, gave birth to that third school to which we have alluded. Campanella recommended the experimental method, and attributed to sensation so large a share in the formation of knowledge, as to seem almost a pure materialist; but then, on the other hand, he granted a *cognitio abdita*, or intuition of primary ideas, affirming that from these, even without the aid of sensation, we derive greater certainty than from all others. But he could not find any mode of connecting these primary ideas with sensations, nor of tracing sensations back to these ideas. Accordingly his doctrine amounted to little more than an imperfect eclecticism, in which experimental philosophy, together with a species of Neo-Platonic idealism (for which the author had a natural inclination) are jumbled with the theology of Aquinas. But these contradictory elements are never brought into fusion, never attain to the unity of a system. From time to time, however, we are dazzled by marvellous flashes of genius, and continually struck by the author's vigorous freedom and independence of thought. In fact Campanella's doctrines were the conceptions of a vast brain, full of daring and enterprise, and that although somewhat disordered and confused, gave frequent proofs of extraordinary penetration and preciseness.[1]

Strangely enough, the conditions of Savonarola's life were almost identical with those which afterwards gave birth to the philosophy of Campanella. He too was a Dominican monk, had diligently studied Aquinas, and assimilated the Saint's doctrines with his own ideas; trained from his earliest years in experimental science and Aristotelian philosophy, he had afterwards come to Florence, and found himself in the headquarters of the Neo-Platonic school, and, with a natural tendency to mysticism, had been thrown in the company of Marsilio Ficino and the rest of the Academy. Even intellectually Savonarola bore no small resemblance to Campanella. He too was a free and daring spirit, yearning to project his mind over the whole world: he too sometimes gave forth flashes of light and unexpected strength, while at others hopelessly involved in the mazes of scholasticism. But the Friar had one great advantage over Campanella; for in the depths of his mind and heart there lay a moral idea, clear, precise, and powerful, constituting the pith of his thoughts, the light of his life, and the unity of his existence.

In short, there is so strong a resemblance between the philosophical systems of these two Dominicans, that it is a matter of surprise that we should be the first to mark it.[2]

[1] Campanella, "Metaphysica." Parisiis, 1638. There is one copy of it in the National Library of Florence. The greater part of Campanella's other works are in the Riccardi and Marucelli Libraries of the same city.

[2] Padre Marchese, "Storia di San Marco," p. 164, attempted to prove a certain resemblance between the political ideas of Savonarola and Campanella, comparing the latter's "Città del Sole" to Savonarola's "Reggimento di Firenze." But, as we shall see, the two friars held very different ideas on politics. The "Città del Sole" was part of Campanella's "Utopia," not of the system he sought to put into practice ; therefore it cannot fitly be compared with the "Reggimento di Firenze." But this

Before treating in detail of Savonarola's philosophical works, we will first remark, that the old catalogues of his manuscripts serve to show that he had devoted much labour to the science, and that some of his works upon it have perished. Among these was a compendium of nearly all the works of Plato and Aristotle.[1] His printed essays are contained in a single volume, consisting of four short tractates: "Compendio di filosofia, di Morale e di logica," and lastly, of a pamphlet on the "Divisione e dignità di tutte le scienze."[2]

His Compendium of Philosophy begins by treating of entity, motion, the primary motive force, heaven, the generation and decay of all things; and thus proceeds to subject the whole of nature to examination, in an ascending scale, from inanimate objects to man. He describes the world as it was then described by the Aristotelians :

point will be treated elsewhere. As to the philosophical works of Savona- rola, Marchese tells us (p. 104) : "We have here a complete compendium of the writings of the Stagirite, in all their variety." Herr Meier, always a very painstaking writer, says with more exactness : "Aristoteles bildet natürlich die Grundlage, doch zeigt sich bei häufiger Berücksichtung des Thomas von Aquino, auch eigenes Urtheil und Kritik. Der Stil ist meistens leicht, und ein Streben nach Klarheit und Bestimmtheit nicht zu verkennen " ("Savonarola," &c., Erst Kap., s. 25). Rudelbach, writing with the sole aim of discovering Protestant ideas, pays no attention to Savonarola's philosophical works. Mons. Perrens, on the contrary, gave them careful examination, but merely translates some passages from them, without pronouncing any judgment upon the value of their doctrines. Nevertheless he expresses an opinion in accordance with the traditional verdict : "Ces écrits sont donc, pour ainsi dire, des catechismes sans prétention." "L'Auteur n'y met rien du sien " (vol. ii. p. 308).

[1] "Aristotelis penè omnia opera, et Platonis abreviati." This is the title given in the catalogue, "De operibus viri Dei non impressis," at the end of the "Biografia Latina," and included in the Appendix (Doc. vi.) to the Italian edition of this work.

[2] "Compendium totius philosophiæ" (to which in other editions are added the words : "tam naturalis quam moralis ") ; "Opus de divisione omnium scientiarum ; " "Compendium Logices." Venetis : Lucæ Antonii Juntæ, 1542. There are many other and some older editions of these works. The treatise on the Art of Poetry, of which we shall speak else- where is often included among them.

namely, as a huge animal informed by three great souls, the vegetative, sensitive, and intellectual (or comprehensive) souls. On this subject it is unnecessary to follow the author in detail, inasmuch as he only repeats the ideas of the school. But in the theory of cognition we recognize Savonarola's own bold touch and freedom of mind, and will therefore give it less summary treatment. "We must start from things best known," he says, "to arrive at the unknown; since only thus is it easy to reach the truth." [1] Sensations are nearest and best known to us; they are stored in the memory, when the mind effects the transformation of many individual sensations into a single general rule or experience. After this it carries on the process until from the union of many experiences universal truths are deduced.[2] Therefore true wisdom is directed towards first principles and first causes; it is speculative, free, and of a very lofty nature.[3] All our knowledge, therefore, proceeds from sensation; hence in philosophy all that is perceptible to the senses must precede that which is imperceptible to and above the senses."[4] Elsewhere he treats in the same fashion of the process by which sensation is transformed into idea. "Sensations are stored in the shape of pictures in our fancy; there the intellect seizes upon them, and by its own virtue transforms them into intellectual acts."[5] From sensation, therefore, without any real process of ratiocination, and *without any doctrinal authority*, our knowledge is derived. Nevertheless the intellect itself could not convert sensation into idea *without pre-existing intellectual cognition*, deprived of which it would be merely a *force*, incapable of achieving the act of knowing, incapable of comprehending even the meaning of words. *Consequently every doctrine must be founded on pre-existing cognitions of the senses, and on the*

[1] Bk. i. p. 17.   [2] Bk. i. pp. 2, 8.   [3] Bk. i. pp. 6, 7, 8, 9, 10.
[4] Bk. i. p. 28.   [5] Bk. xiv. p. 7.

pre-existing cognition of first principles.   These are known
to us without any demonstration, inasmuch as they are true
and self-evident.[1]   They may indeed seem far from us and
very hard to understand, but are substantially the very
essence of truth and evidence.   For not only are they true
in themselves, but constitute the truth of other principles
of experience apparently nearer to us and more easily
understood.   And truly the things best known in themselves are those sharing most in the *actum essendi*, as, for
instance, God Himself, primary intelligences, and primary
principles.   Our intellect proceeds from the power to the
act of knowing ; in the potential state it perceives with
certainty, and almost by intuition, such first principles as it
finds clearest and nearest to itself; but on coming to *the act
of knowing*—that is to say, when we are forced to rise from
the individual to the general—we then find them most
remote and most difficult." [2]   Not that the difficulty consists in knowing the cognitions pre-existing in the intellect,
but in placing primary ideas in relation with primary
sensations, and in filling the immense void between them :
namely, in establishing the first foundations of science.

This was the sagacious way in which Savonarola
attacked the fundamental problem of philosophy, but he
went no farther, and made no attempt to conquer the
difficulties he had so clearly discerned.   He often repeats
that the inductive method is the best by which to

[1] "Logica," Bk. viii. p. 5.
[2] Comp. Phil., bk. i. p. 13.   See also bk. i. pp. 17, 18, bk. ii. p. 4 ;
"Logica," bk. viii. pp. 6, 7, 8.   Perusal of these writings will show that
as regards form, language, and many of their ideas, they are entirely
Aristotelian, but that, nevertheless, the doctrines inculcated show considerable originality and the working of an independent mind.   And
this will be still better understood if we reflect that in lecturing to the
novices Savonarola was compelled to adhere to traditional forms, inasmuch as in his day, and for many following centuries, the scholastic
philosophy alone was allowed to be taught in monastic establishments.
At the present day theology is the only flourishing study in convents, and
even this, as all know, is always taught on the scholastic method.

proceed from the known to the unknown; but as he is content with these vague generalities, there is the same void in his system that was afterwards found in Campanella's. In our author also we may often note a contradictory order of ideas, and in his mind likewise Platonic and Aristotelian doctrines are jumbled with the theology of Aquinas without being brought into complete harmony with it. Nevertheless, of the two philosophers Savonarola is the easier to excuse, inasmuch as he was not solely devoted to philosophy, and in the short tractates, expressly composed for the use of his novices, it was impossible for him to attack, much less to solve, the hardest problem of science.

No more need be said of this first treatise or Compendium of Philosophy in general, for in the rest of it the author is content to borrow from Aristotle, frequently copying and summarising his words.

In the treatise on Moral Philosophy Savonarola treads in the steps of Aquinas, but with a leaning towards Neo-Platonic ideas betraying the influence of Ficino and the Academy. " The ultimate end of man," he says, " is undoubtedly beatitude, the which does not consist, as natural philosophers would have it, in the contemplation of speculative science, but in the pure vision of Deity. In this life we can only have a distant image, a faint shadow of that beatitude ; in the next life alone can we enjoy it in its fulness and reality. And although this beatitude is not to be obtained by human efforts alone, yet man must strive for it by a *motus ad beatitudinem* that will endow him with the disposition required for its reception. God alone is in Himself blessed ; man has need of many efforts, *motibus multis*, and these consist in good works, which are also called merits, *because beatitude is the prize of virtuous deeds*." [1]

[1] Comp. Phil. Mor., bk. i. p. 25.

Here it should be noted that in philosophy as well as in theology Savonarola always insisted on the efficacy and necessity of good works, and consequently on man's free will. " It is free will," he continues, " that distinguishes man from beast, the which free will is neither a quality nor a habit, but the very essence of human will, *est ipsa hominis voluntas.*" [1] He then inveighs against the astrologers' dictum of the human will being influenced by the stars. " Our will can be moved by no extraneous force, neither by the stars, nor by the passions, nor even by God. For the Creator does not destroy, but preserves, moving the world and all created things after the laws of their nature. Now, as we said, if our will is of its nature essentially free, if, indeed, it is freedom itself, God may move it, but always leaves it free, in order not to destroy it." This tractate contains many just and acute remarks, but as we shall find them in still greater abundance in Savonarola's other writings we need not dwell upon them here. It may, however, be useful to quote a few of his ideas concerning veracity, for the instant confutation of those who have accused him of wilfully playing a false part, and claiming to be a prophet in order to increase his influence over the people. We consider this charge to be clearly disproved by the evidence of all Savonarola's acts and words, but meanwhile let us see what he tells us in his Moral Philosophy :—

" By veracity we mean a certain habit, owing to which man shows himself, both in word and deed, as he really is, and rather lesser than greater. . . . This is rather a moral than a legal duty, insomuch as it is certainly a debt of honesty owed by every man to his neighbour, and the manifestation of truth is always a part of justice." [2] We need not dwell here on Savonarola's utterances on Politics

[1] Comp. Phil. Mor., bk. i. pp. 26, 27.
[2] Comp. Phil. Mor., bk. vi. p. 23.

and Economics, which, according to the scholastic doctrines, were both included in Moral Philosophy, for we shall have occasion to mention them in some detail when examining their author's ideas upon politics. Neither shall we analyze his " Logic," since it is a mere summary of the dialectic of the schoolmen, and we have already mentioned the few important ideas contained in it.

Something must now be said of Savonarola's pamphlet on the " Division of all the Sciences," written in answer to the accusation of despising poetry and holding philosophy in no account. In his defence he drew up a general table of the sciences, showing that he assigned to each its proper position, and respected all according to their rank. This table is clear, precise, and well-executed, but is, fundamentally, the same division adopted by the scholiasts. Philosophy consists of two divisions—the rational and the positive ; the first, acting as a guide to reason, is logic ; the second treats of real entities, and is subdivided into practical and speculative philosophy. And practical philosophy is further divided into mechanical and moral, according to whether it treats of the mechanical pro- fessions or moral actions of man ; while moral philosophy is subdivided into ethical, economic, and political. Three sciences—physics, mathematics, and metaphysics—come under the head of speculative philosophy, which can treat of either that which is inseparable from matter, separable from matter only in the abstract, or absolutely immaterial. He proclaims metaphysics to be the queen of all the sciences, since it seeks the highest truths, and more than any other serves to ennoble and elevate mankind.[1] But Savonarola

[1] Mamiani praises Campanella's division of the sciences, and prefers it to that suggested by Bacon. The latter, he remarks, gave us a subjective division, according to our mental faculties (memory, imagination, reason) ; the former made a more rational division, in accordance with the special nature and aim of the various sciences (Mamiani, " Del Rinnovamento dell' antica filosofia Italiana," pp. 37, 38. Paris, 1834). And this has

is careful to add : that is, speaking *secondo puri naturali,* since, Christianly speaking, theology is the true and only science. All the others treat of special things under special aspects; theology alone treats of all under a single and universal aspect ; theology is the first science tracing all things to the first cause; and for this the light of nature is not sufficient, the light of heaven being also required.

From this it is easy to see that this supreme science overshadowed and took precedence of all the rest ; and we can understand the sovereign contempt afterwards shown by Savonarola for philosophy, poetry, and profane studies in general.

been frequently repeated by other writers. In fact, Campanella divides the sciences in several different ways, and never remains constant to one idea. Practically, his arrangement of the sciences is almost the same as that followed in the Middle Ages, placing theology at the head of all. Even in this Savonarola resembles Campanella, for he does the same. Neither showed any real originality in their division of the sciences, and it is impossible to give them the preference over Bacon. The following table will give a clear idea of the division adopted by Savonarola :—

SAVONAROLA'S DIVISION OF THE SCIENCES.

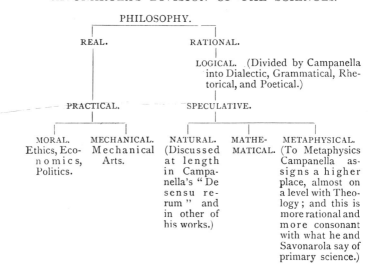

PHILOSOPHY.

REAL.

RATIONAL.

LOGICAL. (Divided by Campanella into Dialectic, Grammatical, Rhetorical, and Poetical.)

PRACTICAL.

SPECULATIVE.

MORAL.
Ethics, Economics, Politics.

MECHANICAL.
Mechanical Arts.

NATURAL.
(Discussed at length in Campanella's " De sensu rerum " and in other of his works.)

MATHEMATICAL.

METAPHYSICAL.
(To Metaphysics Campanella assigns a higher place, almost on a level with Theology ; and this is more rational and more consonant with what he and Savonarola say of primary science.)

We have only dwelt upon the chief divisions of science, without referring to Poetry (classed by Savonarola with Logic, according to the scholastic rules); but of this we shall have occasion hereafter to speak at length. At this point we need only quote what the Friar said of those who were in all things, and especially in poetry, servile copyists of the ancients. "Some have so narrowed their minds and fettered them with the chains of antiquity, that not only do they refuse to speak save as the ancients spake, but will say nothing that has not been said by them. What reasoning is this, what new power of argument? That if the ancients spoke not thus, neither will we speak thus! Therefore if no good deed was done by the ancients must we then do none?"[1] And this was the tone always maintained by him. In an age when every book that appeared sounded the praises of the ancients and inculcated the necessity of imitating them in all things, Savonarola alone raised his voice against these exaggerations. He did still more, when, discarding the ancients altogether, he followed the dictates of his own reason and pressed forward without any other support. This is shown not only by his philosophical writings, but by the still clearer and more abundant proofs of independent thought afforded by his sermons and political and theological treatises. Let us take, for instance, his principal work, "The Triumph of the Cross"—an exposition of Christian doctrines according to natural reason. In the preface we find the following passage : "Whereas in this book we shall only discuss by the light of reason, we will refer to no authorities; but proceed as though no reliance could be placed on any man in the world, however wise, but

---

[1] "Opus perutile de divisione ordine ac utilitate omnium scientiarum. . . . In Poeticen Apologeticus, p. 40. Venetiis : Aurelii Pinci, 1534. There is also a fifteenth century edition undated. There is a singular resemblance between the words quoted above and the ideas expressed by Campanella in his "Poetica" and the tract "De libris propriis."

only on natural reason."[1] And further on, " It is by visible things that we must arrive at the knowledge of the invisible, forasmuch as all our knowledge is derived from sensation, which only comprehends outer, bodily attributes; whereas by intellect, which is subtle, we can penetrate to the substance of natural things, and, after considering these, attain to the knowledge of invisible things."[2] It must not be supposed that these are detached thoughts, scattered here and there in the work, for, on the contrary, they are stated in the preface and serve to indicate the design and method of the whole. Every chapter starts by premising the hypothesis, that nothing has been learnt from any man, and by repeating that we must accept no authority save that of our own experience and reason. Thus it goes on to the end, proceeding from the known to the unknown. And whenever, either in sermons or other writings, Savonarola inculcates virtue, and urges political reform, his practical independence of mind is even still clearer and more visible.

When we remember that he lived in the fifteenth century, when Marsilio Ficino was esteemed the greatest of European philosophers, it must certainly be granted that Savonarola was one of the first to emancipate philosophy from the yoke of the ancients, and that our praises are just and based on a close and impartial examination of his works. The old biographer, Burlamacchi, who was personally acquainted with the Friar, says of him : " that even in his early childhood he would not judge authors according to their fame, nor be content to accept opinions merely because they were in vogue, *but always kept his eye fixed on truth and reason.*"[3] These brief, simple words

---

[1] *Proemio* to the " Trionfo della Croce."

[2] Ibid. chap. i.

[3] Burlamacchi, p. 5. Pico, p. 8, says : " Mirus erat veritatis amator, eo usque provectus eius gratia, ut in his quos coleret doctoribus si quid non placeret. ingenue fateretur." Almost the identical words are to be found

give a better portrait of the man than any furnished by later biographers; and we ourselves, after prolonged study of our author's works, can accept the old chronicler's verdict.

Nevertheless, we have no intention of overrating Savonarola's philosophy in order to exaggerate his scientific merits. He often slighted philosophy, continually censured it, and sometimes spoke of it with contempt. If his short treatises on the subject have been forgotten, it is mainly owing to his own reticence concerning them. They are unmentioned in any history of philosophy, unquoted by any later philosopher, and their existence seems to have been ignored even by Campanella, although, as we have seen, the latter was in some sense a disciple of Savonarola. But although these reasons may diminish the scientific importance of his writings, they cannot detract from the weight of their testimony as to their author's mind.

It was of the highest importance to ascertain the intellectual strength of a man having so large a share in the events of the period during which all Europe was preparing for the renewal of civilization and the reassertion of human reason. Whatever may have been Savonarola's

in the " Biografia Latina," which agrees on this point with Frà Benedetto ("Vulnera Diligentis"), and with all the writers who were personally acquainted with Savonarola. Many learned men of the fifteenth century also held Savonarola's philosophical doctrines in the highest esteem. Ficino (in a letter to Gio Cavalcanti, December 12, 1494) and Poliziano (in a letter to Jacopo Antiquaris, May 18, 1492) both call him a man of *distinguished* learning; Pietro Crinito, in his " De Honesta disciplina," bk. i. chap. 3, says of him : " Qui ætate nostra in omni prope philosophia maxime præstat." Finally, we may quote the opinion of a still higher authority. That Francesco Guicciardini was one of Savonarola's greatest admirers, is clearly proved by his "Opere Inedite." He had closely studied the Friar's writings, and made summaries of some of his sermons, always speaking of them with sincere admiration. As to philosophy he says : " Even his enemies confess him to have been versed in many branches of learning, especially in philosophy, which he had mastered so thoroughly and made so great a use of on all occasions, as though he had been its creator" ("Storia Fiorentina," p. 178).

mission, whatever his temper, whatever his aims, it was imperative for us to define his place as a thinker, and decide whether he was or was not to be ranked among the *new men.*

We are now convinced that, unless we place him at the head of these men, of whom he was the precursor and prophet, and of whose heroic virtues, daring aspirations, and fantastic errors he had so large a share, we shall never be able to understand his true character. So far, in spite of all that has been written upon the subject, no one has yet arrived at an exact definition of its worth. No just comparison can be drawn between Savonarola and the contemporary philosophers and learned men, for he was not only opposed to Paganism, but took a far more serious view of the problems of life. His real originality consisted in recognizing the weight of reason, experience, and conscience in both scientific and practical questions, but without separating science from the religion in which he believed, and without admitting—as many then admitted—that man might hold one faith in philosophy, and another in religion. And in virtue of this, he was the precursor, prophet and martyr of the new epoch.

CHAPTER VII.

N examining the great tide of civilization that began to advance over Europe in the sixteenth century, after the Italian Humanists, and partly by their work, we shall find at the base of the new philosophical and religious doctrines, and in the midst of the hottest struggles and disputes, a general yearning to bring men nearer to God. This yearning was the source of the fresh enthusiasm with which philosophers, theologians, and martyrs were fired. For what was the aim of the new philosophy? The abolishment of every contradiction between the earthly and the heavenly life, between the human mind and nature; the reunion of the creature, animated by the Divine afflatus, with the Creator, so that all things might be fused in one idea by means of the Pantheistic creed taught by Giordano Bruno's pen, and consecrated by his death at the stake. What was the promise held forth by the doctrines of the Reformation? To bring the devout into direct communion with their God, without the intervention of the priest. Ceremonies were superfluous; good works were unnecessary, being valueless of themselves; by grace

alone were the predestined saved, and the believer was an instrument in the hands of God, and must have faith in God alone. This new love and irresistible impulse of the soul, to which Bruno gave the name of "heroic fury;" this faith in the Divine finally rescued mankind from the abyss of scepticism and corruption, in which all at that time were more or less engulfed. It reawakened science, promoted the Reformation, gave new strength to Catholicism, new youth to society, and inaugurated modern culture.

Towards the close of the fifteenth century we can see that men's minds were already stirred by a new warmth ; that they were beginning to have hope in the force of ideas and principles ; were dissatisfied with the actual state of things, and moved by new aspirations. The first sign, or indeed the animating principle, of this renovation appeared in the philosophy of the Alexandrian school, which promised the direct vision of God, and announced that to be the sum of human felicity. This idea, being supported by Ficino and his Academy, gained popularity at once, made rapid way, and penetrated to the hearts of men, at the time when, to all appearance, the reign of materialism seemed permanently assured. But while this idea was still in the preliminary stage of a theory derived from books, we find that Savonarola was possessed by it from his birth, that it ruled his whole life, and may indeed be said to have been his life itself. His sole aspiration was towards God, and his sole desire to make the world share in the blessedness of his hopes.

The writings Savonarola gave to the world about the year 1492 serve to bear out this view, for the greater part of them are filled with manifestations of a religious zeal to which the term of "holy fury" may well be applied. Nearly all of them are short pamphlets, and (especially the tractates on Humility, Prayer, the Love of Jesus Christ, the Widowed Life) in part ascetic, in part purely religious and moral works. It will be our endeavour to describe the ideas contained in them with the utmost fidelity, so that the reader may duly appreciate the means by which Savonarola's ascendency over the people was originally established.

In the first of these tracts he tells us " that the virtues of humility and charity form the two extremities of the spiritual edifice ; [1] because humility is the foundation of the fabric, and charity the perfection and consummation of the whole. Therefore it is meet that the faithful should abase himself before God, recognize that he can do no good of himself, and that without the help of the Lord all his deeds would be sinful. Nor is it enough that he should have an intellectual belief in this ; he must also feel it profoundly in his soul. The will of man is free, therefore he must use all his strength to crush pride, and become a vessel of grace; and for this, outward actions will be not only useful, but necessary. The believer must humble himself before his superiors and before his equals ; let him also humble himself before his inferiors. But if, on reaching this point, he should hold himself to have done a great deed, then outward humility will have increased to the detriment of his inner state, and he will have forfeited all merit. Let him, then, remain steadfast to the idea of his own unworthiness."

In the tract upon Prayer, Savonarola tells us that prayer [2] is one of the most efficacious means of preserving

[1] "Trattato dell' Umiltà," Firenze, per Antonio Miscomini, the last day of June, 1492. Fourteen leaves in all. Other editions : Florence, 1495 ; Venice, 1537, 1547. Both in Audin and in the Guicciardini catalogue several other fifteenth century editions are quoted—undated. In describing the contents of these pamphlets we adhere, as closely as possible, to the author's text.

[2] "Trattato e vero sermone della orazione," Firenze, per Antonio Miscomini, 20th October, 1492. This pamphlet also consists of fourteen leaves. Other editions : Florence, 1495 ; Venice, 1538 ; five of the fifteenth century, undated.

in man a lively feeling of humility.   "Wherefore let him
daily pray fervently and long.   But let us always remember
that prayer must be accompanied by humility and charity,
or it is of no avail.   Where there is fervour, there, too,
is prayer, and therefore, in doing deeds of charity, a man
may be said to pray."

We find these ideas still better developed in a similar
tract on mental prayer.[1]   "He who prays must address
God as though he were in His presence; inasmuch as the
Lord is everywhere, in every place, in every man, and
especially in the soul of the just.   Therefore let us not seek
God on earth, nor in heaven, nor elsewhere; rather let
us seek Him in our own heart, like unto the prophet that
sayeth, 'I will hearken unto that which the Lord shall say
in me.'   In prayer a man may take heed to his words, and
this is a wholly material thing; he may take heed to the
sense of his words, and this is rather study than prayer;
finally, he may fix his thoughts on God, and this is the
only true prayer.   We must consider neither the words
nor the sentences, but lift our soul above our self, and
almost lose self in the thought of God.   This state
once attained, the believer forgets the world and worldly
desires, and has, as it were, a foreshadowing of heavenly
bliss.   To this height it is as easy for the ignorant as for
the learned to rise; indeed, it often comes about that one
repeating the Psalms without understanding them makes a
more acceptable prayer than the wise man who can interpret them.   Words, in fact, are not essential to prayer;
on the contrary, when man is truly rapt in the spirit of
devotion, speech is an impediment, and should be replaced
by mental prayer.   Thus it is seen how great is the error
of those that prescribe a fixed number of orations.   The
Lord taketh not joy in a multitude of words, but rather

[1] "Della Orazione Mentale," Florence, 1492, 1495; Venice, 1538,
1547.   Other fifteenth century editions, undated.

in a fervent spirit. Hereupon we shall be assailed,"
Savonarola adds, " by those whose sole concern is to defend
the ceremonies and exterior rites of the Church. To these
we will make answer, even as our Saviour to the Woman
of Samaria—' Woman, believe me, the hour cometh when
ye shall neither in this mountain, nor yet in Jerusalem,
worship the Father. But the hour cometh, and now is,
when the true worshippers shall worship the Father in
spirit and in truth ' (St. John's Gospel, iv. 21–23). The
which signifies that the Lord desires inward worship, without so many outer ceremonies ; and such was the usage
in the primitive Church, when men could raise their
thoughts to God without need of organ music and chants.
When fervour slackened, ceremonies were introduced, as
medicines to men's souls. In these times, however,
Christians have become like unto a sick man, from whom
all natural strength hath departed, and medicines have no
more power over him. All fervour and inward worship
are dead, and ceremonies wax more numerous, but have
lost their efficacy. Wherefore we are come to declare to
the world that outward worship must give way to inward,
and that ceremonies are naught, save as a means of stirring
the spirit."

But the treatise on the Love of Jesus Christ,[1] of
which many editions rapidly appeared, is a still clearer
expression of the mystic enthusiasm with which, as we
have said, Savonarola's soul was possessed. " The love of
Jesus Christ is the lively affection inspiring the faithful with
the desire to bring his soul into unity, as it were, with that

[1] " Trattato dell' amore di Jesù Cristo," Firenze, per Antonio Miscomini, the 17th day of May, 1492. A pamphlet of twenty-eight leaves.
A second edition appeared in the June of the same year ; there are also
five more, undated, besides those published in the sixteenth century,
one which was issued by the Ginnti Press in 1529. These editions of
Savonarola's pamphlets are very elegant and often illustrated with wood-
cuts by the first artists of the period.

of Christ, and live the life of the Lord, not by external imitation, but by inward and Divine inspiration. He (the faithful) would seek that Christ's doctrine might be a living thing in him, would desire to suffer His martyrdom, and mystically hang with Him on the same cross. This is an omnipotent love, only to be attained by the operation of grace, inasmuch as it raises man above himself, and unites the finite creature with the infinite Creator. Man, in fact, is continually rising from humanity to divinity, when animated by this love, which is the sweetest of all affections, inasmuch as it penetrates the soul, masters the body, and causes the faithful to walk the earth like one floating in ecstasy."

We have here given an almost literal version of Savonarola's words, because this conception of love, recurring continually in his works, and a fundamental point of his doctrine, has never yet received adequate remark. It is true that Savonarola gives no very clear definition of it, since he sometimes declares this love to consist only in grace, and at others only in charity. In truth it partakes of the nature of both, without being exclusively the one or the other. When grace is infused into man, it forthwith generates charity; in fact there can be no true charity without grace. But there is an intermediate state, in which the believer, feeling the nearness and almost the breath of God, experiences a supreme felicity, a species of celestial intoxication. This inner state of the mind, pre-disposing it to grace already indeed conscious of its approach to generate charity, is precisely the state designated by Savonarola as the *love of Jesus Christ*. This conception was an important point in his doctrines precisely because he affirmed that this love, although an entirely subjective state of the mind, sufficed, nevertheless, to predispose it to grace. It is true that no Christian can acquire charity without grace, which is the free gift of

God, and scarcely to be obtained by the help of our own
will; but love, on the contrary, being merely a disposition
of the mind, man may more easily attain to it by his own
effort. Thereupon grace is almost naturally infused in
him, and, as a necessary consequence, charity wells up
in his heart. Thus, *love* has the superhuman power of
joining the finite creature to the infinite Creator, and
explains in some degree the mystery of human freewill
and Divine omnipotence.

The pamphlet concludes with a few stimulating con-
templations (*Contemplazioni infiammative*), in which Savonarola gives vent to all kinds of exclamations on the
goodness and mercy of the Lord, on the ardent longing of
his soul to become as one with Him, to be bound on the
same cross, pierced by the same nails, and crowned by the
same thorns. If we read these things in the sceptic
spirit of the present day, we shall certainly fail to discern
any merit in them; but if we reflect that they were
written for the people, were the utterances of a soul in the
transports of complete prostration before God, and of a
man who found in this holy delirium a species of consolation entirely unknown to ourselves, we shall come to
a juster appreciation of them. And their value will be
increased in our eyes when we remember that Savonarola
succeeded in communicating his enthusiasm to a people
apparently converted to scepticism by the leaders of the
new learning. He was the first to foresee and foretell that
this new love and ecstasy would take possession of the
multitude, and, by rousing religious feeling, help to
regenerate the world.

His " Book of the Widowed Life," [1] published as early
as 1491, consists of sound moral advice to widows.

[1] "Libro della vita viduale," Firenze, issued by Ser Francesco
Bonaccorsi, 1491. It is a pamphlet of thirty leaves. Audin cites three
other fifteenth century editions. Two undated, and one issued by Ser
Lorenzo Morgiani, 26th November, 1496.

This treatise serves to disprove the assertions of those who represented Savonarola as a foe to matrimony, and almost accused him of intending to subject all Florence to monastic rules of life, whereas the doctrines inculcated by him with regard to marriage were full of good sense. " Widows," he says, " like unto orphans, are under the special protection of the Lord. The most fitting life for them would be to renounce the world, give themselves wholly to God, and become ' even as the dove, which is a chaste creature, and therefore, having lost its mate, never couples with another, but spends the rest of ,its life in lonely lamentation.' Nevertheless, if for the education of her children, or through poverty, or from being unable to resist the longings of the flesh, the widow should wish to take a second husband, let her do so ; that is better than being surrounded by adorers, and thus exposed to calumny and dangers innumerable. If a widow be reluctant to preserve the strict decorum and difficult reserve due to her position, rather let her return to the dignified marriage state. But let those conscious of greater strength and of a spirit suited to their condition become models for all other women. The worthy widow should wear robes of mourning ; live alone, and avoid the company of men ; be gravity itself, and so austere in her bearing that no one may dare to address to her a word or smile of disrespect. And, forasmuch as the life of this widow will be a continual lesson to other women, it will be needless for her to strive to speak counsel to others. Let her give no advice save when absolutely required, and seek only to give it to her children or grandchildren. It is unbecoming to a widow's gravity to pry into the life or backslidings of others ; it is unbecoming for her to be, or even appear to be vain ; nor let her, to save others, forget what is due to herself."

By means of these pamphlets, and a few more of

nearly the same kind, which he published from time to time,[1] Savonarola obtained his intent ; for he rose daily higher in the estimation of the learned and the affection of the people. But although in his philosophy he steadily followed the dictates of natural reason, and his religious writings gave free vent to the spontaneous feelings of his soul, yet all this seemed to him insufficient to bring conviction to the minds of men accustomed to be guided by authority. It is true that he was often so dominated and carried away by his own ideas that he was content to assert them as undeniable truths; and in the transports of his devotion, believing himself favoured with direct communications from God, felt no need of offering any proof of his visions and prophecies. Nevertheless, when it was a question of convincing others, silencing the conceit and importunity of the learned, or of winning general belief for extraordinary things, the authority of a book was indispensable in that age. But what authority could he accept save that of the Holy Scriptures,[2] the only book in which he had faith ? Who would dare to resist the word of the Lord ? The Bible had been the surest guide of his youth, the consoler of his griefs ; it had educated and formed his mind. There was no verse in it that he had not committed to memory, no page that he had not com-

[1] Savonarola must have also published at this time his "Confessionale," or "Introductorium Confessorum," of which there is an edition undated, apparently of the fifteenth century. It served as a guide to confessors, and especially to those of the convent, and touches no individual note. It was frequently reprinted, with certain changes and additions, in the course of the sixteenth century, and was very generally used.

[2] At the beginning of the Bible, containing marginal notes in Savonarola's hand, in the National Library of Florence, we find the following note : "Conemur ita Scripturas exponere, ut ab infidelibus non irrideamur," after the title, "Summarium Librorum Sacre Scripture in Biblia comprehensi." The real meaning of his note was plainly this : My visions come directly from God, and would therefore stand in no need of proof, were the men of to-day less incredulous. These private reflections, written by Savonarola for his own use, are naturally of the greatest value to us.

mented, and from which he had not derived some idea for his sermons. By force of study and meditation he had ceased to regard the Bible as a book. It was a world, a living, speaking, infinite world, in which the past, present, and future were all revealed to him. He could not open the Holy Scriptures without feeling exalted by the thought of reading the Word of God, and he discerned in it the microcosm, as it were, of the whole universe, the allegory of the whole history of the human race. It was a study that continually fed upon itself; therefore he covered the margins of the sacred volume with interminable, notes of passing ideas, and many different readings of every passage.

It is only by examination of the sermons that we can realize the varied use that Savonarola made of the Bible. However, to give the reader some idea of it, we may say that, besides literal interpretation of the text, he was accustomed to arrange the reading of every passage under four heads: the *spiritual*, *moral*, *allegorical*, and *anagogical*. As an explanation of his method, let us take, for instance, the first verse of Genesis : "In the beginning God created the heaven and the earth." The spiritual meaning refers to the spirit, hence heaven and earth signify soul and body. The moral meaning, on the other hand, refers to morality, hence heaven and earth signify reason and instinct. The allegorical meaning is double, referring both to the Hebrew and to the Christian Church : in the first case heaven and earth represent Adam and Eve ; the sun and the moon signifying the high priest and the king of the Hebrew people : in the second case heaven and earth signify the chosen people, and the people of the Gentiles, the Pope, and the Emperor. The anagogical meaning refers to the Church triumphant, hence heaven and earth, the sun, moon, and stars signify the angels, men, Jesus Christ, the Virgin, the saints, and so forth.[1]

[1] See note at the end of the chapter.

In this manner Savonarola found confirmation in the Bible for every thought, inspiration, and prophecy that he imagined and for all he beheld.

There was nothing, whether great or small, public or private, sacred or profane, of which he did not find some proof in the Bible. Nevertheless, he recommended that great caution should be exercised in making these interpretations. In one of his marginal notes we find these words : " It is necessary to be acquainted with languages and history, to continually read and have long familiarity (with the Bible) ; it is necessary to be careful not to run counter to reason, nor the received opinions of the Church [1] and the learned. We must not turn the Bible to our own ends, for by so doing the human intellect would usurp the place of the Divine Word.[2] Who then

---

[1] " Ad caritatem, familiaritatemque Christi non pervenerit quisquis Sacre Scripture delitiis abundare non contendit.

" In exponendis Scripturis semper queramus verum sensum auctoris videlicet literalem primo, et ubi sunt plures sensus, eum maxime sequamur, quem plures gravioresque sequunter, *presertim quando sequitur eum Ecclesia Romana : non spernentes tamen expositiones contrarias aliorum Sanctorum."* . . .

"Circa ea que ad fidem pertinent, quædam sunt de substantia, ut articuli, et circa hec non licet contrarium opinari. Quædam non sunt de substantia, ut diversa doctorum expositiones ; et circa hec contingit opinari contraria."

Some of these notes are very beautiful, and prove the independent spirit of their author ; but others are only proofs of his mental excitement and unbalanced fancy. We have only quoted a few of the passages bearing on our theme. These also are at the beginning of the Bible in the National Library, directly after the " Summarium " quoted above.

[2] He seemed to fear lest he should be guilty of this himself, for we find many notes in which he warns himself to take heed, as in some of those we have quoted above, and as may be seen by the following : " Cave ne voluntas precedat intellectum, aut etiam intellectus tuus intellectum Dei in Scriptura, ut velis ipsam exponere sicut prius concepisti, et tuo sensui aptare ; sed potius eius intellectui te ipsum accommoda, ut super dicit Hilarius."

We find a similar thought expressed again further on : " Ne etiam ab infidelibus irrideamur : et falsa pro veris sumamus et asseramus, non debemus Scripturam exponere contra philosophiam naturalem veram.

shall guide the faithful through this sea of peril, and teach him to thread this labyrinth to which the human intellect hath no clue? Divine grace shall be his guide. Therefore let the faithful prepare himself to read the Bible by great purity of heart, by long practice of charity, by raising his thoughts above earthly things; for we may not comprehend this book by the intellect alone, but must also bring our heart and soul to the task. Thus only can we enter without peril into this infinite world of the Holy Scriptures, and obtain the light needed for our salvation. But not unto all is this gift equally granted. From time to time God sends upon earth men favoured with a stronger light than others, and it is their part to enlighten the darkened minds of the multitude. Such are the doctors of the Church, to whom the Lord often speaks in the spirit, revealing hidden things to them by direct communication, so that they may guide and enlighten the faithful." [1]

But, in spite of all these precautions, Savonarola was nearing the brink of a precipice from which it was difficult to avoid falling. With so varied and flexible a method of interpretation, there was nothing that could not be supported on the authority of Holy Writ; and whenever he should let himself be carried away by his imagination, the Scriptures, instead of acting as a check, would only urge him to wilder flights. In fact, whenever his excited fancy evoked strange visions of futurity; whenever he heard voices of sinister omen in the air threatening chastisement to Italy and the Church, he always found this confirmed in some page of the Bible; and the greater his good faith and sincerity the more strongly was he convinced of the truth

Si enim Deus doceret aliud per lumen naturale, aliud contrarium per lumen supernaturale, aut dicerent homines, eum decipere, aut errare. Ergo Scriptura est secundum philosophiam veram, quia verum vero consonat."

[1] *Vide* the same marginal notes in Savonarola's Bible.

of these signs. Nor must we forget that he was encouraged in his system of interpretation by the example of the Neo-Platonist philosopher, Ficino, who was accustomed to interpret the classics on a no less varied nor less arbitrary plan. The traditions and learning of the age, together with his own temperament, combined, therefore, to urge Savonarola irresistibly forward on his dangerous path. But we shall have occasion later to speak of this subject at greater length.

NOTE TO CHAPTER VII.

On the Biblical Exegesis of Savonarola, and on certain copies of the Bible annotated by his hand.

WE shall now give a specimen of Savonarola's various modes of interpreting the Bible, applied to the beginning of Genesis. This specimen is derived from the marginal notes written in Savonarola's hand in two Bibles, one of which is in the National Library, and the other in the Riccardian Library of Florence. From the first and more important of the two we have frequently quoted : it was printed at Basle, 1491, and contains a greater number of notes, besides many dissertations or tractates added at the end. Notes and tractates are alike written in a close, neat hand, and so minutely, and with so many abbreviations, as to be illegible without much study and the occasional use of a microscope. A very exact transcription of them was made by Signor Bencini, of the National Library; and the copy in our own possession forms two stout folio volumes of manuscript. The Riccardi Bible (Venice, 1492) contains fewer and more legible notes and no tractates. The interpretations given are always made on the system we have described. They contain remarks on history and geography, and give the meaning of certain Greek or Hebrew words, from which literal, moral, mystic, allegorical, and anagogical interpretations are derived. It should, however, be remarked that Savonarola, unlike the champions of Reform, seldom raises any purely theological questions in his notes; on the contrary, we constantly find that the passages upon which the Reformers afterwards based most of their controversies are left without comment. But we shall have occasion to recur to this elsewhere. For the moment we need only observe, that Savonarola's chief object in making these notes was for future use in his sermons and devotional writings. The notes frequently cover all the margins, are inserted between the printed lines, and even continued on added leaves.

By placing the National Library Bible, containing the rules for the various modes of interpretation, side by side with the Riccardian copy, in which there is a wider application of these rules to the first chapters of Genesis, we have been enabled to construct the following table. Other and more minute particulars and examples may be found *ad infinitum* in the above-mentioned Bibles, and also in many of Savonarola's sermons ; as, for instance, in No. XXIII. of the series on the Psalm *Quam bonus.*

The reader will be able to form some idea of the manuscript compositions contained in the National Library Bible, in addition to the marginal notes, from the following list of the greater part of them, with their respective titles. As some indication of their bulk, we also note the number of pages occupied by them in our copy :—

" Benedicit nos Deus," &c., pp. 1 2. " In Purificazione : Civitatem adhortaturus ad rectam in Deum intentionem, et mutuam unionem " (this and the preceding are notes for sermons), pp. 2–5. " Cantica Canticorum," pp. 6–44. " Moralitas super 16th Ezechielis," pp. 45–54. " Habacuc " (a complete exposition of that prophet), pp. 54–99. " Circumferatur Arca " (notes for five sermons), pp. 100–107. " In Assumptione," pp. 112–132. Then (pp. 133–247) follow numerous summaries, and notes of different kinds, almost all for sermons, of which the last is addressed *Ad Dominos*, *i.e.*, to the Signory.

We should also remark that there are two ancient parchment Bibles in the Convent of St. Mark, containing numerous marginal notes in a very minute hand somewhat resembling that of Savonarola. This resemblance notwithstanding, and although the words, " *utebatur Hieronymus Savonarola*," were found inscribed on a leaf of one of these Bibles, the notes are certainly not his. We may also add that in the catalogue, " De operibus viri Dei, non impressis," no other Bibles annotated by Savonarola are mentioned, save the following : " Biblie tres glossate ab ipso. Prima, apud Ferrariam, in conventu Angelorum; secunda, Florentia, apud Fratrem Nicholaum di Biliottis ; tertia, Florentia, apud Marcum Simonis de Nigro." It is improbable that the author of this catalogue, who was a friar of St. Mark's, and so careful in noting down his master's manuscript works, should have been unacquainted with Bibles actually contained in the convent while acquainted with those then in the possession of private individuals. Neither are the parchment Bibles in question mentioned in any of the old biographies.

TABLE OF SAVONAROLA'S VARIOUS INTERPRETATIONS OF THE BIBLE, DERIVED FROM HIS AUTOGRAPH NOTES.

Literal Interpretation.	Spiritual Interpretation.	Allegorical Interpretation (with reference to the *Old Testament*).	Allegorical Interpretation (with reference to the *New Testament*).	Moral Interpretation.	Anagogical Interpretation.
First Day.—Heaven, Earth, Light.	Soul, Body, Acting Intelligence.	Adam, Eve, Lights of Grace.	Hebrew People, Gentiles, Jesus Christ.	Soul, Body (in the sense of Reason and Instinct), Light of Grace.	Angels, Men, Vision of God.
Second Day. — The Firmament.	The Will struggling between the Soul and the Body.	Noah's Ark.	The Apostles and Other Saints.	Moral Strength.	Eternal Bliss and Eternal Perdition.
Third Day. — Division of the Waters from the Earth. Dry Places. Grasses and Plants.	The Movement of the Passions and of the Errors possessing the Intellect. The Intellect Craving for Knowledge.	Gentiles separated from the Chosen People. Multitude of the Elect.	Tribulations Separating Many from the Church. The Sound Doctrines of the Church.	Struggle of the Passions against Duty. Reason.	Joy of the Blessed when Freed from Tribulation. Their Praises and Perfect Works.
Fourth Day. — Sun, Moon, Stars.	Metaphysics and Ethics, Natural Science and Logical Science.	High Priest, King, Other Priests.	Pope, Emperor, Doctors.	The Law of Charity, old and new, Minor Precepts.	Christ, The Virgin. The other Blessed.
Fifth Day. — Birds, Fishes.	Contemplation of Higher and of Lower Things.	Maccabees (who always wavered).	Contemplative Life, Active Life.	Contemplation of Things Divine, and of Things Human, to the Benefit of Active and of Contemplative Life.	Angels and Men admitted into the Angelic Choir.
Sixth Day.—Beasts. Land Animals. Beasts of Burden. Man in the Image of God.	Fierce Appetites. Sense, both Inner and Outer. Man, with Control of the Passions.	The Hebrew People (given to Avarice in the time of Christ). The Good. Christ (the expected of the Old Testament).	Antichrist with his Followers. Christians given up to Earthly Things. The Chosen. The Perfect, who will abound in the time of the Antichrist.	The Wicked. Persecutors. He who Becomes Perfect by Tribulation.	Those who were Persecutors. Preachers.

N.B.—It should be observed that, although the second and fifth interpretations—*i.e.*, the spiritual and moral—sometimes appear identical, they must, however, be always understood in two different senses : for instance, in one case *reason* signifies the faculty by which truth is comprehended; and, in the other, signifies the force that controls the passions. Besides, this Table is necessarily imperfect, being drawn up from rough notes, which are often barely traced.

CHAPTER VIII.

*SAVONAROLA PREACHES ON THE GOSPELS IN THE
CATHEDRAL — HE SHOWS HIS AVERSION TO LO-
RENZO THE MAGNIFICENT—HE PREACHES ON THE
FIRST EPISTLE OF ST. JOHN.*

(1491.)

THE Florentines thronged in greater crowds to St. Mark's, until the church could no longer contain them; where-fore, in the Lent of 1491, Savonarola preached in the Duomo, and his voice echoed for the first time within the walls of Santa Maria del Fiore.   From that moment he would seem to have become paramount in the pulpit, and master of the people, who flocked to hear him in increasing numbers, and with redoubled enthusiasm.   The Friar's imagery enchanted the popular fancy; his threats of coming chastisement had a magical effect upon the minds of all, for it truly seemed that all were already oppressed by evil presentiments.   His recently published writings likewise assured his influence over distinguished men who had hitherto stood hesitatingly aloof, but this did not prevent him from condemning, in the plainest and most decided terms, the scepticism and corruption of the most celebrated *literati* of the time.[1]

[1] An autograph codex, in the Library of St. Mark, and of which we shall have more to say hereafter, contains summaries of these Lenten sermons.

All this naturally caused much annoyance to Lorenzo de' Medici, and roused the hostility of his friends. Savonarola began to reflect whether it might not be advisable, for the moment, to cease all mention of visions, revelations, or threats of coming ills, and confine himself to precepts of morality and religion. But he soon realized that it was easier to make this change in theory than in practice. His "Compendium of Revelations" gives us an account of his inward struggles during the second week in Lent. "All that withdrew me from my principal study became quickly distasteful, and whenever I sought to enter on another path, I became instantly hateful to myself. And I remember, when I was preaching in the Duomo in 1491,[1] and had already composed my sermon upon these visions, I determined to omit all mention of them, and never recur to the subject again. God is my witness how I watched and prayed the whole of Saturday and throughout the night ; but all other ways, all doctrines save this, were denied me. Towards break of dawn, being weary and dejected by my long vigil, I heard, as I prayed, a voice saying to me : ' Fool, dost thou not see that it is God's will thou shouldst continue in the same path?' Wherefore I preached [2] that day a terrible sermon, *terrificam prædicationem egi.*" [3]

Of this sermon we have lately discovered an autograph summary, which, although very incomplete, affords a sufficiently clear idea of the whole. It contains a vehement denunciation of the clergy, whom Savonarola declared

---

At sheet 54 we find this passage : "Quidam exponunt cantica de ama-siis, &c. Quidam Scripturas dicunt esse artem poeticam, &c. Quidam cantant versus Loysi Pulici, &c. Quidam habent Biblias in vulgari errantes. Quidam volunt eas corrigere ut grammatici, &c."

[1] In the original 1490 ; but we have adopted the common style of reckoning.

[2] *I.e.*, the second Sunday in Lent, falling on the last day of February, as may be seen in the above-quoted manuscript.

[3] "Compendium Revelationum," Quétif edition, pp. 277-8.

to be devoured by greed of gold, and given up to outer ceremonies of which they made a traffic, while neglecting the inner life of the spirit. " Fathers make sacrifice to this false idol, urging their sons to enter the ecclesiastical life, in order to obtain benefices and prebends ; and thus ye hear it said: *Blessed the house that owns a fat cure.* But I say unto ye : A time will come when rather it will be said : Woe to that house ; and ye will feel the edge of the sword upon you. Do as I bid ye ; rather let your sons follow the way of all others, than undertake the religious life for gain. In these days there is no grace, no gift of the Holy Spirit that may not be bought and sold. On the other hand, the poor are oppressed by grievous burdens, and when they are called to pay sums beyond their means, the rich cry unto them, Give me the rest. There be some who, having but an income of fifty, pay a tax of one hundred, while the rich pay little, since the taxes are imposed at their pleasure. When widows come weeping, they are bidden to go to sleep. When the poor complain, they are told to pay and pay again."

He then went on to speak of the corruption of manners, and wound up by saying : " Bethink ye well, O ye rich, for affliction shall smite ye. This city shall no more be called Florence, but a den of thieves, of turpitude and blood-shed. Then shall ye all be poverty-stricken, all wretched, and your name, O priests, shall be changed into a terror. I sought no longer to speak in Thy name, O Lord ; but Thou hast overpowered me, hast conquered me. Thy word has become like unto a fire within me, consuming the very marrow of my bones. Therefore am I derided and despised of the people. But I cry unto the Lord day and night, and I say unto ye : Know that unheard of times are at hand."

"When Jesus came to redeem the world He found hearers in Judæa alone, and even there the faithful were few.

But He called them to Him on the Mount, and afterwards, by their means, transformed the human race. Ye forsake me, ye deride me, yet shall I gain a few disciples, who will give up all for Christ's sake. They will ask neither benefices nor prebends; will accept neither gifts nor alms, but only their daily bread. They will dress like the poor; they will not seek the great; they will not run after the magistrates in the palace; they will not build houses; they will not visit women daily, to carry them images and rosaries. They will be truthful; they will climb the mount of faith; they will have revelations from heaven and much learning, not, however, the learning of Scotus or the poets, but that of their own conscience and of Holy Writ. They will expound no more their visions until all shall be filled with the glory of God. Then ye shall comprehend that which I say to ye. Now ye cannot comprehend. Wherefore it behoves ye to pray the Lord that He give ye enlightenment. That is your sole need." [1]

[1] In the Museum of St. Mark, in the very cell once inhabited by Savonarola, is now preserved the precious autograph codex from which we have quoted. It is marked E. 5, 10, 76, came from the Palatine Library, and contains summaries in Latin of a great number of Savonarola's sermons, including (at sheets 53–71) those preached during Lent in 1491. To these a contemporary hand, but not that of Savonarola, has affixed the date 1489, which would signify, according to the common style of reckoning, the year 1490. But as we learn from the manuscript, the sermon was preached *Annuntiatione dominica*, that is to say, on the 25th of March, on a Friday, therefore Easter Day must have fallen on the 3rd of April. Now Easter Day fell on the 3rd of April in the years 1485, 1491, and 1496. It could not have been preached in the latter, for that was a Leap Year, and Annunciation Day then fell on Thursday instead of Friday. In 1485 Savonarola was Lenten preacher at San Gimignano; we may therefore take it for granted that his Lenten sermons on the Gospels were preached in 1491. These observations were suggested by Signor Gherardi, and we concur in their justice. We were also able to verify them in another fashion. We found that the sermon for the second Sunday in Lent was precisely the one so minutely described by Savonarola in his "Compendium of Revelations," where he also states that it was preached in the Lent of 1490 (1491 common style). He has noted in his own hand on the margin of the manuscript: "Deinde dixi qualiter fui coactus hec predicare, quia nihil aliud per totam noctem invigilem

From this sermon we may glean some idea of the whole Lenten series of 1491, although the autograph notes of the rest are not only rough and fragmentary, but often almost unintelligible. But we know that Savonarola achieved extraordinary success by them, not, however, without exciting the lively disapprobation of many who felt themselves to be the objects of his attacks. On March 10, 1491, he wrote to Frà Domenico da Pescia, who was then preaching at Pisa, and already one of the most devoted of his followers : " Our work goes on well, for God helps us marvellously, although the chief men of the city are against us, and many fear that we may meet with the fate of Frà Bernardino.[1] But I have faith in the Lord ; He gives me daily greater courage and perseverance, and I preach the regeneration of the Church, taking the Scriptures as my sole guide. Be of good cheer and return quickly, that I may tell ye the marvellous deeds of the Lord." [2]

Further proofs of the signal success of these Lenten discourses are afforded, not only by the testimony of the biographers, but by the remarkable fact that, in spite of his visions, threats, and allusions, and all the murmurs they aroused, Savonarola was invited to the palace by the Signory, and delivered a sermon there on the fourth day of Easter (April 6th). " I am here in the waters of Tiberias," he said. " In the presence of the Signory I do not feel master of myself as in church. Therefore am l constrained to be more measured and urbane, even as

potuit mihi occurrere." These are almost the identical words used in the "Compendium." There is a very incomplete summary of this sermon at sheet 57 of the Codex. *Vide* Appendix of the Italian edition, Doc. vii.

[1] Frà Bernardino da Montefeltro, a Franciscan monk, who, having preached against usury in Florence, and recommended the institution of a Monte di Pietà, was exiled in the time of Piero de' Medici.

[2] This letter was first published by Padre Marchese in an old Italian translation. Gherardi, " Nuovi Documenti," p. 178) brought it out in the original Latin.

Christ in the house of the Pharisee. I must tell you, then, that all the evil and all the good of the city depend from its head, and therefore great is his responsibility even for small sins, since, if he followed the right path, the whole city would be sanctified. We therefore must fish in this sea with nets that can hold the smallest fish, nor must we employ overmuch caution, but, on the contrary, speak frankly and openly. Tyrants are incorrigible because they are proud, because they love flattery, and because they will not restore ill-gotten gains. They leave all in the hands of bad ministers; they succumb to flattery; they hearken not unto the poor, and neither do they condemn the rich; they expect the poor and the peasantry to work for them without reward, or suffer their ministers to expect this; they corrupt voters, and farm out the taxes to aggravate the burdens of the people. Ye must therefore remove dissensions, do justice, and exact honesty from all." [1]

How displeasing this language must have been to Lorenzo, may be easily imagined by all. He was already styled a tyrant by many, and universally charged with having corrupted the magistrates, and appropriated public and private funds. Therefore it was plain that the Friar had dared to make allusion to him. Nevertheless this audacity served to increase Savonarola's fame, and in the July of 1491 he was elected Prior of St. Mark's. This new office, while raising him to a more prominent position, also gave him greater independence. He at once refused to conform to an abuse that had been introduced in the convent, namely, that the new Prior must go to pay his respects, and as it were do homage to the Magnificent. " I consider that my election is owed to God alone," he

[1] A summary of this sermon, but as incomplete as the other summaries, is to be found at sheet 71 of the codex before quoted. *Vide* Appendix to the Italian edition.

said, " and to Him alone will I vow obedience." Lorenzo
was deeply offended by this, and exclaimed, " You see!
a stranger has come into *my house*, yet he will not stoop
to pay me a visit." [1]   Nevertheless, being reluctant to
wage war with the Prior of a convent, or attach too much
importance to a monk, he sought to win him over by
kindness.   He went several times to hear mass in St.
Mark's, and afterwards walked in the garden ; but Savonarola could not be persuaded to leave his studies, in order
to bear him company.   When the friars ran to tell him
of Lorenzo's presence, he replied : " If he does not ask
for me, let him go or stay at his pleasure."   He was very
severe in his judgment of Lorenzo's character ; and knowing the harm wrought on public morals by the prince,
had no wish to approach a tyrant whom he regarded, not
only as the foe and destroyer of freedom, but as the chief
obstacle to the restoration of Christian life among the
people.   Lorenzo then began to send rich gifts, and generous alms to the convent.   But this naturally increased
Savonarola's previous contempt for his character.   And
he alluded to the circumstance in the pulpit, when saying
that a faithful dog does not leave off barking in his master's defence, because a bone is thrown to him.   Nevertheless, soon after this, he found a large sum of money in
gold in the convent alms' box, and, persuaded that Lorenzo
was the donor, immediately sent it all to the congregation
of the good men of St. Martin, for distribution among the
poor, saying that silver and copper sufficed for the needs
of his brethren.   Thus, as Burlamacchi remarks, "Lorenzo
was at last convinced that this was not the right soil in
which to plant vines." [2]

[1] Burlamacchi, p. 20 and fol.; "Biographia Latina," at sheet 7 ; Pico,
p. 23.

[2] Burlamacchi, p. 21.   The " Biografia Latina," at sheet 7, says that
Pietro da Bibbiena, the bearer of the money, when informing Lorenzo
what Savonarola had done with it, added : *Vulpecula ista habet caudam
depilatam.*

But Lorenzo refused to be checked by this rebuff, and presently sent five of the weightiest citizens in Florence [1] to Savonarola in order to persuade him to change his behaviour and manner of preaching by pointing out the dangers he was incurring for himself and his convent. But Savonarola soon cut short their homily, by saying : " I know that you have not come of your own will, but at that of Lorenzo. Bid him to do penance for his sins, for the Lord is no respecter of persons, and spares not the princes of the earth." And when the five citizens hinted that he might be sent into exile, he added : " I fear not sentences of banishment, for this city of yours is like a mustard seed on the earth. But the new doctrine shall triumph, and the old shall fall. Although I be a stranger, and Lorenzo a citizen, and indeed the first in the city, I shall stay while he will depart." He then spoke in such wise on the state of Florence and Italy, that his hearers were amazed by his knowledge of public affairs. It was then that he predicted before many witnesses, in the Sacristy of St. Mark, that great changes would befall Italy, and that the Magnificent, the Pope, and the King of Naples were all near unto death. [2]

Savonarola was extremely tenacious of his independence as an ecclesiastic, and therefore resolutely refused to yield

---

[1] They were : Domenico Bonsi, Guidantonio Vespucci, Paolo Antonio Soderini, Bernardo Rucellai, and Francesco Valori. It is to be noted that almost all of them afterwards became partisans of Savonarola, and the last of the five was indeed the most zealous of his lay followers.

[2] These facts are related in the " Biografia Latina" at sheet 7 ; Cinozzi's " Epistola " ; Burlamacchi, p. 20 and fol. ; Pico, chap. vi. ; and also in the Letter of G. Benivieni to Clement VII., published at the end of Varchi's " Storia," Le Monnier edition of 1857–58. They are also mentioned by Frà Benedetto in the " Secunda Parte delle Profezie dello inclito Martire del Signore, Hieronimo Savonarola," to be found in the National Library of Florence : Rinuccini Codex, II. 8, 123. Among the illuminations in this Codex is a portrait of Savonarola presumably by Frà Benedetto. The first part of this work, bearing the general title of " Nuova Jerusalem," seems to have perished.

on any point. His mystic exaltation daily increased and was more freely displayed in his sermons to the brotherhood. It was then that he indulged in metaphorical utterances and fiery exhortations on the duty of despising carnal things and cultivating the joys of the soul. By opening his whole heart to his brethren, he gained entire mastery over them. One day he said to them : " It is now twenty-seven months since I began to preach on the Apocalypse in this place, that is *nova dicere, novo modo.* Afterwards, being upon a hill, I looked down thence upon a fortified city, which suddenly, as from an earthquake, began to totter and fall. Its inhabitants were quarrelling among themselves. And I bethought me : This city cannot have good foundations, nor its citizens charity. I then went down into the valley, and beheld that there were caverns beneath the houses. I began instantly to build a new city on the plain, asking help from the men ; but instead of aiding in the work, some carried off the stones, while others jeered at me, and shot arrows at me from the old walls. Therefore, I would have withdrawn in despair, but the Lord commanded me to persevere." He then explained that the arrows signified the false teachings of the doctors, who with the string of false knowledge and ill-will bent the bow of righteousness. And the new city was the spiritual life, assailed by worldly men.

" Wherefore pray ye in the spirit," he continued, " so that the Lord may grant ye victory, and persevere, that He may free ye from your many perils." It is easy to lead men to the outer life, to mass, to confession ; but hard to guide them to the inner life and dispose them to grace. It is necessary to shun too many ceremonies. *Oportet viros se ab omni opere exteriori alienare.* These ceremonies are not essential, inasmuch as they vary in different times and places. The ancients lived well without them. Now, by many ceremonies all is converted into shame and gain, as is proved by the universal greed for benefices. Besides, by its effects is the cause known, and your city having no charity cannot have strong foundations. Pray ye then in a fervent spirit, so that the Lord may give victory to the new doctrine. Run not after false knowledge, but examine all things by the light of the Scriptures.[1]

An extraordinary effect was produced on the corrupt and pagan society of Florence by these fervent outbursts of strange, daring and exalted mysticism, which the preacher so suddenly hurled in their midst. Lorenzo fully understood the gravity of the situation ; and although reluctant to hazard extreme measures, had no intention of yielding to what he held to be an audacious aggression. Accordingly, in order to weaken the new orator's growing influence over the people, he persuaded Frà Mariano da Genazzano to resume his sermons, and specially charged him to attack the presumption of uttering prophecies of future events. Frà Mariano had all the impetuosity, hypocrisy, and malice of a courtier-pedant, and although much of his eloquence as a preacher consisted of exaggerated gesticulations, groans and tears, yet he had some reputation for learning, and was in great favour with the creatures of Lorenzo, whom he always flattered from the pulpit.

Up to this time he had always feigned to be Savonarola's friend, and had congratulated him on his fortunate success. But when charged to attack him, he instantly and eagerly accepted the task. On Ascension Day he was to preach in his own convent and church at San Gallo, and take for his text : *Non est vestrum nosse tempora vel momenta* (Acts i. 7). The announcement of this sermon caused great

---

[1] This sermon is given almost in full at sheet 137 and fol. of the previously quoted holograph codex in St. Mark's Library. *Vide* Appendix (of Italian edition), Doc. ix.

excitement in Florence, and the preacher had a very numerous congregation. All the leading citizens were present :
among them Placido Cinozzi, afterwards a friar of St.
Mark's, and Savonarola's biographer; Pico della Mirandola, at that time one of Mariano's admirers ; Poliziano
and even Lorenzo de' Medici, who came to enhance
by his presence the effect of the crushing defeat he
hoped to see inflicted on the Prior of St. Mark's. But
Frà Mariano was betrayed by his own zeal. He began
by hurling all manner of accusations against Savonarola,
styling him a false prophet, a vain disseminator of scandal
and disorder among the people, and this with so much insolence and coarseness of language as to disgust all his
hearers. Thus in a single day his reputation suffered
more than it had gained by the labours of many years.
Indeed, from that moment Cinozzi and Pico forsook
Mariano, in order to attend the sermons of Savonarola,
whose admirers and disciples they subsequently became.
Even Poliziano was greatly shocked, and Lorenzo felt very
humiliated and not a little uneasy.

Thus the threatened discomfiture of the Prior of St.
Mark's was converted into a triumph. The following
Sunday he chose the same verse of the Bible for his text,
interpreting it to the advantage of his own doctrines, and
refuting the charges and accusations of the man who, at a
moment's notice, had changed from a seeming friend to
a declared enemy.[1] The Prior was now master of the
field, for Mariano did not dare to continue his sermons.
Indeed the latter, resuming his old part, feigned indifference, and invited Savonarola to his convent, where they
performed high mass together, and exchanged numerous
courtesies. Nevertheless, the Augustine was cut to the
soul by the humiliation of defeat. To have been once

[1] "Biografia Latina," at sheet 8 ; Cinozzi, "Epistola," &c. ; Burlamacchi, p. 23 and fol.

esteemed the finest preacher in Italy, to have almost anni-
hilated his rival, on the latter's first coming to Florence,
and to be now beaten and vanquished in the sight of all,
was not a blow to be borne without rancour. And from
that moment he cherished the deepest hatred for Savonarola ; vowed eternal vengeance, was indefatigable in raising
fresh obtacles and enemies in his path, and finally succeeded in becoming one of the principal agents of his
fall.

Lorenzo now recognized that he had totally failed in his
intent. He was already suffering from the attacks of the
disease that was soon to have a fatal termination, and weary
of combating a man for whom, in despite of himself, he
felt a growing esteem, no longer attempted to interfere
with his preaching. Nor did Savonarola abuse the privilege.

So far, our only knowledge of his sermons has been
gleaned from his rough preliminary notes. The first
to be printed were those on " The First Epistle of St.
John," which cannot have been delivered before the year
1491. These must now be examined for the sake of a
closer acquaintance with the character of his eloquence.
It is certainly an arduous task to give a detailed account of
a collection of sermons, without unity of subject or links
of connection. And, as the difficulty is increased by the
somewhat disordered nature of the mind and studies of
Savonarola, it will be understood how very difficult it is to
establish the starting-point and goal of our analysis.

The preacher always takes a verse of the Bible for his
text, grouping around it—according to the system of interpretation that we have described—all the ideas, theological, political, and moral, occurring to his mind, and
always quoting other passages of the Bible in their support.
In this way a heterogeneous mass of raw material is built
up, by which the reader is almost overwhelmed. Suddenly,

however, Savonarola shakes off his fetters and thrusts
every obstacle aside : his discourse has touched on some
point of vital interest both to himself and his audience;
his fancy is fired ; colossal images present themselves to his
mind ; his voice swells; his gestures are more animated;
his eyes seem to flame ; his originality is suddenly asserted;
he is a great and powerful orator !   But, all too soon, he
returns to his artificial world of ill-connected, ill-digested
ideas, again issues from it and is again involved in it, without ever leaving it entirely behind, but also without ever
being entirely enslaved by it.   Thus no one can carefully
read and examine these sermons without being forced to confess that Savonarola was a born orator.   Yet, being ignorant
of the rules of oratory, it was only when his subject took
full possession of him, and natural gifts supplied the place
of art, that he could attain to real eloquence.   Nevertheless, if we compare him with his most renowned contemporaries, such as Frà Paolo Attavanti and Frà Roberto
da Lecce, who either remained lost in the mazes of scholastic rhetoric, or stooped to depths of scurrility altogether
unbefitting the pulpit, then indeed Savonarola stands
forth a giant even at his worst moments.   And, in truth,
on patient examination of his sermons, we find an
immense quantity of secondary ideas and details of observation scattered through them which redound to his merit
as a thinker, even when diminishing his worth as an
orator.

All this is abundantly exemplified in the series of sermons to which we have alluded, on the First Epistle of St.
John, probably delivered on the Sundays of 1491.   The
orator gives a lengthy exposition in them of the mysteries
of Mass, together with very useful precepts and directions
for the popular observance of religion.   A minute report
of the order in which they are arranged, and of all the
subjects touched upon, would give so imperfect a notion

of the whole, that it will be more to the purpose to select a few representative thoughts and passages. Among the many occurring to us for quotation, there are some concerning *the word of life*, a theme on which the orator always loved to dwell. His thoughts may appear somewhat artificial and unimportant at the present day, but when we remember what were the theological studies, what was the religious training of his age, we shall see that they prove no little originality of mind, and that Savonarola must have possessed an unusual amount of intellectual vigour.

He treats the subject in the following manner :—" A human word is formed in separate and different ways by a succession of syllables, and therefore when one part of a word is pronounced, the others cease to exist ; when the whole word has been uttered, it too ceases to exist. But the Divine Word is not divided into parts ; it issues united in its whole essence ; is diffused throughout the created world, living and enduring in all eternity, even as the heavenly light of which it is the companion. Wherefore it is *the word of life*, or rather is *the life*, and is one with the Father. It is true that we accept this word in various senses ; sometimes by life we mean the state of being of living men, sometimes we regard it as meaning the occupation of living men : wherefore we say, The life of this man is knowledge, the life of the bird is song. But, truly, there is but one life, and it is God, since in Him alone have all things their being. And this is the blessed life that is the end of man, and in which infinite and eternal happiness is found. The earthly life is not only deceptive, but cannot all be enjoyed, inasmuch as it lacks unity. If thou lovest riches, thou must renounce the senses ; if thou givest thyself up to the senses, thou must renounce knowledge ; and if thou wouldst have knowledge, thou canst not enjoy offices. But the pleasures

of the heavenly life may all be enjoyed in the vision of
God, which is supreme felicity." [1]

Savonarola expounds these ideas at some length, but
more frequently inveighs against the corrupt manners of
the age, denouncing in turn every vice that was then prevalent. This, for instance, is how he speaks against
gambling: "If you see persons engaged in gambling in
these days, believe them to be no Christians, since they
are worse than infidels, are ministers of the evil one, and
celebrate his rites. They are avaricious men, blasphemers,
slanderers, detractors of others' fame, fault-finders, they are
hateful to God, are thieves, murderers, and full of all
iniquity. I cannot permit ye to share in these amusements; ye must be steadfast in prayer, continually rendering thanks to the Almighty in the name of our Lord
Jesus Christ. He that gambles shall be accursed, and
accursed he that suffers others to gamble; shun ye their
conversation, for the father that gambles before his son
shall be accursed, and accursed the mother that gambles
in her daughter's presence. Therefore, whoever thou art,
thou shalt be accursed if thou dost gamble or allow others
to gamble; thou shalt be accursed, I tell thee, in the city,
accursed in the fields; thy corn shall be accursed; and thy
substance; cursed the fruit of thy land and thy body, thy
herds of oxen and thy flocks of sheep; cursed shalt thou
be in all thy comings and goings." [2]

And in speaking against usury and immoderate gains,
he says: "Therefore, owing to avarice, neither ye nor
your children lead a good life, and ye have already dis-

[1] "Sermoni sulla I Epistola di San Giovanni." *Vide* Sermons i., iv.,
v., and vi. *passim.* Our quotation is from the Prato edition of 1846,
which is the easiest to obtain, but although this edition has been collated
with the holograph MS. belonging to Lord Holland, it is incomplete in
some places, and is therefore useless for purposes of study, unless compared with the Venetian editions, of 1547 in Italian, and of 1536 in Latin.

[2] Sermon x. p. 93.

covered many devices for gaining money, and many modes
of exchange which ye call just, but are most unjust, and
ye have likewise corrupted the magistrates and their functions. . . . None can persuade ye that it is sinful to lend
at usury, or make unjust bargains ; on the contrary ye
defend yourselves to your souls' damnation ; . . . nor does
any man take shame to himself for lending at usury, but
rather holds them to be fools that refrain from it. And
thus by ye is fulfilled the saying of Isaiah : ' They declare
their sin as Sodom, they hide it not,' and that of Jeremiah,
' Thou hadst a whore's forehead, thou refusedst to be
ashamed.' Thou sayest that the good and happy life consists in gain ; and Christ says, ' Blessed are the poor in
spirit, for theirs is the kingdom of heaven.' Thou sayest
that the happy life consists in pleasure and voluptuousness ;
and Christ says, ' Blessed are they that mourn, for they
shall be comforted.' Thou sayest the happy life consists
in glory ; and Christ says, ' Blessed are ye, when men
shall revile ye and persecute ye.' The way of life hath
been shown to ye, yet none follows it, none seeks it, none
learns it. Wherefore Christ laments over ye, for having
endured much labour to show ye the way of Life, that all
might be saved, He is justly incensed against you ; and
hath declared by the mouth of the prophet : ' We are
weary with calling, my tongue cleaves to the roof of my
mouth ; for all day do I cry with the voice of the preachers,
and no one hearkens unto me.' "[1]

At other times Savonarola addresses himself to the
hearts of his people, and seeks to lead them to righteousness by rousing their feelings. " Oh ! would that I might
persuade ye to turn away from earthly things, and follow
after things eternal ! Would God grant this grace to me
and to ye, I should assuredly deem myself happy in this
life. But this is a gift from God. None may come unto

[1] Sermon v. pp. 49, 50.

me, sayeth the Lord, unless he be brought by the Father.
I cannot enlighten ye inwardly, I can only strike upon
your ears ; but what may that avail if your intellect be not
enlightened, nor your affections kindled ? " [1]   " And how
may this be done, save by the word of God ?   Labour,
then, to comprehend His word, and do with yourselves as
with corn, which to be made into flour must first be
pounded and ground.   Otherwise what would it avail to
have full granaries, what to have the treasures of the Holy
Spirit unless ye draw out their spiritual meaning ?   Therefore will I strive to do the work of the Apostles,, making
the Holy Scriptures known to ye ; and to ye it behoves to
be doers, and not only hearers of the word of God." [2]

But where Savonarola truly surpassed himself, was in
expounding the Gospel of the Epiphany ; and this sermon
was not only full of feeling and imagination, but also con-
structed with the greatest skill.   " Now when Jesus was
born in Bethlehem of Judæa, in the days of Herod the
king, behold there came to Jerusalem wise men from the
east, saying : Where is He that is born in Judæa ?   For
we have seen His star in the east, and have come to
worship Him with gifts.—Mark the words and observe
the mysteries. . . . Behold then that He by whom all
things were made is this day born upon earth.   Wherefore
the beginning of all things (inasmuch as by Him all things
were created) is now born, and hath a young virgin for
His mother . . . Behold, He who holds the world in His
hand, is brought forth of a maid.   Behold, He that is
above all things begins by having a native land ; He begins
as the compatriot of men, the companion of men, the
brother of men, and the son of man !   See how God
cometh near unto ye !   Seek ye then the Lord, while ye
may still find Him ; call upon Him while He is yet near.
. . . Of a truth this is the bread that comes down from

[1] Sermon vi. p. 52.   [2] Sermon v. pp. 43, 44.

heaven, and gladdens the hearts of angels and of men, so that it may be the common food of men and of angels. . . .

" Hearken then, my brethren, and let not your thoughts go astray. Open your eyes, and behold who are these that are coming. I cry unto ye, O men, and my voice is for the children of men. Behold the Wise men, behold the Chaldeans ; behold those that were not born among Christians ; behold those that were not baptized ; behold those that were not instructed in the law of the gospel ; behold those that did not receive the numerous sacraments of the Church ; behold those that heard not the voices of preachers. *Behold the Wise Men of the East,* from the midst of a perverse and evil nation, from distant and remote regions ; shrinking from no expense, from no weariness, from no danger. *They came.* And when was it that they came ? When all the world was full of idolatry ; when men bowed down before stocks and stones, when the earth was full of darkness and gloom, and all men full of iniquity. . . . When was it that they came ? When Christ was a babe, when He lay upon straw, when He showed nought but weakness, when He had as yet done no miracles. . . . *We beheld His star in the east,* the star that announced His coming. Behold, they saw His star, but no other miracle ; they beheld not the blind restored to sight, nor the dead raised, nor any other visible thing. *And we come to worship Him.* We have made a great journey only to worship the footprints of the Babe. If only we may see Him, may adore Him, may touch Him, if only we may lay our gifts before Him, we deem ourselves blessed. We have forsaken our country, have forsaken our families, have forsaken our friends, have forsaken our kingdoms, have forsaken our great riches ; we have come from a distant land, through many dangers, and with much speed, and solely to worship Him. This is sufficient for us, this is more to us than our kingdoms, this is more precious to us than our very life. . . . What then shall we say to these things, my brethren? What, by our faith, shall we say? O living faith! O highest charity! See ye then how great was the perfidy of the Judæans, how great the hardness of their hearts, since neither by miracles, nor by prophecies, nor by this voice, were they moved!

"But why have we directed our sermon against the men of Judæa, and not rather against ourselves? . . . Why dost thou see the mote in thy brother's eye, yet cannot see the beam in thine own? Behold, the Lord Jesus is no longer a babe in the manger, but is great in heaven. Already hath He preached and performed miracles, hath been crucified, hath risen again, and now sitteth at the right hand of the Father, hath sent His Holy Spirit down upon the earth, hath sent the apostles, hath subjugated the nations. . . . Already the kingdom of heaven is everywhere; behold, its door is opened unto ye; the Lord hath led the way, and the apostles and martyrs have followed Him. But thou art slothful, and all labour is a burden to thee, and thou wilt not follow the footsteps of Christ. Behold, each day avarice grows, the whirlpool of usury is widened, lust hath contaminated all things, and pride soareth to the clouds. Ye are children of the devil, and ye seek to do the will of your father. Oh! well might it be said of ye, in the words of the Bible—' Behold, I go unto a people which kneweth me not, and called not upon my name; daily have I stretched out my hands to an unbelieving people, which walketh in the way of perdition, a people which provoketh me to anger.'"[1]

This description of the wise men coming from distant lands, and through many perils, to seek the infant Jesus, while Christians remain indifferent to Christ the Man,

[1] Sermon xvii. pp. 164–9.

even when He has risen to the splendour of His glory, and opens His arms invitingly to them, was undoubtedly one of the appeals that acted most magically upon the people ; and the whole sermon was one of the best Savonarola ever gave. Natural, spontaneous, heart-stirring eloquence of this kind, was entirely unexampled in that age of pedantic and imitative oratory.[1]

The simple eloquence of the thirteenth century, of which, with all its childishness and ingenuous charm, St. Bernardino of Siena was the last and most famous example, had now long died out. The preachers of the time, as we have before remarked, when not rhetoricians of the Frà Mariano type, indulged in vulgar theatrical displays, or spoke a scholastic jargon that was no longer understood. Accordingly, the secret of Savonarola's enormous success may be entirely attributed to his mystic religious ardour, and to the earnest affection he felt for the people and elicited from them in return. His was the only voice

---

[1] In the holograph manuscript of Cerretani's " Storia di Firenze," preserved in the National Library of Florence (II., III. 74, sheet 174[1]), we find the following remarks on Savonarola's sermons : " He introduced an almost new manner of preaching the Word of God, namely the Apostolic manner, without dividing the sermon into parts, without proposing questions, and shunning cadences and all the devices of eloquence ; for his sole aim was to expound some passages of the Old Testament, and introduce the simplicity of the primitive Church." Guicciardini states, in his " Storia Fiorentina," that having read and considered Savonarola's sermons, he found them " to be very eloquent, and with a *natural and spontaneous, not artificial, eloquence*." He adds that for centuries no man had been seen so versed as he in Holy Writ, and that whereas no one had ever succeeded in preaching for more than two Lenten seasons in Florence without the public growing weary of him, Savonarola alone was able to continue preaching for many years, and always rising in the estimation of the people. As we have before remarked, Guicciardini was one of the warmest admirers of Savonarola, and made summaries of all his sermons. The manuscript of these summaries, written in Guicciardini's own hand, was published some years ago by his heirs and descendants. His opinion is the more valuable because he was a constant adherent of the Medici, and far from being a fanatic, was by no means of a very religious turn of mind.

that addressed them in familiar[1] and fascinating tones. He used language that stirred the hearts of the multitude, and spoke of subjects which came home to them. He was the only one who fought sincerely for truth, was fervently devoted to goodness, and deeply commiserated the sufferings of his hearers; accordingly he was the one really eloquent speaker of his age. Since the holy eloquence of the early Christian Fathers and Doctors passed away, no voice had been heard worthy of lasting fame. Frà Girolamo was the first to restore pulpit preaching to its old post of honour, and to give it fresh life, and accordingly he well deserves to be styled the first orator of modern times.

NOTE.

On the Language employed by Savonarola in his Sermons.

IT will be clear, from what we have already said, that Mons. Perrens and many other writers were mistaken in their belief that Savonarola frequently delivered his sermons in Latin. This error was caused by finding that the holograph manuscripts of many of the sermons, including those on the First Epistle of St. John, as well as their first printed edition, were in Latin. But at that time it was the general habit to write in that tongue. When, however, the sermons began to be reported as they were spoken (as, for instance, in Ser Lorenzo Violi's collection), they were always published in Italian; although, even then, when Savonarola himself sketched or wrote them out for the press he found it easier to write them in Latin. It is an undoubted fact that he always preferred to write in that tongue. All the marginal notes in his Bibles are in Latin, so too all his rough sketches for sermons preserved in the Florence National Library, and the holograph codex at St. Mark's. But even in these first rough notes, we often find that when Savonarola wished to put a thought into shape, and reduce it to the form in which it was to be delivered as part of a sermon, he wrote it out in Italian; whereas in jotting down ideas as they first occurred to him, he always used Latin, and probably preached sometimes to his monks in that language when no other

---

[1] *Vide* Note to the following page.

hearers were present. Many of his works, originally written in Latin, were afterwards translated by himself into Italian, for a second edition, and *for the use of believers in general.* These words being prefixed by Savonarola to every translation of his works, it is plain that there is no foundation for the belief expressed by some writers that Latin was commonly understood by the people at that period. But as it was the language of the learned classes throughout Europe, it was naturally employed in all theological and philosophical works, and all the more so because, in order to treat of these themes in Italian, it would have been requisite to coin new phrases and forms of speech, almost, indeed, to create a new language. Accordingly it was found easier to write first in Latin, and then translate into the vulgar tongue. To conclude these remarks, we need only add that Savonarola's sermons on " Noah's Ark," delivered in 1494, were taken down from his lips in Italian, but were afterwards, in order to *improve their literary form* (as their editor informs us), translated into dog-Latin, and thus published and reprinted at Venice several times during the sixteenth century. The sermons on " The Book of Job " were similarly taken down in Italian and translated into Latin, and then again rendered in the Vulgate, *as at first they were truly composed and preached;* so we are told by the editor of the Italian edition (Venice : Bascarini. 1545). All this serves to convince us that, although some of Savonarola's sermons are found to be in Latin, both in their first printed edition and in the holograph manuscript, this by no means implies that they were delivered in that language.

CHAPTER IX.

DEATH OF LORENZO DE' MEDICI AND OF POPE INNOCENT VIII.—ELECTION OF ALEXANDER VI.— SAVONAROLA'S JOURNEY TO BOLOGNA. — SEPA- RATION OF THE CONVENT OF ST. MARK FROM THE LOMBARD CONGREGATION.—REFORMS IN THE CONVENT.

(1492-93.)

LORENZO DE' MEDICI had retired to his pleasant country house at Careggi. He was wasting away from severe internal disease, and by the beginning of April, 1492, all hope of his recovery was at an end. His doctors had ex- hausted all the resources of their skill; the renowned physician, Lazzaro of Pavia, had been summoned in vain, even his marvellous potion of distilled gems having failed to take effect. The Magnificent was near unto death. A few faithful friends cheered his last hours by their devoted affection. Ficino and Pico paid him frequent visits, and Angelo Poliziano never left his bedside. The latter was sincerely attached to Lorenzo; and felt that in losing him, he lost the patron to whom he owed everything and to whom he was bound by stronger ties of gratitude than to any other man upon earth. In vain he sought to hide his grief, to repress his tears. Lorenzo fixed his eyes upon him with the

enigmatic glance peculiar to the dying, and then, unable
longer to restrain his feelings, Poliziano burst into a flood
of tears.[1]

These proofs of affection gave solemnity to these last
hours, and the Magnificent, having now turned his
thoughts to religion, seemed to be a changed man. In
fact, when the last sacrament was about to be administered
to him, he insisted on rising, and leaning on the arms
of his friends, tottered forward to meet the priest, who,
seeing how much he was overcome by emotion, was
obliged to order him back to his bed. But it was
extremely difficult to soothe his agitation. Lorenzo's
mind was haunted by spectres of the past; and as his
last moments drew near, all his sins rose before him in
increasing magnitude, became more and more threatening.
The last offices of religion were powerless to conquer his
terrors, for having lost all faith in mankind, he could not
believe in his confessor's sincerity. Accustomed to see
his slightest wish obeyed and all the world bow to his
will, he could not realize that any one would dare to
deny him absolution. Accordingly the blessing of the
Church was powerless to lighten the weight burdening his
conscience, and he was more and more cruelly tortured
by remorse. No one has ever dared to refuse me anything—he thought to himself, and thus the idea that had
once been his chief pride became his worst torment.

Suddenly, however, he thought of Savonarola's stern
face; here, he remembered, was a man who had been
equally unmoved by his threats and his blandishments,
and thereupon he exclaimed, "I know no honest friar save
this one," and expressed his desire to confess to Savonarola.
A messenger was instantly despatched to St. Mark's,
and the Prior was so astounded by the strange and
unexpected summons, that he almost refused to believe

---

[1] Politiani, "Epistolæ." Jacopo Antiquario, xv. kalendas iunias 1492.

it, and answered that it seemed useless for him to go
to Careggi, since no words of his would be acceptable
to Lorenzo. But on learning the desperate condition
of the sick man, and his earnest desire to confess to him,
he set forth without delay.

On that day Lorenzo thoroughly realized that his end
was at hand. He had sent for his son Piero, and given
him his 'final counsels and last farewells. His friends had
been dismissed during this interview, but when they were
allowed to return to the room and had persuaded Piero to
retire, as his presence agitated his father too much, Lorenzo
expressed a wish to see Pico della Mirandola once more,
and the latter immediately came to him. The sweet aspect
of the kindly, gentle young man seemed to have a soothing
effect upon him, for he said : I should have been very
sorry to die, without first being cheered a little by thy
presence. And thereupon his face grew calm, his discourse almost cheerful ; and he began to laugh and jest
with his friend. Pico had scarcely left the room before
Savonarola entered it, and respectfully approached the
bed of the dying prince. Lorenzo explained that there
were three sins on his conscience which he was specially
anxious to confess, in order to be absolved from them :
the sack of Volterra ; the robbery of the *Monte delle
Fanciulle,* whereby so many girls had been driven to
a life of shame ; and the bloody reprisals following the
conspiracy of the Pazzi. In speaking of these things,
even before beginning his private confession, the Magnificent again fell into great agitation, and Savonarola
sought to calm him by repeating: God is good, God
is merciful . . . But, he added, directly Lorenzo had
ceased speaking, three things are needful. What things,
Father ? replied Lorenzo. Savonarola's face grew stern,
and extending the fingers of his right hand, he began
thus : Firstly, a great and living faith in God's mercy.—

I have the fullest faith in it. Secondly, you must
restore all your ill-gotten wealth, or at least charge your
sons to restore it in your name.—At this the Magnificent
seemed to be struck with surprise and grief; nevertheless,
making an effort, he gave a nod of assent. Savonarola
then stood up, and whereas the dying prince lay cowering
with fear in his bed, he seemed to soar above his real
stature as he said : Lastly, you must restore liberty to
the people of Florence. His face was solemn; his voice
almost terrible; his eyes, as if seeking to divine the
answer, were intently fixed on those of Lorenzo, who,
collecting all his remaining strength, angrily turned his
back on him without uttering a word. Accordingly
Savonarola left his presence without granting him absolution, and without having received any actual and detailed
confession. The Magnificent remained torn by remorse,
and soon after breathed his last, on April 8, 1492.[1]

The death of Lorenzo de' Medici wrought great changes
not only in the affairs of Tuscany, but of all Italy. His
skilful mode of action, the prudence with which he had
maintained his position with regard to other potentates,
and his dexterity in keeping them all, if not united, at
least in balance, had rendered him the arbiter, as it were,
of Italian politics, and Florence the centre of the gravest
affairs of state. Piero de' Medici, on the contrary, was
in all respects the opposite of his father. Handsome
and robust in person, he cared only for sensual pleasures
and athletic sports. He had a great aptitude for spinning
improvised verses, and a graceful and pleasant delivery ;
but he only aspired to excel as a horseman and in the
lists, at football, boxing, and tennis. Indeed he was so
proud of his skill in these games as to challenge all the
best players in Italy, and persuade them to come to Florence.
He inherited from his mother all the pride of the Orsini

[1] *Vide* Note at the end of the chapter.

house, but had none of the courteous refinement of
manner that had so largely contributed to his father's
popularity. On the contrary, he gave offence to all by
his uncouthness, and indulged in such violent transports
of anger, that on one occasion, before many witnesses,
he boxed the ears of one of his cousins. Behaviour of
this kind was far more intolerable to the Florentines than
any open violation of the laws, and was quite sufficient
to raise numerous enemies against him.[1]

And he not only offended private individuals, but
contrived, at the very beginning of his reign, to so
thoroughly disgust all the Italian princes, that Florence
speedily lost the proud pre-eminence Lorenzo had gained
for her. Even the most pressing affairs of state were
entirely neglected by Piero, whose sole concern was to
find opportunities for increasing his personal power, and
who daily swept away some of the semblances of freedom,
which the Magnificent had so shrewdly preserved, and
to which the people were still so attached. Hence, there
were growing murmurs among the bulk of the citizens,
and a hostile party had been already formed, and was
continually gaining fresh recruits from the ranks of those
who, in Lorenzo's time, had been staunch adherents of
the Medici. A presentiment of coming change was
already in the air, and there was a growing desire and
necessity for a change of some sort, inasmuch as Piero,
being forsaken by men of good repute, was obliged to
lean more and more upon untried and incapable persons.

Meanwhile the multitude assembled in increasing
numbers round the pulpit of Savonarola, who was now
considered the preacher of the party opposed to the
Medici. That Lorenzo, on his death-bed, should have
wished to confess to him had infinitely raised him in the

[1] Nardi, " Storia di Firenze "; Guicciardini, " Storia d'Italia," and
" Storia Florentina "; Sismondi, " Hist des Rép. Ital.," &c.

estimation of all those admirers of the prince, who were now alienated by the violence and uncertain policy of his son. And the lower classes, on their side, were beginning to recall how Savonarola had once predicted to several influential citizens,[1] in the Sacristy of St. Mark's, the approaching death of Lorenzo, the Pope, and the Neapolitan king. One part of this prophecy had been almost immediately fulfilled; and another seemed about to come to pass.

In fact, the vital powers of Innocent VIII. were rapidly sinking: he had been lying for some time in a lethargic state, that was occasionally so death-like as to make his attendants believe that all was over. Every means of restoring his exhausted vitality had been tried in vain, when a Jewish doctor proposed to attempt his cure by means of a new instrument for the transfusion of blood. Hitherto this experiment had only been tried upon animals; but now the blood of the decrepit Pontiff was to be transfused into the veins of a youth, who gave him his own in exchange. Thrice, in fact, was the difficult experiment made. It did no good to the Pope, and three boys, costing the sum of one ducat apiece, lost their lives, through the introduction of air into their veins.[2] The Jewish doctor then fled, and on July 25, 1492, Innocent VIII. finally expired. Intrigues for the election of his successor were immediately set on foot.

The corruption of the Roman Court had now reached so high a pitch, that enormities formerly carried on in secret, and even thus causing much scandal and universal

---

[1] These citizens were: Alessandro Acciaioli, Cosimo Rucellai, and Carlo Carnesecchi. As we have before stated, this prediction is mentioned by many writers (*vide* Note 2, to page 131); and Savonarola frequently alluded to it in his sermons.

[2] " Iudeus quidem aufugit, et Papa sanatus non est," are the concluding words of Infessura. But the Florentine ambassador, does not give this incident, although it is recorded by many historians.

lamentation, were now openly practised and almost un-remarked. The number of cardinals sitting in conclave was only twenty-three; and the election being a simple matter of traffic, was carried by Roderigo Borgia, the candidate able to bid the highest price and promise the greatest number of preferments. Mules laden with gold were seen entering the palace-yard of Ascanio Sforza,[1] Borgia's most dreaded competitor, who also gained, in return for his vote, the office of Vice-Chancellor and other almost equally lucrative appointments. The Romans viewed these things with indifference, and discussed the details of their bargain as though it were all in the natural course of events.[2]

The name of the new Pope, Alexander VI., has too evil a notoriety for it to be necessary to speak of him at much length. Roderigo Borgia was of Spanish birth, and had studied law in Italy. Owing to his great facility of address, astonishing aptitude for business, particularly in the management of finance, and above all by the favour of his uncle, Calixtus III., he had risen step by step to the rank of Cardinal and the possession of large revenues. One of his strongest passions was an insatiable greed for gold; and he accordingly formed intimate relations with Moors, Turks, and Jews, regardless of all the prejudices and customs of his age. In this way he was enabled to accumulate the immense fortune that served to raise him to the papacy. Addicted to license and sensuality, he was always the slave of some woman. At the time of his election he was the lover of the notorious Vannozza, by whom he had several children. This woman's mother was said to have been his former mistress, just as he was afterwards accused of a shameful connection with his own

[1] Brother of Ludovic the Moor.
[2] *Vide* Infessuræ, "Diarium"; Burchardi, "Diarium"; Guicciardini, "Storia d' Italia"; and almost every historian of Rome and the Popes.

and Vannozza's daughter, Lucrezia, known to all the world as the cause of the many scandals and sanguinary jealousies by which the name of Borgia became a disgrace to humanity. Such was the character of the man now raised to the papal chair; and therefore, in spite of official rejoicings, the announcement of his election was received throughout Italy with universal dismay. According to Guicciardini, Ferdinand of Naples burst into tears at the news, although never before known to weep, even for the death of his own children.[1]

Nevertheless the beginning of the new pontificate did not seem to justify the evil expectations formed of it. For the first time some order was introduced into the administration of the papal revenues. During the past years crimes of every kind had been rampant in the Campagna and all the provinces, acts of violence being committed almost by the hundred each week. These were now rigorously repressed, and their number diminished with marvellous speed. But it was soon found that the aim of all these improvements was to give the Pope increased facility for extorting money from his subjects, and establish stronger principalities for his children, who were already notorious for the enormity of their lusts and the atrocity of their crimes.

These things began to have a terrifying effect on men's minds, and every one thought of the future with the utmost trepidation. All eyes, therefore, were turned towards the man who had already prophesied evil to Italy and the Church, and whose words now seemed to be so strangely fulfilled. Two of the princes whose deaths he had foreseen were already in their graves; the third was

---

[1] Guicciardini, " Storia d' Italia," vol. i. p. 9. Gregorovius and Reumont have recently written on the history of the Borgia family, and fresh light has also been thrown on the subject by the " Dispacci " of A. Giustiniani, edited by ourselves. Florence : Successori Le Monnier, 1876, 3 vols.

too decrepit to last much longer; and for ages the Church
had never been in so deplorable a state.   The three
famous " Conclusions" pronounced by the Friar passed
therefore from mouth to mouth; true believers, in their
unhappiness, began to place implicit faith in them; and
thus the confused terror oppressing the public mind,
served to the increase of Savonarola's fame.   He himself
was at once the source and the victim of these gloomy
presentiments.   His predictions spread alarm on all sides,
and seeing that nearly all believed them and adopted his
ideas, he became more excited by them himself, and more
convinced of their truth.   The times he had prophesied
seemed at last near at hand;   he read and re-read the
prophets; his sermons in the churches of St. Lorenzo and
Santa Reparata were marked by greater vehemence; nor
is it any wonder that, in this state of mind, he should have
again beheld visions.

In fact we learn from his own words that, during this
year 1492, two visions were shown to him, which he was
forced to accept as revelations from heaven.   The night
before his last Advent sermon, he beheld in the middle of
the sky a hand bearing a sword, upon which these words
were inscribed : " *Gladius Domini super terram cito et
velociter.*"   He heard many clear and distinct voices
promising mercy to the good, threatening chastisement
to the wicked, and proclaiming that the wrath of God was
at hand.   Then, suddenly the sword was turned towards
the earth ; the sky darkened ; swords, arrows, and flames
rained down : terrible thunderclaps were heard; and all
the world was a prey to war, famine, and pestilence.   The
vision ended with a command to Savonarola to make these
things known to his hearers, to inspire them with the fear
of God, and to beseech the Lord to send good shepherds
to His Church, so that the lost sheep might be saved.[1]

[1] " Comp. Revelationum," p. 231, and following.

SAVONAROLA MEDAL.

("GLADIUS DOMINI SUPER TERRAM CITO ET
VELOCITER.")

This vision was afterwards recorded by innumerable medals and engravings ; and it almost served as a symbol of Savonarola and his doctrines.[1] During Lent, and precisely on Good Friday, he saw another vision, in which a black cross rose from the city of Rome, and reaching the heavens, stretched its arms over the whole earth. Upon the cross was written, " *Crux iræ Dei.*" The sky was densely black, lightning flashed, thunder pealed, there came a storm of wind and hail. From the centre of Jerusalem rose a golden cross, shedding its rays over the whole world, and upon this was written, " *Crux Misericordiæ Dei,*" and all the nations flocked to adore it.[2]

[1] Many medals were struck in Savonarola's honour. They are minutely described by all writers on the Italian medalists of the Renaissance, and two of these authors' names may be quoted : Friedländer, " Die Italienischen Schaumüngen des fünfzehnten jahrhunderts " (Berlin, 1880–82) ; and A. Heiss, " Les Médailleurs de la Renaissance" (Paris : Rothschild, 1881–86). Two of the Savonarola medals are, as it were prototypes of all the others, and are preserved in the Uffizii Gallery at Florence.

The first of the two, attributed by Heiss and a few other writers to one of the Della Robbia family, bears on the obverse the Friar's head, cowled, but with the rather high forehead left uncovered. The legend encircling it is, " *Hieronymus Savonarola Ferrariensis vir doctissimus ordinis prædichatorum.*" Cn the upper part of the reverse is a hand with a dagger ; beneath a city (Florence or Rome), and round it the words, "*Gladius Domini super terram cito et velociter.*" This medal gave origin to several others, among them one of much later date, with the bust of Savonarola, crucifix in hand. The reverse is divided by a vertical line, on the right side of which there is a hand with a dagger above a city ; on the left side the emblem of the Holy Ghost, and the earth beneath. The legend is almost identical with those of the older medals.

The second prototype shows Savonarola's head with the cowl drawn forward, very like the head in Giovanni delle Corniole's engraving. The only inscription is, " *F. Hieronimus Savonarola ordinis prædicatorum.*" On the reverse, a hand with a sword in the sky ; and to the left of this, the Holy Spirit and a shower of flames falling on the earth. There should be the same inscription as on the other medals, " *Gladius Domini,*" &c., and " *Spiritus Domini super terram copiose et abundanter.*" But neither was given in the medal shown to us.

[2] In the " Compendium Revelationum," pp. 244–5, Savonarola says that this vision appeared to him on Good Friday, while he was preaching in

Savonarola was now increasingly earnest in proclaiming his doctrines of chastisement and regeneration, basing his arguments not only on reason and the Bible, but even on the authority of his visions. He continued to do this throughout the year 1492, and particularly during Lent. It was then that he began those celebrated discourses on " Noah's Ark " which made so great a sensation, were afterwards continued, and concluded, with still greater success, in 1494. But more will be said of them hereafter, when reviewing the whole series.

Meanwhile, we often find him unexpectedly absent from Florence. In February and May, 1492, he made journeys to Venice, either shortly before or shortly after his visit to Pisa, where he gave a few sermons in the Monastery of Santa Caterina, and contracted a friendship with Stefano da Codiponte,[1] afterwards one of the most faithful and devoted of his followers. But in the Lent of 1493 he made a still longer absence, and preached in Bologna. It appears that Piero de' Medici, being less

S. Lorenzo, during the Lent of 1492. It is proved by Signor Gherardi's " Documenti " (p. 12) that his Lenten sermons for 1492 were delivered in that church, and from Violi's " Giornate " (*vide* doc. xvi. of appendix to Italian edition) we learn that Savonarola then began his course of sermons on Noah's Ark. This year could not be that of 1493, common style, for it is well known that in 1493 Savonarola was Lenten preacher in Bologna. The Easter of 1492 fell on the 22nd of April, and this seems to explain why the Lent was dated 1492 both in the Florentine and the common calendar.

[1] He was a young man from Liguria, who had come to study law in the Pisan University. Being tired of the world, he became a monk in 1491, and then wearying of the cloister, asked leave to return to it. But just then Savonarola came to Pisa, and Codiponte was so deeply moved by his sermons that he not only recurred to his first purpose, but adhered to it most firmly, and became very zealous in the faith and devoted to Savonarola. One of the most beautiful of the Friar's letters is addressed to Codiponte, and dated 22nd May, 1492. This letter was discovered by us in the Riccardi Library (Codex 2053), and is given in Document x. of the appendix to the Italian edition. For facts concerning Codiponte, see the " Annali del Monastero di Santa Caterina di Pisa," published in the " Archivio Storico Italiano," vol. vi. part ii. p. 615.

TOMB OF SAN DOMENICO IN BOLOGNA.

judicious than his father, wished to be rid of this too popular preacher, round whom all his enemies were beginning to rally. He accordingly arranged with the superiors of the Order in Rome or Milan to have the Friar removed from Florence, and wished Frà Mariano to come back and resume his sermons.[1] The brethren of St. Mark's were sorely grieved by the prolonged absence of their Prior, and Savonarola endeavoured to console them by letter. "Your tender affection is ever in my mind, and I often speak of it with Frà Basilio, my very dear son and your true brother in Christ Jesus. . . . We lead a very solitary life, like unto two turtle-doves, awaiting the spring to return again to the soft climate where we once dwelt, amid the blossoms and joys of the Holy Spirit. . . . But if your sadness seems too great for ye to deem life possible without me, your love is still imperfect, and therefore God has taken me from ye for some space of time."[2]

Nevertheless, Savonarola remained at Bologna very reluctantly. Banished from Florence as too great a partisan of the people, he found himself ill at ease in a city ruled by the iron hand of a Bentivoglio, and where he was obliged to keep strictly within bounds. Being thus constrained to preach in a manner opposed to his inclination, he spoke coldly, and was styled "a simple man, and a preacher for women."[3] But his name proved an

---

[1] Proofs of this are given in the documents published by Cappelli, "Frà Girolamo Savonarola," &c., pp. 28-30.

[2] This letter, which is full of affection and Christian counsel, is given in Quétif's "Additions" to Pico's biography of Savonarola, vol. ii., p. 99. Quétif says "*quando praedicabat Bononiæ, anno millesimo quadringentesimo nonagesimo secundo.*" But this was the year 1493, according to the common style, as is also proved by another of Savonarola's letters published in Cappelli's "Frà Girolamo Savonarola," p. 30. As usual, the biographers are somewhat confused in their dates.

[3] "Biografia Latina," chap. x., at sheet 9; Burlamacchi, p. 26; Padre Marchese, "Scritti Vari" (we always quote from Le Monnier's first edition of the work), p. 136.

attraction to the crowd, and numbers flocked to hear him. Among them was Bentivoglio's wife, who always, arriving very late with a long train of ladies, cavaliers, and pages, daily interrupted the sermon. This was an irregularity that Savonarola would by no means tolerate. For the first day or so he paused in his discourse, thinking that this would be a sufficient reproof; but finding that the annoyance was continued and increased, he made some remarks on the sin of disturbing the devotions of the faithful. Thereupon, her pride being offended, the lady came later and later, made more noise, and behaved with haughtier disrespect. At last, one morning, Savonarola being interrupted in the heat of his discourse, could no longer restrain his anger, and cried out:—" Behold, here cometh the devil to interrupt God's word." At this Dame Bentivoglio was so enraged, that she directed two of her grooms to strike him dead in the pulpit. They, however, shrank from so great an atrocity. Then, increasingly indignant at the thought of having been put to humiliation by a monk, she despatched two other satellites to fall upon the preacher in his cell, and do him, at least, some grievous bodily hurt. But Savonarola faced the men with so much firmness, and addressed them in so dignified and commanding a tone, that they were awed by his words, and slunk away in confusion. Fortunately Lent was nearly over, and he was soon to bid the people farewell. Nevertheless, in order to show that he was not easily cowed, he publicly announced from the pulpit: " This evening I set forth on my journey to Florence, with my little staff and a wooden flask, and I shall rest at Pianoro. If any man have aught to say to me, let him come before I leave. But I tell ye that my death is not to take place in Bologna." [1]

On his arrival in Florence he found the city in a worse

---

[1] *Vide* the same authors quoted above.

state than before, Piero's insolence having so much increased, that each day brought fresh proofs of the popular
discontent. Consequently the Prior of St. Mark's found
himself in a position of great difficulty. He had either to
keep silence or run the risk of being again banished by
order of his superiors in Lombardy or Rome. While
reflecting on this state of things, Savonarola remembered
that the Tuscan Congregation had always been separate
from that of Lombardy, down to the year 1448, when it
was joined to the latter, because the Tuscan convents were
deserted on account of the plague : consequently it might
not be impossible to restore the Congregation to its former
independence, now that it numbered so many more
brethren.[1] Accordingly he applied all his energy to
effect this change on which depended the success of
all his future designs, and it is possible that he began
to negotiate the affair as far back as 1492, during his
various visits to Venice, where the General of the Order,
Giovacchino Turriano, was then resident. It is certain
that this affair first brought his great shrewdness and
practical energy to light, and made the frivolous incon-
sistency of Piero de' Medici still more clearly apparent.
For Piero let himself be persuaded to favour a measure
tending to neutralise his own authority over the convent
of St. Mark, and caused the magistrates to write letters
pressingly recommending it to the Florentine ambassador
in Rome, and to the Cardinal of Naples, the patron of the
Order.[2] His conduct was all the more inexplicable, since
he had now taken under his protection the Frati Minori
(Franciscans), who had always been hostile to the Dominicans, and who, by urging from the pulpit the expulsion of

[1] Padre Marchese, p. 83. Savonarola frequently spoke on this subject, and it was also mentioned by the Council of Ten in the despatches
they sent to Rome, as we shall have occasion to see further on.

[2] *Vide* Appendix to the Italian edition, doc. xi. and xiv.

the Jews, against the express orders of the Signory, had caused many disturbances in Florence.[1] Either failing to see the importance of the request, and, as usual, wishing to spite Ludovico the Moor, or because the idea of a Tuscan Congregation tickled his fancy, and made him hope to win the hearts of the friars of St. Mark's, by promoting its formation, it is certain that, on this occasion, Piero played into Savonarola's hands. Accordingly the Prior seized the opportunity by instantly despatching to Rome Frà Roberto Ubaldini, Frate Alessandro Rinuccini, and Frà Domenico da Pescia.[2] The latter monk was already his most sincere and zealous disciple. Born at the foot of the Pistoian Apennines, he had all the daring of a mountaineer : his ingenuous, faithful soul was full of enthusiastic devotion for Savonarola, he believed him to be a prophet sent to Florence from God, and would have gone to the stake for him without a moment's hesitation.

When the three friars arrived in Rome they found that the official support of Florence was not sufficient to defeat the Lombards, who, through the intervention of Ludovico the Moor, were energetically seconded by many ambassadors. Thus a convent quarrel had assumed the proportions of an affair of state. On the one side the Signory of Florence, the Cardinal of Naples, Piero, and Cardinal dei Medici, were writing and exerting their

[1] There is a minute account of these riots in Parenti's "Storia di Firenze," vol. i., at sheet 23 ; and passim, Codex ii. 129, in the Florence National Library.

[2] Frà Roberto Ubaldini, author of the "Annali di San Marco," states that he went to Rome to accompany Frate Alessandro, who was old and in bad health ; he does not mention Frà Domenico, who may have followed afterwards. ("Annales Conventus S. Marci," at sheets 13 and 14.) On the other hand, Burlamacchi (p. 47), makes no mention of Ubaldini. In the "Biografia Latina" (at sheet 11[t]) we find these words : "Pro hac re Romam miserunt fratrem Alexandrum Rinuccinum senem, et fratrem Dominicum pisciensem." In the despatch sent by the Signory to the Cardinal of Naples, only Rinuccini and Frà Domenico are mentioned. (Vide Appendix to the Italian edition, doc. xiv.)

influence in favour of St. Mark's; on the other, the Lombard friars, Ludovico the Moor, Venice and Rome, were against it. Thereupon Savonarola's envoys wrote to him that there was no hope of success; but he only replied, " Fear not, remain firm, and you will conquer : the Lord scattereth the counsels of the nations, and over-throweth the designs of princes." [1]

In fact, victory was finally gained in a very strange and unexpected manner. A rumour was spread in Rome to the effect that many of the brethren of St. Mark's were opposed to the separation proposed by Savonarola. Thereupon the latter called a grand assembly of all his friars and made them sign a special petition, attested by the Signory.[2] Nevertheless, on the 22nd of May, 1493, all hope of success seemed at an end, for the Pope dissolved the consistory in a fit of ill temper, saying that he was not disposed to sign briefs that day. Being left alone with the Cardinal of Naples he fell into lively conversation with him, indulging as usual in many extravagant jests. It seemed to the Cardinal that the right moment had come, and quickly producing the Brief (which was already drawn up) from his pocket, besought the Holy Father to sign it. He laughingly refused, and the Cardinal laughing also, drew the Pope's ring from his finger, and sealed the Brief.[3] This was scarcely done when, as though with a presentiment of what had occurred, messengers arrived in hot haste from the Lombards, armed with new and more powerful recommendations. But the Pope was already so sick of the affair,

[1] " Biografia Latina," chap. xiii. ; Burlamacchi, p. 47. On this affair of the separation from the Lombard Order, many new documents have been published in Gherardi's collection, p. 12 and fol.

[2] Gherardi, " Nuovi Documenti," p. 12, and fol.

[3] There is a very incorrect copy of this Brief in the Riccardi Library, Codex 2053 ; but a more exact version was given in the "Bullarium Ord. Praedicatorum." (*Vide* Appendix to the Italian edition, doc. xii.

that he refused to hear another word about it, saying,
" Had you come sooner your request would have been
granted, but now what is done is done." [1]   In this way
the independence of St. Mark's was achieved, and Savonarola's words were fulfilled.

The Lombards, being thus unexpectedly worsted, made
many attempts to get the Brief annulled, or to at least
attenuate its effects, and in this they were encouraged by
Piero de' Medici, who, after having opposed them, now
wished to come to their aid.[2]   But it was too late ; for
St. Mark's, as the head and centre of a congregation, was
now subject only to Rome and the Superior of the Order.
The latter at once transferred Savonarola and Frà
Domenico to Florence, since both were still on the rolls of
the Bolognese brotherhood ; and at the same time issued
strict orders to the Lombard friars to discontinue their
fruitless opposition, and abstain from giving further
annoyance to St. Mark's.[3]   Savonarola was re-elected
Prior, and the General, in a letter of the 15th November,

[1] " Biografia Latina," and Burlamacchi, loc. cit. ; " Annales Conventus
S. Marci," at sheet 13.

[2] Before the Roman Brief was signed, the Lombards had sent an order
from Milan, commanding Savonarola to leave Florence without delay.
Fortunately, however, the order was directed to the Prior of Fiesole, who
chanced to be absent.   Accordingly it only reached Savonarola after the
Brief had arrived.   Trusting to the aid of Piero de' Medici, whom they
expected to retain the Brief for some time, the Lombards had made
Savonarola agree to a convention stipulating that the Lombard Congregation should preserve its old authority in Tuscany, until the Brief was
actually deposited at St. Mark's.   But they failed at all points.   Savonarola having foreseen how the affair would turn, had accepted the convention in a short letter of two or three lines, the only one (as far as we
know) that he ever wrote to Piero de' Medici.   Mons. Perrens reports,
and cites it as a proof (vol. i. p. 51, note 2), that " le prieur sut fort bien,
dans l'occasion, faire acte de soumission, si non à Laurent, du moins à
son fils Piero " (vol. i. p. 51).   But it is to be found in the Archivio
Mediceo, with the convention to which we have alluded, and also another
letter to Jacopo Salviati.   These three documents (given in the Appendix
to our Italian edition, doc. xiii.) show that the Prior's submission was only
apparent.   (See, too, the " Biografia Latina," ch. xiii.)

[3] Gherardi, p. 24 ; Burlamacchi, p. 48.

conferred on him the post of Provincial of the Order.[1]
Thus, at last, his independence was assured, he was his
own master, could speak freely, and could not be easily
removed from his established headquarters in Florence.
He alone had seen from the first the importance of
obtaining the Brief ; others perceived it afterwards,
Nevertheless new and greater dangers were rapidly
drawing near ; and Savonarola foresaw and did his best to
prepare for them by hastening on his work.

First of all it was requisite to re-establish order and
discipline in the convent. At one time he had thought of
withdrawing with his brethren to some mountain solitude,
to lead a poor and hermit-like existence, and had discussed
the matter with his disciples ;[2] but these juvenile dreams
had now yielded to riper ideas. It was no question of
forsaking the world, but of living in its midst, in order
to purify it ; it was his business to train men, not to be
good hermits, but worthy monks, living an exemplary life,
and ready to shed their blood for the salvation of souls.
To purify manners, rekindle faith and reform the Church,
were the objects Savonarola sought to promote. And
if enabled by the Lord's help to accomplish these holy
desires, he would then depart from Italy with a chosen
band of courageous brethren, in order to preach the

[1] Turriano's letter says : " Cum igitur continue multa possint accidere,
quae mei officii requirant auctoritatem, ne vobis huc atque illuc post me
sit cursitandum, &c." For these reasons he conferred this fresh authority
upon him. (Gherardi, p. 23.)

[2] The author of the " Biografia Latina " was so affected by Savonarola's
enthusiastic description of the life to be led in the new convent, that he
wrote : " Et ego tunc in corde meo dixi : Illo in tempore efficiar religi-
osus, et non tempore tepiditatis," chap. xii. at sheet 10. But he adds
that some of the friars were of a different opinion, and showed themselves adverse to the severity of the new discipline proposed by Savonarola, saying : " Hoc futurum macellum fratrum." (Ibid., at sheet
11.) It seems that Savonarola was so intent on carrying out this idea,
that he had already caused a wood to be cut down on the hill where he
wished his hermitage to be built. (Burlamacchi, p. 46 and fol.)

Christian religion in the East.   Constantinople was one of
the dreams of those days : it was there that statesmen
desired to crush the enemy of Europe and re-establish the
Latin Empire ; it was there that the clergy wished to convert the infidels and replace Jerusalem under the Christian
rule ; many men shared Savonarola's belief that the times
announced by his prophecies were at hand, and that at last
there would be *but one fold and one shepherd.*

FRA GIOVANNI DA FIESOLE.

To return to the convent, the first reform introduced
by Savonarola was the re-establishment of the rule of
poverty.   St. Dominic had, in fact, pronounced a terrible
curse on all who should allow monks of his order to
possess property, nevertheless, after the death of St.
Antonine, only the letter of his command remained on the
convent walls.[1]   A change in the constitution of the con-

[1] " Have charity, preserve humility, observe voluntary poverty : may
my malediction and that of God fall upon him that shall bring possessions
to this Order."   Such were the last words of St. Dominic to his disciples.

vent had given St. Mark's the right to hold property, and in a short time its wealth had been largely increased. Savonarola, therefore, revived the old rule and sold the possessions held by the convent in disobedience to the precepts of the founder of the Order.[1] But as free gifts had long diminished in quantity, it was requisite to find some other mode of supplying the brethren's needs. He reduced expenses by clothing them in coarse robes, stripping their cells of all superfluities and forbidding them to have illuminated books, gold or silver crucifixes, and similar vanities. But all this was insufficient. He therefore ordained that the friars should work for their bread, and opened schools for the study of painting, sculpture, and architecture, and the art of transcribing and illuminating manuscripts. The lay brethren and such of the monks as were unfitted for higher spiritual work, were to exercise these arts, in order to supply the needs of the convent.

These men were also to be charged with the cares of administration. In this way priests and prelates could more freely devote themselves to the duties of the confessional and the cure of souls, and to the spiritual and intellectual training of the novices. Those more advanced in the spirit of charity and in theological doctrine were to devote themselves to preaching and journey from city to city. Each of these missionaries was to be attended by a lay brother who was to work incessantly to provide for his wants, so that he might not be withheld from speaking unwelcome truths by fear of receiving no alms.[2] The three

Fra Beato Angelico had decorated the outer wall of the dormitory with a Virgin and many saints, and among the latter was St. Dominic holding an open book, in which these words were written. (*Vide* Lacordaire, " Vita di San Dominico;" Padre Marchese, " Storia del Convento di San Marco," in the " Scritti Vari," pp. 80 and 139.)

[1] "Annales Conventus S. Marci," at sheet 13 and fol. " Biografia Latina," chap. xiii., at sheet 13.

[2] " Predicare veritatem ne timerent, dicendo : si dicimus veritatem omnibus, non dabunt elemosinas nam veritas odium parit, et sic desistent a veritate et sint canes muti." (" Biografia Latina," at sheet 11.)

studies Savonarola specially encouraged in his convent were theology ; philosophical and moral science ; and above all, the examination of the Holy Scriptures by the aid of Greek, Hebrew, and other Eastern tongues. These languages were also taught with a view to the time when, as he hoped, the Lord would send him and his brethren to preach the gospel to the Turks.[1]

It was far from easy to carry out all these ideas, nor were they altogether unopposed ; but the convent soon began to flourish : there was a growing zeal for study, and love for the Bible and a spirit of religion were continually on the increase. There was every incitement to progress under a Prior who was a living example of the principles he inculcated. If severe to others, he was still more severe to himself : his clothes were the coarsest, his bed the hardest, his cell the poorest of all. From letters written by him at this period, it is plain that he was in a very excited state of mind, convinced that a new and startling reform was at hand, and that this was clearly inspired by the will of God. " You ask what we are doing," he replied, in a letter dated September 10, 1493, to an abbess of Ferrara, who had expressed some doubts as to the in. novations he had made. " What are we doing ? only casting away superfluities, and returning to the simplicity and poverty enjoined by the original rules of our Order. The real innovation was when mendicant friars were seen to build sumptuous palaces. We first devoted long hours to prayer, and then awaited the voice of the Lord, which hath now been heard. Could I speak with you, I should

---

[1] " Biografia Latina," chaps. xii. and xiii. ; Burlamacchi, p. 44 and fol. ; "Padre Marchese," p. 31 and fol. Savonarola often alludes in his sermons to the various languages taught in the convent, and to the use that was to be made of them. The "Biografia Latina" tells us at sheet 12 : " Perfectio trium (sic) linguarum, videlicet : Hebree, Grece, Latine, Caldee, Maure et Turche." Mons. Rio (Art Chrétien) speaks eloquently of the schools of fine arts in St. Mark's, but gives an exaggerated idea of their importance.

be able to make you understand that the world is all darkened, all depraved, and that it is time to regenerate God's people. It is time, it is time, it is time, my well beloved mother. The Lord is weary, and it behoves us to despise the judgment of the lukewarm ; we must be ready to face the persecutions inevitably directed against any good work. And we are ready." [1]

This spirit of enthusiasm had now spread through the whole population which was entirely favourable to St. Mark's. Many of the lower classes, many of the nobles sought leave to join the brotherhood ; and it was said that even Angelo Poliziano and Pico della Mirandola were disposed to take the same step. The number of the friars increased so prodigiously that before long the original building was too small to contain them.

Nor was this enthusiasm confined to Florence, for we find it extending to convents in other parts of Tuscany. The communities of St. Dominic at Fiesole, Prato and Bibliena, and the two Magdalen hospices at Pian di Mugnone and Lecceto asked to be enrolled in the new Tuscan Congregation, and gained admittance at different times.[2] Things reached to such a pitch, that the Camaldolesians of the Monastery degli Angioli signed a legal contract, binding themselves to change their Order on purpose to join the brethren of St. Mark's. But Savonarola refused their request, as one he was unable to grant, without far exceeding the authority conferred upon him by the Brief.[3] He was unwilling to afford his enemies any

---

[1] This remarkable letter is given in the appendix to the Italian edition, doc. xv.

[2] "Biografia Latina," at sheet 12 and fol. Burlamacchi, p. 49 and fol. ; "Annales Conventus S. Marci," at sheets 14 and 15 ; Gherardi, "Nuovi Documenti," p. 25 and fol. ; Marchese, "Storia di San Marco," in the "Scritti Vari," p. 138 and fol.

[3] Ibid. at sheet 24. Burlamacchi, at p. 81 follows his usual custom of translating literally from the original Latin, and his additional words : "It was I who brought the contract" were inserted by another hand in the printed edition.

excuse for attacking him ; and although desirous to gather
all the Dominicans of Tuscany about him he saw it would
be difficult to accomplish on account of the party hatreds
dividing the country.[1]   In fact he had found it very hard
to introduce his reforms in Pisa, although he went there
in person ; and of the forty-four Dominican friars in that
city, only four, of whom Stefano Codiponte was the first,
adhered to his views.   The others quitted the city.   And
even this poor attempt at union came to nothing when
Pisa rose against the Florentines.[2]   At Siena he was received
with still more disfavour, there was almost a riot, and the
local Signory commanded him to depart.[3]   He at once
returned indignantly to Florence, where the congregation
of St. Mark continued to flourish, increase in numbers, and
effect fresh improvements.   All the convents aggregated
to it were zealous in the cause, and it received encouragement and sympathy from all the citizens of Florence.

NOTE TO CHAPTER IX.

*On the Death of Lorenzo the Magnificent, and the Last
Words addressed to him by Savonarola.*

SOME historians, especially those who always side with the Medici,
deny that Savonarola really addressed Lorenzo in the terms we have
described.   One of the arguments they adduce in support of their
assertion deserves to be taken into consideration.   In his well-known
letter to Jacopo Antiquario, Poliziano (book iv. epistle 11) gives a

---

[1] In a letter to the Pope, of which we shall have occasion to speak
hereafter, Savonarola treats of these enmities and of the dangers they
caused him to incur.

[2] *Vide* " Annali del Convento di Santa Caterina et Pisa, published in
the " Archivio Storico Italiano," vol. vi. part ii. p. 609 and fol.

[3] " Biografia Latina," chap. xiii. at sheet 12.   Some new documents on
this subject were published by Signor V. Mattii, in the appendix to his
translation of the " Apologetica ec. di Frate Girolamo Savonarola." Siena :
Bargellini, 1864.

minute account of Lorenzo's illness and death, relates Savonarola's visit, but does not give the words we have quoted. Now, say these historians, he was the only eye-witness of the scene, and when narrating it in a private letter to a friend could have no motive for altering the facts ; accordingly, his authority is more trustworthy than that of Savonarola's biographers, who have probably coloured the facts in their own way to their hero's advantage. But, first of all, we have no certain proof of Poliziano's presence during Savonarola's interview with Lorenzo. Without dwelling on the point that some of the biographers expressly assert that directly Savonarola entered *the others left the sick room*, it is certain that Poliziano himself states that he was frequently dismissed to the adjoining chamber, and it is most probable that he was sent away when Lorenzo was about to confess. Even if he remained present, it is hard to believe that the Magnificent would have spoken aloud of his sins, or that Poliziano, even had he known them, would have cared to make them public. As to his having communicated them privately to a friend, this is a reason only to be urged by some one ignorant of the fact that in the fifteenth century the private letters of learned men were as public as their works, and frequently collected and published by their authors.

We will now proceed to examine the authorities on whose account of the scene we have relied. Their number is infinite. It may be said that almost all the biographies of Savonarola, whether ancient or modern, in print or in manuscript, describe the interview in the same way, those of Perrens and Rastrelli alone excepted. Rastrelli was the author of the anonymous work (dated Geneva, 1781) to which we have before alluded, and which is a libel rather than a biography. We will confine ourselves to naming the principal contemporary authorities, from which all the other accounts are more or less derived. These are Placido Cinozzi's "Epistola ; " G. F. Pico della Mirandola's "Vita," &c. ; and the "Biografia Latina." It is needless to add that the same account is reported in Burlamacchi, Barsanti, Razzi, Frà Marco della Casa, and all the numerous biographies compiled from Burlamacchi's. Cinozzi reports the words pronounced by Savonarola, expressly remarking that all this was a preliminary to the confession that was never made after all, and saying in conclusion :—"And these words were repeated to me by Frà Silvestro, who died with his superior, Frà Ieronimo, and who, as I well believe, had them and heard them from P. F. Ieronimo's own lips." He omits Lorenzo's first words to Savonarola, and these are also omitted by Pico (chap. vi.), whose statement is identical with that of Cinozzi. The "Biografia Latina," on the other hand (chap. xi. at sheet 50), gives the entire dialogue, and adds :—Hæc verba retulit frater Silvester Maruffus, et dominus Dominicus Benevienus, canonicus

Sancti Laurenti. . . . De visitatione ista loquitur etiam Angelus Politianus," &c.

The first writer to question the authenticity of this dialogue, and founding his doubts on the authority of Poliziano, whose account is somewhat different from that of the others, was Fabroni, in his " Life of Lorenzo the Magnificent;" next came Roscoe, the frequent plagiarist of Fabroni ; and lastly Mons. Perrens, who is so often misled by Roscoe's assertions. Of Rastrelli it is needless to speak, for his book is a pile of blunders and insults, and proves absolutely nothing. A judicious reply to Perrens was published by Ermolao Rubini in " La Polimazia" (year 11, Nos. 3 and 4 : Florence, 1854), calling the French writer's attention to the fact that Poliziano's authority was by no means so valuable as he had supposed. In truth, the whole question hinges upon this point, whether we are to give more credence to Poliziano, who, being a courtier, was bound to speak of Lorenzo in a flattering sense, or to Cinozzi and the author of the " Biografia Latina," who, although staunch partizans of Savonarola, were nevertheless sincere and honest men ; and to G. F. Pico, who was not only honest and sincere, but learned, intelligent, independent, and of a family bound by friendship to the Medici. Accordingly, whether we are to have greater faith in a courtier, who withholds a fact that he could not relate without injury to himself, or in honest men, contemporaries and friends of Savonarola, who, writing in times hostile to the latter's memory, would have been roughly called to account by followers of the Medici had they ventured on any false statements concerning Lorenzo.

Nor is this all. If Poliziano's letter is attentively read, it will be seen that, far from contradicting the fact as described by others, he merely alters it in so transparent a way that we may cull from his own words proofs of all that he sought to conceal :—"Abierat vix dum Picus, cum Ferrariensis Hieronymus, insignis et doctrina et sanctimonia vir, cœlestique doctrinæ prædicator egregius, cubiculum ingreditur, *hortatur ut fidem teneat ; ille vero tenere se ait inconcussam : ut quam emendatissime posthac vivere destinet ; scilicet facturum obnixe respondit : ut mortem denique, si necesse sit, æquo animo toleret ; nihil vero, inquit ille, iucundius, si quidem ita Deo decretum sit. Recedebat homo iam, cum Laurentius :* Heus, inquit, benedictionem, Pater, priusquam a nobis profisceris. Simul demisso capite vultuque, et in omnem piæ religionis imaginem formatus, subinde ad verba illius et preces rite ac memoriter responsitabat, ne tantillum quidem familiarium luctu, aperto iam, neque se ulterius dissimulante, commotus. Diceres indictam cæteris, uno excepto Laurentio, mortem."

Now, who could really believe that Savonarola would have come to the dying Lorenzo of his own accord, and said to him—" First, have

faith ; secondly, seek to lead a righteous life ; thirdly, prepare for
death ; " and that when the Magnificent had replied in the affirmative
to all these demands, the friar would have gone away without even
according him his blessing ? There can be no doubt that if Savonarola
went to Lorenzo it was at Lorenzo's request, for neither was he one
to present himself unannounced, nor would the courtiers, in that case,
have granted him admittance. Besides, why should Lorenzo have
required Savonarola's presence at that moment, save for the purpose of
confessing his sins and receiving ghostly comfort and absolution ?
And of what sins would he chiefly speak, if not of such as were
known to all the world as the deepest crimes of his life ; exactly
those mentioned by Cinozzi, Burlamacchi, and others ? Finally, if
the friar prepared to depart, as it would seem, according to Poliziano,
without bestowing his benediction, it is plain that Lorenzo had not
been absolved from his sins. Therefore the question turns, neither
upon the visit nor upon the absolution, which was certainly unaccorded,
but upon Lorenzo's words (which seem to us the least important), and,
above all, on the expressions used by Savonarola. Concerning the
latter, Poliziano's narrative only differs from the others as regards the
words said in conclusion ; that is to say, he is silent as to Savonarola's
last condition, " *You must restore liberty to the Florentines ;* " and as to
Lorenzo's refusal of it. But this was precisely the point that Poliziano
could not repeat without danger to himself, and accordingly it was
only too natural for him to change the real words into the general
command, " *Prepare for death.*"

Of late years several weighty writers have revived the dispute, and
have settled it, as it seems to us, in a manner giving additional confirmation to our own view of the case. Von Reumont, who is a
learned admirer of the Medici, and hardly less enthusiastic than
Roscoe, denied the scene *in toto* in the first edition of his work on
Lorenzo de' Medici, and declared it to be altogether fictitious. Then
came Professor Ranke (" Historisch-biographische Studien," p. 350),
who went more minutely into the question, but without having consulted Cinozzi, the " Biografia Latina," or the numerous other old
manuscripts in which the dialogue is given. He only referred to
Pico and Burlamacchi, and (as we have before said) erroneously considering the latter a mere compilation from Pico, compared them
together. Finding that Burlamacchi gives words spoken by Lorenzo,
which are omitted in Pico, he concluded the latter to be purely
fictitious and incredible, since they could have been only related by
Savonarola, who, in that case, must have divulged the secrets of the
confessional. He was unaware that the identical words were given
in the " Biografia Latina," failed to observe that Savonarola could
scarcely have apostrophized Lorenzo *ex abrupto* unless the latter had

first spoken, and did not notice that, like Cinozzi, Pico states that no actual confession was made, as indeed may be ascertained from the pages of Poliziano and others. Cinozzi writes that Lorenzo, having spoken a little, concluded by saying that he wished to confess, and that Savonarola replied: "*That before confession he had three things to say to him*." Pico : "Si antequam noxas contractas confiteretur, tria præstaret" (p. 24). The "Biographia Latina" and Burlamacchi both relate that directly Lorenzo beheld Savonarola he said that he wished to make confession, but was tormented by three things. Therefore he spoke before confession. In any case, even according to Professor Ranke, Pico has preserved Savonarola's words, which is the important point, and, in spite of his doubts, the modern historian cannot decide to reject them. So we see in the end that the historic sense and profoundly critical intelligence of Professor Ranke prevented him from altogether rejecting the fact, even though he was ignorant that it had been narrated by several of the older biographers. His doubts would have probably disappeared had he been acquainted with their works. His verdict has rather shaken that of Baron von Reumont, who, in the second edition of his work on Lorenzo de' Medici (vol. ii. p. 443), expresses a far less absolute opinion, and merely says that the question is still unsettled. Nevertheless, he still finds it strange that Savonarola should exact from a dying man the restoration of Florentine liberty. How was he to restore it? But Lorenzo was not yet dead ; he might have lingered for a time ; and, in any case, it was a question of intention. On the other hand, Poliziano's narrative would be altogether inexplicable unless it were admitted that he coloured the facts in his own way, while it is also clear that he could not make a genuine report of them, like that of other and more independent contemporaries, without offending the friends and memory of his deceased patron.

In connection with our theme we may here mention a very badly restored picture, attributed by some authorities to Sandro Botticelli, preserved in the store-rooms of the Uffizii Gallery. At first sight its subject might appear to be an Adoration of the Magi, but on closer examination we find it to represent a great multitude engaged in adoring the Virgin and Child. In the midst of the crowd there is seen the figure of a Dominican friar addressing an apparently terror-stricken man, and pointing with an energetic gesture of his out-stretched arm and hand to the child Christ, as though in the act of saying, "Repent and adore !" The friar certainly bears a resemblance to Savonarola, and the man addressed by him to Lorenzo de' Medici. The first person to notice and call public attention to this was Mr. Charles Heath Wilson, the learned English connoisseur of Italian art, and author of a life of "Michelangelo Buonarotti."

CHAPTER X.

(1493–1494.)

N the Advent season of 1493 Savonarola resumed his preachings in Florence, and, with a continually increasing public, was encouraged to greater hardihood and freedom of speech. He now spoke, not only as a saintly friar whose prophecies had been wonderfully fulfilled, but also as the independent head of the Tuscan Congregation. Accordingly his words carried double weight, and he was able to express himself as daringly as he chose without fearing the vengeance of Piero de' Medici. In fact, the infamous manners of the princes and priests of Italy ; the corruption of the Church ; the approach of the threatened scourges ; and the anxiety of the righteous to put an end to the general depravation, were the themes of the twenty-five sermons preached by him, on the Psalm *Quam bonus*, during Advent this year. But these discourses also contained minute examinations of important points of Christian theology ; for he aimed at giving a complete exposition of his doctrines, tracing them in firm lines, so

as to impress them thoroughly on his hearers' minds, and thus enable the latter to prepare for the chastisements by which they were about to be assailed. From the theological point of view, these sermons were undoubtedly among the best Savonarola ever delivered.

We may begin by citing his own words upon faith : " Faith is the gift of God, given to every believer for his salvation ; therefore, my children, share not the errors of those who say to ye, ' If I saw some miracle, or some man raised from the dead, then would I believe.' Those men are deceived, for faith cometh not of our own strength, but is a supernatural gift—that is, a light shed from above into the mind of man. And he that would receive this light must prepare his inner man and abase himself before God." [1]   Here it might be urged—if all things be ordained to an end, they reach that end by natural means ; how, then, should it be that the nature of man may not suffice of itself to attain the end to which it is pre-ordained? Is man, then, inferior to the beasts? No ; this must be attributed to his nobility and his excellence, inasmuch as he is ordained to a Divine end, an end that transcends nature. [2]   But mayhap, thou wouldst then ask, Wherefore are some chosen and others cast out? Matters of faith, my son, must be studied by the light of faith, in the manner prescribed unto thee by the Scriptures ; further than this thou mayest not go, lest thou shouldst stumble.

[1] " Prediche sul Salmo *Quam bonus :* " Prato, Guasti, 1846. *Vide* Predica iv. p. 237. These sermons were reported *verbatim.* After their delivery in the Duomo, Savonarola wrote them out in Latin in a somewhat abbreviated form, as may be ascertained from the holograph codex at St. Mark's. They were afterwards translated and published in an amended form by Girolamo Giannotti during the sixteenth century. In every edition of them we have seen we find the statement that they were delivered in Advent, 1493, and we accordingly mention them in this chapter. But it should be noted that, in his " Compendium Revelationum," Savonarola states that during every Lent and Advent from 1491 to 1494, he always preached from the Book of Genesis.
[2] Ibid.

Who art thou to make answer unto God ? Hath not the potter power over the clay, to knead from the same mass vessels of honour or vessels for base uses ? God shows mercy to the elect, justice to the wicked. But shouldst thou ask wherefore God hath predestined this man rather than that, wherefore John is chosen rather than Peter ? Then I shall tell thee that such is the will of God, nor can any other answer be given. Origen sought to overstep these limits, and said that predestination depended upon the merits of another life anterior to this. The Pelagians declared it to depend upon our good deeds in this life; for, according to those heretics, the principle of well-doing is in ourselves, its consummation and perfection coming from God. They sought to pass the bounds assigned to us, and fell into heresy. The Scriptures are very plain : they tell us, not in one place, but in many, that not only the end of well-doing, but likewise its beginning, cometh to us from God ; even as in all our good works it is God who works through us. " It is therefore untrue that the grace of God is obtained by pre-existing works and merits, that through them we are predestined to everlasting life, as though works and merits were the cause of predestin-ation, *cum sit,* it is all the contrary, for works and merits are the effect of predestination, and the Divine will the cause of predestination, as we have before said." [1]

" Tell me, O Peter, tell me, O Magdalen, wherefore are ye in Paradise ? Ye sinned even as we sin. Thou, Peter, who hadst testified unto the Son of God, hadst conversed with Him, heard Him preach, beheld His miracles, and, alone, with two other disciples, hadst beheld His transfiguration on Mount Tabor, hearkened unto His paternal voice, and who, despite all this, at the word of a base woman didst deny Him thrice, yet thou wert restored to grace, and made the head of the Church, and

[1] Predica, viii. pp. 299–302.

dost now enjoy heavenly bliss; how hast thou gained these guerdons? Confess that not by thine own merits hast thou attained salvation, but by the goodness of God, who didst bestow so many blessings on thee, and vouchsafed to thee in this life so much light and grace. And thou, Magdalen, vulgarly called the sinner, thou didst hearken many times to the preaching of thy master Jesus Christ, and nevertheless wert deaf to His words; and although Martha, thy sister, didst admonish thee and exhort thee to change thy life, thou didst heed her not. But when it pleased unto the Lord, and He touched thy heart, thou didst hasten as in a frenzy, with thy vase of alabaster, to the house of the Pharisee, and casting thyself at thy sweet Master's feet, didst bathe them with thy tears, and wast deemed worthy to hear the sweet words— '*Dimittuntur tibi peccata multa.*' Later, thou wast so favoured by the Saviour as to be the first to behold Him risen from the dead, and wert made an apostle unto the Apostles. This grace, these gifts, were not vouchsafed to thee for thy deserts, O Mary! but because God loved thee and willed thy salvation." [1]

By limiting ourselves to quotations of this kind without giving their context, it would be very easy to find evidence supporting the theories of those German and English writers who have sought to prove that Savonarola was a precursor of the reformed doctrine of justification by faith alone, without works; the believer being little more than a passive instrument in the hand of the Lord, at whose good pleasure he is either chosen, or rejected without being able to attain to salvation by freewill. Certainly Savonarola was most profoundly convinced of the nullity of the creature before the Creator; and in his submission to the Divine will he earnestly sought to enforce the same conviction on his hearers. But that is no reason for

[1] Predica, ix. p. 323.

tampering with the fundamental points of his creed, which he so often reiterated and so clearly explained, as to leave us in no doubt concerning them. In fact, no sooner were his works thoroughly examined than the foreign authors to whom we have referred were convicted of error by their own countrymen.[1]

The necessity of good works, freewill, and the co-operation of human effort with grace, even although the latter be a free gift from God, are arguments to which Savonarola constantly recurs, and without failing to add that not only is it in our power, but that it is also our duty, to prepare ourselves for the reception of this gift of faith and grace, which is never withheld from those who do their utmost to obtain it.[2] According to him, there are three things required to prepare and dispose us for its reception, namely, determined belief, prayer, and good works.[3] Consequently we must not condemn the sinner, but only his sins, and must have compassion on him; for so long as freewill and the grace of God endure, he may always turn to the Lord and be converted.[4] If any one ask why the will is free, we reply unto them, Because it is will.[5] Therefore man must needs co-operate in the act of justification, and do all that in him lies, for God will not fail him. Art thou fain, my brother, to receive the love of Jesus Christ? Seek, then, to hearken unto the Divine voice that calleth thee. Daily the Lord calleth unto thee, Do thou also somewhat for thyself." [6]

When very young Savonarola had adopted this motto:

[1] Rudelbach ("Savonarola und seine Zeit," chap. iii. of part 3; "Savonarola's dogmatischer Standpunct"). This author is undoubtedly the staunchest supporter of the former opinion; but even in Germany has been victoriously confuted by Herr Meier, who, although anxious to prove that Savonarola was a Protestant, has tried to modify to some extent the exaggerations of Herr Rudelbach.

[2] Sermon iv. pp. 237, 238.　　[3] Sermon v. p. 246.
[4] Sermon xii. p. 373.　　[5] Sermon xiv. p. 399.
[6] Sermon xvi. p. 443.

"*Tanto sa ciasenno quanto opera*" ("As much as one knows, so much one does").[1]   And truly we should be disposed to entitle his doctrine the doctrine of works, were it not rather the doctrine of love, taking the word in the acceptation given to it above, *i.e.*, as the state in which a soul, being already spontaneously disposed to grace, feels its approach and is inflamed with charity.   "This love," Savonarola tells us, " is likewise a gift of the Lord ; it is a fire that kindleth all dry things, and whoever is disposed unto it shall forthwith find it descend into his heart and set it aflame.   Earnest love is truly a great might, 'for it can do all things, overcome and conquer all things. . . . Nought can be done save by the impulse of love. . . . And inasmuch as charity is the greatest love of all, therefore charity worketh great and marvellous things.   Charity easily and sweetly fulfilleth the whole law of God, being the measure and rule of all measures and of all laws.   For, in fact, every individual law is the measure and rule of some special action and of no other ; but it is not thus with charity, which is the measure and rule of all things and of all human acts.   And therefore he that hath this rule of charity ruleth well both himself and others, and interpreteth all laws rightly.   This is clearly proved when we find that those charged with the cure of souls allow themselves to be guided solely by that which is written in the canonical laws, which, being special laws, can never rule justly without charity, the universal measure and law.   Take, for example, the physician that bringeth love and charity to the sick, for, if he be good and kind, and learned and skilful, none can be better than he.   Thou wilt see that love teacheth him everything, and will be the measure and rule of all the measures and rules of medicine.   He will endure a thousand

---

[1] All the biographers give this as his motto, and it is repeated in his Sermons.   See, for instance, Sermon v., on the Book of Job.

fatigues as though they were of no account, will inquire
into everything, and will order his remedies and see them
prepared, and will never leave the sick man. If instead,
gain be his object, he will have no care for the sufferer,
and his very skill will fail him." " Behold what love can
effect. Take the example of a mother with the child.
Who hath taught this young woman, who hath had
no children before, to nurse her babe ? Love. See what
fatigue she endureth by day and by night to rear it, and
how the heaviest fatigue seemeth light to her. What is the
cause of this ? It is love. See what ways she hath, what
loving caresses and sweet words for this little babe of hers !
What hath taught her these things ? Love. . . . Take
the example of Christ who, moved by the deepest charity,
came to us as a little child, in all things like unto the sons
of men, and submitting to hunger and thirst, to heat and
cold and discomfort. What hath urged Him to do this ?
Love. He spoke now with just men, now with publicans
and sinners, and He led a life that all men and all women,
small and great, rich and poor, may imitate, all after their
own way and according to their condition, and thus undoubtedly win their salvation. . . . And what made Him
lead so poor and marvellous a life ? Undoubtedly,
charity. . . . Charity bound Him to the pillar, charity
led Him to the cross, charity raised Him from the
dead and made Him ascend into heaven, and thus
accomplish all the mysteries of our redemption. This is
the true and only doctrine, but in these days the preachers
teach nought but empty subtleties." [1]

He then goes on to speak of the clergy. " They tickle
men's ears with talk of Aristotle and Plato, Virgil and
Petrarch, and take no concern in the salvation of souls.
Why, instead of expounding so many books, do they not
expound the one Book in which is the law and spirit of

[1] Sermon ii. pp. 208–210.

life ! The Gospel, O Christians, ye should ever have with
ye ; not merely the letter, but the spirit of the Gospel.
For if thou lackest the spirit of grace, what will it avail
thee to carry about the whole book. And, again, still
greater is the foolishness of those that load themselves
with briefs and tracts and writings, so that they are like
unto stalls at a fair. Charity doth not consist in written
papers ! The true books of Christ are the Apostles and
the Saints ; the true reading of them is to imitate their
lives. But in these days men are made books of the
devil. They speak against pride and ambition, yet are
plunged in both up to the eyes ; they preach chastity, and
maintain concubines ; they prescribe fasting, and feast
splendidly themselves. Those are useless books, false
books, bad books, and books of the devil, for the devil
hath filled them with his malice."[1] " These prelates exult
in their dignities and despise others ; these are they that
would be feared and reverenced ; these are they that seek
the highest places in the synagogues, the chief pulpits of
Italy. They seek to show themselves by day in the public
squares, and be saluted, and called masters and rabbis,
they make broad their phylacteries and enlarge the hems
of their garments ; [2] they spit roundly ; step gravely and
expect their slightest nod to be obeyed."[3]

From the prelates he goes on to describe the princes of
Italy. " These wicked princes are sent to chastise the
sins of their subjects ; they are truly a sad snare for souls ;
their courts and palaces are the refuge of all the beasts and
monsters of the earth, for they give shelter to ribalds and

---

[1] Sermon vii. 271–275.

[2] " Dilatant enim philacteria sua, et magnificant fimbrias " (Matthew
xxiii. 5). Phylacteries are strips of skin, with a capsule also of skin,
containing a parchment inscribed with some passages of the Pentateuch.
The Jews wear these round the left arm and on the forehead, when reciting the early morning prayers, on certain days of the week.

[3] Sermon viii. p. 296.

malefactors. These wretches flock to their halls because it is there that they find ways and means to satisfy their evil passions and unbridled lusts. There are the false councillors, who continually devise new burdens and new taxes to drain the blood of the people. There are the flattering philosophers and poets, who, by force of a thousand lies and fables, trace the genealogy of those evil princes back to the gods; but, and worse than all, there are the priests who follow in the same course. This is the city of Babylon, O my brethren, the city of the foolish and the impious, the city that will be destroyed of the Lord."[1]

He then minutely describes the construction of this city, which was erected by the twelve follies of the impious. "They behold light and darkness, and they prefer darkness to light; they find an easy way and a rough and perilous way; and they prefer the latter to the former. Behold, now they plunge into the sea and mount upon a whale, which they believe to be a rock, and they settle upon it. What generation of men is this? What purpose can be theirs? especially, as I would have ye to know that they intend to build a city on the whale's back. What do ye? I say. Ye will weigh down the beast and will drown. Nevertheless they labour and dispute, build fortifications and come to blows, and one seeks to subjugate the other, and finally there arises a tyrant to oppress them all. He persecutes his enemies to the death, has spies everywhere, hence there are fresh wars and fresh dissensions. At last, the whale, wearied by all this tumult, makes a plunge, and thereupon all are drowned, and the city of Babylon is destroyed. Thus," concludes Savonarola, "it is made manifest that the impious perish by the labours of the foolish, and that the foolish shall be chastised."[2]

It was very easy to see that by this city of fools

[1] Sermon x. pp. 344–345.   [2] Sermon xiii. pp. 382–384.

Savonarola had dared to symbolize the rule of Piero de' Medici and his friends, which, according to the friar's predictions, was soon to be overthrown. But he did not stop here. After speaking of the corruption of the people and princes of Italy, he again touched with equal audacity on the much graver subject of the priesthood and the Church. Giving a very strange interpretation to certain words of the Bible, he said : " *In securi et in ascia deiecerunt eam*— When the devil sees that a man is weak, he strikes him with a hatchet in order to make him fall into sin ; but if he sees that he is strong, he then strikes him with an axe. If a young girl be modest and well brought up, he throws some dissipated youth in her way, and causes her to yield to his flatteries and fall into sin. Thus the devil strikes her with his axe. Here is a citizen of good repute ; he enters the courts of the great lords, and there is the axe so well sharpened, that no virtue can resist its strokes. But we are now living in still more evil days ; the devil has called his followers together, and they have dealt terrible blows on the very gates of the temple. It is by the gates that the house is entered, and it is the prelates who should lead the faithful into the Church of Christ. Therefore the devil hath aimed his heaviest blows at them, and hath broken down these gates. Thus it is that no more good prelates are to be found in the Church." " Seest thou not that they do all things amiss ? They have no judgment ; they cannot distinguish *inter bonum et malum, inter verum et falsum, inter dulce et amarum ;* good things they deem evil, true things false, sweet things bitter, and *vice versâ.* . . . See, how in these days prelates and preachers are chained to the earth by love of earthly things ; the cure of souls is no longer their concern ; they are content with the receipt of revenue ; the preachers preach for the pleasure of princes, to be praised and magnified by them. . . . And they

have done even worse than this, inasmuch as they have not
only destroyed the Church of God, but built up another
after their own fashion. This is the new Church, no
longer built of living rock, namely, of Christians steadfast in the living faith and in the mould of charity ; but
built of sticks, namely, of Christians dry as tinder for the
fires of hell. . . . Go thou to Rome and throughout
Christendom ; in the mansions of the great prelates
and great lords, there is no concern save for poetry and the
oratorical art. Go thither and see, thou shalt find them
all with books of the humanities in their hands, and telling
one another that they can guide men's souls by means of
Virgil, Horace, and Cicero. Wouldst thou see how the
Church is ruled by the hands of astrologers ? And there
is no prelate nor great lord that hath not intimate dealings
with some astrologer, who fixeth the hour and the moment
in which he is to ride out or undertake some piece of business. For these great lords venture not to stir a step save
at their astrologer's bidding.

"But in this temple of theirs there is one thing that
delighteth us much. This is that all therein is painted and
gilded. Thus our Church hath many fine outer ceremonies for the solemnization of ecclesiastical rites, grand
vestments and numerous draperies, with gold and silver
candlesticks, and so many chalices that it is a majestic
sight to behold. There thou seest the great prelates
with splendid mitres of gold and precious stones on their
heads, and silver crosiers in hand ; there they stand at the
altar, decked with fine copes and stoles of brocade,
chanting those beautiful vespers and masses, very slowly,
and with so many grand ceremonies, so many organs and
choristers, that thou art struck with amazement ; and
all these priests seem to thee grave and saintly men, thou
canst not believe that they may be in error, but deem
that all which they say and do should be obeyed even as

the Gospel ; and thus is our Church conducted. Men
feed upon these vanities and rejoice in these pomps, and
say that the Church of Christ was never so flourishing,
nor divine worship so well conducted as at present . . . .
likewise that the first prelates were inferior to these of our
own times. . . . The former, it is true, had fewer gold
mitres and fewer chalices, for, indeed, what few they
possessed were broken up to relieve the needs of the
poor ; whereas our prelates, for the sake of obtaining
chalices, will rob the poor of their sole means of support.
But dost thou know what I would tell thee ?   In the
primitive Church the chalices were of wood, the prelates
of gold ; in these days the Church hath chalices of gold
and prelates of wood.   These have introduced devilish
games among us ; they have no belief in God, and jeer at
the mysteries of our faith !   What doest Thou, O Lord ?
Why dost Thou slumber ?   Arise, and come to deliver
Thy Church from the hands of the devils, from the hands
of tyrants, the hands of iniquitous prelates.   Hast Thou
forsaken Thy Church ?   Dost Thou not love her ?   Is
she not dear unto Thee ?   O Lord, we are become the
despised of all nations ; the Turks are masters of Constantinople ; we have lost Asia, have 'lost Greece, we
already pay tribute to the Infidel.   O Lord God, Thou
hast dealt with us as a wrathful father, Thou hast cast us
out from Thy presence !   Hasten then the chastisement
and the scourge, that it may be quickly granted us to
return to Thee.[1]   *Effunde iras tuas in gentes.*   Be ye not
scandalized, O my brethren, by these words ; rather, when
ye see that the righteous desire chastisement, know that it
is because they seek to banish evil, so that the kingdom
of our Blessed Lord, Jesus Christ, may flourish in the
world.   The only hope that now remains to us, is that the
sword of God may soon smite the earth." [2]

[1] Sermon xxiii. pp. 562–572.
[2] Sermon xxiii. pp. 578–579.   We find the same idea repeated in
many of these sermons, of which indeed it is the principal theme.

Thus Savonarola devoted this Advent to preaching on morals, politics, religion, and the Church; he inveighed against the princes and clergy, and came to the conclusion that the scourge was at hand, and was to be desired by the righteous. In this way, after expounding his doctrines, the Friar threw down the gauntlet in defiance of all earthly potentates. All princes, both temporal and spiritual, all the wealthy, all ecclesiastical dignitaries and worldly rulers were equally attacked by him. " I am like unto the hail," he said, " which pelts every one who is out in the open air." Consequently, these sermons of 1493, although by no means the most eloquent and daring of Savonarola's discourses, are those most completely representative of his whole train of thought. They bring him before us not only as an acute theologian and fearless denouncer of the corruptions of the Church, but also as the declared champion of liberty and the people.

It is impossible to ascertain the precise nature of his Lenten sermons in the year 1494, but during the autumn he carried on and concluded the famous series of sermons on Noah's Ark (*Prediche sopra l'Arca di Noé*), begun, as we have seen, in Lent, 1492. Thus, we find both series printed together in the same volume. They are mentioned by all the biographers, who are unanimous as to the strong impression these sermons made on the people ; how they amazed and transported all hearers, and how strangely the predictions contained in them had been fulfilled. But, unfortunately, it is very difficult for us to pass any decisive judgment on them, the edition being so faulty and incomplete, as to have lost almost every characteristic of Savonarola's style. Their reporter, unable to keep pace with the preacher's words, only jotted down rough and fragmentary notes. These were afterwards translated into barbarous dog-Latin—by way of giving them a more literary form—and published in

Venice.[1] For this reason Quétif and some other writers entertained doubts of their authenticity. It is true that they are in too confused a condition for continuous reading ; nevertheless the ideas expounded, or rather referred to, in them are so evidently those of Savonarola, and the testimony of the biographers is so unmistakably clear, that it is impossible to share Mons. Quétif's doubts.

Having demonstrated in his previous sermons on Genesis the necessity and approach of chastisement, Savonarola now devoted this next series to the representation of a mystical Ark, in which all should take refuge who wished to escape the coming flood. In the literal sense, this was the Ark of Noah as described in Genesis, while in the allegorical sense it portrayed the gathering together of the righteous : its length representing faith ; its width, charity ; its height, hope. He enlarged upon this strange allegory during the whole of Lent, 1492, and giving each day a different interpretation of the ten planks of which the Ark was composed, again expounded the virtues good Christians were bound to possess and the duties they should fulfil. Finally, on Easter morning, he declared the Ark to be complete, and ended his sermon with the following words : " Let all hasten to enter into the Lord's Ark ! Noah invites ye all to-day, the door stands open ; but a time will come when the Ark will be closed, and many will repent in vain of not having entered therein." In these Lenten discourses, and also in some others, he continued to dilate on the threatened scourges, and foretold the

---

[1] Venetiis, in officina divi Bernardini, 1536. The volume contains the forty-three Lenten sermons, and the thirteen others erroneously supposed to have been given in Advent. Both sets were also published separately, the same year, in Venice. In order to understand how many gaps occur in them, it is necessary to read the sermons before looking at the remarks made on them by their editor, and by the publisher of the " Sermons on Job."

coming of a new Cyrus, who would march through Italy in triumph, without encountering any obstacles, and without breaking a single lance. We find numerous records of these predictions, and the terrors excited by them, in the historians and biographers of the period, and Frà Benedetto reports his master's words in the following verses :—

> Presto vedrai summerso ogni tiranno,
>   E tutta Italia vedrai conquassata
> Con sua vergogna e vituperio e danno.
> Roma, tu sarai presto captivata ;
>   Vedo venir in te coltel dell' ira,
> El tempo è breve e vola ogni giornata.
>
>   *   *   *   *   *   *
>
> Vuol renovare la Chiesa el mio Signore,
>   E convertir ogni barbara gente,
> E sarà un ovile et un pastore.
>   Ma prima Italia fatta fia dolente,
> E tanto sangue in essa s'ha a versare,
>   Che rara fia per tutto la sua gente.[1]

---

[1] Frà Benedetto, "Cedrus Libani," a little poem published and edited by Padre Marchese in the "Archivio Storico Italiano," Appendix to vol. vii. pp. 59-95. *Vide* chap. ii : " Summary of the prophecies which the compiler heard delivered by the prophet Ieronimo in expounding the subject of Noah's Ark, at a time when no one was in dread of any tribulation."

The following is a literal translation of the verses :—

> Soon shalt thou see each tyrant overthrown,
> And all Italy shalt thou see vanquished,
> To her shame, disgrace, and harm.
> Thou, Rome, shalt soon be captured :
> I see the blade of wrath come upon thee,
> The time is short, each day flies past.
>
>   *   *   *   *   *   *
>
> My Lord will renovate the Church,
> And convert every barbarian people.
> There will be but one fold and one shepherd.
> But first Italy will have to mourn,
> And so much of her blood will be shed,
> That her people shall everywhere be thinned.

So extraordinary was the effect produced by these sermons on the whole public, that every day greater numbers thronged to the Duomo. Savonarola seemed to be the most important personage in Florence, and Piero de' Medici could no longer restrain his uneasiness. But it was a matter of general surprise that the Friar should devote so much time to the building of the Ark, and that even on resuming the same theme in the autumn of 1494, his exposition of this short chapter of Genesis should still be left unfinished. He has said himself that he could not explain his own slowness, and that some superior power seemed to be holding him back. Suddenly, however, he hurried to a conclusion.[1] The third of these sermons was to treat of the 17th verse of chap. vi., describing the Deluge, and it was given on September 21, destined to be a memorable day for Savonarola and Florence. The Duomo was scarcely large enough to contain the vast crowd which had been waiting since the early morning in a state of great excitement and expectation. At last the preacher mounted the pulpit, and on looking round upon his hearers and noting the extraordinary agitation prevailing amongst them, cried out in a terrible voice : " *Ecce ego adducam aquas super terram!* " His voice resounded through the church with the strength of a thunder-clap ; his words seemed to impress all present with a strange alarm. Pico della Mirandola said that he felt a cold shiver run through him, and that his hair stood on end ; and Savonarola has also declared that he himself was no less moved than his hearers.[2]

[1] The Venetian editor calls this series of thirteen sermons "Advent Sermons," makes them precede the forty-three Lenten discourses, and prints them all with the same inaccuracies : Venetiis in officina divi Bernardini, 1536. But the "Advent Sermons" of 1493 were those on the Psalm *Quam bonus*, and in Advent 1494, Savonarola preached on Haggai. The thirteen sermons on the Ark should therefore follow, not precede, the Lenten series (1492), as will be clearly seen on perusal.

[2] " He had preached in Santa Liperata (an old name for the Duomo), and closed the Ark just before the descent of the French king into Italy,

The extraordinary agitation of the Florentine public is easily explained. Unexpectedly as a thunderclap from a clear sky, came the news' that a flood of foreign soldiery was pouring down from the Alps to the conquest of Italy. And rumour, with its usual exaggeration, declared the invaders to be an innumerable host, of gigantic stature, great ferocity, and invincible strength. All felt taken unawares. Excepting the King of Naples, not one of the Italian princes was in the least prepared for resistance : the native armies were very feeble, the foreign forces hostile ; and all men were so overwhelmed by terror, that they already seemed to see blood flowing on all sides. Accordingly the people thronged to the Duomo, as though to seek aid from Savonarola. For all his words were now verified : the sword of God had come down upon earth ; the threatened chastisements had begun. The Friar alone had foreseen the future ; he alone would know the remedy for all this disaster. Hence all Italy rang with his name ; all eyes were turned towards him, and, by the irresistible force of events, he was almost instantaneously transformed into a political authority. The whole population applied to him, the most influential citizens sought his advice ; and as if by magic his followers became masters of the town. But by this time, so total a change had taken place in the affairs of Florence and of Italy in general, that it is necessary to go back a little, and explain at length in what manner this change had been wrought.

with certain sermons so full of terrors and alarms, cries and lamentations, that every one went about the city bewildered, speechless, and, as it were, half-dead." (Cerretani, "Storia," an autograph MS. loc. cit. sheet 185. See, too, the "Compendium Revelationum," loc. cit.)

BOOK II.

CHAPTERS I.—VII.

(1494–1495.)

CARLO VIII.

CARLO VIII. Re di Francia acquistò il Regno di Napoli, cacciandone Ferrante II. e lo tenne da vn'anno, e mezo.

CHAPTER I.

THE COMING OF THE FRENCH INTO ITALY.

(1494.)

A FTER the death of Lorenzo de' Medici, and the election of Alexander VI., the state of affairs in Italy grew rapidly worse. The Borgian Pontiff, with his devouring ambition to create principalities for his children, turned a greedy eye on every feeble or timid potentate; he made and unmade treaties, alliances, and solemn engagements, and was ready to expose Italy and the whole of Europe to any catastrophe, in order to gain his ends.[1] No less dangerous was the temper of Ludovico the Moor, for he was equally dominated by fear and ambition. His duplicity and bad faith were notorious throughout Italy; he concluded treaties only to violate them at the first opportunity; sometimes, indeed, in the act of signing them he was scheming how best to break the contract, should it seem expedient to do so. He prided himself on being the craftiest man in Italy, and was incessantly

---

[1] Machiavelli, "Legazioni"; Francesco Guicciardini, "Storia d'Italia"; Sismondi, "Hist. des Répub. Ital."; Michelet, "Renaissance." All historians and Italian ambassadors are unanimous on this point. See, too, De Cherrier, "Hist. de Charles VIII." Paris: Didier, 1868. Two Vols.

weaving fresh designs and fresh plots in order to strengthen his sovereignty, crush his enemies, and increase his power. And when suffering from attacks of fear, all his mental faculties were quickened and developed into a kind of spasmodic activity ; so that at these moments it was impossible for any one to foretell what he would decide to do next.[1] Unfortunately, both for himself and for Italy, he was a prey to fear at the time of which we are now speaking, and consequently in a state of continual suspense.

He had made himself lord of Milan by an act of cruel usurpation ; he kept his nephew, Giovan Galeazzo, the rightful duke, a prisoner at Pavia, and has been suspected of having compassed his death by slow poison. The young man was already weak and ailing, and his strength daily declined. Accordingly he could make no attempt to resist his uncle ; but his wife, Isabella of Aragon, daughter of Alphonso of Naples, refused to submit tamely to the loss of their rights, and the humiliating confinement imposed by their usurper. Therefore she proclaimed her grievances to all Italy, and repeatedly summoned her father and grandfather to come to avenge her wrongs and replace herself and husband at the head of their State. King Ferdinand and his son Alphonso, sovereigns of a vast kingdom and proud of the military renown they had won in their wars with the Barons, and at the siege of Otranto, treated the Moor with the utmost contempt. In their despatches they addressed him either as the Duke of Bari, or merely as Messer

---

[1] "Le dit Seigneur Ludovic estoit homme très sage, mais fort craintif et bien souple quand il avait peur (j'en parle comme de celuy que j'ai congnu et beaucoup de choses traicté avec luy) et homme sans foy, s'il voyait son profit pour la rompre" (Philippe de Comines, "Mémoires," &c., bk. vii. chap. ii. p. 491. Paris : Rollin, 1747). Excepting when quoting from this author we shall refer to him under his real name of Commines.

Ludovico,[1] and they continually threatened to deprive him of his ill-gotten power, and restore it to Isabella and Galeazzo. It is impossible to describe the agonies of fear endured by Ludovico at these moments, nor the wild plans he conceived. Had it been in his power, he would have unhesitatingly set all Italy and the whole world on fire, in order to be freed from these alarms.

Lorenzo de' Medici had always shown much prudence in acting as mediator between the two parties, and while preserving his own neutrality, maintaining friendly relations with both. He contrived to effect this by means of a kind of political see-saw, and was therefore styled by his contemporaries the beam of the Italian scales. As early as 1480 he had concluded a treaty of union between the States of Naples, Milan, and Florence; and later, by throwing his weight alternately to this side and that, had always contrived to keep this alliance intact.[2] But after his death the aspect of affairs instantly changed, and Ludovico's first thought was to test in some way the disposition of his allies. He therefore proposed that, to do honour to the newly-elected Pope, the ambassadors from the three courts should go to Rome at the same moment, and be presented together as friends to Alexander. But Piero de' Medici, being desirous to figure as the head of a special embassy from Florence, for which he had already made splendid preparations, induced the King of Naples to find some excuse for rejecting Ludovico's proposal. Ferdinand eagerly seized the opportunity to wound his

---

[1] These despatches, chiefly written by Pontano, are of great importance. We found them in the Neapolitan Archives and have made use of them in the present work. One is given, as a specimen, in the Appendix to the Italian edition, doc. xviii. The whole collection has since been published, in four volumes, by the Directors of the Archives, in the " Codice Aragonese." Naples, 1866–74.

[2] This is not only affirmed by the historians, but clearly proved by Lorenzo's published and unpublished correspondence.

personal enemy, giving him to understand, at the same time, that it was in compliance with the wishes of Piero. It is difficult to imagine to what an extent Ludovico's suspicions were aroused by this reply. And before long he was forced to regard it as a token of profound and general hostility, and of his own isolation in Italy, inasmuch as the Orsini had accepted commands in the pay of the Neapolitan king, and already won Piero de' Medici over to their side. Accordingly Ludovico began to give serious attention to his own safety, and could not rest until he finally hit upon the plan of inviting the French to undertake the conquest of the Neapolitan kingdom. This proved to be the beginning of the long string of disasters which was to desolate Italy for ages to come, destroy her commercial prosperity, stifle her literary and scientific culture, and extinguish every spark of her liberty. Ludovico undoubtedly gave the first impetus to these woes, but he has been unjustly execrated as almost the sole author of events for which, in truth, the way had long been prepared. He has thus been raised to an historical importance, to which even the evil he wrought upon his country can give him no claim.

Italy had been so worn out by the over-active and restless life of preceding times, that now, in the fifteenth century, she had fallen into a state of premature decrepitude, was politically aged, divided, and feeble. Great and powerful States had sprung up around her, and were rapidly gaining maturity and strength. The Turks, now at the height of their power, had already established a firm foothold in Europe, and were threatening Italy and the whole Western continent, both by sea and by land. Spain had united the kingdoms of Aragon and Castille, expelled the Moors, and, guided by the daring genius of Christopher Columbus, was already traversing the Atlantic. In France the iron despotism of Louis XI. had lowered

the aristocracy and raised the people, re-established the
finances, united the country, and extended its frontiers
towards the Rhine and the Pyrenees. At the same time
the decease of René of Anjou, by giving the French king
possession of that Duchy and Provence, had invested
him with all the boasted rights of the Angevins to the
Neapolitan throne. Germany, although apparently weakened by the feeble and vacillating rule of Maximilian I.,
was nevertheless developing increased energy as a military
power. And lastly the Swiss, now the best foot soldiers
of Europe, were ready to cross the Alps in formidable
numbers at the bidding of any paymaster.

At this moment, partly from consciousness of their own
strength, spirit of enterprise, desire for advanced civilization, but, above all, from a certain national jealousy, all
these races were disposed to attack Italy. They deemed
it unpardonable that Italy should still be the world's
preceptress ; that students from all parts of Europe should
flock to her universities ; that she should be the sole centre
of art and literature ; that her manners should be imitated,
her language studied in every Court throughout Christendom ; that the writers, artists, philosophers, physicians,
astrologers, and navigators of Italy should still surpass all
others in glory, as much as her princes and merchants
eclipsed all others in wealth. Hence the mingled sentiment of love and hate that instinctively attracted the rest
of Europe to Italy. And as Italy scattered the seeds of
culture all over the world, while no longer able to conquer
by force, it was inevitable that she should now be conquered.
In fact, during the fifteenth century *the Italian enterprise*
was regarded by Europe in the light of a crusade ; captains
and statesmen expected to reap from it precious and easy
victories ; scholars looked to it as to a revelation of the
world of art and science ; soldiers dreamt of the rich
booty to be gleaned from the sack of palaces and villas ;

and all coveted the blue skies and fruitful soil of Italy.[1]

But of all these nations, the first destined to pass the Alps was inevitably the French. The position of France, in the centre of Europe and on the confines of Italy, the temper of her people, her political and military standing— everything, in short, summoned her to the van of the mighty movement that was to bring life to Europe by Italy's death. Besides, at this juncture France had a new sovereign, Charles VIII., a youth of twenty-two years, filled with a strange passion for adventure. Of weakly constitution, stunted and almost deformed, scarcely able to read the alphabet, and devoid both of judgment and prudence, he was eager to rule, while incapable of maintaining his authority even over his courtiers.[2] He was always surrounded by men of low origin, who, by winning his favour, were raised to the highest dignities of the State ; and these satellites continually stirred his childish ambition to emulate the deeds of St. Louis of France, and immortalize his name by a crusade against the Turks, of which the conquest of Naples was to be the first step. And while these men were urging him to assert the claim to the Neapolitan throne, supposed to have devolved upon the sovereign of France from the House of Anjou,[3]

[1] Guicciardini, Sismondi, Leo, &c. The subject is treated in Michelet's "Renaissance" in terms of great eloquence and originality. See also De Cherrier, op. cit.

[2] The character of Charles VIII. is admirably described in Guicciardini's "Storia d'Italia," vol. i. p. 87. See also De Cherrier's remarks on it in his "Histoire de Charles VIII.," and those of Nardi, Parenti, and Cerretani in their respective histories of Florence. But the best author to consult on this period of history is Philippe de Comines (from whose "Memoires" we have already quoted), who was one of the finest observers and diplomats of the fifteenth century.

[3] Gibbon once entertained the idea of writing the history of the descent of Charles VIII. into Italy ; "an event," as he says, "which changed the face of Europe." In vol. iii. of his "Miscellaneous Works" (London, 1814) he gives the scheme of this projected history, and explains the nullity of the French pretensions to the Neapolitan throne.

the Neapolitan exiles were always at his side striving to
direct his ambition to the same end. The princes of
Salerno and Bisignano, who had escaped the massacre of
the Neapolitan Barons, were incessantly declaiming against
the cruel tyranny of Ferdinand and Alphonso, declaring
that there was a powerful Angevin party in the kingdom,
and that King Charles would be welcomed with open
arms by the population at large. In fact the distressed
condition of the Neapolitans was a matter of universal
notoriety ; and, apart from the exaggerations of the
exiles, it was also true that there was a general desire
for a change of some sort.

Throughout the rest of Italy it was plain that all friends
of liberty looked forward to the coming of the French with
much greater pleasure than alarm. The easy and yielding
temper of that people, and the known element of uncertainty and unexpectedness in their character, caused all
to hope from them that which they most desired, so that
every oppressed city or republic expected relief from its
woes at the hands of the French. Louis XI. had been
frequently solicited by this or that party to cross the
Alps, and now that Ludovico the Moor was sending
ambassadors to tempt Charles VIII., it appeared that even
the Pope was by no means averse to the plan. Whether
it was that Alexander wished to frighten the King of
Naples, in order to make peace with him on more advan-
tageous terms, or had let himself be ensnared by the
subtle devices and crafty policy of the Moor, or merely,
like so many others, hoped in the unknown, it is positive
that he also encouraged the French to come down into
Italy.[1]

Indeed, by a strange anomaly, the French invasion,

---

[1] Guicciardini, " Storia d'Italia " ; " Codice Aragonese " (previously
quoted) ; De Cherrier, op. cit. ; Michelet, " Renaissance" ; Sismondi,
" Histoire des Français."

fated to bring so many woes on our country, was, at that moment, positively desired by almost all Italians, and only opposed by the French. The Barons of France met in council and openly declared themselves adverse to so ill-judged and perilous an enterprise. No reliance, they said, could be placed on the aid of an ally such as the Moor, nor of a Pope so fickle and changeable as the Borgia ; the forces of the Neapolitan king were no contemptible foes, and France, with her exhausted treasury, had no means of pursuing a lengthy campaign. At bottom, their chief distrust was in their own king, whom they judged to be quite unfit to be the leader of so great an enterprise. But Charles paid no heed to their advice, and allowed himself to be guided by two individuals who were totally unversed either in war or in statesmanship. One of these was Etienne de Vers, originally a lackey, and now Seneschal Beaucaire ; the other, Guillaume Brissonet, a petty tradesman, first made Minister of Finance, and afterwards a cardinal. Incited by the hope of fresh gains, and the promises of Ludovico and the Pope, they were the only Frenchmen who favoured the war, and urged Charles VIII. to undertake it.

The monarch finally dismissed the agents of the Neapolitan king and sent four envoys to ascertain the intentions of the other Italian States. But they received no real sympathy from any of the Governments : the Venetian Republic was neutral ; Piero de' Medici entirely devoted to the House of Aragon, and the Pope, in spite of his invitation to the French, had now changed his views, and seemed to be on the Neapolitan side. King Ferdinand had done his utmost to win Borgia's friendship as soon as his own fortunes were threatened with danger, but his lavish attentions and promises had produced no effect. He died on January 25, 1494, tormented by agonies of remorse, and his last hours were also embittered by the

thought of bequeathing a tottering throne to his heirs.
Thus, after a long and prosperous life, he ended his days
—to use the words of a contemporary writer—*sine luce,
sine cruce, sine Deo.*[1] But his son Alphonso made the
most vigorous preparations for war, and, while collecting
soldiers and re-organizing the fleet, succeeded in buying
the Pope's alliance at the price of thirty thousand ducats
to Alexander himself, and generous donations to his sons.[2]

But although the French envoys found that all the
Italian powers, excepting Ludovico of Milan, were opposed to the coming of King Charles, they also ascertained that the masses regarded it very favourably. This
was particularly the case in Florence. Savonarola, from
the pulpit, boldly invited the new Cyrus to cross the Alps,
and public opinion was decidedly friendly to the French
and opposed to Piero de' Medici. The latter had been
compelled to relegate his own cousins to their country
houses because they had joined the popular party and
declared their almost unanimous hostility to the Medicean
rule, at the time when he had sent envoys to France
to explain and justify his policy to Charles. Piero
Capponi, always a man of extreme measures, had been
one of these ambassadors, and had advised the king to

[1] Joh. Burcardi, "Diarium," recently edited by Mons. L. Thuasne
(3 vols. Paris : Leroux, 1883-85). *Vide* to vol. ii. p. 89. This excellent
work may be consulted with great profit for details of the period.

[2] Besides the authors already quoted, the reader may be referred to
the Introduction of our own work on Machiavelli, &c., vol. i. p. 236
and fol., and likewise to Marin Sanuto's "La Spedizione di Carlo VIII.
in Italia." This very important work, preceding the author's celebrated
"Diarii," to which it serves as an introduction, is preserved in manuscript in the National Library of Paris. Finding that Venice had no
copy of it, and that it was not generally known, we succeeded, by the aid
of the Government, in having it sent to Italy on loan and copied in the
"Archivio dei Frari." This copy is now in the Marcian Library at
Venice. It was afterwards published by Professor R. Fulin in his
"Archivio Veneto," and also in a separate form. (Venice, 1883.)
Unfortunately the Paris MS. contains some inaccuracies which have
been preserved in the printed version.

expel all Florentine merchants from France, and by this severe blow to the material interests of the Republic, rouse the whole population against the Medici.[1]

These things might have been supposed to hasten King Charles's movements, but, apparently, hesitation was his normal state of mind. When all was prepared, and the moment for action arrived, he always began to have doubts. Thus, no sooner was it ascertained that the masses had declared in his favour, than he instantly recognized the full difficulty of the undertaking. But now, while he was at Lyons, there came to him the Cardinal of St. Piero in Vincoli, who had escaped from

[1] "Memoires de Philippe de Comines," livre vi. chap. vi. p. 444. The author says that Piero de' Medici sent two embassies to Charles VIII., and that the Bishop of Arezzo and Piero Soderini formed part of the first. "A la seconde fois envoya le dit Pierre (de' Medici) à Lion, un appelé Pierre Cappon, et autres, et disoit pour excuse, comme javoit fait, que le roy Louys onziesme leur avoit commandé à Florence se mettre en ligue avec le roy Ferrand. . . . En tous les deux ambassades yavoit toujours quelq'un ennemy dudit de Medicis, et par especial cette fois le dit Pierre Cappon, qui soubz main advertissoit ce qu'on devoit faire pour tourner la cité de Florence contre le dit Pierre, et faisait sa charge plus aigre qu'elle n'estoit, et aussi conseilloit qu'on bannist tous les Florentins du royaume, et ainsi fu fait. Cecy je dis pour mieux vous faire entendre ce qui advint après ; car le Roy demoura en grande inimitié contre le dit Pierre ; et lesdits general et seneschal (Brissonet and Beaucaire) avoyent grande intelligence avec ses ennemis en ladite cité, et par especial avec ce Cappon, et avec deux cousins germains dudit Pierre, et de son nom propre." It is therefore plain, according to Commines, that Capponi was adverse to Piero de' Medici, by whom he had been sent to France. Baron Kervyn de Lettenhove says in his Lettres, &c., de Philippe de Commines (vol. ii. p. 98. Brussels, 1868), that the charge is doubtful, since Commines was not Capponi's friend. And this opinion is corroborated by others and supported by the fact that during this time Capponi's letters to Piero de' Medici always seemed to be written in a very friendly spirit. Nevertheless the orator, Francesco della Casa, who was sincerely attached to Piero de' Medici, wrote from Lyons at this time warning him to be on his guard against Capponi and Capponi's adherents. And in fact, directly Capponi returned to Florence, he showed himself to be one of the most determined opponents of the Medici. He was an extremely courageous man, but a somewhat inconsistent politician, and, as Guicciardini neatly said of him, "he sometimes wavered, and sometimes shammed" ("Storia Fiorentina," p. 140).

the Castle of Ostia, where, after having defied and alarmed the Pope, he had been so strictly besieged and in such danger that he had been barely able to save his life by flight. He was the mortal enemy of Borgia, whom he always designated as a heretic and unbeliever, was one of the few cardinals who had refused to sell him their votes, and afterwards became Pope Julius II. For a long time he warred against Alexander with untiring energy, did his best to assemble a Council for the purpose of deposing him, and, in spite of his years, undauntedly faced every kind of danger and hardship. When admitted to the king's presence his fiery words swept away all Charles's doubts, and at last decided him to set forth towards Italy.[1]

But first of all funds had to be provided, and money was very scarce in France just then, although Ludovico the Moor was ready to pay down 200,000 ducats, and had given his promise for more.[2] Meanwhile a loan was obtained at high interest from Genoese bankers, and the Crown jewels were pledged, together with those of several nobles of the Court. It was also requisite to arrange an agreement with Spain and the emperor, in order not to be attacked in the rear. Accordingly Charles concluded a treaty of alliance with the former Power, ceding Perpignan and the county of Roussillon, which had been gloriously gained to France by the hard-fought victories of Louis XI., and formed the key of the Pyrenean district. The county of Artois, also conquered by the late king, was yielded to Maximilian. The emperor's daughter was likewise restored to him, for although long repudiated by Charles, the latter had hitherto refused to send her back, in spite of her father's repeated demands. The French were naturally enraged by all these concessions. They

[1] Guicciardini, "Storia d'Italia," vol. i. p. 58.
[2] Guicciardini, p. 83 and fol. ; De Cherrier, vol. i. p. 351.

considered the surrender of such important provinces a
grave offence to the national honour, and that Charles had
lowered the dignity of the country by his treaties and
burdened it with new debts which it was in no position to
redeem. Therefore every one augured ill of an enterprise
disapproved by all captains and statesmen, and that could
only be undertaken at the price of degrading acts of submission to neighbouring Powers. Nevertheless France
had Providence on her side, and her fortunes were bound
to prosper since Italy was incapable of resistance.

Our military strength was then very low, if not entirely
extinguished, for the reputation gained by the troops of
the Neapolitan king in their petty warfare against the
Barons was not likely to stand the test of pitched battles.
The celebrated Condottieri and free captains, who had
formerly encountered foreign armies with so much honour,
been the first to found the science of war, and instruct all
Europe in modern strategy and tactics, had now ceased to
exist. None of their best qualities had been inherited by
their successors, who had converted war into a shameful
trade, in which their chief concern was to get the highest
pay without risking their skins. Those were the times of
which Machiavelli said that two armies would often fight
for hours without any one falling by the sword, and that
the only men killed were those who were thrown down
and trampled under the horses' hoofs.[1] In fact the chief
strength of the Italian armies of the period lay in the
cavalry, and the trooper and his horse were both so
loaded with armour that, once down, neither could rise
without help. The infantry, on the other hand, was too
lightly armed, the arquebuse and pike having been only
just introduced ; so the foot soldiers fought in skir-

[1] Of course Machiavelli's words are not to be taken quite literally, for
though he often repeats the assertion, it was undoubtedly exaggerated.
Nevertheless those were sad times when similar accusations could even
be hazarded !

mishing form, or behind trenches and embankments, and, when drawn up in bands, formed so wide a line and so shallow a flank as to be very easily routed. The artillery consisted of a few heavy guns drawn by oxen, very difficult to load, and the large balls fired from them, being generally of stone, inflicted little damage on the foe.[1] The French army, on the other hand, was a model to all Europe in the art of war. It had adopted all the latest improvements, and its main strength lay in the infantry, which, moving in large and compact bodies, and being excellently drilled, could execute many new and startling manœuvres, and be handled with the utmost rapidity. The vanguard consisted of eight thousand Swiss, and the strength of the cavalry force was increased by the spirit of emulation existing between the great French lords and the flower of Scottish chivalry who rode in its ranks. The French also used the best weapons which had then been invented. Their infantry were armed with shining halberds and pikes, and every thousand foot soldiers comprised one hundred arquebusiers. Besides culverins and falconets, they had thirty-six guns drawn by horses and mounted on four-wheeled carriages. Two of these wheels were detached when the pieces had to be placed in position. On the march the guns moved almost as quickly as the infantry, which was considered a great marvel in those days.[2] Every one talked of the prodigies to be expected from the French cannon ; and the Florentine ambassadors had already given minute descriptions of " these fearsome things." [3]

---

[1] In Porzio's " Congiura dei Baroni," bk. i. and ii., there is a minute and masterly description of Italian warfare at that period. See also Guicciardini, Sismondi, &c.

[2] Sismondi, " Hist. des Répub. Ital." and " Histoire des Français " ; Michelet, " Renaissance " ; Guicciardini, &c.

[3] Desjardin, vol. i. p. 400. A despatch from Vespucci and Capponi, dated June 8, 1494.

It is almost impossible to arrive at any certainty as to the number of the French forces, for the old writers are always very inexact in their figures, and their mode of counting by *men at arms* [1] greatly adds to the confusion. Nevertheless most of them calculate that King Charles's army consisted of 22,000 foot and 24,000 horse, and with the addition of all his other followers, and the Milanese soldiery that was to join him in Italy, his whole force must have amounted to 60,000 men. [2]

Meanwhile King Alphonso of Naples was actively preparing for war to the best of his strength. His brother, Don Frederic, was leading an army against Genoa, where the French fleet was assembled ; Don Ferdinand, Duke of Calabria, together with the Count of Pitigliano and Gian Jacopo Trivulzi, two of the most renowned captains of the day, was advancing into Romagna to divert the war from the Neapolitan frontier.

This state of things made it imperative for King Charles to hasten his movements, and the very generals who had opposed the expedition were now anxious to begin it, being convinced that its difficulties would only be increased by delay. But at this juncture fresh doubts assailed the king. He was perplexed by a thousand uncertainties, and seemed, indeed, to have changed his intentions altogether, for some of his troops, who were already on the march, received orders to retrace their steps. Thereupon the Cardinal of St. Piero in Vincoli again sought his presence and addressed him in an almost violent

---

[1] A *man at arms* generally signified one mounted trooper, two bowmen, and two reserve horses, thus three men and five horses in all. But the number often varied, as also the numbers of the swarm of pages, workmen, attendants, and other supernumeraries added to the army.

[2] There are too many discrepancies on this point among the old historians for it to be worth while to quote them, all their calculations being made by hearsay, or at random. We have followed the computation given by Nardi and accepted by Sismondi, Michelet, and other modern writers.

tone. His Majesty, he said, was endangering not only his own honour, but that of the whole nation. His vehemence carried the day, and all hesitation was at an end.

So, at last, on the 22nd of August, 1494, the king set forth with his army, and crossing Monte Ginevra, halted at Asti, where he was met by Ludovico the Moor, together with his wife and the Duke of Ferrara.

But, amid festivities and women, Charles again forgot the war and indulged in so many excesses, that he fell seriously ill, and was detained at Asti for a month. He then went on to Pavia, where he found the unfortunate Giovan Galeazzo wasting away, bedridden, in the prime of his youth, and heard the lamentations of the prince's wife, who, casting herself sobbing at his feet, besought him to deliver them from their misery. The king appeared to be greatly moved and promised to give them effectual help. But he had hardly reached Piacenza before news arrived of the poor young prince's decease, and rumour added that he had been poisoned by his uncle, the Moor. The whole army was stirred to indignation by this event, for it revealed the nature of the ally with whom they had to deal. The king alone seemed to attach no importance to it. He had relapsed into his usual state of uncertainty, could not decide whether to march towards Romagna or through Tuscany, and meanwhile again halted in order to give himself up to fresh excesses.

During this time good news poured in from all sides of successes achieved by the French. The valiant General D'Aubigny, who had been sent to Romagna to hold the Neapolitans in check, had succeeded in harassing them so cruelly with his small force, that, without coming to a pitched battle, he had succeeded in driving them back across their own frontiers. At Genoa the Duke of Orleans with a powerful fleet had forced Don Frederic to withdraw his troops. At Rapallo the scanty Neapolitan garrison was surprised by a small body of Swiss, who effected a landing under cover of the ship's guns, sacked and fired the town, and although the garrison had surrendered, put them and all the inhabitants to the sword without even sparing forty sick persons, who were killed in their beds. The news of this deed spread indescribable terror throughout Italy, where warfare of so ferocious a kind was then unknown. The Neapolitan army beat a retreat; every city, down to the smallest town within range of the hostile fleet, expected to share the sad fate of Rapallo; the name of the French became a word of terror, and scarcely any resistance was offered to their advance.

About this time Piero de' Medici's cousins, Giovanni and Lorenzo, who had joined the popular party, and escaped from the villas to which they had been banished, arrived at the royal camp and assured the king that all Tuscany would welcome the passage of the French. Accordingly the army at last set out through the Lunigiana territory and skirted the banks of the Magra. On reaching Fivizzano they took its castle by assault, and rivalled the cruelties of the Swiss. But they soon discovered that their way was beset with dangers. They were in a barren district, shut in by mountains to the left; on the right lay the sea, where the enemy's vessels might appear at any moment; and before them rose the fortresses of Sarzana, Sarzanello, and Pietrasanta, which, even with scanty garrisons, were enough to check the advance of any army, no matter how formidable. Had Piero de' Medici possessed the courage to strike a bold blow, even at this moment, he might have inflicted on the French a severe and ignominious defeat. But their armies seemed to be miraculously guided by Providence to work our ruin, and, notwithstanding the blind indolence of their king, and their neglect of the most ordinary precautions, all was fated to go well with them.

Meanwhile the utmost confusion reigned in Florence. The popular party had always been favourable to France ; but now, owing to Piero's mad policy, the king was advancing as an enemy, and devastating the land by fire and sword. What was to be done in this state of things ? To open the road to the French, without first coming to terms with them, would be both imprudent and cowardly ; while to refuse them passage would be equivalent to a declaration of war. The government of the city was still in the hand of the weak and incapable Piero, the sole cause of all these disturbances ; accordingly every one waited to see what line of conduct he would adopt, and amid the general danger all took pleasure in witnessing his discomfiture. In fact Piero's position was the worst that could be conceived. The victorious enemy now drawing near was personally incensed against him ; he was penniless, with no friends to whom he could turn for supplies ; the country was against him, and he had no one to give him advice ! He sent Paolo Orsini with a few horse and three hundred foot to reinforce the garrison of Sarzana ; but no sooner had he done this than, assailed by fresh fears, he resolved to go to the royal camp and sue for peace. In this way he thought to imitate his father's journey to Naples, when, by daringly putting himself in King Ferdinand's power, Lorenzo had succeeded in obtaining honourable terms from him. But it is very difficult for history to reproduce itself, and Piero, urged by fear to that which Lorenzo had done from courage, reaped nothing but humiliation and ruin by an act that had brought increased power and prestige to his father.[1]

---

[1] Parenti (in the holograph MS., from which we have already quoted, in the National Library, II., IV., 169, at sheet 187) writes that Piero said on this occasion : " Every one must act for himself." Commines, Guicciardini, Nardi, Cerritani, &c., are all perfectly agreed as to these facts. See also De Cherrier, vol. i. chap. i. ; Cappelli, op. cit., p. 34 and fol.

On his departure he sent letters to Florence full of dis-
couragement and confusion, in which he tried to explain
his intentions. He felt that he was rushing to his ruin,
traho[1] *ad immolandum ;* he was forsaken by all, and this
w s his last resource. He should always remain faithful to the King of Naples.[2]   Meanwhile, on the 2nd
Nov mber, the Florentines despatched seven ambassadors
to overtake Piero. They were to keep a strict watch on
his actions, and endeavour to obtain easy terms, without giving too much offence to the king.[3]   But Piero
was already at Pietrasanta, and had there learnt that
Orsini had been defeated on the march by a small body
of French. This news having increased his anxiety to
obtain peace at any price, he sent to demand a safe-con-
duct, and directly he received it, repaired to the camp.
There he found that the king and his advanced guard had
been attacking the fortress of Sarzanello for three days
without success.   Any other man would have known how
to turn this failure and the perilous position of the enemy's
forces to his own advantage ; but Piero was unable to
shake off his terrors, and was additionally cowed by the
cold and haughty reception he met with from the king.
Without even questioning the ambassadors, he had the
incredible folly to cede all the three fortresses to Charles,
despatching peremptory orders to their governors for their
consignment to the French, who lost no time in taking
possession of them.   He also promised Charles 200,000
florins and permission to hold the fortresses of Pisa and
and Leghorn so long as the war should last.

[1] Instead of *trahor*, according to the original manuscript in the Florentine Archives. Piero meant to say : I go to immolate myself of my own
accord.
[2] Desjardin, vol. i. p. 587 and fol.   See also Guasti, " Relazioni diplomatiche tra la Toscana e la Francia," in the " Archivio, Stor. Ital.,"
N.S., vol. xvi. part ii. pp. 54 and 55.
[3] Desjardin, vol. i. p. 594 and fol.

Being now masters of the Tuscan territory the French made a rapid advance, scarcely able to believe in the change, by which they had been so miraculously delivered from danger. They all accepted it as a sign that Heaven favoured their enterprise ; and this belief was not only shared by generals as well as soldiery, but even by the king, who was now convinced that he was really the new Cyrus, foretold by the preacher of St. Mark's.[1] When the news of these events reached Florence, it roused the public to indescribable fury, and led to startling and most important events.

[1] Philippe de Comines, " Memoires," livre vii. cap. ix. p. 451. This writer says that the French could not believe their own eyes, and laughed at Piero de' Medici on seeing how readily he yielded everything : "Comme si tost accorda si grande chose." And he frequently repeats that : " Dieu monstroit conduire l'entreprise.

CHAPTER II.

(NOVEMBER, 1494.)

HE month of November, 1494, began under sinister auspices in Florence. The unexpected, almost incredible news of the surrender of fortresses which had cost the Republic prolonged sieges and enormous expense,[1] and formed the key of the whole Tuscan territory, instantly raised a tumult among the people; and the general fury was increased by letters received from the French camp, and the accounts of the returned envoys. For they told with what ease honourable terms might have been wrested from the king; with what a mixture of cowardice and self-assertion Piero de' Medici had placed the whole Republic at the mercy of Charles VIII., without waiting for the ambassadors or interrogating any one. All gave free vent to their indignation, and the people began to gather in the streets and

---

[1] The fortress of Pietrasanta cost the Republic 150,000 ducats and a two months' siege; that of Sarzana, 50,000 florins. *Vide* Rinuccini "Ricordi Storici," p. cxli. This diary was brought out by Aiazzi, in Florence, 1840, and may be consulted with profit. *Vide* also Cerretani, "Storia di Firenze," cod. cit. II., III., 74, at sheet 180.

squares. Some of the crowd were seen to be armed with old weapons which had been hidden away for more than half a century; others flourished daggers, which, as they said, had done work in the Duomo on the day of the Pazzi plot; and from the wool and silk manufactories strong, broad-set, dark-visaged men poured forth, reminding the beholder of Michele di Lando's Ciompi.[1] On that day it seemed as though the Florentines had leapt back a century, and that after patient endurance of sixty years' tyranny they were now decided to reconquer their liberty by violence and bloodshed.

Nevertheless, in the midst of this general excitement, men's minds were daunted by an equally general feeling of uncertainty and distrust. It was true that the Medici had left no soldiers in Florence, and that the people could at any moment make themselves masters of the whole city; but they knew not whom to trust, nor whom to choose as their leader. The old champions of liberty had nearly all perished during the last sixty years, either at the block or in persecution and exile. The few men at all familiar with State affairs were those who had always basked in the favour of the Medici,[2] and the multitude just freed from slavery would inevitably recur to licence if left to themselves. This, therefore, was one of those terrible moments when no one could foretell what excesses and what atrocities might not be committed. All day the people streamed aimlessly through the streets, like an impetuous torrent; they cast covetous glances on the houses of citizens

---

[1] Jacopo Nardi, Istoria di Firenze," vol. i. p. 37 and fol.

[2] " Florence, thou knowest that for sixty years thou hast had an armed man in thy home. . . . He robbed thee of thy goods and he robbed thee of thy women, and thou wast compelled to bear all with patience. . . . Where couldst thou find support? Under what government didst thou live, but a government made I know not how? Tell me what brains hadst thou on thy side? On his were better brains than on thine—I would say those of his adherents" (From a sermon preached by Savonarola on the third Sunday in Lent, 1496).

who had amassed wealth by acts of oppression ; but they
had no one to lead them ; only at the hour of Savonarola's
sermon they all flocked instinctively to the Duomo. Never
had so dense a throng been gathered within its walls ; all
were too closely packed to be able to move ; and when at
last Savonarola mounted the pulpit he looked down upon
a solid and motionless mass of upturned faces. Unusual
sternness and excitement were depicted on every countenance, and he could see steel corselets flashing her᷉ and
there in the cloaked crowd.

The Friar was now the only man having any influence
over the people, who seemed to hang on his words and
look for safety to him alone.   One hasty word from his
mouth would have sufficed to cause all the houses of the
principal citizens to be sacked, to revive past scenes of
civil warfare, and lead to torrents of blood.   For the
people had been cruelly trampled on, and were now
panting for a cruel revenge.   He therefore carefully
abstained from all allusion to politics ; his heart was overflowing with pity ; he bent forward with outstretched arms
from the pulpit, and in tones which echoed throughout
the building, proclaimed the law of peace and charity and
union : " Behold ! the sword has come upon you, the
prophecies are fulfilled, the scourges begun ! Behold !
these hosts are led by the Lord ! O Florence ! The
time of singing and dancing is at an end ; now is the
time to shed floods of tears for thy sins. Thy sins, O
Florence ! thy sins, O Rome ! thy sins, O Italy ! They
have brought these chastisements upon thee ! Repent
ye, then ; give alms, offer up prayers, be united ! O
my people ! I have long been as thy father ; I have
laboured all the days of my life to teach ye the truths of
faith and of godly living, yet have I received nought but
tribulation, scorn, and contumely ; give me at least the
consolation of seeing ye do good deeds ! My people,

what desire hath ever been mine but to see ye saved, to see ye united? 'Repent ye, for the kingdom of heaven is at hand!' But I have said this so many times, I have cried to ye so many times; I have wept for thee, O Florence, so many times, that it should be enough. . . . To Thee I turn, O Lord, to Thee, who didst die for love of us and for our ʂins: forgive, O Lord, forgive the Florentine people, that would fain be Thy people."[1] And in this strain he continued to exhort his hearers to charity, faith, and concord with such exceeding earnestness and fervour that he was exhausted and almost ill for several days after.[2] These sermons were less eloquent than some of the others, since he was too deeply moved for reflection or for studied effects; but the tenderness with which he spoke dominated and soothed the people, who, fresh from the tumults without, entered this place of peace to hear the words of the Gospel. So magical was the power of Savonarola's voice in those days, that, in all this great stir of public excitement, not a single excess was committed, and the revolution that seemed òn the point of being effected by violence on the Piazza was quietly and peaceably accomplished within the walls of the palace. And this miracle, unprecedented in Florentine history, is unanimously attributed by the historians of the time to Savonarola's beneficial ascendency over the minds of the people.[3]

[1] "Sermons on Haggai," delivered in Advent, 1494. Venice, 1544. Frate Stefano da Codiponte transcribed them as they were spoken. See the first sermon. Haggai was the prophet who addressed the Hebrews on their return from captivity in Babylon, in order to urge them to rebuild the temple. It is easy, therefore, to understand why Savonarola made choice of the subject at this moment.

[2] "Calendis igitur Novembris, id est Sanctorum omnium solemnitate, et duobus proximis diebus, voci et lateri non peperci, et (ut omni populo notum est) tantum ex pulpito declamavi, quod infirmior corpore factus, paene langui" ("Compendium Revelationum," p. 236).

[3] All the historians are unanimous in asserting that Savonarola was the soul of the Florentine people during those days. If much was owed to

On November 4th the Signory called a special meeting of the Council of Seventy, in order to decide what course to adopt. All the members were adherents and nominees of the Medici, but were so enraged by the cowardly surrender of the fortresses that they already had the air of a republican assembly. According to the old Florentine law and custom no one was allowed to speak unless invited to do so by the Signory, and was then only expected to support the measures which they had proposed. But in moments of public excitement neither this nor any other law was observed in Florence. On this day there was great agitation in the Council ; the safety of the country was at stake ; the Signory asked every one for advice, and all wished to speak. Yet so much were men's minds daunted by the long habit of slavery, that when Messer Luca Corsini broke through the old rule, and, rising to his feet, uninvited, began to remark that things were going badly, the city falling into a state of anarchy, and that some strong remedy was required, every one felt amazed. Some of his colleagues began to murmur, others to cough ; and at last he began to falter and became so confused that he could not go on with his speech.[1]

However the debate was soon reopened by Jacopo di

him for having roused them during the previous years from their prolonged slumber, a still greater debt was due to him for having maintained peace and concord in those days of disturbance. This will be more fully seen in the ensuing chapters, and the sermons on Haggai will supply us with excellent proofs. Guicciardini was one of those who best judged and appreciated Savonarola. In his dialogue, " Sul Reggimento di Firenze," p. 28, he makes Bernardo del Nero address the following words to Capponi, who sided with the government of the " Ottimati " : " I hold you to be deeply indebted to this Friar, who, having early quieted the tumult, has prevented any trial being made of the results of this form of government of yours ; for I cannot doubt that it would have given birth to civil discords of such a sort as would have speedily produced some disorderly and tumultuous change." As Savonarola was the only man who saved the State from anarchy, Guicciardini also writes of him at some length in his " Storia Fiorentina."

[1] Cerretani, " Storia di Firenze," Cod. cit., at sheet 181.

Tanai de' Nerli, a youth of considerable spirit, who warmly seconded Corsini's words ; but he too presently began to hesitate, and his father, rising in great confusion, sought to excuse him in the eyes of the assembly by saying that he was young and foolish.

Lastly Piero di Gino Capponi rose to his feet. With his finely-proportioned form, white hair, fiery glance, and a certain air of buoyant courage like that of a warhorse at sound of trumpet, he attracted universal attention, and reduced all to silence. He was known to be a man of few but resolute words, and of still more resolute deeds. He now spoke plainly, and said : " Piero de' Medici is no longer fit to rule the State ; the Republic must provide for itself ; *the moment has come to shake off this baby govern-ment.*[1] Let ambassadors be sent to King Charles, and should they meet Piero by the way, let them pass him without salutation ; and let them explain that he has caused all the evil, and that the city is well disposed to the French. Let honourable men be chosen to give a fitting welcome to the king ; but, at the same time, let all the captains and soldiery be summoned in from the country, and hidden away in cloisters and other secret places. And besides the soldiery, let all men be prepared to fight in case of need, so that when we shall have done our best to act honestly towards this most Christian monarch, and to satisfy with money the avarice of the French, we may be ready to face him and show our teeth if he should try us beyond our patience, either by word or deed. And above all," he said in conclusion, " it must

---

[1] Cerretani has bequeathed us a minute account of this debate (Cod. cit., at sheet 181 and fol.). It is also mentioned by Gaddi, the " Priorista," who, however, puts into Nerli's mouth the concluding words really spoken by Capponi, to whom, as a man of mature years, they are far more appropriate than to the very youthful Nerli. *Vide* Acciajoli, "Vita di Piero Capponi," in the " Archivio Storico," vol. iv. part ii. In the appendix to the biography a portion of the " Priorista Gaddi " is given.

not be forgotten to send Father Girolamo Savonarola as
one of the ambassadors, for he has gained the entire love
of the people."[1]   He might have added : because he has
the entire respect of the king ; for Charles had conceived
an almost religious veneration for the man who had so
long foretold his coming, and declared it to be ordained
by the Lord.

The new ambassadors were elected on the 5th of November, and consisted of Pandolfo Rucellai, Giovanni Cavalcanti, Piero Capponi, Tanai de' Nerli, and Savonarola.[2]
The latter allowed the others to precede him to Lucca,
where they hoped to meet the king, while he followed on
foot according to his usual custom, accompanied by two
of his brethren.[3]   But, before starting, he again addressed
the people, and preached a sermon ending with these
words :   " The Lord hath granted thy prayers, and
wrought a great revolution by peaceful means.   He alone
came to rescue the city when it was forsaken of all.   Wait
and thou shalt see the disasters which will happen elsewhere.   Therefore be steadfast in good works, O people
of Florence ; be steadfast in peace !   If thou wouldst
have the Lord steadfast in mercy, be thou merciful towards thy brethren, thy friends, and thy enemies ; otherwise thou too shalt be smitten by the scourges prepared
for the rest of Italy.   *Misericordiam volo,* crieth the Lord
unto ye.   Woe to him that obeyeth not His commands ! "[4]

[1] Cerretani and Acciaioli, from whom we have already quoted. Capponi had a great veneration for Savonarola and the brotherhood of St.
Mark's, but did not show himself unfailingly constant. He used to confess to Frà Silvestro, and his published letters in the Archivio Storico, at
the end of Acciaioli's biography of him, give frequent proofs of his high
esteem for the Prior.

[2] *Vide* the portion of the " Priorista Gaddi," published in the Appendix
of the Life of Capponi, to which we have before referred, and Desjardin,
vol. i. p. 598 and fol.

[3] Parenti, " Storia," already quoted ; Cod. already quoted, sheet 190.

[4] "Prediche sopra Aggeo," Sermon iii.

After delivering this discourse he started for Pisa, where the other ambassadors and also the king speedily arrived.

When Piero de' Medici found that these envoys came in the name of the Republic, without offering any sign of allegiance to himself, he at once understood that some important change had occurred in Florence. He therefore earnestly besought the king's assistance, and promised immediate payment of the required 200,000 ducats.[1] Then, after bidding Paolo Orsini to collect his troops, hire as many men as possible in the neighbourhood, and follow him to Florence, he hastily returned to the city on the evening of the 8th of November.[2] The ensuing day, towards the twenty-first hour, he presented himself at the palace with a numerous retinue, for the purpose of calling a general parliament of the people, and of taking the government into his own hands. But the Signory being forewarned of his designs, only allowed him to bring in a few of his companions, and, receiving him with studied coldness, advised him to dismiss his hired troops in order to avoid involving himself and the city in a fruitless struggle. Piero was so confounded by this cold and determined reception, that he knew not what course to adopt, and withdrew muttering that he would first see what was to be done and then return to announce his decision to the Signory. Repairing to his own house, he sent orders to Orsini to seize the San Gallo Gate ; and after providing himself with weapons, and an armed escort, went again to the palace. But several members of the Government stood in the doorway and barred his entrance, telling him they were forbidden to let him pass that way, and could only admit him, alone and unarmed, by the little postern gate. Thereupon, boiling with rage, and

[1] Parenti, " Storia," already quoted ; Cod., already quoted, at sheet 94. See also the " Priorista Gaddi," p. 41 and fol.

[2] Jacopo Nardi, vol. i. p. 42 ; Rinuccini, " Ricordi," p. clii.

with threatening glances, he turned away. But he had scarcely gone two steps, when he was hailed by one of the mace-bearers to the Signory, sent by Messer Antonio Lorini, the only member of the Government still remaining faithful to the Medici, on purpose to call him back. This Lorini, chancing to be Proposto [1] that day, had the sole right of proposing measures for discussion, and had thus been able to prevent the issue of any decree hostile to Piero. Also, having the care of the tower keys, he had prevented the bell from being rung to summon the people. But he had gone too far in venturing to recall Piero, in defiance to the general will ; so now Messer Luca Corsini, together with Jacopo de' Nerli and Filippozzo Gualterotti, came to the gate expressly to prevent his admittance. Lorini's invitation had restored Piero's courage, so he now tried to take an arrogant tone and force his way in ; but Nerli drove him back with words of insult, and shut the door in his face

On witnessing this scene the populace began to riot, and, by way of proving their contempt for Piero, drove him off with scornful cries and gestures, wagging the tips of their hoods at him, while the street boys assailed him with hisses and volleys of stones. Piero had drawn his sword, but, unable to decide whether to use it or sheathe it, shrank timidly away surrounded by his followers and cowed by the mere voice of the people, upon whom he had so arrogantly trampled. While he and his band were retreating with the mob at their heels, they encountered the Bargello,[2] Pico Antonio dell' Aquila, who, attempting to give aid to the Mediceans, was immediately seized by the unarmed crowd, and, together with his men, stripped of all weapons and valuables. He was then led to his

[1] The Proposto was generally changed twice a week and sometimes every second day.
[2] Captain of Justice.

palace (the Bargello) and compelled to release all the prisoners confined there. Thereupon the rioters hurried away, and it was a strange sight to see that the arms taken from the Bargello, were the first brandished in the cause of liberty. But already the great bell of the Signory was heard pealing the alarm, and the whole population rushed to the Piazza. All left their houses, closed their shops, and issued forth armed with billhooks, spits, stakes, or any other implement that came handy. On that day some old citizens were seen dressed in quaint-cut garments and with rusty weapons, recalling the times of the perished Republic, and their appearance was everywhere hailed with cries of joy by the crowd.[1]

Hardly was the throng gathered in the Piazza than Francesco Valori appeared mounted on a mule and covered with dust, having just returned from the camp whither he had been sent as one of the first embassy from Florence. The crowd pressed round him to ask for news, and in a moment he was in the thick of·the riot. Valori was an old partisan of the Medici, had filled many posts under Lorenzo, and been one of the five citizens sent by that prince to urge Savonarola to alter the tone of his sermons. But that interview had excited Valori's sympathy for the Friar, and he had gradually become one of his most devoted followers. Disgusted by Piero's misrule, he was now an energetic member of the popular party, where he was more in his place than among the Mediceans. For he had all the qualities of a popular leader, being impetuous and daring, narrow-brained, large-hearted, rashly eager in all his resolves, and perfectly at home in popular tumults. So, now, without even dismounting from his

[1] Jacopo Nardi, vol. i. p. 41 and fol. ; Rinuccini, "Ricordi Storici," p. clii. and fol. ; Gaddi, " Priorista," p. 41 and fol. ; Parenti, " Storia" (already quoted), sheet 192 and fol. ; Cerretani, " Storia di Firenze," sheet 192 and fol. ; Landucci, " Diario," p. 73 and fol.

mule, or shaking off the dust of the journey, he began to harangue the multitude. He told how at first the king had seemed well disposed towards the ambassadors, but that on following him to Pisa they had been very coldly received, thanks to Piero de' Medici, who, before leaving the camp, had accepted disgraceful terms, and made numerous promises and requests to the injury of Florence. And on seeing that his narrative had inflamed the popular fury, he put himself at the head of the mob and marched them with cries of *Abbasso le palle* (Down with the balls)[1] to attack the Medici Palace.[2]

Pierò meanwhile had summoned Orsini and his troops, assumed his armour and determined to force his way into the public palace. His brother, Cardinal Giovanni,[3] set out first and rushed through the town trying to rally the people in his favour to the cry of *palle, palle !* But there was no response, and he was threatened on all sides, in the streets and from the windows. On reaching the Church of St. Bartolommeo, he descried the approach of the furious crowd led by Valori, and beat a rapid retreat, seeing that weapons were flashing and blows begun. Returning to the Medici house he found that Piero had already taken flight. For the latter, having received a decree from the Signory, proscribing himself and the Cardinal as rebels, and learned that his brother was being driven back, had not even the courage to wait for him, but had fled to the San Gallo Gate with his few remaining followers. There he made a desperate attempt to raise the inhabitants of that quarter—people of the lowest class, who had been always strongly attached to his House. But his words and the gold he scattered in the streets were equally fruitless. Even these dregs of the populace treated him

---

[1] Six balls were the Medici arms.—TR.

[2] See the authors quoted above.

[3] Afterwards Pope Leo X.

with contempt and turned away towards the palace of the Signory. Then at last he saw that all hope was gone, and that the best he could do was to save his life. Humiliated and overwhelmed by these sudden reverses, he set forth on the road to Bologna, and before he had made a dozen steps beheld the city gates closed behind him. He was accompanied by a handful of soldiers, who, sharing his fears of being attacked on the way and cut to pieces by the peasantry, nearly all deserted him before he came to the Tuscan frontier. Reaching Bologna with his scanty and miserable escort, worn out and exhausted by his long journey, he met with a very rough reception from Bentivoglio, who said : " I would rather have been hacked to pieces than abandon my State in this fashion." Yet before long, in the presence of a similar danger, the haughty Bentivoglio was himself reduced to cowardly flight. Meanwhile Piero, increasingly depressed by his adverse fate, pursued his journey to Venice, where he at last found courtesy and rest. But while there, he was pained to find that Soderini, the Florentine ambassador, had already declared in favour of the new government. The Venetians, however, received him with all the honours they usually accorded to fallen potentates, and this was balm to his troubled spirit.

His experiences during the last few days seemed to have lasted a century. He now awoke as from a weary dream, and began to realize the enormous folly of his conduct, and his cowardice in leaving the State, when threatened by no positive danger, and when the French king seemed ready to assist him. It is certain that, had he shown a determined spirit during those days, he might have succeeded in putting down the budding revolt and relied on the speedy assistance of the French.[1] In

---

[1] This was the opinion not only of Nardi and the other historians, but also of Savonarola, who consequently attributed the expulsion of the

fact the king was so favourably disposed towards him, that he sent messengers to Venice to invite his return. But Piero shrank from the thought of again exposing himself to the tumultuous throng whose cries still rang menacingly in his ears. Meanwhile the Cardinal, who had shown greater courage during his flight, also arrived in Venice.[1] The latter had remained in Florence for some time, disguised as a monk and exposed to much hardship and danger ; he had collected all the more precious valuables which he was able to find in the hurry and confusion, and ensured their safety by conveying them to the convent of St. Mark. His example was followed by several other citizens who were conscious of having incurred the hatred of the people. The integrity of Savonarola and his brotherhood was held in such great esteem, that, although their convent was practically the headquarters of the popular party, the partisans of the Medici, and even the Cardinal himself, knew of no safer place for the bestowal of their treasures.

About this period the Signory proclaimed a reward of 2000 florins for the dead bodies of Piero and the Cardinal, of 5000 for their delivery alive.[2] At the same time

Medici to the Divine intervention. "God hath freed you of this strong man of war ; let no one say to thee : It was I that overcame him, for thou hadst not the strength to uproot so great a House and so powerful a man. . . . God hath been stronger than he ; He hath taken his spoils from him and his own possessions and his dominion over thee " (Sermon delivered the third Sunday in Lent, 1496).

[1] Guasti, " Della relazioni diplomatiche tra la Toscana e la Francia," in the " Archivio Storico Italiano," N.S. vol. xiv. part ii. p. 57. On November 9th the Signory announced to their ambassadors that Piero and Cardinal Giovanni had been expelled by the people and had fled towards Bologna.

[2] So says Giovanni Cambi, " Storia," vol. ii. p. 78. Landucci (p. 75) only says that they put the price of 2000 florins on Piero's head, and of 1000 on the Cardinal's ; others give different versions. But we learn from the official documents (" Deliberazioni della Signoria, ad annum," sheets 95 and 95ᵗ) that on November 20th a reward of 2000 *lire* was offered for Piero's head, without any mention of the Cardinal's. It is difficult to

efforts were made to destroy all memory of the past
despotism. The effigies of the rebels of 1434 painted on
the walls of the Podestà's palace were effaced, and likewise
those of the rebels of '78 by Andrea del Castagno on the
door of the Custom House.[1]

The Neroni and Pazzi families were recalled, together
with many others who had been exiled or relegated to
certain places. Among these were Piero's cousins, Lorenzo
and Giovanni de' Medici, who, immediately after their
return, stripped the shield with the *palle* from their houses,
put the arms of the Florentine people in its place, and
changed their name from Medici to Popolani. Thus the
hitherto despised multitude was now beset with flattery !

Meanwhile disturbances went on increasing, and the
populace seemed already intoxicated with licence. The
dwellings of Giovanni Guidi, notary and chancellor of the
Riformagioni, and of Antonio Miniati, manager of the
Monte,[2] were put to the sack, for both these men having
been faithful tools of the Medici, and their subtle coun-
sellors in the art of burdening the people with insupport-
able taxes, were objects of general hatred.[3] The house of
Cardinal Giovanni de' Medici was also pillaged, together
with the garden by St. Mark's, in which so many treasures
of art had been collected by Lorenzo. So far, with the
exception of a few dagger thrusts, no blood had been shed ;
but many were eager for conflict, and it would have
certainly begun, had not Savonarola's partisans done their

ascertain how matters really stood in that period of confusion. Many
decrees were passed, which remained unregistered, and were afterwards
changed, for different reasons. And rumours were purposely spread of
decrees which had never been passed. It is extremely probable that the
Government did not dare to register its proceedings against the Cardinal,
on account of their respect for his ecclesiastical dignity.

[1] So says Nardi. But, according to Vasari, the effigies of the rebels of
'78 had also been painted on the Podestà's palace. Cosimo returned
from exile in 1434 ; the conspiracy of the Pazzi took place in 1478.

[2] State Bank.　　[3] Nardi, vol. i. p. 46.

best to keep the peace, and had not the Friar been hourly expected from Pisa, whither he had repaired on the 13th day of the month with a second embassy.[1] The Signory also endeavoured to quell the disturbances by means of edicts of the severest kind.

But the popular discontent was now heightened by the arrival of other envoys from Pisa with very unsatisfactory tidings. They had informed the king that Florence was friendly to him, and already preparing to welcome him with all the honours due to his royalty; they only asked that, being received as a friend, he should bear himself in that light, and deign to name his terms at once, so that free vent might be given to the public joy. But the only reply Charles condescended to give was that "Once in the great town, all should be arranged."[2] And it was evident from his Majesty's coldness that the solicitations of Piero de' Medici, his earnest prayers, lavish promises of money, and submissive obedience, had turned him in his favour. Consequently the ambassadors had to leave without any definite answer, and could only say that the monarch was by no means well disposed to the Republic.

But when the foiled envoys had left Pisa, Savonarola repaired to the French camp, and passing through that great host of armed men, made his way to the king's presence. Charles, who was surrounded by his generals, received him very kindly, and thereupon, without wasting much time in preliminaries, the Friar, in sonorous and almost commanding accents, addressed him with a short exhortation beginning as follows : " O most Christian king, thou art an instrument in the hand of the Lord, who sendeth thee to relieve the woes of Italy, as for

---

[1] During these days successive embassies were sent to the king. That of the 13th comprised Savonarola, Benedetto Nerli, Lorenzo Lenzi, Piero Vittori, and Bernardo Rucellai. On the 15th of the same month two others were despatched and a third appointed. See Guasti, op. cit., p. 58.

[2] " Dentro alla gran *villa* s'assetterebbe ogni cosa."

many years I have foretold; and He sendeth thee to
reform the Church which now lieth prostrate in the
dust. But if thou be not just and merciful ; if thou
shouldst fail to respect the city of Florence, its women,
its citizens, and its liberty ; if thou shouldst forget the
task the Lord hath sent thee to perform, then will He
choose another to fulfil it ; His hand shall smite thee,
and chastise thee with terrible scourges. These things
say I unto thee in the name of the Lord."[1] The king and
his generals seemed much impressed by Savonarola's
menacing words, and to have full belief in them. In fact
it was the general feeling of the French that they were
divinely guided to fulfil the Lord's work, and Charles felt
a strong veneration for the man who had prophesied his
coming and foretold the success of his expedition. Consequently the Friar's exhortation inspired him with real
terror, and decided him to behave more honourably to the
Florentines. Thus, when Savonarola returned to the city
shortly after the other ambassadors, he was the bearer of
more satisfactory intelligence.

[1] This discourse is to be found at p. 237 and fol. of the " Compendium
Revelationum." For the compilation of our narrative of these events
(besides using the documents given to the world by Desjardin and Guasti,
we have relied not only on Nardi's minute account, but also on the evidence of Cerretani, Parenti, Rinuccini, Gaddi, Landucci, and Guicciardini,
&c. All these writers agree as to the main facts, while differing as to
minute and insignificant details.

CHAPTER III.

(NOVEMBER, 1494.)

WING to fresh disasters, Tuscan affairs were now at a sad pass. On the very day that the Medici were expelled from Florence, the Pisans rose in revolt and regained their liberty by force. Ever since their subjection to the Florentine, or, as they called it, the foreign yoke, their sole aim had been to cast it off. Loss of independence had been almost immediately followed by the ruin of their commerce and industry. They had seen their population thinned, every free institution destroyed, and accordingly the greater part of the citizens had preferred exile to slavery. But, at the approach of the French, their hopes had revived, and Ludovico the Moor, who always fished in troubled waters, and already cherished the design of becoming master of Pisa, continually urged them to revolt, promising all kinds of assistance and causing secret hopes to be held out to them by persons in attendance upon the king. Hence, the moment Charles VIII. entered the city, the populace rose, tore down the Florentine arms, cast into the Arno the Marzocco[1] that stood on the bridge, and set up the king's statue in its place. The Florentine authorities were forcibly expelled and their houses sacked by the mob. Liberty and independence were instantly proclaimed, all exiles recalled, and preparations begun for the celebrated and ill-omened Pisan war, that was fated to exhaust the strength of both the revived republics, and cost the lives of many gallant citizens without any profit to either side.

The king was a spectator of these revolutionary acts, and at first seemed inclined to encourage them ; but his mood changed on beholding the expulsion of the Florentine rectors. He apparently expected the Pisans to reclaim their liberty without ceasing to yield obedience to the Florentines ! But the people, having once begun the revolt, proceeded to accomplish it with the utmost rapidity. Thereupon Charles placed a French garrison in the fortress, and, thinking that this was all that was required, resumed his journey, scarcely noticing what had happened, and without troubling himself as to the consequences of having encouraged the Pisans. Thus, even before entering Florence, he had dealt a cruel blow to the Republic by allowing its subjects to rise in rebellion before his eyes and with the French army within their walls. It was truly a dangerous example for the whole State, and one that was soon followed by Arezzo, Montepulciano, and other cities. Meanwhile he continued his march, with a few days' halt at Signa, in order to give time for the tumults in Florence to subside, and for suitable preparations to be made for his entry. Another embassy was sent to implore him to settle the terms of the treaty before he proceeded farther ; but

[1] The Florentine Marzocco is the figure of a lion seated on its haunches, with one paw resting on a shield bearing the emblematic lily of the Republic. It was always erected in public places. The derivation of the word is unknown.—TR.

he replied as before : " We will arrange everything within the great town (ville)." [1]

All this combined to keep the city in a state of confusion and suspense. The Medici only just driven out, the old government overthrown, and the new still unorganized ; the king about to arrive without having been brought to terms, and at the head of a powerful army, already stained with Italian blood ! There was excellent cause for alarm ; but fortunately citizens of noted prudence and determination came to the Signory's aid. Among others there was Piero Capponi, who in these days seemed to be the right hand of the Republic, even as Savonarola was its heart and soul. The latter preached charity, peace, and union, while the former flew wherever his presence seemed needed, providing arms and collecting men. All the houses were stocked with war material of every kind ; stakes and planks were prepared for barricading the streets ; hired troops, amounting, it is said, to the number of six thousand, were quartered in courtyards and in cloisters, ready to sally forth in defence of the Republic at the first sound of the alarm bell. [2]

As the king's intentions were still unknown, fresh relays of ambassadors were sent out to him. But meanwhile French officers and men passed the gates in little bands of fifteen or so at a time, and were seen roving about the town unarmed, jaunty, and gallant, bearing pieces of chalk in their hands to mark the houses on which their troops were to be billeted. While affecting an air of contemptuous indifference, they were unable to hide their amazement at the sight of so many splendid buildings, and at every turn were confounded by the novel scenes presented to their

[1] Nardi, vol. i., p. 47. See also the other historians before quoted, and more especially Cerretani, Parenti, Gaddi, and Guicciardini.

[2] Guicciardini, "Storia d'Italia," i. 117, and "Storia Fiorentina," chaps. xi. and xii. See also Nardi and the other authors before quoted.

gaze. But what struck them most of all was the grim severity of the palaces which appeared to be impregnable strongholds, and the towers still scarred with the marks of fierce and sanguinary faction fights. Then, on the 15th of November, they witnessed a sight that sent a thrill of fear to their souls. Whether by accident or design, a rumour suddenly spread through the town that Piero de' Medici was nearing the gates. Instantly the bell of the Signory clanged the alarm; the streets swarmed with a furious mob; armed men sprang, as by magic, from the earth, and rushed towards the Piazza; palace doors were barred; towers bristled with defenders; stockades began to be built across the streets, and on that day the French took their first lesson in the art of barricades. It was soon ascertained that the rumour was false, and the tumult subsided as quickly as it had risen. But the foreign soldiers were forced to acknowledge that their tactics and their stout battalions would be almost powerless, hemmed in those streets, against this new and unknown mode of warfare. In fact the Florentines looked on the Frenchmen with a certain pert assurance, as if they would say: " *We shall see!* " For having now regained its liberty, this people thought itself master of the world, and almost believed that there was nothing left for it to fear.[1]

Meanwhile splendid preparations were being made in the Medici palace[2] for the reception of King Charles; his officers were to be lodged in the houses of the principal citizens, and the streets through which he was to pass were covered with awnings and draped with hangings and tapestries. On the 17th of November the Signory assembled on a platform erected by the San Frediano Gate; and numbers of young Florentine nobles went forth to meet the king, who made his state entry at the

[1] Nardi, Parenti, Cerretani, Rinuccini, &c.
[2] Now known as the Riccardi Palace in Via Cavour.

twenty-first hour of the day.[1] The members of the
Signory then rose and advanced towards him to pay their
respects, while Messer Luca Corsini, being deputed to that
office, stood forth to read a written address. But just at
that moment rain began to fall, the horses grew restless
and hustled against one another, and the whole ceremony
was thrown into confusion. Only Messer Francesco
Gaddi, one of the officers of the palace, had sufficient
presence of mind to press his way through the throng and
make a short speech suited to the occasion in French ;
after which the king moved forward under a rich canopy.[2]
The monarch's appearance was in strange contrast
with that of the numerous and powerful army behind
him. He seemed almost a monster, with his enormous
head, long nose, wide, gaping mouth, big, white, purblind
eyes, very diminutive body, extraordinarily thin legs, and
misshapen feet. He was clad in black velvet, and a
mantle of gold brocade ; bestrode a tall and very beautiful
charger, and entered the city riding with his lance levelled—
a martial attitude then considered as a sign of conquest.
All this rendered the meanness of his person the more gro-
tesquely conspicuous. By his side rode the haughty Cardinal
of St. Piero in Vincoli, the Cardinal of St. Malò, and a few
marshals. At their heels came the royal body-guard of
100 bowmen, composed of the finest young men in France,
and then 200 French knights marching on foot with
splendid dresses and equipments. These were followed
by the Swiss vanguard, resplendent and parti-coloured,
bearing halberds of burnished steel, and with rich waving
plumes on their officers' helmets. The faces of these
men expressed the mountaineer spirit of daring and the
proud consciousness of being the first infantry in Europe ;

[1] *I.e.*, about two o'clock in the afternoon.
[2] Gaddi, " Priorista," in the "Archivio Storico Italiano," vol. iv. part ii.
p. 42.

while the greater part of them had scornfully thrown aside the cuirass, preferring to fight with their chests bared. The centre consisted of Gascon infantry, small, light, agile men, whose numbers seemed to multiply as the army advanced. But the grandest sight was the cavalry, comprising the flower of the French aristocracy, and displaying finely-wrought weapons, mantles of gorgeous brocade, velvet banners embroidered with gold, chains of gold, and other precious ornaments. The cuirassiers had a terrible aspect, for their horses seemed like monsters with their cropped tails and ears. The archers were men of extraordinary height, armed with very long wooden bows ; they came from Scotland and other northern countries, and—in the words of a contemporary historian— *seemed to be beast-like men (parevano nomini bestiali)*.[1]

This well-ordered and disciplined army, composed of so many different nationalities, with such varied attire and strange weapons, was as new and amazing a sight to Florence as to almost all Italy, where no standing armies were as yet in existence, and mercenaries the only soldiery known. It is impossible to give the number of the forces accompanying the king to Florence ; for his artillery were marching towards Rome by another route, he had left garrisons in many strongholds, and sent on another body of men by Romagna. Gaddi,[2] who witnessed the entrance of the French, says that their numbers amounted to

[1] Cerretani, "Storia di Firenza," at sheet 201, Parenti ; Gaddi, Nardi. See also Albèri, " Relazioni degli Ambasciatori Veneti," vol iv. p. 16. In the midst of the terror spread by this army it was the theme of many satirical remarks, especially from the Venetians, whose pride was always the greatest. Marin Sanudo tells us—in his " Spedizione" di Carlo VIII. in Italia," p. 134—that the French weapons seemed " better suited for splitting doors than for fighting." And, at the head of all the soldiers, he adds, there marched " a monster of a man (*omaccione*) with a polished sword like a spit for roast pork, and then four big drums played with both hands, and accompanied by two pipes, making an infernal noise, such as one hears at a fair."

[2] Gaddi, " Priorista."

12,000 ; Rinuccini, who was also present, estimated them at a lower figure ; others at a higher. In any case the city and suburbs were crammed with them.

The procession marched over the Ponte Vecchio (Old Bridge), which was gay with festive decorations, and sounds of music, wound across the Piazza amid a crowd of triumphal cars, statues, &c., and, passing the Canto dei Pazzi, made the tour of the Cathedral Square, and halted before the great door of the church.[1] The people shouted the name of France with cries of applause, but the king only smiled inanely and stammered some inappropriate words in Italian. Entering the Duomo, he was met by the Signory, who, to avoid the pressure of the armed host, had been obliged to come round by the back streets. After joining in prayers with their royal guest, they escorted him to the sumptuous palace of the Medici, and the soldiers dispersed to their quarters. That night and the next the whole city was a blaze of illuminations ; the intervening day was devoted to feasting and amusements, and then the terms of the treaty began to be discussed.

The arbiters or syndics chosen by the Signory for this purpose were : Messer Guidantonio Vespucci, Messer Domenico Bonsi, Francesco Valori, and Piero Capponi— all citizens of the highest reputation. Vespucci was thoroughly versed in law and the management of State affairs ; Bonsi had won honourable distinction in many embassies ; Valori, afterwards entitled the *Florentine Cato,* had become, as we have seen, one of the leaders of the

---

[1] This narrative is mainly derived from the accounts of Gaddi and Rinuccini, who were spectators of the king's entrance. Cerretani supplies a very minute description of the French army ; and Nardi, Parenti. Guicciardini, Sanudo, and Commines all give many particulars of it. Among modern writers we may mention Sismondi, " Hist. des Répub. Ital." and " Histoire des Français " ; and Michelet, " Renaissance." De Cherrier's work is more recent, but contains little fresh information.

people ; and Capponi, to whom we have so frequently referred, was in truth a man of extraordinary gifts. He was born in 1447, of an old Florentine stock that had always been friendly to freedom and distinguished for many noble deeds. His father had trained him to commerce, recommending him to keep out of politics, now that the times were going badly, and accordingly Piero devoted himself so energetically to trade, that many accused him of being over greedy of gain. When about thirty years of age, Lorenzo de' Medici, who knew how to turn capable citizens to account, offered him several missions, which he willingly undertook and accomplished with admirable skill. On these occasions Capponi showed himself possessed of a singular insight into character, and a special power of gaining influence over the potentates with whom he had to deal, and more especially over those who prided themselves on their reticence and impenetrability. In fact Ferdinand and Alphonso of Naples frequently trusted to his advice rather than to that of their own generals and ministers. Capponi had done well in exchanging commerce for diplomacy, but he did still better in forsaking the latter for the business of war, and then realized that his true mission was neither to sit in a banking office, nor negotiate treaties, but rather to fight, sword in hand. His vocation was revealed to him by chance. He was acting as Commissary of the Republic to Alphonso of Aragon's camp when this monarch was marching to the assistance of the Duke of Ferrara. The Neapolitan army being defeated by the Papal forces, Alphonso was so deeply discomfited that he would have certainly ordered a retreat had not Capponi contrived to infuse fresh courage both in him and his men. And adding deeds to his words, the Florentine led the men into action in so gallant a way as to prove to himself that he was a good soldier, and not only capable of facing the enemy, but of making an excellent leader to all brave enough to follow him. [1] From that day he was always to be seen in the thickest of the fight, and the Republic, delighted to possess so valiant a captain, continually charged him with the most difficult enterprises. And the harder the task, the more readily Capponi assumed it, always acting both as soldier and commander — a fatal readiness that afterwards led to his death.

He had always been one of the most powerful men in Florence, and, from love of activity, frequently given his services to Lorenzo the Magnificent. But when that prince was dead, and Piero reigning in his place, Capponi, as we have seen, soon lost patience with the latter's feeble, vacillating, and undignified rule, and, declaring himself an irreconcilable foe to the Medici, was one of those who did most to drive them from Florence. He was accordingly held in the highest estimation by the people, and the safety of the whole Republic was now entrusted, almost exclusively, to him. No better man could have been found to deal with Charles, and, if necessary, firmly resist him. Having been sent on several missions to France, he had learnt to understand the national character, and was accustomed to say : " When our Italians have once smelt the French, they will cease to have so great a fear of them." [2] Hence the whole weight of these grave and difficult negotiations naturally fell upon his shoulders, and the knowledge that the fate

---

[1] This circumstance, while doing much honour to Capponi, is an additional proof of the miserable state to which the art of war in Italy had then been reduced. Acciaioli, "Vita di Piero Capponi," in the " Archivio Storico Italiano," vol. iv. part ii.

[2] *Vide* Capponi's Letters given in the appendix to the "Vita di Capponi," quoted above, p. 55. See also the fine remarks of Marquis Gino Capponi on the same subject in the first volume of the " Archivio Storico Italiano," p. 348 and fol.

of the entire nation was in his hands, only swelled his courage and raised him, as it were, above himself.

Meanwhile the mother and wife of Piero de' Medici had gained the ear of the king and his advisers, and, in the words of the chronicler, "gave, and promised, and offered that if Piero could succeed in returning, he would share the government with the French."[1] These solicitations inclined the monarch still more in favour of the Medici, and the syndics of the Republic were now treated with great haughtiness. Charles gave them audience surrounded by his generals, advanced new and more exorbitant demands, and declared, among other things, that he had come to the city as a conqueror, having entered with levelled lance ! These speeches only served to exasperate the people against him, without leading to any conclusion, and matters dragged on from bad to worse. When at last the king ventured to say a few words in Piero's favour to the syndics, the faces of the Republicans grew very stern, and there was a speedy change in the aspect of the city. The Signory instantly met in council at the palace, summoned the principal citizens, and informing them of the public danger, bade them make ready to fly to arms, and head the people at the first peal of the tower bell. Rumours of the expected crisis were already afloat ; consequently Florentines and French began to exchange defiant glances and insulting words, and even occasionally came to blows.

One day a quarrel of this kind led to a serious disturbance. A band of French soldiers were seen going about the city dragging some Italian prisoners of war bound with ropes, whom they had taken in Lunigiana, forcing them to beg money in the streets to pay their ransom, and threatening to kill them if they did not obtain enough. The Florentines were so enraged by this barbarous sight,

---

[1] Parenti, " Storia," MS., at sheet 203.

that some of the more daring spirits cut the cords and
allowed the prisoners to escape. The French were furious,
and vainly tried to recapture their victims. A fight
ensued, the citizens stood their ground, and recruits
poured in from all sides to swell the fray. The Swiss,
hearing of the riot, thought that the king's safety was
threatened, and made a rush towards his palace ; but their
passage was barred in Borgo Ognisanti, and on trying to
force their way through, they were assailed by such a hail-
storm of stones from the windows that they were driven to
retreat. The struggle went on for an hour, but then some
of the royal officers and many of the principal citizens
came to quell the disturbance by the Signory's command.
However, this was a severe lesson for the French ; their
pride was lowered, and they realized that Florence was not
to be conquered by entering it *chalk in hand and lance to
hip*.[1] A city, that at the first stroke of the alarm bell,
could be converted into a menacing stronghold, that bar-
ricaded its streets, and rained down stones, fire and all
sorts of projectiles from its windows, was a place of
mystery and terror even for the haughty Swiss infantry,
who were dismayed by seeing how easily an army could
be destroyed in those narrow streets.[2]

Thereupon the Signory took advantage of the opportunity, and, with the aid of many of the foreign ambassadors, at
last succeeded in bringing the king to a more reasonable
frame of mind. Some of his extravagant pretensions were
abated ; he said nothing more of Piero or the *conquered
city*, and almost all the terms of the treaty were fixed.

[1] It was in these terms that the king and his officers boasted that they
were masters of Florence. As we have seen, the French made chalk
marks on the houses they intended to occupy.

[2] *Vide* the descriptions of this riot given by Cerretani and Parenti.
Cerretani (MS., loc. cit., sheet 211) concludes his narrative of the event
in the following words : "A most courageous defence was made, the
which inspired no little fear in the French ; for the greater part of them,
armed soldiers though they were, gathered together trembling like women."

THE MEDICI PALACE—NOW PALAZZO RICCARDI—WHERE THE TREATY WITH
FLORENCE WAS SIGNED.

The king was to receive the title of Protector of the liberty of Florence, and have the right to hold the fortresses for two years, on condition that he restored them sooner, should the war be ended before that date. The Florentines also agreed to pay him a large sum of money ; but fresh dissensions then arose as to its amount. Charles VIII. having been much impressed by the lavish promises of Piero de' Medici and his kindred, demanded a far larger sum than the Republic was able to pay, without most unjustly burdening all the citizens. Thus there was again much exasperation on either side, and messengers were continually sent backwards and forwards between the Signory and the king, without anything being settled. Charles clung obstinately to his demands, and Capponi found it very difficult to control his temper and restrain his indignation. At last the monarch ordered his secretary to read his *ultimatum,* saying that he would yield no more upon any point. Naturally the syndics again refused to accept it ; whereupon the king turned on them in great fury and exclaimed, in a threatening tone : " Then we will sound our trumpets." At this Capponi became red as fire, and, snatching the paper from the secretary's hand, tore it in the king's face, and made his celebrated reply : " And we will ring our bells."[1] And thanks to the energy of his tone, the agreement was signed and sealed in a few hours, after so much entreaty and so many days of negotiation had been devoted to it in vain.[2]

[1] The historian, Marquis Gino Capponi, says, in reference to Capponi's reply : " Fortune enabled him to seize one of the rare moments which only come once in a lifetime (" Archivio Storico Italiano," vol. i. p. 361.) *Vide* Cerretani, Parenti, Guicciardini, Nardi, Machiavelli ; and the before quoted " Vita di P. Capponi."

[2] Machiavelli's " Decennali " contains some well-known lines on this theme :—

> Lo strepito dell' armi e de' cavalli
> Non potè far che non fosse sentita
> La voce d'un Cappon fra cento Galli.

(Even the clash of arms and stamping of steeds could not drown the crow of a Capon among a hundred cocks.)

The terms of the treaty stood as follows :—That there should be a good and faithful friendship between the Republic and the king ; that their subjects should have reciprocal protection ; that the king should receive the title of Restorer and Protector of the liberty of Florence ; that he should be paid 120,000 florins in three instalments ; that he was not to retain the fortresses for more than two years ;. and if the Neapolitan expedition finished before that date, he was then to give them up without delay ; that the Pisans were to receive pardon as soon as they should resume their allegiance to Florence. It was also stipulated that the decree, putting a price on the heads of the Medici, should be revoked, but that the estates of Giuliano and Cardinal Giovanni were to remain confiscated until all Piero's debts had been paid, and that the said Piero was to remain banished to a distance of 200 miles, and his brothers, of 100 from the Tuscan border. After the agreement had been drawn up in regular official form, the contracting parties met in the Duomo to swear to the observance of all its clauses, and in the evening there was a general illumination of the city, although the people gave no signs of their previous goodwill towards. the King.[1]

But no sooner was one difficulty disposed of, than another arose. When all was concluded Charles relapsed into his normal state of inertia, and showed no disposition to depart. The city was thronged by the French quartered in the houses, and the Italian soldiery hidden on all sides; the shops were shut up and all traffic suspended ;. everything was in a state of uncertainty and disorder, and the continual quarrels between the natives and the foreigner might at any moment provoke the most serious

[1] The treaty between Charles VIII. and the Republic was published in the first volume of the " Arch. Stor. Ital.," with some interesting remarks by Marquis Gino Capponi.

complications. There were perpetual robberies and murders by night—a most unusual state of things for Florence ; and the people seemed to be on the verge of revolt at the least provocation. Thus matters went on from day to day, and consequently all honest citizens vainly did their utmost to hasten the king's departure. And the universal suspense was heightened by the impossibility of finding any way of forcing him to a decision.

At last another appeal was made to Savonarola, who was exerting all his influence to keep the people quiet, and whose peaceful admonitions during this period of danger and confusion had been no less efficacious than the heroic defiance of Piero Capponi. The Friar's sermons at this time were always directed to the general welfare. He exhorted the citizens " to lay aside their animosities and ambitions ; to attend the councils at the palace in a righteous spirit, and with a view, not to their personal interest, but to the general good, and with the firm resolve to promote the unity and concord of their city. Then, indeed, would they be acceptable in the Lord's sight." [1] He addressed himself to every class of the people in turn, proving to all that it would be to their own advantage, both in this life and the next, to labour for the defence of liberty and the establishment of union and concord. When asked to seek

[1] " Prediche sopra Aggeo," before quoted. Venice, 1544. But, as in most of the Venetian editions of Savonarola's works, there are many blunders in this collection of sermons. For instance, sermon iv. is said to have been delivered after the expulsion of the Medici, and sermon v. after the Friar's return from Pisa. This has led several biographers to believe that Savonarola's journey from Florence to Pisa was made after the Medici had been driven out. But by careful perusal and by noticing that sermons i., ii., and iii. were preached on the 1st, 2nd, and 6th November, it will be ascertained that No. iv. is the sermon preached after Savonarola's return from Pisa, and that he was not in Florence when the Medici were expelled. This too is clearly proved by the chroniclers who give us the dates of the election of the ambassadors and of the day of their departure. And there are official documents to prove the accuracy of these dates,

the king and endeavour to persuade him to leave, he cheerfully undertook the task and hastened to the royal abode. The officers and lords in attendance were at first inclined to refuse him admittance, fearing that his visit might defeat their plan of pillaging the treasures of this sumptuous palace. But remembering the veneration in which the Friar was held by the king, they dared not refuse his demand and allowed him to pass. Charles, surrounded by his Barons, received him very graciously, and Savonarola went straight to the point by saying :— " Most Christian Prince, thy stay here is causing great injury both to our city and thine own enterprise. Thou losest time, forgetful of the duty imposed on thee by Providence, and to the serious hurt of thy spiritual welfare and worldly fame. Hearken now to the voice of God's servant ! Pursue thy journey without delay. Seek not to bring ruin on this city and thereby rouse the anger of the Lord against thee." [1]

So, at last, on the 28th November, at the twenty-second hour of the day, the king departed with his army, leaving the people of Florence very badly disposed towards him. Among their many just causes of complaint was the sack of the splendid palace in which he had been so liberally and trustfully entertained. Nor were common soldiers and inferior officers alone concerned in this robbery ; the hands of generals and barons were equally busy, and the king himself carried off objects of the greatest value : among other things a precious *intaglio* representing a unicorn, estimated by Commines to be worth about seven thousand ducats. With such an example set them by their sovereign, it may be easily imagined how the others behaved ; and Commines himself tells us that " they shamelessly

---

[1] These facts have been repeatedly narrated by Savonarola himself, as well as by his biographers. *Vide* sermon xxvi., *sopra Michea* (on Micah), delivered the 28th October, 1496.

took possession of everything that tempted their greed."[1]
Thus the rich and marvellous collections formed by the
Medici were all lost, excepting what had been placed in
safety at St. Mark's, for the few things left behind by the
French were so much damaged that they had to be sold.[2]
Nevertheless the inhabitants were so rejoiced to be finally
rid of their dangerous guests, that no one mourned over
these thefts. On the contrary, public thanksgivings were
offered up in the churches, the people went about the
streets with their old gaiety and lightheartedness, and
the authorities began to take measures to provide for the
urgent necessities of the new Republic.

During this interval the aspect of Florentine affairs had
entirely changed. The partisans of the Medici had disappeared from the city as if by magic ; the popular party
ruled over everything, and Savonarola ruled the will of
the whole population. He was unanimously declared to
have been a true prophet of all that had occurred, the
only man who had succeeded in controlling the king's
conduct on his entry into Florence, the only man who
had induced him to depart : accordingly all hung on
Savonarola's lips for counsel, aid, and direction as to their
future proceedings. And as though the men of the old
State saw the need of effacing themselves to make way for
new blood, several prominent representatives and friends
of the Medici House died during this period. Angelo
Poliziano had passed away this year, on the 24th September,
" loaded with as much infamy and public opprobrium as a
man could well bear."[3] He was accused of numberless
vices and unlimited profligacy ; but the chief cause of all
the hatred lavished on him was the general detestation
already felt for Piero de' Medici, the approach of his

---

[1] Commines, "Memoires," liv. viii. chap ix.
[2] Ibid. and Sismondi, "Hist. des Rép. Ital.," chap. xciii.
[3] Parenti, "Storia Fiorentina," MS. cit., loc. cit., sheet 479.

downfall and that of all his adherents.[1] Nor was the public rancour at all softened by the knowledge that the last utterances of the illustrious poet and learned scholar had been the words of a penitent Christian. He had requested that his body should be clothed in the Dominican habit and interred in the church of St. Mark, and there his ashes repose beside the remains of Giovanni Pico della Mirandola, who expired on the very day of Charles VIII.'s entry into Florence.[2] Pico had long entertained a desire to join the fraternity of St. Mark's, but delaying too long to carry out his intent, was surprised by death at the early age of thirty-two years.[3] On his death-bed he,

[1] "The vituperation poured upon him (Poliziano) was caused less by his vices than by the hatred Piero de' Medici had excited in our city " (Parenti, loc. cit.).

[2] These are the inscriptions to be found in the Church of St. Mark :

"D.M.S.
Johannes iacet hic Mirandula cætera norũt
Et Tagus et Ganges forsan et Antipodes
Ob. an. Sal. MCCCCLXXXXIIII. vix. an. xxxii.

Hieronimus Benivienius ne disiunctus post
Mortem locus ossa separet quor. animas
In vita coniunxit amor hac humo
Supposita poni curavit ,
Ob. an. MDXXXXII. vix. an. lxxxix. Mens. vi."

Below this tablet is the one dedicated to Poliziano :

"Politianus
In hoc tumulo iacet
Angelus unum
Qui caput et linguas
Res nova tres habuit
Obiit an. MCCCCLXXXXIV.
Sep. xxiv.—Aetatis
XL."

[3] Pico's long hesitation led Savonarola to doubt for a moment whether his friend could be saved, since he had apparently resisted the call vouchsafed him by the Lord. But the Friar afterwards had a vision in which he beheld Pico borne up to heaven by angels. Thereupon he felt assured that his friend was in Purgatory, and stated his belief to the people from the pulpit. *Vide* the conclusion of sermon vi. in the "Prediche sopra Aggeo."

too, had besought Savonarola to allow him to be buried in the robe he had yearned to wear.

The end of these two celebrated Italians recalled to mind the last hours and last confession of Lorenzo the Magnificent, and was by many regarded as a sign that the Medicean adherents had been unwilling to pass away without acknowledging their crimes, without asking pardon from the people whom they had so deeply oppressed, and from the Friar, who was, as it were, the people's best representative. It was certainly remarkable that all these men should turn to the Convent of St. Mark, whence had issued the first cry of liberty, and the first sign of war against the tyranny of the Medici.

CHAPTER IV.

(December, 1494.)

IT had always been the old custom in
Florence to accomplish changes of
government by means of *Parlamenti*.
When the great bell rang the summons
to Parlamento, the people assembled,
unarmed, on the Piazza, which was
guarded by the armed attendants of the Signory. Then
the members of the Signory appeared on the balcony [1]
(ringhiera) in front of the palace, and asked the right
of Balìa for themselves or their friends. The Balìa really
signified *carte blanche* to do as they chose, for it was a
species of dictatorship, conferred either for months or for
years ; it might be frequently renewed, and gave its
holders the power of electing magistrates, or of even
changing the form of government. In the latter case
the population was again summoned to *Parlamento*, and
deceived by this false show of liberty, always proved a

---

[1] The *ringhiera* was on the platform attached to the façade of the
palace, in the place where the Marzocco now stands, beside the outer
steps.

docile instrument in the hands of ambitious and powerful citizens, and was always eager to applaud any proposal for Balìa, in the belief that it was thus giving a proof of its independence at the very moment that it was rivetting its bonds. This was the origin of the ancient Florentine proverb: " *Chi disse Parlamento, disse guastamento* " (To speak of Parliament was to speak of detriment). It was by the help of *Balìe* and *Parlamenti* that the Albizzi so long dominated Florence, and the tyranny of the Medici had been carried on by the same means. Nevertheless, so strong was the force of custom, that on December 2nd, 1494, a few days after the French had gone, the great bell of the palace rang forth a summons to Parlamento. The armed servants of the Signory guarded all the issues of the square, and the people, highly satisfied with their own importance, assembled *in the old way*, *i.e.*, ranged in different *Compagnie*, each under its own gonfaloniere.[1] Then the Signory read out a *provvisione* (proposal), in which they begged for authorization to name twenty *Accoppiatori* with the *Balìa*, or right of electing the Signory and all the principal magistrates for the term of one year. These Accoppiatori were authorized, subject to certain rules and restrictions, to nominate some of their own number to all the offices of State, including that of Gonfalonier of Justice.[2] The multitude, almost crazed

---

[1] Parenti, "Storia di Firenze" (Cod. orig. cit.), sheet 209ᵗ.

[2] This law, after treating of the election of the *Accoppiatori*, goes on to say : "The which Twenty thus elected, shall be held as, and to be Accoppiatori for one year from the present time. And during the said year they shall have authority to elect (*imborsare*) the Signory, the Gonfalonier of Justice, and their Notary. . . ." Archivio Fiorentino, "Consigli Maggiori, Provvisioni, Registri," vol. clxxxvi, at sheet 1 and fòl.

Rinuccini, "Ricordi Storici," p. clv., says : "The Signory appeared in the Ringhiera, and there had a petition read aloud, asking, among other clauses, that the *Otto di Balìa* should be elected by open choice (*a mano*) once for all ; and that the election to the three chief offices should also be made at the free pleasure of the Twenty Accoppiatori for the term of one year ; and that of the *Dieci di libertà e pace* for the term of six

with delight, burst into shouts of applause ; and in this way the new government, known as that of The Twenty, came into existence.

In past times the government of the Florentine Republic was vested in eight Priors and a Gonfalonier of Justice, who constituted the supreme magistracy or Signoria, and were changed every two months. The functions of the sixteen Gonfaloniers of the Companies, under whom, at one time, all arm-bearing citizens were enrolled, together with the twelve *Buoni Uomini* (*Worthies*), were afterwards reduced to acting as an escort for the Signory ; the whole number together constituted the Collegii (Colleges), and these were also designated the Three Higher Offices. Then came the Ten of War (*Dieci di Guerra*), elected every six months, and the Eight of Guard and Custody (*Otto di guardia e balìa*), whose chief duty was to act as a tribunal for criminal and political cases, and who were elected every four months. Lastly, there were the two Councils or Assemblies of the People and the Commune, dating from the time when the city was divided into the people proper and the powerful

months ; and that the *Otto di guardia e balìa*, now in office, should be superseded."

Nardi, vol. i. p. 60, gives almost identical details. Here it may be useful to explain the terms—*imborsare, tenere le borse serrate, tenere le borse aperte*, &c.—so frequently met with in all accounts of the Florentine Republic. Two *borse* or purses were generally provided in the election of the principal officers of the State. One of these *borse* was used by the Greater Guilds (*Arti Maggiori*), the other by the Lesser Guilds (*Arti Minori*), to hold the names of the different candidates proposed for office (*a sedere*). The process of drawing the names being termed *lo squittinio*, the candidates thus drawn were called *squittinati* or *imborsati*. The election might be for six months, one year, or even for a longer period. At every election of magistrates the names of the candidates were drawn by lot from the purses, and this was termed an election by closed purses (*tenere le borse serrate*) ; but if it was decided that the Accoppiatori were to have the right of choosing at their own pleasure any of the names contained in the purses, instead of choosing them by lot, this was called an election by open purses, or by purses in hand (*tenere le borse aperte, le borse a mano*).

citizens (potenti), who claimed for themselves the special right of constituting the Commune. These Councils were charged with the enactment of laws and the election of magistrates, and the latter duty was considered to be the highest function of government and chief safeguard of liberty.[1] When the Medici began to take the lead in Florence they levelled all distinctions between the different orders of citizens, subjecting all alike to their tyranny. Thus the two Councils of the People and the Commune lost all their special functions, but nevertheless still continued to hold meetings, both as a matter of form, and because their new masters recognized that the people were more tenacious of nominal rights than of real liberty. Lorenzo the Magnificent adhered to the same policy and sanctioned both the Assemblies ; but, at the same time, created another Council, known as the Seventy, solely composed of his own partizans. By transferring to this body the chief functions of the old Councils, especially the election of the magistrates, he thus succeeded in becoming master of the Republic.[2]

But now, when the general Parliament was convoked, all the old institutions were left intact, the Council of Seventy alone being abolished, and its functions transferred to the Twenty Accoppiatori ; so that although persons and names were altered, there was little real change in the form of government. The magistrates' duties were then so imperfectly defined that each one of them believed himself omnipotent. The real administration of the State

[1] *Vide* Giannotti, " Della Repubblica Fiorentina " ; Guicciardini, " Del Reggimento di Firenze," vol. ii. of the " Opere inedite" ; our own articles on the same subject in the " Politecnico" of Milan (March, 1866, and following numbers), and the " Nuova Antologia " (July, 1869) ; and particularly the original *Statuti* and *Provvisioni*, which alone can give the reader an exact idea of these imperfectly investigated details.

[2] The Marquis Gino Capponi published the law by which Lorenzo called this Council into existence, with an explanation of the full importance of this tyrannical institution. *Vide* " Arch. Stor. It.," vol. i.

was entirely in the hands of the Signory. They passed
the laws, despatched ambassadors, declared war, and frequently acted as a tribunal of justice, pronouncing sentences of death and confiscation. Besides, in addition
to· the great authority conferred upon them by their
statutes, they could always find special means of extending
their rights.[1] But some check was put upon their arbitrary power by their term of office being limited to two
months ; and accordingly the members of the Signory had
practically less authority than their electors, since, whereas
they were displaced at the end of this short period, the
latter preserved the direction of State affairs, if not permanently, at least for many years.[2] Lorenzo had skilfully
carried out this plan by means of his Council of Seventy,
and every one expected that the people would be equally
successful with the help of the Twenty.

But, as was soon perceived, the course of events by no
means fulfilled these expectations. The Republic was in
the hands of the Accoppiatori, but the wheels of the State
stood still, and although the Accoppiatori had nominal
authority over all things, they were practically masters of
none. The Medici, Albizzi, and other powerful families,
surrounded by friends of great wealth and enormous
prestige, had found it possible to rule the city on this
plan ; but what could be done by twenty citizens of
various conditions, views, and modes of thought, many
of whom moreover were quite inexperienced in State
affairs ? So, notwithstanding their legal authority, they
soon found that they had neither the capacity nor the
strength to govern, and their chief source of weakness
was the want of harmony among themselves. The first

---

[1] Guicciardini, in his " Reggimento di Firenze " (p. 282 and fol.),
makes admirable remark on this subject ; so, too, Giannotti in his
"Della Repubblica Fiorentina."

[2] Guicciardini, *ibid.;* Giannotti, *ibid.*

instance of this was given when they had to elect the Gonfalonier. None of their candidates obtained more than three votes, so that at last, to their great disgrace, the Accoppiatori decided to choose the first who obtained a majority, even if less than the number prescribed by law.[1]

Thus the old custom of *Parlamenti* quickly gave birth to the old disturbances, and before the new Government had fairly begun, all were proposing to change it. Every one recognized the folly of hoping to resuscitate the Republic by means of old institutions which had been reduced by the Medici to mere phantoms. It was clear that only a corpse had been placed in the hands of the Accoppiatori, and accordingly they could not be expected to breathe fresh life into it. Therefore the Florentines began to cogitate some radical change and reconstruction of the Government ; but on setting to work they found that the stringency of their need greatly increased the difficulties of the task. For they were harassed on all sides by new and unexpected obstacles.

The rebellion of Pisa was daily assuming graver proportions. In that city the pressure of danger had produced concord : a Government had been speedily constituted ; men, arms, and money collected ; and all the citizens were inspired by an ardent zeal for liberty and independence. The rest of the Florentine territory was in a very tottering condition. Arezzo and Montepulciano, encouraged by the example of Pisa and by money and advice from Siena, had already risen in revolt, and other cities and towns were preparing to do the same. Thus Florence was hard-pressed to meet the expenses of three wars, and fulfil its engagements to the French king, who was already clamouring to be paid in advance. Soldiers had to be hired, recruits levied, captains engaged, and new and heavier taxes imposed on the already over-

[1] Nardi, " Istorie di Firenze," vol. i. p. 82.

burdened people. Even a strong and united Government would have found it difficult to meet all these demands, and the present one was so weak and disunited that some change was imperatively required.

Unfortunately, during the sixty years which had elapsed since the return of Cosimo de' Medici, the Florentine citizens had entirely lost their former marvellous political aptitude for framing new laws and institutions, so that now, when suddenly emancipated and their own masters, they seemed only confused and bewildered by their independence. There was no longer, as in the days of the Albizzi, a patrician class fitted to take the lead in public affairs. Under the Medici, the only privilege allowed to the wealthier citizens had been that of enjoying their riches ; so that they had been content to live at ease, filling what public offices were to be obtained by favour, and going through life without any experience of, or liking for, business of the State. As for the lower classes, they were thoroughly disorganized. The ancient trade associations, or guilds, once the centres of industrial and political life, whose workshops had supplied the enormous wealth expended on long and difficult wars, and which had formed the arena wherein artizans had been trained in politics by their struggles among themselves, and learnt the art of giving good counsel and brave service to the State—all these ancient associations now existed only in name. The multitude had no longer a corporate existence, nor any confidence in itself. Therefore the organization of a new Government was a task of exceeding difficulty, not only because the city was burdened with wars, the old institutions devoid of vitality, and the people of political training ; but likewise because none of the ancient Republican forms was at all suited to the new state of things.

And, besides lacking the necessary aptitude, the people

had no leaders to guide it in the hard and important enterprise of framing a new constitution. We have seen that
Francesco Valori was able to sway the mob and lead it on
to expel the Medici ; but although incomparably well
fitted for a street orator, he was disqualified for any high
position in the State by his impetuous temper and want of
self-control. We have seen how Piero Capponi won
immortality by his defiance of the sovereign and captains
of France, but he also lacked statesmanlike patience in
debate. At moments when it was best to cut short discussion by grasping the sword, Piero Capponi was in his
true element, but to sit quietly in cloak and hood, through
lengthy, hair-splitting debates, was simply unendurable to
him. He was far more at ease in his armour, exposed to
sunshine or storm or the enemy's shots. In fact his most
earnest desire was to be sent to the camp before Pisa, and
to open the campaign without delay.

In this dire emergency Florence knew not in whom to
trust, nor was it easy to hope that new men might be
found to meet the occasion. For, as we have already
shown, there had been sixty years of tyranny, and during
two generations men had lost all familiarity with public
affairs. Nevertheless, as there is always some compen-
sation for every ill, a school of Italian politicians was
already rising up in Florence, destined to give good
fruit in Niccolò Machiavelli, Francesco Guicciardini, and
Donato Giannotti, and these men were all in their first
youth at the moment when their country regained its
freedom. So great was the inborn love of liberty distinguishing the Florentines, that from the moment Republican
institutions were destroyed, they began to discuss Government affairs, and created the science of statesmanship.
On opening their works we find that they always begin by
stating that man's greatest happiness on earth consists in
having a share in the government of his country, and that

when deprived of this by tyranny, his sole resource is to
seek happiness in intellectual pursuits, wait for better
times, and accumulate experience for the benefit of posterity.   But this budding science could offer no efficacious
remedy for the load of ills then burdening the city.   As
yet none of the new school of thinkers had attained
sufficient eminence to be able to impose his will upon the
people ; and further, the youths of most talent, having
nearly all led a lonely student life, had no practical knowledge of politics, were unknown to the crowd, and had no
chance of attracting notice in times of disturbance when
the world is to the strong.   Nevertheless, it was during
this revolution that their minds were trained and their
theories shaped.   And as their ideas then began to spread
and prevail, it is important for us to examine their ground-
work and substance.

Modern political science is based upon general principles ; while the modern art of government consists in
an endeavour to obtain the most equal division of power,
the soundest administration of justice, the greatest official
independence, and the widest extension of individual
liberty.   But at the close of the fifteenth century Italian
political science was little more than a studious analysis
of the passions of mankind.   Starting from the sole pre-
mise that to govern was the greatest happiness and highest
ambition of man, it was naturally concluded that all men
must be ambitious of power, and every one aspire to grasp
the reins of government in his own country, to the ex-
clusion and injury of his fellow-citizens.   This state of
things necessarily led to continual danger of tyranny ;
and, in fact, almost all the Italian States had fallen a prey
to despotism.   In those days, when Italian politicians were
asked to define a perfect form of government, they invariably replied, " That in which tyranny is impossible."
But what is the form of government under which tyranny

is impossible ? That which is so ordered as to satisfy the aspirations of all classes of citizens at one and the same time. In every city, they said, there will always be a few men eager to hold command over the rest ; patricians (ottimati) who will always strive for honours, and people for freedom.[1] Hence, all endeavoured to find some mixed form of government, an amalgamation of the monarchical, aristocratic, and democratic elements, fitted to satisfy alike the cravings of ambitious leaders, patricians, and people. This, they judged, was the only means by which liberty could be firmly established.

On passing from theory to practice, Florentine politicians always took Venice as their model. This was the only Government in Italy that had survived the general ruin ; the only Government that had increased its power and prestige without falling under the sway of a despot. Consequently Florence, like the other extinguished Italian Republics, longed to be revived in the form of the Venetian commonwealth, that seemed to them the perfection of government. And, in fact, on comparing the interminable vicissitudes of the Florentine State with the strict and lasting repose of the Venetian lagoons, the same impression was produced that is felt by ourselves when comparing the political state of France with that of England. But in planning to bestow the Venetian form of government upon Florence, the citizens were met by the same difficulties which the French would have to face if they attempted to adopt the English constitution. From the remotest times Venice had possessed a strong and powerful aristocracy ; but this order having long dis-

---

[1] Giannotti gives a minute exposition of this theory as the basis of his own political creed. It is also repeated in Machiavelli and Guicciardini, although presented by these authors in a new and original shape. It frequently occurs in the writings and speeches of Savonarola's contemporaries, and was afterwards lucidly formulated by Savonarola in his " Trattato circa il Reggimento e Governo della città di Firenze."

appeared in Florence, there now seemed to be no alter-
native save between absolute tyranny or equally absolute
anarchy.   Nevertheless there was a general desire to introduce some modified form of the Venetian government ;
some wished to establish it on a wider, some on a narrower
basis ; but every one agreed that of all models this was the
best and most practicable.   And wherever men gathered
together in Florence, in the streets, or under the arcades,
this was the main theme of discourse and argument.

But while the scheme remained in the abstract, and as a
mere topic of street talk, it was as fruitless as steering a
vessel without a compass.   Some one was needed to stand
forth in the councils of the State to guide and persuade
his colleagues, and above all to win the favour of the
Twenty Accoppiatori, without whose consent no change
could well be effected.   In this condition of affairs, when
men of learning had little practical experience, and men of
action little prudence or ability, another order of citizens
began to rise into notice.   This was the legal class, in
whose hands fortune often places the helm of the State
during a nation's passage from servitude to freedom.
Owing to their professional training and knowledge of
legal matters, lawyers are commonly credited with all the
doctrine and practice required to cope with similar emergencies ; nor have the painful results of past experience
availed to teach the world that no nation has ever been
enabled to found a stable constitution by the help of that
class.

Accordingly, after long hesitation in the palace councils,
the measures proposed by Messer Guidantonio Vespucci
and Messer Paolo Antonio Soderini, both doctors of law,
finally carried the day.   Soderini belonged to the popular
party, and having long been ambassador to Venice, had
enjoyed special opportunities of gaining a thorough
acquaintance with its method of government.   He

proposed, therefore, to replace the two Councils of the People and the Commune by one greater General Council of the People, similar to the Grand Council of Venice, for the purpose of electing magistrates and passing laws ; and one Lesser Council, composed of *ottimati*, or men of greater weight and experience on the pattern of the Council of the Pregati, for the discussion of delicate affairs best settled by a few. He also proposed to abolish the Twenty without delay, but to maintain the Signory, the Council of Eight, the Council of Ten, and the Gonfaloniers of the Companies. No opposition was made to the latter clauses of his proposal ; but there was great divergence of opinion regarding the formation of the councils, especially of the Greater. The *ottimati* were strongly opposed to this measure, and Vespucci threw his weight on their side. He dilated at length on the incapacity and excesses of the multitude, recalled all the worst episodes of Florentine history, and added that the Greater Council of Venice was composed of gentlefolk, not of the people, although the lower classes of that city were far more serious, quiet, and sober-minded than those of Florence, where men had keener wits, quicker imaginations, and less controlled passions. But his adversaries declared in return that a Venetian gentleman was no more than a Florentine citizen, since the populace held no rights of citizenship in Florence, that as no patrician order existed, a limited government would always lead to the tyranny of the few ; and, finally : that inasmuch as the expulsion of the Medici was owed to the people, it would be unjust to exclude from all share in the government the very class by whose means the restoration of liberty had been accomplished.[1] Not only the people at large, but all the wiser heads in the city were in favour of Soderini's views ; but Vespucci had

[1] The speeches of Soderini and Vespucci are well known, and are given in Guicciardini's "Storia d'Italia."

the majority in the councils at the palace. There were many secret partisans of the Medici in their ranks, and the Twenty Accoppiatori, while aware that they were about to be dismissed, still hoped that the new constitution might be framed in such a manner as to leave all real power in their hands. But all were forced to recognize that no one was in favour of a limited government, save those who would have a share in it ; and that it would probably give rise to new disturbances, which might result in anarchy, followed by the forcible restoration of the banished Medici.[1]

The palace continued to be the scene of vehement debate, and the councils prolonged their sittings far into the night.[2] As the discussion was mainly carried on by two advocates, who were proud of their suddenly acquired importance, there was little chance of bringing it to a speedy termination. Time was wasted in talking, wrangling, and chattering, when the moment for action had come. For there was pressing danger of war ; many cities subject to Florence were on the point of revolt, the people were wearying of prolonged suspense as to their future fate, and might at any moment fly to arms and commit some sanguinary excess. Many of the citizens, therefore, were so confused and terrified that they could neither speak nor act. As the scholars were not men of action the people gained no help from them ; men of action could give none, for want of practical experience of liberty ; but most incompetent of all were the legal men, who, as usual, had only one-sided views and false

---

[1] All the historians of the time concurred in this view, and it is emphatically expressed by Guicciardini in his " Reggimento di Firenze " and his " Storia Fiorentina."

[2] " They carried on very long disputes among themselves, and sometimes remained in council to the fifth or sixth hour of the night " (Burlamacchi, p. 67).

theories of State affairs. Nothing but good sense, ardent
devotion to the public welfare, and a strong determination
to achieve it, could avail to save the people in the midst
of all this confusion. Undoubtedly the grandest lesson
taught us by history is that of seeing how in terrible
moments such as these, when the world seems to be at the
mercy of brute force, and the earth threatened with chaos ;
when rank and power, science and wealth are alike impotent ; when courage itself is vanquished by the unbridled audacity of the mob—help is only to be obtained
from virtue, generous resolve, and unselfish love of goodness. Thus Friar Girolamo Savonarola was fated to be the
saviour of Florence. The hour had struck for his appearance in the arena of politics ; and notwithstanding the
firm determination with which he had hitherto held aloof
from it, he was now compelled to obey the summons by
the pressure of events.

The history of the Florentine Republic records numerous instances of ecclesiastical intervention in the business
of the State—more than one of the intervention of saints
—notably that of St. Catherine of Siena. Savonarola,
however, absorbed in his Biblical studies, in his sermons
and his convent, had been unwilling to turn his attention
to other things. Even now, when his human will was
bending to the irresistible force of events, when he saw
the people languishing in idleness and misery in the midst
of the general suspense, and his heart was admonishing
him that charity knows no law, he still struggled against
his fate. But although he continued to preach on his
accustomed themes, new ideas were forced upon his mind
by the altered aspect of his surroundings. "Forsake
pomps and vanities," he cried, " sell all superfluous things,
and bestow the money on the poor. Citizens ! let
us collect alms in every church, for the poor in the
city and outside the walls. Devote to the poor for

one year at least, the funds of the Pisan University ; [1] if these should not suffice, let us take the church plate and decorations, and I will be the first to set you the example. But, above all, pass a law that shops may be opened and work provided for the populace now idling in the streets." [2] Afterwards, in treating of the state of the Church, he declared that the Lord would renovate all things ; and gave a sermon in which he continually repeated the text : "Let us sing a new song unto the Lord," and expounded it to the Florentines in the following manner :—" It is the Lord's will that ye should renew all things, that ye should wipe away the past ; so that nought may be left of the old evil customs, evil laws, and evil government." But, then, as though fearing to touch too nearly upon politics, he again spoke of the Church, saying : "This is the time for words to give place to deeds, vain ceremonies to real feelings. The Lord said : 'I was a hungered, and ye gave Me no meat ; I was naked, and ye clothed Me not.' He did not say : Ye built Me not fine churches, nor fine convents. He did but exhort ye to works of charity ; therefore by charity shall all things be renewed." [3] Thus, his first sermons on Haggai show that he was still hesitating and doubtful whether or no to plunge into politics.

But as public agitation increased, these sermons made less effect on his flood of hearers, and the Friar was almost driven by force to act as a citizen. He beheld a whole people bewildered, desolate, in need of help, and with no confidence in any one save himself. He saw the

---

[1] The University re-established by Lorenzo de' Medici was now closed in consequence of the revolt of Pisa, and a few only of its chairs had been transferred to Prato. Consequently its revenues were available for other purposes, and it was certainly best to apply them to the relief of the poor.

[2] Sermon vii., *sopra Aggeo* (on Haggai).

[3] Sermon viii., ibid.

vanity of learning, the incapacity of prudent men, the wickedness of others, while his own common sense, strong determination, and sincere love of goodness left him in no doubt as to the path to be pursued. He rose above himself, was conscious of having the power to soothe discord and direct men's wills towards religion and liberty ; he felt able to infuse his own devotion and his own soul into the whole people. It was then that he cried, " O Florence ! I cannot express to thee all that I feel. . . . Could I but tell thee all, thou wouldst behold a new vessel, a sealed vessel, full of boiling must, that vainly seeks to force an issue." [1]

He uttered these words on December 12th, the third Sunday in Advent, and the same day made more decided allusions to politics. He began by explaining a theory already much diffused in the schools, namely, that an absolute monarchy is the best of all governments under a good prince, but the worst under a bad one, inasmuch as it is the strongest and most united both for good and for evil, and is typical of God's empire over nature, which seeks unity in all things.[2] Such was the language of the school, and such the text of Savonarola's first political discourse. But as he went on his good sense came to the rescue, and he left the old formulas behind. " These principles," he added, " should be modified according to the nature of the people to whom they are applied. Among northern nations, where there is great strength and little intellect, and among southern nations, where, on the other hand, there is great intellect and little

[1] Sermon xiii., *sopra Aggeo* (on Haggai).
[2] These ideas are fully expounded in the treatise, " De Regimine principium," attributed to St. Thomas Aquinas, and were still very generally diffused among Florentine politicians in Savonarola's day. They had been adopted by Ficino ; certain traces of them are visible in Guicciardini's " Reggimento di Firenze," and Savonarola treated them at greater length in his " Trattato circa il Reggimento e governo della città di Firenze."

strength, the rule of a single despot may sometimes be the best of governments. But in Italy, and above all in Florence, where both strength and intellect abound, where men have keen wits and restless spirits, the government of one can only result in tyranny. The sole form of government suited to our needs is a civil and general government. Woe to thee, Florence, if thou choosest a head to dominate and oppress all the rest! From heads come all the evils by which cities are ruined. The word 'tyrant' signifies a man of evil life, of greater wickedness than other men, an usurper of others' rights, a destroyer of his own soul and the soul of the people. Wherefore let this be the first of thy laws, that henceforth no man shall be head of thy city, for otherwise thou wilt have built on the sand. Those who would fain rise above other men, and cannot tolerate civil equality, are always desperately wicked, destroyers of souls and of States.

"O my people! thou knowest that I have always refrained from touching on the affairs of the State; thinkest thou that I would enter on them at this moment, did I not deem it necessary for the salvation of souls? Thou wouldst not believe me, but now thou hast seen how all my words have been fulfilled; that they are not uttered of my own will, but proceed from the Lord. Hearken ye, then, unto Him that desireth nought but your salvation. Purify the spirit, give heed to the common good, forget private interests, and if ye reform the city to this intent, it will have greater glory than in all past times. In this wise, O people of Florence, shalt thou begin the reformation of all Italy, and spread thy wings over the earth to bear reform to all nations. Remember that the Lord hath given plain tokens that it is His purpose to renew all things, and that thou art the people chosen to begin this great enterprise, provided thou dost follow the commands of Him who calleth and inviteth thee to return to the spiritual life. Open, O Lord, the heart of this people, so that it may comprehend the things which are in me, and which Thou hast revealed to me and commanded.

" Your reform must begin with spiritual things, for these are higher than material things, of which they are the rule and the life ; and likewise all temporal good must be subordinate to the moral and religious good, from which it depends. If perchance ye have heard it said ' that States cannot be governed by Paternosters,' [1] remember that this is the maxim of tyrants, of men hostile to God and the common welfare, a rule for the oppression, not for the relief and liberation of the city. For if, on the contrary, ye desire a good government, ye must submit it to God. Certainly I would take no concern for a State that should not be subject to Him.

" Hence, when ye shall have purified your hearts, rectified your aims, condemned gambling, sensuality, and blasphemy, then set to work to frame your government, first making a rough draft of it, afterwards proceeding to details and amendments. And let your first draft, or rather model and basis of government, be conceived in such wise : *that no man may receive any benefit save by the will of the whole people, who must have the sole right of creating magistrates and enacting laws.* The form of government best adapted to this city would be that of a Grand Council on the Venetian plan. Therefore, I would have ye assemble all the people under the sixteen Gonfaloniers, and let each of the companies propose a form ; from the sixteen forms thus obtained let the Gonfalonier select four, and present them to the Signory, who, after first engaging earnestly in prayer, will choose the best of the four forms. And whichever shall be chosen

---

[1] This was a well-known saying of Cosimo the Elder, who was also accustomed to declare *that with two ells of red cloth one could make a good citizen* ("Con due canne di panno rosato si fa un uomo dabbene ").

by the people in this manner, ye may be assured that it cometh from God. I believe that the Venetian model will be the one chosen, and ye need hold it no shame to imitate the Venetians, because they, too, received it from the Lord, whence all good things come. Ye have seen how, since that government has been established in Venice, no factions nor dissensions of any sort have arisen, there-fore we must needs believe that it exists by God's will." [1]

After the sermon he added a few words regarding certain special measures that were no less urgently required. One of these was a revision of the taxes, which, while weighing on the lower classes with incredible injustice, gave such scanty returns, that, although all complained of being too heavily taxed, the city was always hard pressed for money. He also suggested that all important posts should be filled by chosen nominees, leaving only minor offices to be drawn by lot ; in this way every citizen might hope to obtain a share in the government. He then concluded by recom-mending public prayers, and a general reconciliation of all the citizens both of the old and the new State. [2]

In his preceding sermons, [3] Savonarola had touched lightly on some of these ideas ; but from this day (December 12th) he devoted himself to their exposition, and with so much acumen as to excite the marvel of all hearers. Considering what his life and his studies had been, no one would have believed him capable of this minute discussion of State affairs. And the measures he proposed were deemed so wise and prudent, that the Signory frequently asked his advice at St. Mark's, and even sent for him to the palace, where he occasionally consented to deliver a sermon. [4] At last the day came when he

---

[1] See the whole of Sermon xiii., *sopra Aggeo* (on Haggai).
[2] Sermon xiii.   [3] Especially in Sermon viii.
[4] Violi, as quoted by Barsanti (p. 86), says in his " Giornata," xi.
(Cod. cit., sheet 157[t]) : " When the form of the new Government was under consideration, he (Savonarola), together with several other monks,

gathered all the magistrates and people—women and children excepted—in the Duomo and exhorted them to turn their minds chiefly to the following points : first, to the fear of God and reformation of manners ; secondly, to zeal for the popular government and public welfare, in preference to all private interests ; thirdly, to a general reconciliation, whereby the friends of the past Government should be absolved of all their crimes, even their fines remitted, and indulgence be shown towards all debtors of the State ; fourthly, to a form of *universal government*, comprising all citizens who, in virtue of the city's ancient statutes, were entitled to a share in the State.[1] And the preacher suggested, as the best model, a Government on the pattern of the Grand Council of Venice, with certain modifications suited to the temper of the Florentine people.[2]

These proposals, made from the pulpit of Sta Maria del

was asked to discuss and consider what form would be best and most adapted to the city, in order to preserve their recently recovered liberty ; and it was agreed to accept the opinion of Frà Hieronimo, that an universal government shared by all the citizens was better fitted than a government of few, or under a single head, to maintain the peace of the city ; and accordingly that government was chosen as the best." The biographers frequently allude to Savonarola's visits to the palace. See " Vita Latina," sheet 18 ; Burlamacchi, p. 69. At the conclusion of the marginal notes to the Bible preserved in the National Library of Florence, and also in other of Savonarola's holographs, there are some memoranda of sermons given in *Palatio, ad Dominos*, and so on.

[1] We shall see that their number was by no means too large, but on the contrary too small.

[2] This sermon is unpublished, but Savonarola gives a minute account of it in his Sermon xxix. upon Job (*sopra Giobbe*). Nardi also speaks of it in detail (vol. i. pp. 58-59), and adds the following remarks : " At that time it was believed that this man knew little of active life, and could only speak of morals in general and with special reference to true Christian philosophy. As to his doctrines, had they been listened to in a right spirit, they would have undoubtedly disposed the minds of our citizens to accept some good and holy form of government. And when he had preached the said things, and repeatedly impressed them on his hearers, the greater part of them were finally carried and decided upon after much difficulty and opposition " (Ibid. p. 60).

Fiore by the Friar Savonarola, whose prophecies had all
been fulfilled, and at a moment of general suspense, had
great weight with the public, and produced an extraordinary effect. Indeed, all the best historians and
politicians of Florence unanimously agree that, but for
these sermons, Vespucci's proposal would have been carried
at the palace, and led to fresh tumults and revolutions.[1]
But when the Friar's voice was raised in the cause of
liberty, no further resistance was possible. Up to this
time the people had been in a state of uncertainty without
knowing what to decide, but now all doubt disappeared,
their way was clear ; nothing would content them but *a
Grand Council on the Venetian plan* (*Il Consiglio Grande
al modo Viniziano*), and they shouted their decision aloud
in the streets.

The element of Divine authority introduced by
Savonarola into politics was particularly effectual in
Florence, inasmuch as the Republic had always been under
the special protection of some saint, and on many occasions religion had joined with the State in the defence of
liberty. And, if the spectacle of a Friar preaching politics
from the pulpit excited some amazement, this very amaze-

[1] "In the councils, which were composed of no great number of
citizens, the proposal for a somewhat limited form of government would
certainly have prevailed, had not the Divine authority mingled in the
counsels of men through the mouth of Girolamo Savonarola of Ferrara,
a friar of the preaching order. He . . . in these days publicly expressing his detestation of the form of government proposed in Parliament, declared it to be the will of God that an absolutely popular
government should be chosen, and in such a way that it should be out of
the power of a few citizens to infringe the security or liberty of the rest ;
and thus, reverence for so great a name according with the desires of
the majority, even those who felt differently were unable to resist the
general inclination" (Guicciardini, "Storia d'Italia," chap. ii. pp. 164-165).
In his "Storia Fiorentina," Guicciardini wrote that Savonarola did not
treat politics from the sole standpoint of general principles, but in full
detail, so that one might have supposed him born and trained to the
government of States. See the note at the close of the next chapter,
and Nardi's remarks in the "Discorso" given in the Appendix to the
Italian edition, doc. xviii.

ment helped to exalt his authority. Indeed, on studying, not
only the historians of the period, but the statements afterwards made in the political writings of men such as
Giannotti, Guicciardini, and Machiavelli, regarding the
government as it was then constituted, we are almost
tempted to believe that a miracle had been wrought in
Florence, when a Friar, totally unversed in worldly matters,
could succeed in confounding the wise, redeeming his
country, and establishing a new Republic. But, on the
other hand, this seemed to confirm the old experience, that
in great social emergencies one force alone is powerful to
save ; the pure and unselfish moral force of really great
men, namely : fervid earnestness for truth, firm and
steadfast aspirations after goodness. In Savonarola all
these elements were combined, and formed, indeed, the very
essence of his noble character. In moments of trial what
learning could compare with wisdom such as this?
what prudence boast the victories and conquests such
devotion could achieve?

Is any excuse, then, required to justify the Friar's
entrance into politics ? Is it necessary to repeat that he
sought to establish liberty, and assure the triumph of
faith? Must we cite the example and authority of other
churchmen and monks who pursued the same course ?
We need only dwell on the fact that Savonarola did not
enter into politics of his own choice, but only, as we have
seen, when impelled by the irresistible force of events.
It may also be added that no profession, no vows, no laws
are binding against the laws of nature, or against the
vow that every honest man has sworn to himself—to
strive to do good in every way and in all times and
conditions.

But these hypotheses may be left aside ; the step was
taken and led to many and unavoidable consequences.
Savonarola suddenly found himself the head of all

Florence, and had to hasten the organization of the new government in order to checkmate its many assailants. Piero de' Medici had already gone to the French camp near Naples, and been favourably received by the monarch who so unworthily justified his title of *Protector of Florentine liberty.* At the first turn of fortune there was a tyrant ready to pounce upon Florence. Hence the most strenuous labour was required to complete the constitution of the popular government, and give it unity, power, and prestige, to save the republic from again falling a prey to oppression. We shall now see the masterly prudence and wisdom shown by Savonarola in all the fundamental laws he proposed for the new State, and how the whole people became so inspired and penetrated by his influence, that every one seemed suddenly to share his ideas and echo his speech.

CHAPTER V.

CONSTITUTION OF THE NEW GOVERNMENT THROUGH SAVONAROLA'S EFFORTS—THE GREATER COUNCIL AND THE COUNCIL OF EIGHTY—A NEW SCHEME OF TAXATION, BASED ON THE "DECIMA," OR TAX OF TEN PER CENT. ON REAL PROPERTY—DISCUSSION ON THE LAW FOR A GENERAL PACIFICATION AND THE REPEAL OF THE LAW "DALLE SEI FAVE," THE WHICH REPEAL IS CARRIED—THE ESTABLISHMENT OF THE TRIBUNAL OF MERCHANDISE OR COMMERCE—RESIGNATION OF THE ACCOPPIATORI —THE ABOLITION OF "PARLAMENTI"—FOUNDATION OF THE MONTE DI PIETÀ — VERDICT OF ITALIAN POLITICIANS ON THE REFORMS INTRODUCED BY SAVONAROLA.

(1494-1495.)

FOR the full comprehension of Savonarola's importance as a statesman, it is requisite to follow step by step the formation of the new Government, and also to read the sermons he delivered during that period. When we see that every new law was preceded by one or more discourses setting forth the subject with explanatory advice to the people—when we attend the debates of the Signory [1] in the Palace, and

---

[1] When the Signory, together with the colleges, and other magistrates and a few specially invited citizens (designated, therefore, as the *Richiesti*), met in Council for the purpose of discussion, they were said to hold a *Pratica*. After 1494 this term was likewise applied to any meeting held by the Signory conjointly with other magistrates and with the Council of Eighty. In the *Libri di Pratiche* of the period there are summaries of the speeches made on these occasions.

hear all these citizens carrying on their discussions in the Friar's own language, and propounding his arguments in his very words, so that we might almost believe their speeches to be copied from his sermons, and the law under consideration quoted from one of his epistles, we shall then be able to realize how this man had become the leading spirit of the entire people.[1] And when, this examination ended, we shall have gathered all the various laws together, and reconstructed the government as a whole, we shall find it admirable in all its parts, and completely harmonious in its entirety ; and hearing the assurances of all the greatest historians and politicians of Italy that this was the best, or indeed the only good government ever possessed by Florence in the whole course of its long and turbulent history, then at last we shall be qualified to form an accurate judgment of Savonarola.

His sermons in the Duomo, while the new constitution of the Republic was being organized at the Palace, were the Advent series *on Haggai*, to which must be added eight others on *the Psalms*, delivered on the Sundays after Advent. They are chiefly important from a political point of view, but always retain their religious character, since political reform was only one item of Savonarola's scheme of universal reformation ; and the new Government merely the first step towards the regeneration of morals and of the Church. Hence he never suspended his discourses on good morals and true religion : on the contrary, political questions afforded continual opportunities for recurring to those themes. These sermons are not distinguished from the others by any surpassing eloquence, but are undoubtedly the most valuable of all with regard

[1] This is also confirmed by all the historians of the time. *See*, too the " Discorso ". of Jacopo Nardi, in the Appendix to the Italian edition, doc. xviii.

to the history of the times and the story of Savonarola's life. While the other sermons enable us to appreciate his goodness and vast theological learning, these reveal his immense force of character and another side of his intellect. For they contain a complete exposition of the new scheme of government, and, by showing the vicissitudes attending its birth, almost enable us to reconstruct the whole political history of the Florentine Republic during that time.

We have already noted how, on the 12th December, Savonarola resolutely entered on his new career, and what principles of government he recommended. We see that by the 22nd and 23rd of the same month, a law of the highest importance was already drawn up in complete conformity with the Friar's views, and that it was passed by an overwhelming majority in the Councils of the People and of the Commune.[1] This law or *provision*, as it was then called, fixed the basis of the new government, and therefore demands our minute examination.[2] For it established a Great Council (*Consiglio Maggiore*) empowered to create all the chief magistrates, and approve all the laws : thus, in other words, rendering it the sovereign power in the State. All citizens were eligible as members of this Council, provided they had attained the age of twenty-nine years, and were *netti di specchio*, *i.e.*, had paid their taxes ; and were *beneficiati*,[3] which, by the terms of an ancient law, signified those who had been

---

[1] It was carried in the former by 229 black beans against 35 white, and in the latter by 195 against 16. Archivio Florentino, "Provvisioni Registri," No. 186, sheet 1 and fol., second numbering. It is well known that it was the Florentine custom for the opposition to vote with white beans ; hence the expression to *whiten* a law meant to reject it.

[2] It is designated by contemporary historians as the Great or General Council ; but in official documents it is called the Greater Council (*Consiglio Maggiore*).

[3] *Vide* Pitti, p. 227 of his " Apologia dei Cappucci " (published in the "Arch. Stor. It.," vol. iv. part ii.).

seen or *seated* (*veduti o seduti*)[1] in one of the higher magistracies, or had enjoyed this *benefit* (*beneficio*) in the person of their father, grandfather, or great-grandfather. It is needless to inquire into the origin and purport of this ancient law : we are only concerned here with the fact that instead of all the citizens being eligible for the Greater Council (as was asserted by those who objected to the new government on the score of its being too democratic), only the *beneficiati* could sit in it. And the new law further provided that whenever the *beneficiati* exceeded the number of 1,500, they were to be *sterzati,* *i.e.*, divided into three parts, each of the which parts was to constitute the Council for the term of six months. At the first election it was found that in all the population of Florence, amounting to about 90,000 souls,[2] there were only 3,200[3] *beneficiati* of the required age, so that for eighteen months the Council had to be formed of little more than a thousand members in turn.[4] No meeting was valid unless two-thirds of the members called were present. Another provision of the new law was, that " to encourage the younger and incite the elder men to virtue," every three years sixty *non-beneficiati* citizens, and twenty-four youths aged twenty-four years, were to be

---

[1] Giannotti, " Della Republica Fiorentina," bk. ii. chap. vii. pp. 113-114.

[2] Zuccagni Orlandini derives this number from the number of births registered in San Giovanni, and the same figure is also given by other writers. Marin Sanudo (" La Spedizione di Carlo VIII.," p. 133) says that Florence " counts 128,000 souls, and 15,000 foreigners." We do not know on what grounds the Venetian chronicler based this assertion, and it is known that all calculations were made very loosely in those days. Pagnini (" Della Decima," vol. i. p. 35) does not believe that the number of inhabitants amounted to 90,000.

[3] Rinuccini, " Ricordi Storici," p. clvi.

[4] Pitti contradicts the charge of excessive democracy brought against the new Government in his " Apologia dei Cappucci" (p. 277 and fol.) ; it is also treated at length in Guicciardini's " Reggimento di Firenze," " Storia Fiorentina," and " Storia d'Italia " ; also in the " Storia," and " Discorsi " of Jacopo Nardi.

chosen to sit in the Greater Council.[1] And, from the 15th January next ensuing, the Council was authorized to elect eighty citizens of forty years and above to form the Council of Eighty, which was to change its members every six months. This Council was always in attendance on the Signory, who were obliged to consult with it at least once a week ; and conjointly with the colleges, and other magistrates, it nominated ambassadors and commissaries of war, engaged mercenaries, and arranged other important affairs, such as could not be decided in public.

. In this way the basis of the new Government was formed of a Grand Council and a Council of Eighty answering to an assembly of the people and a Senate. When a law was to be passed, whichever member of the Signory was on duty as *Proposto*, rose and proposed it to that body ; and if a measure of special importance, after being approved by the Signory and the Colleges, it was further discussed by a *Pratica* of experienced citizens ; if not, it was brought at once before the Eighty, and then before the Grand Council, by whom it was finally sanctioned. The Councils were not empowered to discuss laws, but only to vote them ; and no member had the right to speak save by the express request of the Signory, and then only in favour of the proposed law. But on every occasion when the Signory asked the opinion of the citizens assembled in *Pratica*, the latter took their places on their respective benches (*nelle pancate*) according to the offices they filled or the order in which they had been elected, and, after consulting together, deputed one of their number to collect their votes and report their different opinions ; but if a new law was in question, even then no

[1] Thus, the number of those eligible to the Council went on increasing. By an old MS. bequeathed to the National Library of Florence by Passerini (" Libro della riforma del governo fatta del Savonarola ") we find that in 1510 they already amounted to 4,501.

one was allowed to speak against it. All this was in accordance with the ancient customs of a state, that having freely opened the doors of government to the masses, then sought to keep them in check by ineffectual or injurious expedients.[1] In any case the above regulation concluded with these words : " Forasmuch as the laws of the city are in great confusion, and no magistrate, either within or without the walls, knows his precise duty, it is decreed that a number of citizens should be appointed to gather all the laws together in one volume." The utility of this decree can only be appreciated by those, acquainted with the ancient statutes of Florence, and the terrible disorder they were in. For new laws and old were jumbled together, and under the Medicean rule all the laws and institutions of the Republic had been thrown into the wildest confusion.

During the two days when the establishment of the Greater Council was under discussion, another decree was passed,[2] for the nomination of a committee of ten citizens, to decide on the whole or partial remittance of unpaid taxes, of fines incurred for non-payment of the same, and to make a general revision of the taxes, levying them upon all real property, even including that of ecclesiastics, provided the requisite permission could be obtained from Rome.

Thus all the measures proposed by Savonarola were

---

[1] " They were deprived of the right (to speak) in order that the Councils might be driven by weariness to approve the provisions (of the law), whether reasonable or not ; and might pronounce judgment after only hearing one side of the question " (Guicciardini, " Opere Inedite," vol. ii. p. 296). Every means was tried to enable the Signory to carry all measures proposed by them : in fact they were authorized to bring forward the same laws repeatedly during the same day. Even the law by which the Great Council was established empowered the Signory to bring forward the same proposal eighteen times, *i.e.,* at the rate of six times a day.

[2] Archivio Fiorentino, " Registro di Provvisioni " (before quoted), sheet 5 and fol.

carried into effect, and the laws drawn up almost in his own words. The new government was established ; the Accoppiatori were forced to resign their now useless office, and the old Councils of the People and the Commune were both to be speedily abolished. The last law of any importance voted by these Councils had been that of the 28th December, repealing for a certain period the duty on weapons brought into the city, in order that all might have facilities for obtaining arms.[1] Under the Signory in office during January and February, 1495, laws were passed by the Council of Eighty,[2] and the Greater Council, who were now charged to complete the new government and bring it to perfection.

The first matter demanding attention was the revision of the taxes.[3] Savonarola continually urged this in his sermons. " Levy taxes on real property alone, abolish continual loans, abolish arbitrary imposts : " such was his advice to the authorities. But to the people he said : " Citizens ! I would have ye steadfast in devotion and help to your Commune. The son owes so much to his father that he can never do enough for him. Wherefore I say unto ye—your Commune is your father, and thus each one of you is bound to give it assistance. And if thou wouldst say, I get no good from it, know that thou mayest not say this, inasmuch as the Commune protects thy property, thy household, and thy children. Rather thou shouldst step forth and say : Behold, here are fifty florins, a hundred, a thousand. Thus do good citizens who love their country."[4] And while, on the one hand, the whole

---

[1] In the Council of the People this law was carried by 203 black beans against only 2 white ; and in the Council of the Commune by 166 against 9 (" Registro di Provvisioni " (before quoted), sheet 10).

[2] Rinuccini, " Ricordi," p. clvii., and " Registro " (above quoted), sheet 46 and fol. The first law was that voted the 29th and 31st of January.

[3] See the Sermons " sopra Aggeo," among others, No. xiii.

[4] " Prediche sopra Amos," and especially the sermon delivered on Easter Tuesday.

system of taxation was undoubtedly most unjust, and in greater disorder than can well be described; on the other, the popular discontent, although justly excited in the first instance, had now reached so excessive a pitch, that many expected the new government to relieve them of all burdens.

In the days of the first Florentine Republic men lived so frugally that the revenues of the customs sufficed for the maintenance of the State. Afterwards voluntary ' ,ans were raised to carry on wars, but as these loans became more and more frequent, and were scarcely ever repaid, the credit of the State was so much depreciated that forced contributions had to be levied instead. Then, in all public emergencies the Signory began to tax every citizen *ad arbitrio*, namely, according to their own estimation of his means ; and as powerful men always tried to evade these calls, the chief burden consequently fell upon the lower classes and caused general discontent. In 1427 the Medici, in order to win favour with the people and keep down the great families, decreed a *Catasto*, or valuation of the property of all the citizens, so that every one might be justly taxed according to his means. But, despite its apparent fairness, this Catasto proved most unjust and cruel in practice ; for even the fluctuating incomes derived from industry and commerce were assessed at a fixed rate, and this innovation roused such tremendous discontent in Florence, that many citizens entirely withdrew from trade. Thus the Catasto dealt the last blow to Florentine commerce. And while causing all this positive injury it remedied none of the existing abuses, for the system of loans was continued, the amount always fixed (*ad arbitrio*) at the discretion of the authorities, and the State was very seldom in a position to repay its creditors. Besides, the assessment of fortunes derived from trade was so un-certain, that it always afforded the Medici a convenient means of favouring their friends and oppressing their enemies.[1] This state of things was still in force when the new law of taxation was brought before the Greater Council on February 5, 1495. It had been drawn up according to Savonarola's ideas, and on such prudent, sound, and sagacious principles, that almost to our own day the taxation of Florence has been regulated on the system introduced by the Friar. For the first time, not only in Florence but in Italy, the new law established a general and regular tax upon property, abolishing all loans and arbitrary assessments, and obliging all citizens to pay ten per cent. on all income from real property, without any right to repayment. This was called the *Decima*, and a new office was created for the just valuation of property and yearly receipt of taxes.[2]

After this weighty undertaking, in which Savonarola played the part of one of the greatest of political reformers, had been thus prudently and wisely concluded, two other measures of no less importance had to be taken under consideration. The first of these was the proposal for a general pacification and pardon, and, thanks to Savonarola's continual exhortations from the pulpit, all seemed unanimous in its favour. Not so with the second, known as the *law of the six beans*, of which a few words must be said, since it led to lengthy discussions in the "Pratica," and was afterwards the cause of great danger and disturbance to the Republic, and of serious and unjust charges against the memory of Savonarola. According to the statutes all

---

[1] Machiavelli, "Opere," Italia, 1813, vol. i. p. 221.

[2] The subject was fully treated by Pagnini, "Della Decima," 4 vols. Lisbon and Lucca (Florence), 1765–66. This work also contains the provisions of the law for the new tax. The office of the *Decima* lasted down to our own day ; and the "Libri della Decima," dating from 1494, are now in the Florence Archives. Some time passed, however, before the law could be brought into effective working order, and permission to impose a permanent tax on ecclesiastical property was only granted by Rome in the year 1516.

political and criminal offences were to be tried by the Eight (*Gli Otto di guardia e balià*), excepting in special cases, when judgment was pronounced by the Signory. The Tribunal of Eight could pass sentences of imprisonment, exile, confiscation, and death, by means of six votes (*sei fave*), and these magistrates being so frequently changed, and party hatreds so rife in Florence, cruelly unjust and preposterous sentences were constantly pronounced. Accordingly all legal men agreed in the necessity of creating some court of appeal which, by curbing the excessive authority of the *Six Beans*, should put a stop to these acts of tyranny ; and the proposal was seconded by Savonarola.[1]

Having concluded his course of sermons on Haggai in January and February, 1495, the Friar gave a few upon the Psalms,[2] in which he continually urged the necessity of a general reconciliation, and of appealing from the decisions of the *Sei Fave*. Almost every day he said from the pulpit : " Florence, forgive, and make peace, and cry not again : flesh, and more flesh, blood, and more blood ! "[3] And he went on to say : " Some check must be applied to the authority of the *Six Beans*, *by means of appeal to a council of eighty or a hundred*, chosen from the members of the Grand Council. Thou sayest that this would diminish the power of the Signory ; but I tell thee it would rather increase it. Either the Signory seeks to

[1] This opinion was shared by the most distinguished politicians of Florence. *Vide* Giannotti, " Della Republica Fiorentina," and Guicciardini, " Del Reggimento di Firenze."

[2] " Prediche sui Salmi." It should be noted that Savonarola began these sermons on the 6th January, 1495 (new style), and gave eight of them ; but preached on Job during Lent. Afterwards, on the 1st May, he resumed the course on the Psalms, and continued it to the 28th July, and then gave three more in October. The first series of eight are regarded as a sequel to the Advent sermons on Haggai. *Vide* doc. xvi. (already quoted) in the Appendix to the Italian edition.

[3] " Predica I. sui Salmi."

do ill, and should be deprived of all power; or strives to do well, and merits the help of a council of honest citizens." [1] On another occasion he pressingly urged reform in the administration of justice; inveighed against the prevalent use of torture; exhorted men to peace, and again wound up by saying : " I said to thee concerning the Court of the *Six Beans*, that it was needful to give it *a staff to lean upon, in the shape of a Council of Appeal.*" [2] And he continued to insist upon this point, until the Signory was induced to frame a decree, which, after being repeatedly discussed, was at last, on the 15th March, 1495, brought before an unusually numerous *Pratica*, which, in consequence of the special importance of the case, [3] all the principal citizens and magistrates had been summoned to attend. Custom forbade that laws should be in any way made public before being presented ; but in this case, although all were acquainted with the new provision, the reading of it was heard with the utmost attention.

The first portion was in complete accordance with Savonarola's views ; might, indeed, have proceeded from his pen, and ran to the following effect : " Considering the weighty need for union and concord in a well-constituted republic, and in order to follow in the footsteps of our Lord, who, in all that He did, whether journeying, preaching, or resting, always enjoined peace ; and considering that the same is to be seen in natural things, which ever seek for unity, according to their kind, wherefore it was said by the philosopher : the strongest virtue is united virtue ; and finally, being admonished by the supernatural events we have witnessed this year, in the establishment of our new government, and the mercy

[1] Sermon i. " sui Salmi."

[2] " *Un certo bastoncello, cioè quel Consiglio dello appello.*" Sermon ii. "sui Salmi."

[3] It was brought forward on the 6th, 8th, 9th, and finally on the 15th March.

vouchsafed us by the Lord, the which mercy it behoves us to imitate—

" The magnificent Signory and Gonfaloniers hereby ordain that a general peace be made, that all offences be pardoned and all penalties remitted unto the supporters of the late government." [1]

The second part, consisting of an entirely distinct law, was less in accordance with Savonarola's advice, and was to the effect : " That every citizen eligible to public office who, for any political offence, should be sentenced by the Signory or the Eight either to death, to corporal punishment, or to any fine above the sum of three hundred florins, or to reprimand, imprisonment, &c., should have the right of appeal, for the term of eight days, to the Greater Council. That, in case of such appeal, the Signory should be bound to allow any one to speak in defence of the accused ; and within the term of fifteen days to bring the case before the said Council as many as six times in the space of two days, and, furthermore, to acquit the accused if two-thirds of the assembly voted in his favour." [2]

The point on which this law differed from that proposed by Savonarola was one of very decided importance. For instead of establishing, as he had proposed, a right of appeal to a limited Court composed of wise experts in legal matters, appeal was to be made to the Greater Council, whose decisions would be influenced by party spirit rather than justice, and where the ignorance of the many would prevail against the wisdom of the few. The Ottimati had been opposed from the first to any right of appeal, since, being accustomed to have the office of the Eight almost always in their own hands, they could not

[1] Archivio Fiorentino, " Registro di Provvisioni " (before quoted), sheet 82[t] and fol.
[2] Same, " Registro di Provvisioni," sheet 83[t].

tolerate the idea of any infringement of its absolute
authority. But, on the other hand, the people regarded
the Greater Council as the highest power in Florence, on
which all authority legally devolved. Party spirit had
been rekindled by the conflict in the palace, and the
popular side, aware of its superior strength, went to
the length of demanding that the mob should pass judgment on the gravest political offences. And the law
being already drawn up and brought forward, there
was great difficulty in modifying it. As no one was
allowed to speak in opposition, it had either to be rejected
or accepted. Yet, to reject it was impossible, since its
promoters had purposely tacked it on to the law for a
general reconciliation which was deemed imperative by all,
and also because some right of appeal from the Tribunal
of the Six Beans was considered equally expedient.

Nevertheless it is evident, from the debates in the
Pratica, that all honest citizens were aware of the abuses
to which the bill would lead, and did their best to prevent
them. And they might have succeeded but for the
artful and almost diabolic devices of the enemies of the
new government. For when the latter perceived that not
only the people, but men of wisdom and Savonarola himself, alike demanded an appeal from the *Six Beans*, they
were convinced that nothing could serve their designs
better than the new law, which, being an excessive
measure, would give rise to disturbances at the first
opportunity ; and only in times of disturbance could they
hope to change the government and vest all power in the
hands of a few of their own party. Therefore, after strenuously combating the right of appeal to a limited council of
wise and prudent citizens, they all joined in energetic and
almost furious efforts in favour of appeal to the Greater
Council. In the Pratica, accordingly, it was seen with
much surprise that, whereas the men of the people mode-

rated their tone, and the partizans of Savonarola positively ventured to express their disapproval of the law proposed by the Signory, the Ottimati, foes of the new government and adherents of the Medici, employed their best eloquence in its favour. In a volume of fragments of the Pratiche [1] we had the good fortune to find reports of these speeches made by the government notary, and are thus enabled to realize one of the chief and most animated debates of the period. The question was one of high importance, and the speakers were men of authority who brought all their mental powers to bear on its discussion. Their speeches not only serve to show us how laws were discussed and voted on those exceptional occasions, but also throw new light on a little understood event, and exonerate Savonarola from one of the heaviest charges ever brought against him.

The law being duly presented and the opinion of the meeting asked by the Signory, the citizens withdrew to their respective benches, and, after holding noisy consultation, Messer Domenico Bonsi, one of the Accoppiatori, a friend of Savonarola, was the first to speak. Reporting the verdict of his bench, he recommended peace, proving its expedience and necessity by many quotations from the Gospel and St. Paul, and by others from Demosthenes and Aristotle. Proceeding to the question of appeal, he acknowledged that the measure would be useful, but reported that his colleagues were very divided in their views; and then, as though hardly daring to speak against a law proposed by the Signory, he suddenly came to a stop. Thereupon Messer Francesco Gualterotti rose and, after extolling the plan of a general reconciliation, spoke of the necessity of sanctioning appeal from the tyrannical Tribunal of the Eight, who had always oppressed the city with sentences of exile and confiscation. Yet even he found the new law to be so excessive in its tendency, that he ventured to propose that it should not be permanently sanctioned, but only for a time (*a tempo*).

The discussion now became lively, and one of those who, on the first day of the revolution, had closed the palace door in Piero de' Medici's face, now rose to speak. This was Messer Luca Corsini, a very influential and eloquent man, and one of the most fervent advocates of the popular party. He gave a vivid description of the miserable state of the country, saying : "We behold all Italy stirred by new and terrible dangers; and we ourselves, being in the centre of the land, are exposed to even worse suffering than the rest. Wherefore unity and concord are the only remedies which will avail to preserve us from the attacks of neighbouring potentates, who are already preparing to fall upon us at the first sign of disturbance. Besides, having now given to all the right to sit in our councils, unless we are careful to conciliate some at least of the friends of the old State, they will oppose us, both by the beans and in secret. For if no other reason avail to persuade you," he added, in louder and more impressive tones, "the example of our Lord should suffice, since, after smiting us with His sword of justice, He hath mercifully averted it from our heads and vouchsafed us His pardon. Let us, then, also be merciful ; let us ordain a general pardon ! And should any one deem this an extraordinary remedy, let him remember that in extraordinary cases the wisest rule is to follow none."

On coming to the question of the "*Six Beans*," he spoke with still greater warmth, asserting the absolute necessity of some new measure. And moved by the democratic spirit which so easily runs to exaggeration, he

added : " The Republic consists of one body alone, and this
body is the whole people, which, unable itself to attend
to every branch of the administration, therefore appoints
magistrates. But when doubts, disorders, or dissensions
arise, even as we see to be of daily occurrence, there is no
injustice in recurring to the Greater Council which repre-
sents the people and has conferred office on the magistrates ;
nor can the authority of the Signory be diminished by an
appeal to the people to whom the whole of the Republic
belongs. For if we consider what things have come to
pass in these latter days, we shall say that it is the highest
wisdom and prudence to desire that these laws should be
carried."

When Corsini had finished this animated address, all
eyes were turned towards Messer Guidantonio Vespucci,
who was noted for his eloquence and experience, and one
of the most powerful members of the *Ottimati* party.   It
was he who, during the preceding December, had alleged
so many reasons in the palace for opposing the new form
of popular government.   His learning gave added weight
to his opinions ; and, conscious of this, he spoke with
much emphasis, and displayed his well-known oratorical
gifts.   He began by carefully praising the discourses of the
preceding speakers ; who, as he said, " were all labouring
in different ways towards the same end—the consolidation
of liberty.   Also I am well content to see that many have
frankly expressed opinions opposed to that of the Signory,
for this is the only way to arrive at tru n.[1]   For my own
part," he went on, entering at once into the question of
the " Six Beans," " the only plan seems to be to seek a mode
of establishing perfect equality among the citizens ; if the
old road will lead us to that goal, let us follow it ; if not,

---

[1] He intended this as an ironical reproof to those who, in violation of
the statutes, had ventured to express views somewhat inimical to the
measure proposed by the Signory.

we must choose another path. I certainly deem the old law to be very perilous, and if carefully considered, it will be seen to be neither well-ordered, nor practically good; nor, indeed, does it appear just to give so much power to the Signory, without also granting right of appeal against their decisions. In France appeal can be made to the Council of Paris against the verdict of the King; imperial decisions can be reversed by the Pope, and the sentence of the Papal Chair itself can likewise be appealed against.[1] Hence no one should be angered if others correct errors into which he has been betrayed by haste or inadvertence. And if princes, who are bound by no law, are willing to allow right of appeal, why should it be refused by magistrates whose authority is wholly derived from the people? By granting this power of appeal we shall only restore to the people its own right, and repress the immoderate pretensions of the over-ambitious. It will certainly act as a great check upon tribunals to know that their sentences are subject to the approval of the Greater Council. Accordingly, I see not what harm can be caused by destroying the pernicious authority of the ' *Six Beans.*'

" Regarding the peace, unanimously desired by the citizens, nothing need be said, save that the speedier and the more general it be the greater the good. But," he said, finally, " the most useful peace that can be concluded will be to deprive the ' *Six Beans* ' of the accursed power that has been the source of all discord." [2]

---

[1] At this time the Council of Trent had not yet taken place, and that of Constance was still fresh in men's minds; accordingly the doctrine of the right of appeal from the Pope to the Council was still uncondemned by the Church of Rome.

[2] These speeches are all given in the " Frammenti di Pratiche," above quoted. We have endeavoured to reproduce their exact sense and almost their exact words in translating them back from the Notary's Latin reports into the Italian in which they were delivered.

There was great amazement in the assembly on hearing
Vespucci so vigorously defend the rights of the people
after having opposed them with equal force in the previous
December. Nevertheless his speech turned the scale, and
on the 18th of March the new law was passed in the Council
of Eighty, by 80 votes against 38 ; and on the 19th in
the Greater Council by 543 votes against 163.[1] Such is
the true history of a discussion on which all writers
have been silent, while charging Savonarola with the
authorship of an extreme measure. The accusation is
most unjust, for whereas his sermons testify that he was in
favour of a far more temperate law, the orator's speeches
show that the Friar's adherents almost violated the old
parliamentary usages of the Republic in their endeavours
to check the excesses of both secret and declared opponents. The latter, however, were triumphant.[2]

[1] Florence Archives, "Registro di Provvisioni" (before quoted), sheet
84[t]. The Signory, Colleges, &c., sat in the Council of Eighty (and in
the Greater Council also) ; so that its members exceeded the number indicated by its name.

[2] It should be noted that many contemporary writers either refrained
from repeating this charge against Savonarola, or merely spoke of it as
an unfounded rumour. But in the sixteenth century, his adversaries
maintained the charge, and brought many worshippers of his memory to
believe in its truth. Thus, Guicciardini ("Reggimento di Firenze,"
p. 165) makes Del Nero, when speaking of the Eight *di guardia a balìa*,
say these words : "And I would add that which I understand is proposed by this Friar, namely, that whenever a citizen is condemned for
political offences—but for no other reason—right of appeal should be
allowed ; not however as he proposes, to the Greater Council, but to the
Senate "[*here the author added in a marginal note to the MS.*] : "It might
perhaps be better for this appeal to be made to the *Quarantia* (Forty), so
that the magistrate who had given sentence could appear in defence of his
verdict." Thus, without being aware of it, Guicciardini maintained the
same opinion held by Savonarola, and that is so decidedly expressed in
the latter's sermons. Machiavelli, who still more explicitly charges Savonarola with the authorship of this law, also says : "After the year 1494,
when the government of Florence had been reconstituted by the aid of
Frà Girolamo Savonarola, whose writings demonstrated the learning,
wisdom, and goodness of his mind : and when, among other institutions
to insure the safety of the citizens, he had caused a law to be passed, for
making appeal to the people against all condemnations for political

This law may indeed be considered the first step and first victory of the party whose aim it was to destroy the Republic. We shall presently witness the untiring efforts of this faction to compass the Friar's downfall, and its readiness to resort to arts of dissimulation and double-dealing with a refinement of political skill surpassing that of the best diplomatists of our own times. It is true that Savonarola made no spoken protest after the law was once carried ; for it would have been useless to excite dissensions and rancour between the Signory and the people. It may also be, that neither he nor others could then foresee the sinister and dangerous consequences of this intemperate enactment of a law, that, after all, was based on a just principle inculcated by himself. Yet none of the evils to be feared in the future was so great as the patent evil that had just been accomplished ; when, at the very moment that by the will of the people a general peace and amnesty was declared, the enemies of the new government banded together to effect the ruin of the Republic by which they had been so magnanimously treated. Certainly, great exasperation was felt that day, and Savonarola's frank sincerity must have been singularly chafed by the spectacle of all this ingratitude and craft. For although maintaining strict silence at the time, the sermons he gave shortly after were marked by an unprecedented irritation and violence of tone. So true is the old saying that : *One drop of vinegar spoils a whole cask of honey !*

The passing of this law of appeal against the sentences

offences pronounced by the Eight and the Signory ; the which law after long persuasion, and with the greatest difficulty, he successfully carried, &c." ("Discorsi," bk. i. chap. 95). This opinion of Machiavelli, and other writers of his time became very widely diffused, for although totally contradicted by documentary evidence, the leading part played by Savonarola in the formation of the new government caused people to regard him as the author of all the new laws passed, including those that he disapproved.

of the " Six Beans" was, however, the beginning of
judicial reform, for in all his sermons Savonarola continued to insist on the due administration of justice.[1]   In
this, as in every other branch of public affairs, there
was the greatest disorder; an indescribable confusion
of laws and tribunals.   This state of things had been
purposely contrived by Lorenzo de' Medici, who in order
to hold the life and property of the citizens at his own
disposal, threw old and new laws, old and new institutions into so strange a jumble, that it was almost impossible to disentangle them.   In earlier times the supreme
jurisdiction in nearly all criminal and civil cases had been
assigned to two foreign magistrates, the Podestà and the
Captain of the People, who passed sentence on all important cases and heard appeals [2] from the decisions of petty
magistrates presiding over civil tribunals in different quarters of the town.   But in 1477 the office of Captain of
the People [3] was abolished, and that of the Podestà near
its end ; and as the greater part of their functions now
devolved on the Signory and the Eight, the power of these
bodies became greatly increased.   In the same year the
tribunal of commerce, known as the *Casa della Mercatanzia*, situated next to the Palace of the Priors, also
began to decline.   It had been a very important institution
in the Republic as the nucleus and chief meeting-place
of the Florentine guilds.   And no steps having been
taken with regard to these tribunals, suitors scarcely
knew to which to apply, and justice was very badly administered.   Accordingly Savonarola urged the necessity
of a general reform ; recommending the creation of a
Ruota, or tribunal of citizens who were to be wise, wealthy,

[1] *Vide* the "Prediche sopra Aggeo" and the "Prediche sui Salmi."
[2] *Vide* the "Statuti Fiorentini" (3 vols.), published in 1778, and dated
Friburg.
[3] Florence Archives, "Provvisioni, Registro," No. 19b, sheet 5ᵗ.

and well-paid in order to ensure their incorruptibility. " But should this be too great an expense for the moment," he said, " hasten, at least, to appoint a good and competent judge of appeal ; [1] and likewise see to the re-establishment of the Mercatanzia with a foreign judge, elected according to the ancient statutes." [2] The institution of the Ruota was so novel an idea for Florence, that it was only decided upon some years later,[3] but measures were instantly taken to restore the Mercatanzia to its original importance.

On the 20th and 21st May, 1495, both Councils passed a new law to the following effect : Considering that there is nothing more important than the administration of justice, and seeing how the reputation of the *Casa della Mercatanzia* has been lowered by the confused laws introduced subsequently to the ancient statutes,[4] the Magnificent Signory and Gonfalonier are resolved to remedy the said confusion by following the example of ancient and well-digested laws, and restoring the said Casa to its former high reputation, and hereby provide and ordain :—

" That the Signory of the Mercatanzia shall elect thirty-eight sagacious citizens, aged thirty-five years, to be drawn by ballot (*squittinio*) from the members of the Greater Council ; and that the thirteen having the largest number of votes, shall be appointed *Statutarii e Riformatori della Casa e Corti della Mercatanzia ed Università dei Mercatanti*, with the same authority held by the *statutarii* down to the year 1477, *i.e.*, that of changing, enlarg-

---

[1] *Vide* " Prediche sopra Aggeo," and " Prediche sui Salmi." See also the " Prediche sopra Rut e Michea," given on Sundays and other festivals during 1496, and particularly the sermon of the 3rd July.

[2] Ibid.

[3] On the 20th April, 1498, it was decided to re-establish the office of Captain of the People, and to strengthen the authority of the Podestà. *Vide* the " Provvisioni " to that effect in the " Registro " (before quoted), No. 190, sheet 5. In 1502 the advice given by Savonarola was followed, and the Ruota instituted.

[4] *I.e.*, the statute that was thoroughly reformed in 1393.

ing, and entirely reforming the statutes, which, after being approved by the Signory and their Colleges, will be fully enforced." [1]

Thus was re-established the old and illustrious *Casa della Mercatanzia*, and the new commercial code of Florence compiled, known to merchants as " the Statute of '96." [2] This document is another proof of the revival of civic wisdom among the Florentines, and proved of great advantage to the people, the guilds, and the cause of justice.

While the machinery of the Republic was thus being rapidly brought to perfection, it became necessary for the Accoppiatori to resign their functions, which, unless reduced to mere sinecures, would inevitably clash with the duties of the new magistrates. Savonarola gave much help in overcoming the difficulty, and his friend, Messer Domenico Bonsi, was one of the first *Accoppiatori* to spontaneously resign his post. The others seemed willing to follow his example ; and on the 8th and 10th of June a *provvisione* was carried giving the *Accoppiatori* " authority, power, and charge to renounce and transfer to the Greater Council every privilege and power conferred on them by the Parliament." [3] The same law established the new rules and mode of procedure to be observed in all future elections of the Signory.[4]

---

[1] Florence Archives, " Provvisioni, Registro," 187, sheet 42.

[2] In the National Library of Florence, class xxix. cod. 143, there is an old copy of the " New Statute," prefaced by the above-mentioned provision.

[3] " Provvisioni, Registro " (above quoted), sheet 44[t] and fol.

[4] According to this Provvisione the Signory was to be elected in the following manner : First, the Greater Council was assembled, and ninety-six electors chosen by lot ; *i.e.*, twenty-four for each quarter of the town. Each of the ninety-six nominated some individual of his own quarter, and the ninety-six thus chosen were the candidates for the Signory. From those obtaining most votes (provided they had more than half of the total number) eight candidates were then selected (*i.e.*, two for each

The dismissal of the *Accoppiatori* having been thus successfully and peacefully accomplished, another very important measure had to be carried. This was for the abolition of *Parlamenti* which had brought so many disturbances, changes, and tyrannies on Florence. Now that the Greater Council could make and unmake every institution at will, Parliaments were no longer required ; and henceforth there could be no object in summoning them, save for the overthrow of the Republic. Besides, if Piero de' Medici—who was known to be busily intriguing and had already gained some support from the French and among Italian potentates—were to succeed in returning to Florence, the only mode in which he could gain the suffrage of the mob would be by means of a Parliament. Also, if his friends, neither few nor feeble, unluckily, should think of rousing the city in his favour, they too would infallibly resort to a *Parlamento*, which had always been found the best engine of tyranny in Florence, and the easiest means of effecting a change in the government.

Florentine historians and politicians have frequently indulged in long dissertations on the dangers of these

quarter), and their names put into the general bag (*borsa*), that of the senior candidate, however, being placed in the little bag (*borsellino*). Then for each of the acting members of the Signory, two new names having a majority of more than half of the total number of votes, were placed in the bag *for respect*, and were considered to be *veduti*, or seen. The reason why the name of the senior member was placed in the little bag (*borsellino*) seems to have been because on him devolved the duty of being the first *Proposto*, an office alternately held by each of the Signory, sometimes for one day, and sometimes only for part of one sitting.

For the office of Gonfalonier twenty electors were drawn by lot. Each of the first ten of these elected two candidates, one as *sitting* Gonfalonier, the other as a *veduto*, or prospective Gonfalonier ; then each of the second ten chose two other candidates for the offices of Gonfalonier and Notary. The twenty names thus obtained were then balloted, and the one obtaining most votes, provided these exceeded half of the total number, was elected Gonfalonier ; the two coming next according to the number of their votes, took the rank, by courtesy (*per rispetto*) of *veduti*. *Vide* the same " Provvisione."

popular assemblies and the enormities sanctioned by them ; [1] but at this moment the question touched the citizens to the quick. They all knew that the banished Medici were plotting to return ; they had discovered by the debates on the law of the " Six Beans " that there were enemies of liberty in their midst ; therefore all minds were in a very excited state, and even Savonarola was moved to speak from the pulpit in terms which were not only unusual but most unsuited to the lips of a minister of peace.

" I have taken thought of this Parliament of thine, and I hold it to be nought but a means of destruction, wherefore it were best to be rid of it. Come forward, my people ! Art thou not sole master now ?—Yes !—See then that no Parliament be called, unless thou would'st lose thy government. Know, that the only purpose of Parliament is to snatch the sovereign power from the hands of the people. Keep ye this in mind, and teach it to your children. And thou people, at the stroke of the bell calling thee to Parliament, rise and draw thy sword and ask— ' What would'st thou ? Cannot the Council decide all things ? What law would'st thou make ? Hath this Council no power to make it ? ' And therefore I would have ye frame a provision to the effect, that the Signory, on taking office, should swear to summon no Parliament ; and that should any one scheme to call a Parliament, let him that denounces that man receive thirty thousand ducats, if he be a member of the Signory ; if not of it, one thousand. And if he that would summon a Parliament be of the Signory, let his head be cut off ; if he be

---

[1] For example, this is what Guicciardini says of the matter in his "Discorsi," "Opere inedite," vol. ii. p. 299) : " To firmly maintain this form of government, it is requisite to firmly observe the law against Parliaments, which only serve to destroy the popular life, . . . forasmuch as by terror and force of arms, they compel the people to consent to all that they propose ; and make them believe that all that is done, is done by the will and pleasure of the whole population.'

not of it, let him be proclaimed a rebel and all his goods confiscated. Likewise let all Gonfaloniers, on taking office, swear that on hearing the bell ring to Parliament, they will at once hasten to put the abodes of the Signory to the sack ; and let the Gonfalonier who doth sack one of the houses of the Signory receive one-fourth of the spoil ; and the remainder be distributed among his comrades. *Item*, that should the Signory seek to call a Parliament, the instant they set foot on the *ringhiera*, they shall no longer be considered the Signory, and all may cut them to pieces without sin." [1]

This was a momentary licence of speech ; and it is only just to add that confiscation, pillage, and capital punishment were the usual penalties at that time for political offences. Nevertheless, in spite of the general usage, and although Piero de' Medici and his adherents were already plotting against the Republic, and already, as we shall presently see, nearing the gates of Florence, it was inexcusable for Savonarola to indulge in so virulent an outburst.

Anyhow, this sermon was delivered on the 28th of July, 1495, and by the 13th of August a law was passed to the following effect : Seeing that the reform of the present State was made to secure the liberty of this most flourishing people ; and it being desired to maintain this government for ever, so that not ourselves only, but also our children may enjoy this sacred liberty, and no one dare to raise his head as a tyrant and subjugate the free citizens, also knowing that in no way can our liberty be so easily subverted and this new and good rule and government overthrown as by means of Parliaments ; and finally, seeing that no circumstance could arise in which a Parliament would be necessary, inasmuch as the government is in the hands of the people, which is the true and lawful master

---

[1] "Prediche sui Salmi." Sermon xxvi., given on the 28th July.

of our City, and able to pass new laws, without need of other popular convocations, &c.—

The Magnificent Signory and Gonfalonier do hereby provide and ordain, that no Parliament be held in future ; that henceforth the Signory shall swear never again to convoke one ; and that whoever may plot to do so, shall be put to death, and 3,000 florins awarded to his denouncer.[1] But after this burst of fury Savonarola calmly resumed his work of peace and turned his attention to the establishment of a *Monte di Pietà.* " I recommend this *Monte di Pietà* to your care, that all may come to its aid; all women especially should devote to it their every superfluity. Let all contribute, and let them give ducats not farthings.[2] He frequently preached in favour of this institution, and exhorted his female hearers, the wealthy, and all the citizens in general, to bestow their charity on the poor.

In fact, a *Monte di Pietà* was the best possible means for relieving the people's distress. In those days the

[1] " Registro di Provvisioni " (before quoted), sheet 84ᵗ and fol. Shortly afterwards Savonarola had the following lines inscribed in capital letters in the hall of the Greater Council. They cannot be said to possess any poetic merit—

> " Se questo popolar consiglio e certo
> Governo, popol, della tua cittate
> Conservi, che da Dio t' è stato offerto,
> In pace starai sempre e 'n libertate.
> Tien, dunque l'occhio della mente aperto,
> Chè molte insidie ognor ti fien parate ;
> E sappi che chi vuol far parlamento
> Vuol torti dalle mani il reggimento."

Of which the literal translation is as follows : " O people ; if thou dost preserve this popular Council, this sure Government of thy city, which God has vouchsafed to· thee, in peace and in liberty shalt thou dwell for evermore.   Keep open, then, thy mind's eye ; for many snares will be laid for thee.   And be assured that he who would call a Parliament would fain take the government from thine hands." *Vide* Varchi, " Storia Fiorentina " (Arbib edition), vol. ii. p. 202.

[2] " Prediche sopra Amos."   The Sermon preached on Easter Tuesday.

Jews of Florence lent money at $32\frac{1}{2}$ per cent., and with compound interest, so that a loan of 100 florins was found to increase in fifty years to the sum of 49,792,556 florins, 7 *grossi*, and 7 *denari* (and several fractions),[1] consequently they were held in the utmost detestation by the populace, and many attempts had been made to check their extortions. In past years Frà Barnaba da Terni had urged from the pulpit the necessity of founding a *Monte di Pietà*, and established one at Perugia in 1462. Later Frà Bernardino da Feltre endeavoured to diffuse the system throughout Italy, and preached upon it in Florence during the reign of Lorenzo de' Medici. On the 27th March, 1473, a decree for its institution was already drawn up when a Jew contrived to corrupt the magistrates, and even Lorenzo de' Medici, with a bribe of 100,000 florins, and the scheme fell to the ground. In the days of Piero de' Medici the Minorite Friars again excited the populace against the Jews, although more prudent citizens blamed the attempt, and when Frà Bernardino resumed his propaganda in favour of the *Monte*, so many riots took place that the preacher was finally banished from Florence.[2]

Savonarola had never taken part in these idle controversies, nor uttered a word against the Jews ; and when questioned on the subject by the Lucchese in May, 1493, had urged the duty of tolerance, saying that he sought not to persecute but to convert the Jews ;[3] but after the

[1] This is no exaggerated calculation made by historians, but is recorded in the decree for the establishment of the *Monte di Pietà.*

[2] Parenti ("Storia di Firenze," cod. cit., sheet 141 and fol.), gives an account of these events, adding that the more cultivated classes were in favour of the Jews, and that Piero de' Medici was very foolish to second the Minorites and oppose the views of the magistrates.

[3] Letter of Savonarola, dated 18th May, 1493, published by Signor Bonzi in the "Giornale Storico degli Archivi Toscani," April—June, 1859. It is worthy of remark that in this letter Savonarola says that usury could not be permitted by the Pope, thus already formulating the opinion that no one should have a recognized authority to permit evil.

liberation of the people he raised his voice in favour of the Monte di Pietà, and its establishment in Florence was solely owed to him. On the 28th December, 1495, a law was passed beginning with these words : " Blessed be he that cherisheth the poor and needy : in the day of adversity the Lord shall give him freedom." It then went on to speak of " the pestiferous gulf and gnawing worm of usury, already endured for some sixty years in Florence through that perfidious sect of the Hebrews, the foes of God." It wound up with a decree for the election of eight unsalaried citizens, who were to frame the statutes of the Monte; after which all contracts with Jewish money-lenders were to be considered void, and the said lenders were to leave the city within the space of one year.[1] By the 15th April, 1496, the statute was drawn up, and was passed by the Greater Council on the 21st. It was planned entirely to the advantage of the people : the expenses of its administration were restricted to 600 florins annually ; the interest exacted from borrowers pledging their effects was to vary between 5 and $7\frac{1}{2}$ per cent., the said borrowers, however, being obliged to swear not to gamble with the money received from the Monte.[2] Savonarola's object in promoting this righteous institution being solely the good of the people, he had first proposed that the officials employed at the Monte should be paid by the State and no interest taken on loans.[3] This proved

[1] " Provvisioni, Registro" (before quoted), sheets 167–68.

[2] " Provvisioni, Registro," 188, sheet 5ᵗ, and fol. See also Passerini, "Storia degli Stabilimenti di Beneficenza," Florence, Le Monnier, 1853. The author is however mistaken in saying that Savonarola never favoured the Monte di Pietà, which was promoted by his enemies, the Minorites. This statement is not only contradicted by the unanimous verdict of the historians and biographers of Savonarola, but likewise by all the Friar's public utterances from the pulpit. Nor is Passerini quite right in his other assertion that all the Jews were driven out, since only Jew money-lenders or usurers were in question. It must, however, be allowed that nearly all the Jews in Florence belonged to that class.

[3] " Prediche sopra Amos," Sermon xxi.

to be impracticable, but the new statutes of the Monte afforded great relief to the lower classes, and rendered it needless to persecute the Jews or drive them all from Florence, as the Minorites had suggested ; for, despite the fervent zeal of Savonarola and his followers, they were never betrayed into intolerance.

Such were the laws by which the liberty of Florence was consolidated and a new constitution framed. Many others may of course be found in the records of the Provisions passed during these years, but being of no general importance we have left them aside. One of them, however, dated June, 1495, is deserving of mention. It runs thus : The Magnificent Signory and Gonfalonier, " considering that Messer Dante Alighieri, great-grandson of Dante the poet, cannot return to the city, owing to his inability to pay the tax levied on him by the Signory in November and December last ; and deeming it were well to give some proof of gratitude to the descendants of the poet, who is so great an ornament to this city ; do hereby provide that the said Messer Dante be held exempt from every fine or penalty, &c." [1] This was a tardy proof of pardon to the memory of the great Ghibelline, a very slight act of justice to the name of the " divine poet;" yet such as it was, it is a title of honour to the new-born Republic.

Thus, in the space of one year, the liberty of Florence was established, the people authorized to carry arms, the system of taxation revised, usury extinguished by the Monte di Pietà, a general peace made, justice re-organized, *Parlamenti* were abolished for ever, and the Greater

---

[1] It was discussed by the Signory on the 3rd June, approved by the Eighty on the 8th, and passed by the Greater Council on the 10th. " Registro di Provvisioni," 187, sheets 49ᵗ–50. It had been previously debated by the Signory, the 31st December, 1494. These documents have been made public by Professor Del Lungo in his work, " Del 'Esilio di Dante," Florence, Succ Le Monnier, 1881, pp. 180–181.

Council was constituted, to which the Florentines showed a tenacious attachment, such as they never accorded to any other of their political institutions. It was then that Donatello's noble group of Judith and Holifernes was placed on the platform (*ringhiera*) in front of the palace as a symbol to the people of the triumph of freedom over tyranny, and with the following inscription: *Exemplum sal: pub: cives posuere*, MCCCCXCV.[1]

And all this had been accomplished in a short time, without a sword being drawn, a drop of blood spilt, without any internal dissensions; and this in Florence, the city of riots! But the crowning marvel was to see how one man, a simple Friar, swayed all Florence from the pulpit, and always swayed it for good; an example without precedent in history of the might of human utterances and the human will. This Friar made no harangues in the streets, had no seat in the Councils of the State, yet he was the soul of the whole people, and the chief author of every law of the new government.[2] In all the laws sub-

---

[1] This statue originally belonged to the Medici, and after their expulsion was placed on the *ringhiera*, where Michael Angelo's David afterwards stood. Later it was removed to its present position under the Loggia de' Lanzi, with the same republican inscription. Some writers assert that Cellini's masterpiece of Perseus with the head of Medusa was placed beside the former work by the Medici in reply, and as a symbol, as it were, of the slaying of the Republic by tyranny restored. Some learned adulators alleged that the Medici could trace their descent from Perseus.

[2] On the 1st April, 1495, Savonarola spoke of the changes in the new government and of the principal laws ordained by himself in the following terms: "Seeing that a change of government was at hand, and considering that it might lead to much scandal and shedding of blood; . . . I decided, being thereto inspired by God, to begin to preach and exhort the people to repentance, in order that He might show mercy. And on the Feast of St. Matthew the Apostle, *i.e.*, the 21st day of September, 1494, I began, and with what strength was vouchsafed me by God, did exhort the people to confession and fasting and prayer; and whereas these things were done willingly, by the goodness of God justice was changed to mercy, and on the 11th November the State and the government were miraculously changed in your city, without bloodshed, or any other

sequent to the revolution of 1494, the influence of the
democratic monk is clearly to be traced in every word and
detail. They were now drawn up in Italian instead of
Latin ; [1] in a new form, a new style, and animated by a
new spirit. They often seem the echo of Savonarola's
own accents, and are frequently composed of fragments of
the sermon in which he had urged their adoption. If we
enter the Council Hall we find the citizens maintaining
his ideas and speaking in his very words ; and, on looking
back at the close of this year 1495, we shall find that
never before had Florence been so wisely and prudently
ruled, and that the form of government then constituted
was the best and most stable that in all its years of turbulent
life its people had ever been able to create. Can we, then,
be astonished to see that the greatest of Florentine politicians thought it worthy of examination, and could not
refrain from extolling it to the skies ? [2]

Machiavelli, Guicciardini, and Giannotti, whose works
were composed after the liberties of Florence were crushed

scandal. Then, O people of Florence, since thou hadst to form a new
government, I did summon ye all, excepting the women, to your cathedral, in the presence of the Magnificent Signory and all the other magistrates of the City ; and after speaking many things concerning the good
government of the city conformably with the doctrines of philosophers
and the holy fathers, I instructed thee as to the natural governments of
the Florentine people ; and then, continuing my sermon, went on to propose four things which it behoved thee to do. Firstly, to fear God ;
secondly, to love the general welfare of the city, and prefer it to private
interest ; thirdly, to make a general reconciliation between thee and those
who had ruled thee in the past ; and added to this the right of appeal
from the 'Six Beans!'" Sermon 29, "Sopra Giobbe." It should be
noted that this sermon was delivered after the new law of appeal was
passed, and that both now and on other occasions Savonarola always
states that he counselled the appeal from the "Six Beans" but never the
appeal to the Greater Council.

[1] In fact, all Provvisioni previous to 1494 are in Latin ; those following
the expulsion of the Medici began to be written in Italian. In the same
way, in the second half of 1495 even the reports of speeches made at the
Pratiche were in Italian, but later were again transcribed in the Latin
tongue.

[2] *Vide* the note at the end of the chapter.

and the hopes of patriots extinguished, ransacked the whole history of Rome, Florence, and Italy, in search of the best form of government for their native city, in case of some fortunate turn of events ; and they all three arrived at the conclusion that with certain modifications suited to the alteration of the times, no better form of government could be found than that of the Greater Council and the Republic of 1494. And it is truly amazing to see that even the modifications proposed by these great intellects were in harmony with the Friar's conceptions. They suggested that the post of Gonfalonier should be a permanent appointment, and Savonarola frequently advised the same before his death ; they demanded a new tribunal for criminal offences, and he had propounded the same idea in his sermons ; they proposed allowing freedom of discussion in the Councils, and he had urged this more constantly than anything else.

It is true that some writers endeavour to prove that Savonarola could not have originated the idea of the Greater Council, because Soderini had borrowed the scheme from Venice ; nor invented the *Monte di Pietà*, because it had been previously suggested by others, and so on. But this is labour lost ; Savonarola did not invent any of the institutions he persuaded Florence to adopt, and this really constituted his chief merit. Institutions are neither created nor conceived ; they come into existence as the result of the times and condition of the people. He re-discovered them, as it were ; and recognizing their value succeeded in persuading the nation to adopt them ; and what higher meed of praise can be given to his political sagacity ! [1] We repeat that Savonarola was

[1] Later, when the persecutions against Savonarola began, the Republie abolished a law of the 13th of August, 1495, concerning the mode of electing and proclaiming the Signory, and stated that this law had been passed *opera et ordine fratris Ieronomi Savonarolæ*. Signor Gherardi

more clear-sighted than other men, simply because his eyes were sharpened by natural good sense and earnest benevolence, and his mind was unperplexed by theories, his heart undisturbed by party spirit. He therefore deserves to be ranked among the greatest founders of republican states.

For, if the evidence of historical events, the written testimony of the laws we have almost literally transcribed, and the opinion of the greatest of Italian political thinkers, do not suffice to enforce our verdict, we are at a loss for fresh arguments. We are aware that many are now of opinion that Savonarola should be mainly judged in the light of a mystic and seer of strange visions. But, it should be remembered, that during the first year of his political life, all his visionary ideas were kept in the background, and although at a later period, they are too often intruded in his religious, scientific, and even political discourses, many of the greatest men of his time were guilty of the same error. Yet no one thought of denying the competence of these men in science, letters, or public affairs, because they chanced to be mystics. Why, then, should Savonarola be robbed of his fame as a statesman and held up to ridicule, when we behold a people called back to life, as it were, by his breath, and see that the government he framed is the admiration of all writers, both in old times and new ? And, should the strange shadow of Savonarola the mystic obscure the reader's mind, and prevent him from forming a clear and accurate judgment of Savonarola the man, we will beg him to patiently follow this narrative, assured that on coming to a closer and more detailed view of the Friar's visions and prophecies, they will appear in a very different light from that in which other biographers have placed them.

("Nuovi Documenti," pp. 214–25) justly remarks, that this is an almost official recognition of the great share taken by Savonarola in the formation of the new government.

NOTE TO CHAPTER V.

Of the opinions professed by great Florentine politicians concerning Savonarola and the government framed by him.

MACHIAVELLI seems originally to have felt little sympathy for Savonarola, since in one of his early letters he only alludes to him as an astute and sharp-witted monk ; but this gives increased weight to the respect with which he spoke of him in riper years. For while noting what he thought to be political errors on the part of the Friar —especially concerning the law of the " Six Beans," which we have already mentioned and shall have to mention again—he makes far more frequent allusions to his learning, prudence, and goodness of soul (" Discorsi," bk. i. chap. xlv.) ; declares him to " be inspired with Divine goodness " (" Decennale primo ") ; and asserts that " so great a man should be mentioned with reverence " (" Discorsi," bk. i. chap. xi.). Then, in treating of the institutions founded by Savonarola, he is forced to acknowledge their high importance, as we see by his " Discorso " to Leo X., in which he expressly states, that the only way to re-establish the Florentine State is by opening the Greater Council. " No stable republic was ever formed without satisfying the masses. The general mass of the Florentine citizens will never be satisfied, unless the hall (of the Council) be re-opened ; . . . and your Holiness may rest assured, that whoever should wish to deprive you of the State, will hasten to throw it open before thinking of anything else." It might perhaps be urged that Machiavelli shows greater heartiness in praising the laws suggested by Savonarola and the latter's enormous influence over the people, than in praising the Friar himself ; this is quite true, and easily explained by the great difference between these two almost antagonistic characters—the one, all spontaneous enthusiasm and faith ; the other, all analysis, doubt, and inquiry. Both were great men, but each was singularly unfitted to comprehend the other. Savonarola would have judged the ideas of the Florentine Secretary with undue severity ; and the latter, much as he admired the founder of the republic of 1494, could not refrain from passing sarcasms on the monk and the prophet. In fact, the irony piercing through his praise, and the esteem and respect always tempering his blame, give us a better idea of Machiavelli's mental attitude than had his verdict on Savonarola shown more logic and coherence.

As to Giannotti, the noble and generous citizen who twice witnessed the downfall of his country's freedom; twice endured exile, and sought to mitigate his grief by studying how best to reconstitute the government, in case liberty should again be restored to Florence; he cannot mention Savonarola's name without his brave *popolano* heart throbbing faster within him. His admiration for the institutions counselled by the Friar, is expressed with an ingenuous eagerness that almost moves us to tears. "He that made the Great Council," he says, "was even wiser than Giano della Bella; for the latter sought to lower the great in order to ensure the safety of the people; whereas the former sought to secure freedom to all" ("Della Repubblica Fiorentina," bk. i. p. 87, in the "Opere," vol. i., Florence, Le Monnier, 1850). The whole book is impregnated with this admiration. Wishing to reprove the abuse common to the Friars of his day of continually preaching sermons on matters of state in the palace, he is careful to add: "For although Frà Girolamo preached them, no Frà Girolamo now exists adorned with equal learning, prudence, and wisdom; therefore, none should be so presumptuous as to deem it fitting to do that which was done by one in all things superior to all other men" ("Della Repubblica Fiorentina," bk. iii. p. 233).

But to learn the real views of great statesmen concerning Savonarola, and their minute investigations of the form of government he instituted, and of his great services to liberty in Florence, it is necessary to turn to the "Opere inedite" of Francesco Guicciardini. In his "Storia d' Italia," written at a riper age and in times hostile to Savonarola, he was cautious in his expressions; but in these works composed in the privacy of his closet and never intended for publications, he becomes another man. Sometimes he seems to be trying to lighten a load too heavy for his conscience to bear, by giving vent to feelings he had long been forced to suppress from motives of personal interest. We can almost see the sumptuous mantle of the diplomat drop from his shoulders, and reveal the simple republican jerkin beneath. An eloquent hymn to liberty gushes from his soul, and he seems forced to cry it aloud to the walls of his room, after having lacked the courage to proclaim it to his fellow-citizens. In these writings, no praise is too high for Savonarola and the Greater Council promoted by him. He says, in his "Ricordi": "The affections of the Florentines are so strongly set on the liberty given to them in 1494, that no devices, nor caresses, nor tricks of the Medici, will suffice to make it forgotten. It was easy to do so once, when only a few were robbed of their liberty; but now, after the Grand Council, all are robbed of it alike" ("Ricordi," xv., xxxviii., ccclxxvi.). And in his "Reggimento di Firenze," he continually repeats: "You owe a great debt to this Friar, who made the revolution at the right moment, and accomplished without blooodshed that which, but for him, would have cost much blood and disorder. For, but for him, you would have had first a restricted patrician government, and then an excessively democratic one; which would have led to riots and bloodshed, and possibly ended in Piero's restoration by force. He (Savonarola) alone had the wisdom to hold the reins loosely at first in order to apply the curb at the right moment" (p. 28, and *passim*). In his youthful work, the " Storia Fiorentina," Guicciardini has almost the air of a *Piagnone*. Extolling the prudence of Savonarola, his practical and political abilities, he speaks of him as the saviour of the country, in terms of such genuine eloquence, that, being unable to quote the whole passage as it stands, we refrain from reducing it to a colourless summary.

It cannot be denied that some writers of the present day have begun to speak slightingly of Savonarola ; to deny his political merit, and, failing other arguments, have put him to ridicule and shown incredible flippancy in their estimate of his worth. But every modern writer of importance who has devoted serious attention to the subject has always ended by concurring in the views of the elder historians. And if we may venture to quote any political writer of our own time in the same breath with the great Italians referred to above, we would mention the name of the young Tuscan, Francesco Forti, who, but for his untimely death, would have gained well-deserved celebrity. This writer was gifted with a special intuition of all points connected with our old laws and institutions, and this is what he says of Savonarola : " The reforms accomplished by the Friar, gave Florence the only just republican government it ever possessed. In fact, all the best men in favour of a popular government in Florence down to 1530 were unanimously devoted to Savonarola's ideas. The history of all Italy in the fifteenth century can reckon few names greater than his ; and the political history of the Florentine Republic perhaps none so great " (Forti, " Istituzioni Civili ").

It would seem superfluous to lengthen this note by more quotations, when the facts are so plain. But it may be as well to add that Professor Cipolla's criticisms on Savonarola, in his learned paper, " Frà Girolamo Savonarola e la Costituzione Veneta " (" Archivio Veneto," April–October, 1874), do not seem particularly well founded. He quotes and reiterates charges urged against the republican constitution of Florence by Savonarola's admirer Giannotti. But he fails to observe that the latter's remarks do not apply to Savonarola's reforms in particular—for these are praised by Giannotti—but to the constitution of the Commune of Florence in general, and indeed to that of all Italian Communes, where there was never any just division of power, or legitimate check on the authority of the magistrates. Continual change of magistrates was the expedient resorted to, but this led to other evils. The Florentine Republic was always marred by these defects, which although recognized in the fifteenth century by political writers, such as Guicciardini, Machiavelli, and Giannotti, were still left unremedied. In fact, they only disappeared with the destruction of the Italian Communes and the birth of the modern state. The objections urged by Professor Cipolla against Savonarola's reforms apply with equal force to the reforms suggested by Machiavelli to Leo X. For, although the first idea of the modern state is to be found in the secretary's writings, even he proved unable, when reducing theory to practice, to cast entirely off the mediæval conception of communal government.

CHAPTER VI.

SAVONAROLA'S PROPHECIES AND PROPHETICAL WRITINGS.

HAT, at this juncture, was the state of Savonarola's mind? From the events narrated in the preceding chapter, one might be led to interpret it very wrongly. One might naturally expect to find him if not uplifted, at least rejoiced by his success, and the great good achieved for his people. But, on the contrary, just at that time, as a glance at his sermons will show, he was plunged in the deepest depression. While ruling the whole people from his pulpit, with all hanging on his words, and the whole city obedient to his will, he could yet feel no joy. The future looked dark to his eyes, and he vainly tried to throw off his gloomy presentiments. "I am weary, O Florence, after the four years of incessant preaching, in which I have spent my strength for thee alone. Likewise am I bowed down by constant thought of the scourge I behold drawing near, and by fear lest it overwhelm thee. Wherefore I offer up unceasing prayers for thee to God." [1] And it was

---

[1] Predica xxiii., " sopra Aggeo."

true that the tempting hopes and promises he had held out to Florence had always been conditional : " If ye turn not to the Lord, the joyful tidings shall become tidings of woe." And the people being so hardened in sin, the future of Italy, Florence, and the Church naturally seemed to Savonarola to be threatened with increasing danger and suffering.

SAVONAROLA PREACHING.

Thus, precisely at the time when he might have been supposed to be full of calm and content, he was most burdened by these presentiments. After the victorious result of his first political conflict ; after seeing the law carried for the establishment of a popular government with a grand council ; when all Florence was thronging round his pulpit in the hope of hearing some joyful out-burst of thanksgiving to the Lord—he again began to preach in his former allegorical strain, describing the sad-

ness weighing on his soul, and prophesying the violent death
to which he had always, apparently, known himself fore-
doomed. "A youth," he began, "left his home and went forth
in a bark to fish, and, while fishing, the master of the bark
steered far to sea, and out of sight of the port ; whereupon the youth burst into loud lamentations.   O Florence !
the lamenting youth standeth here in this pulpit.   I was
led from mine own home to the port of religion, and I
went thither at the age of twenty-three years in search of
the two things most dear to me—liberty and quiet.   But
then I looked on the waters of this world, and by preaching I began to win a few souls ; and seeing that I found
my pleasure therein, the Lord led me on board a vessel
and out to the open sea, where I now lie tossed and
beyond sight of land.   *Undique sunt angustiæ.*   Storms
and tempests are gathering before mine eyes ; I have lost
sight of the port behind me, and the wind bears me farther
forward.   On my right hand are the chosen, imploring
my help ; on the left the demons and the wicked, who
assail and molest us ; I look above, and there is the
eternal goodness urging me to hope ; I look below, and
there is hell, and as a mortal man I fear it, since without
the help of God it would certainly be my portion.   O
Lord ! Lord ! where hast Thou led me ?   Through seeking to save a few souls, I have come into a place whence
there is no return to peace.   Why hast thou made me a
man of disturbance and discord over the whole earth ?
I was free, and am now the slave of all men.   From all
sides I behold war and discord coming upon me.   Ye, at
least, O my friends, ye chosen of God, for whom I travail
by night and by day, have mercy on me !   Let me
say, in the words of the canticle : give me flowers, *quia
amore langueo.*   Flowers are good works, and I only yearn
for ye to please God, and save your souls."   And while
giving this discourse he was so overcome by emotion as

to be obliged to pause, saying, " Now let me rest awhile
in this storm."

Presently, resuming his sermon, he cried : " What
reward, O Lord, what reward shall be given in the life to
come to the winner of a battle such as this ? That
which the eye cannot see nor the ear hear—bliss eternal.
And in this life what shall be his reward ? The servant
may not be greater than his master, replieth the Lord.
Thou knowest that after preaching to thee I was crucified ;
thus martyrdom shall also be thy portion. O Lord,
Lord," now cried Savonarola, his powerful tones ringing
through the church, " grant me then this martyrdom, and
quickly let me die for Thee, even as Thou hast died for me.
Behold, the sharpened blade already appears before mine
eyes. . . . But the Lord sayeth unto me : wait yet a little
while, so that all things may be duly fulfilled, and then
thou wilt use the strength that shall be vouchsafed thee."
Thereupon he broke off, resumed his exposition of the
text from the Psalms, *Laudate Dominum, quia bonus,* and
went on with his sermon.[1]

This was one of the moments when, as Savonarola was
accustomed to say, " an inward fire consumes my bones
and compels me to speak." Rapt in a species of ecstasy,
he then seemed to have real revelations of the future. If
he chanced to fall into this state in the solitude of his cell,
he would be visited by a long series of visions, and maintain
his vigil night after night, until at last, overcome by
sleep, his wearied body found rest. But if he fell into this
state while in the pulpit, his excitement surpassed all
bounds. Words fail to describe it ; he was, as it were,
swept onwards by a might beyond his own, and carried his
audience with him. Men and women of every age and
condition, workmen, poets, and philosophers, would burst
into passionate tears, while the church re-echoed with their

[1] Predica xix., " sopra Aggeo."

sobs. The reporter taking notes of the sermon was obliged to write : "At this point I was overcome by weeping and could not go on." Savonarola sometimes sank exhausted in his seat, and was occasionally confined to his bed for several days after.[1] It is impossible to form any just estimate of the nature of his eloquence at moments such as these, for his words were either left unrecorded, or coldly and lifelessly rendered. But our belief in the orator's extraordinary state of excitement, in his vehement words and eloquent gestures, is all the greater when we find nothing in the written reports of his sermons to justify the tremendous effect they produced on the Florentine public, which was certainly the most cultured in Europe. We shall also find, on impartial consideration of Savonarola's life and doctrines, that his strange and inexplicable presentiment of his future fate served to endue his writings, sermons, and life with an extrordinary charm.

When his predictions are stripped of all secondary details and accessories, we note with surprise that nearly all were fulfilled. Nor do we merely refer to the political acumen, enabling him to be the first to announce the coming of the French, the expulsion of the Medici, and many other subsequent events; although it was precisely this gift of acumen that roused the amazement of all the keenest statesmen of his age.[2] Neither need we dwell

---

[1] He mentions this himself in his "Compendium Revelationum."

[2] As we have already noted, and shall again have occasion to show, Philip de Commines felt convinced that Savonarola was a true prophet, continually mentioned him in his "Mémoires" in terms of admiration, and always repeated that—"He foretold the coming of the king, when no one else thought of it ; he afterwards wrote and told to my own ears things which no one believed, and which nevertheless were all fulfilled. No one could have suggested them to him, for they were known to none." Nardi and numerous other contemporary authorities styled and believed him a prophet ; and even Machiavelli, though certainly not one of those who best understood Savonarola and judged him with the most impartiality, never attempted to deny his gift of prophecy. He says that " of

upon Savonarola's fixed presentiment of dying a violent death, and the truly marvellous and unaccountable certainty with which he so frequently announced it. The chief point to be noted is that he was the first to feel that a great regeneration of mankind was at hand; that the religious sentiment would reawake in men's hearts to achieve this regeneration, and that society would be re-invigorated by sanguinary conflict. For on close examination we shall see this to be the real gist of his well-known "Conclusions." " The church shall be renovated, but must first be scourged, and that speedily." His continual predictions of the coming conversion of all unbelievers, the triumph of Christianity upon earth, where soon there would be but one fold and one Shepherd, affords us the best proof of his belief that the human race was about to be welded into true unity, and christianity acknowledged as the sole religion of the civilized world. On attentive perusal and consideration of his works, we are positively amazed by his constant insistence on these " Conclusions," and his faith in their speedy fulfilment. And when we find him proceeding to describe the future woes of Italy in minute and strangely graphic detail; when we see how deeply his own spirit is stirred and touched, so that in speaking of these things he is seized with a species of delirious excitement— we are forced to recognize that we are in the presence of an extraordinary fact, even though it be one that admits

such a man one can only speak with reverence," and adds that infinite numbers believed in him " because his life, his doctrines, and the subjects he treated, were sufficient to inspire them with faith " (" Discorsi sulla prima Deca," bk. i. chap. xi.) Guicciardini, who, on the whole, judged him more fairly than any one else, and warmly extolled his goodness, learning and intellect, says that some of his prophecies were fulfilled ; but is uncertain, notwithstanding the excommunication, whether he was to be considered a saint and a prophet. But he winds up by saying, " At all events, we have seen him to be a truly extraordinary man, who wrought the greatest good to our city " (" Storia Fiorentina," chap. xvii.). And these verdicts were pronounced after Savonarola's death and the downfall of his party.

of no explanation. Here is a man who, foreseeing the wretched future awaiting his country, has so distinct a prevision of its woes, that he already seems to suffer them in his own person.

This, it seems to us, is the view to be taken of Savonarola in his character of a prophet, when, after glancing at his entire career, and all his predictions, we concentrate our attention on such of his prophecies as are of general importance, leaving all of secondary interest aside. For if we pause to notice these, everything is changed, and we are driven to examine another side of his character. We shall then perceive that his was a dual nature, composed of two opposite individualities, and that whereas the one spurred him towards the future, the other almost chained him to the past. Having considered the first half of his nature, we must now try to arrive at some comprehension of the second.

The scholastic studies, forming so great a part of Savonarola's training, had given him an irresistible tendency to the subtleties of the sophists. And his early application to Thomas Aquinas had inspired him with a strange ardour for all the Father's utterances concerning the angelic operations, and the nature and visions of the prophets ; he had strenuously pored over the minute and hair-splitting distinctions drawn by the "angelic doctor," and made at the same time so close a study of the Old Testament and Revelations, as to be thoroughly acquainted with every dream or vision of the prophets and patriarchs. These things had absorbed his youthful mind for days at a stretch, inflamed his already over-heated fancy, and excited and shaken his sensitive nerves to an indescribable degree. He had seen spectral apparitions even as a child ; they were now multiplied, haunted him even in public by day, and became almost threatening by night. On finding, in after years, that by study of the Bible and the Fathers, by fervent prayer and prolonged vigils, these ghostly visions were increased, he began to believe them inspirations from Heaven, mental pictures shown to him by the angels even as the visions of the prophets described in St. Thomas. From that time he let no dream or phantasy pass without seeking some parallel case in the Bible, and scrutinizing it by the rules of the "angelic doctor." He spent whole nights kneeling in his cell, a prey to these visions, until, his strength exhausted, his brain more and more inflamed, he ended by perceiving in all things some revelation from the Lord.

It should also be remembered that Ficino's Platonic philosophy was then much diffused in Florence, and that its continual reference to spirits, angels, and visions undoubtedly exercised great influence on the Friar's mind. And there was another circumstance that should be specially noted. Among the brethren of St. Mark's was a certain Silvestro Maruffi, who played a great part in Savonarola's life. In consequence of some disease contracted in infancy, this man was subject, even by day, to attacks of somnambulism, during which he saw curious visions and uttered strange words. But, evidently, he did not attribute these manifestations to any mysterious or supernatural agency, for on learning that Savonarola was beginning to speak of Divine revelations and predict the future, he sternly reproved him, saying that this was mere folly unworthy of a man of his gravity. Thereupon Savonarola, with the earnestness of look and tone that gained so much ascendency over men's minds, counselled him to address fervent supplications to the Lord for enlightenment as to the truth in this matter. Maruffi himself, when at the point of death, and with no courage left to defend his master, distinctly confessed that, "Whether from bodily ailments or other causes, it certainly appeared to me that I was then rebuked by the spirits for mine unbelief." [1] Doubtless, this was only another of his strange hallucinations; but it produced so great an effect on both the monks, that they never again doubted, even for a moment, that these visions and revelations did not come directly from the Lord. Savonarola began to regard Maruffi with an almost reverential esteem totally unmerited by that weak and frivolous man. [2] His blind faith in Silvestro's hysteric utterances involved him in a maze of error and confirmed his strange belief in the truth of his own visions. Temperament, chance, study and prayer, all combined to urge him forward, irresistibly as it were, on the perilous path.

In fact, Savonarola's self-delusion on this point passes description. He was a slave to these so-called visions, and, indeed, often spoke of them as though they were the most important part of his divinely appointed task.

[1] This fact is clearly proved by the documents of Savonarola's second and third trials, and of the trials of Frà Silvestro and Frà Domenico, all of which were discovered by us in the Florentine libraries. These documents are included in the Appendix to vol. ii. of the Italian edition of this work. Frà Silvestro describes his visions, distinctly avows that physicians declared them to be caused by disease, and adds, that when by reason of another illness eight pounds of blood were drawn from him his visions suddenly diminished. The records of Frà Domenico's trial confirm all that Frà Silvestro said on the subject, together with the depositions of the other prisoners, which we have also included among the documents.

[2] The reports of the above-mentioned trials give the best evidence of the truth of this assertion. Frà Domenico stated in his confession that he and Savonarola put so much faith in Maruffi's words, that on one or two occasions they gave out, as if seen by themselves, certain visions which Maruffi declared to have been shown him by the angels on purpose that he might describe them to his two friends, who were likewise commanded to proclaim them to the people as though seen by themselves. And, although on the brink of death, Frà Domenico tries to prove that this was not only a justifiable fraud, but a positive duty, inasmuch as it was imposed by the angels. All these particulars are given in Frà Domenico's holograph confession, a most important document, first discovered by us in the Codex 2053 of the Riccardi Library, and afterwards in other MSS. It affords a luminous proof of the heroic firmness of Frà Domenico, for, while openly confessing his own and Savonarola's superstition, his words place the sincerity of both beyond doubt.

He made them the object of continual study and profound
meditation, devoting much time to defining the angelic
method of revealing visions to mortals, enabling them to
hear supernatural voices, and so on. Some of his theories
on the subject are to be found scattered through his
sermons, epistles, and other writings; but in his "Dialogo
della verità profetica," published in 1497, he has put them
all together, almost in the shape of a scientific treatise.
This composition is an indubitable proof of the Friar's
innocent credulity and the confusion of ideas in his brain.
It is impossible to discover what was his precise view of
his own prophecies and prophetic mission; he seems to
have bewildered himself with conflicting theories, and been
unable to decide to which to cling. Sometimes his
prophecies of the future appear dictated by a simple
process of reasoning, and, as though he considered that
study of the Bible and of the corruption of the Church
must convince all wise men that chastisement was at
hand.[1] But at other times he evidently believed his
knowledge of the future to be derived from celestial visions
expressly vouchsafed to him by God for the benefit of the
Italian people. According to him this gift of prophecy
was quite independent of his merits as a good Christian.
A prophet, as such, is a mere tool in the hands of God,
and may even be unfit to save his own soul. It was on

---

[1] In chap. v. of Pico's "Vita Fr. H. Savonarolæ," entitled "De
divinis citra velamen revelationibus, quarum particeps factus Hieronymus, futuras predixit clades," this author clearly shows that Savonarola
deduced his "Conclusions" from the evidence of the Scriptures. For
in all his works the Friar makes continual allusion to the *natural reasons*
enabling him to foretell future events, and frequently styles prophecy a
part of wisdom : "Inter alias partes prudentiæ tres principales ponuntur,
videlicet : memoria præteritorum, intelligentia præsentium, et previdentia
futurorum." *Vide* "Expositio Abachuch prophetæ," an unpublished
work of Savonarola, written in his own hand on sheets added to the
Bible containing his marginal notes, preserved in the National Library.
An old copy of this composition is to be found in the Marcian Library at
Venice.

the strength of this theory, deduced from the teachings of
St. Thomas Aquinas, that he claimed to be a prophet,
and attributed to his visions the same explanations and
same importance accorded by the " angelic doctor " and
the Church to those of the prophets of old. "These
visions come directly from God," he said, "and are
impressed by the angels on the intellect and not on the
heart ; hence it does not follow that their recipient is
assured of salvation." [1]

But in other parts of his works we suddenly come upon
an almost opposite theory, which, leaving puerile dreams
and visions aside, no longer attributes to Divine inspiration apart from Divine favour or assurance of salvation, the marvellous instinct, or divination of the future
that he undoubtedly possessed, but asserts it to be
a result, and almost an essential element of the evangelic spirit with which every Christian must be imbued.
" I am neither a prophet, nor the son of a prophet," he
says at these moments ; " I would not assume so terrible
a name; but I am certain that the things announced by me
will be fulfilled, for they are derived from Christian learning and the evangelic spirit of charity.[2] . . . Truly your
sins, the sins of Italy, make me a prophet perforce, and
should make all ye prophets. Heaven and earth
prophesy against ye, and ye neither see nor hear. Ye are
inwardly blind, ye deafen your ears to the voice of the
Lord calling unto ye. Had ye the spirit of charity, all would
see, even as I see, the scourge that draweth near."[3] These
different theories clash against each other at every step in

[1] *Vide* " Compendium Revelationum ;" "Dialogo della verità profetica ; "
" Predica del 27 Marzo, 1496 " (among those upon Amos) ; " Prediche
sopra Giobbe."
[2] " Prediche sopra Amos e Zaccaria," Violi's collection, sheet 40 and
passim : Florence, 1497.
[3] " Epistola a certe divote persone," ec., given in vol. ii. of Quétif's
work, p. 181 ; " Prediche sopra l'Esodo " (Florence, 1498), sheet 12 ;
" Prediche sopra Amos e Zaccaria," sheet 39.

Savonarola's works, without either being absolutely predominant. Similar contradictions are frequent in the sermons, but are still more abundant and more forcibly expressed in the works specially devoted to the subject of prophecy. And for a due comprehension of this remarkable side of Frà Girolamo's mind and character these must be carefully examined.[1]

In the "Dialogo della veritá profetica," to which we have before referred, Savonarola is supposed to carry on a discussion with seven allegorical speakers representing the seven gifts of the Holy Spirit, and to refute their various

---

[1] Herr Rudelbach deserves praise as the first writer to note the opposition between Savonarola's principal theories on prophecy. His remarks are based on a diligent examination of the author's works ; but, as usual, he arrives at the most arbitrary conclusions. *Vide* the long chapter entitled "Uber die prophetische gabe, und die Prophezeihungen Savonarolas." After justly noting the difference between the two conceptions, he tries to refute the first and exaggerate the second in order to prove that Savonarola was an *evangelical* prophet, or prophet of the Reformation. He places him in the same category as Abate Gioacchino, St. Bridget, and St. Catherine, who, in his opinion, were all more or less prophets of the Reformation.

Herr Meier, on the other hand, while also seeking to prove that Savonarola was a Protestant, tries to tone down Rudelbach's exaggerations, and confesses that the latter was too prone to let his fancy run away with him. He, too, notes the contradiction between Savonarola's two theories ; but while destroying one of them, he tries to keep the other out of sight, and seems almost persuaded that the Friar neither was nor believed himself a prophet, but merely tried to divine the future by the light of the Scriptures. This biographer does not appear to keep his own aim very distinctly in view, and treats the subject so coldly and vaguely, that, instead of satisfying or convincing, he only wearies his readers. Nevertheless honour is justly due to these two German writers as the first to study the prophetic works of Savonarola, and appreciate the necessity of treating the subject at length, instead of eluding it, as so many other biographers of the Friar had done.

Some years later Professor Döllinger published a paper on Christian Prophecy, in Riehl's "Historisches Taschenbuch" (Leipsic, 1871). He concurs in our own views with reference to Savonarola, saying, "Aber mehr und mehr wird doch erkannt werden dass dieser ausserordentlicher Mann, wie es der beste seiner Biographen, Villari, ausgesprochen, wirklich eine irgenthümliche Gabe der Divination bessessen habe." *Vide* p. 354.

objections. They first ask him—Whether he ever feigns
to be a prophet the better to convince the people of the
truths of religion. To this Savonarola indignantly replies,
That there is but one truth, and that every falsehood is a
sin ; and that the greatest sin of all would be to deceive a
whole people in the name of the Lord, and thus make
God Himself an impostor. Might not all this, asks
another of the seven, be some arrogance of thine, hidden
beneath the garb of false humility ? Thereupon, quoting
the authority of St. Thomas, Savonarola replies : Man is
not justified of this light ; what foundation, therefore,
could I have for my pride and arrogance ? May it not
be, adds a third, that in all good faith thou dost deceive
thyself ? No, that is not possible. I know the purity of
my intentions ; I have sincerely adored the Lord ; I try
to follow in His footsteps ; I have passed my nights in
prayer and watching ; I have renounced my peace ; I have
consumed health and strength for the good of my neighbour. No, it is not possible that God should have
deceived me. This light is truth itself ; this light is the
aid of my reason, the support of my charity." [1]   And then,
with much eloquence, he proceeds to expound a theory
totally opposed to that which he had proposed a few pages
back. To one interlocutor he proves the truth of his
light, by saying that it is independent of grace ; and then
tries to prove it to another by asserting that light is almost
identical with grace.

But the most noteworthy point of this dialogue is the
reply made to the demand : What certainty hast thou of
the truth of these revelations of thine ? It is curious to

[1] "De veritate prophetica, Dialogus in lib. viii." (without date).
Another edition, dated Florence, 1497, is entitled, " De veritate prophetica libri seu dialogi ix." The alteration in the number of the
dialogues is caused by one of the editors having included the introduction.
A third edition was brought out in Italian during the same year, 1497,
and a reprint of the work was produced in Venice in 1548.

see how he then flounders among a thousand arguments and syllogisms, which are the merest sophistry. He was in the unfortunate position of one trying to prove by reason that he was above reason, and demonstrating by human arguments that he was above humanity. Unconsciously to himself, Savonarola was treading dangerous ground on the verge of an abyss. His supernatural powers could only be proved in one way—*i.e.*, by a miracle. And at any moment a miracle might be required of him by the multitude, whose blind credulity was impelling him to ever wilder extremes ; and such a request would inevitably prove a most powerful weapon in the hands of his adversaries. But his beliefs were so fixed, that it never occurred to him to waver in them ; to do so would have seemed an act of ingratitude to the Almighty. Nor could he ever admit that those who refused to share them might be sincere in their incredulity. Savonarola also wrote another pamphlet on the subject of prophecy, entitled " Compendium Revelationum," which was published in August, 1495.[1] This contains a compendium of his principal visions, and many highly interesting details of his life, some of which refer precisely to the time and

---

[1] "Compendium Revelationum." Impressit Florentiæ ser Franc Bonaccorsio, 1495 ; v nonas mensis octobris. The same printer had published an Italian version on the 18th of August, 1495, which was reprinted twelve days afterwards by ser Lorenzo Morgianni. In 1496 it was republished both in Paris and Florence ; at Venice in 1537, and again in Paris, under Quétif's direction, in 1674.

Besides Savonarola's own writings on prophecy, we may refer to many tractates on the same subject written by his disciples. *Vide* Girolamo Benivieni, " Lettera a Clemente vii.," published by Comm. G. Milanesi at the close of Varchi's " Storie " (Florence : Le Monnier, 1857–58) ; Domenico Benivieni, various " Epistole " and " Trattati," giving expositions of his Master's doctrines ; Lorenzo Violi, " Giornate " (among the MSS. of the Magliabecchi collection) ; Frà Benedetto, the Florentine, in nearly all his works (to which further reference will be made elsewhere), and especially in the " Secunda parte delle profezie di Frà Girolamo " ; and finally, leaving aside many minor writers, G. F. Pico and all the elder biographers, by whom the subject is treated at length.

manner of his first prophecies, and record how he combated the impulse to narrate his visions, and then finally
yielded to it. Savonarola has written this composition
in unusually correct and even almost elegant Latin ; and
the visions described in it have a certain imaginative force,
like those mentioned in a previous chapter, concerning the
Sword of God menacing the earth ; the black cross rising
to heaven from the centre of Rome, amid flashes of lightning, thunderbolts, and storms, and the cross of gold
rising from Jerusalem, and shedding light and consolation
over the earth. As their meaning was clear, and the hopes
symbolized in them were easily understood, these visions
became popular, and were reproduced in numerous medals
and illustrations to the Friar's works. But what can be
said of Savonarola's subsequent phantasies, when, in the
character of Christ's appointed messenger to the
Florentines, he narrates, in minute detail, his long and
strangely incomprehensible journey to Paradise, reporting
the speeches there addressed to him by various allegorical
personages, including the Virgin herself, and even describing the Madonna's throne and the exact number and
quality of the precious stones with which it is set ? This
mysterious journey concludes with a sermon from Jesus
Christ to the Florentines, transmitted through Savonarola's
lips, and confirmatory of all that he taught. He first
related this vision in a sermon given in May, 1495, and
it apparently excited much adverse criticism; for in a
letter addressed *ad amicum deficientem*,[1] Savonarola
complains of his critics, declaring them to have been inspired by malignity : " for, had they listened attentively,
they would have understood that I did not intend to say
that my mortal body had been in Paradise, but only that
I had seen it in a mental vision. Assuredly in Paradise
there be neither trees, nor waters, nor stairs, nor doors,

nor chairs ; therefore, but for their ill-will, these men
might have easily understood that all these scenes were
formed in my mind by angelic intervention." We leave
the reader to judge whether these fantastic dreams were
produced by angelic intervention or by the preacher's
excited fancy !

Nevertheless the puerility of these visions is a strong
proof of Savonarola's sincerity, and helps to rebut the
numerous charges of fraud and bad faith urged by those
who would have us believe that he merely fostered the
credulity of the mob, in order to augment his own
influence. Were we to accept this view of the man,
it would be impossible to form any judgment of his
character ; for his whole life would be then reduced
to chaos, and not only his best qualities, but his worst
errors be alike inexplicable. How could it be credited
that a man of Savonarola's genius, wisdom, and experience
would indulge in so clumsy and childish a fraud ? Had
he been a wilful deceiver, would he have exposed his own
fictions and bared his weaknesses to all the winds of
heaven ? If his sole purpose was to beguile the people,
why should he have written abstruse and difficult treatises
on his visions, described them to his friends and his
mother, or made them the theme of marginal notes in
his Bibles ? [1] All that his warmest admirers would
be most willing to conceal ; things which the clumsiest
impostor might indeed have narrated to the people, but
would have never allowed to be printed, are precisely
what he published, republished, and enforced by quotations from Scripture and St. Thomas Aquinas. Indeed
the strangest side of his character and most noteworthy

[1] In fact, he expresses the same views as to the importance of his
prophecies in many holograph notes written in his Bibles for his private
use ; and in letters to his mother, brothers, and friends, constantly
maintains the same principles, feelings, and contradictions.

point of his career lies in the fact that the ruler of an
entire people, who filled the world with his eloquence, who
was one of the most original philosophers of his age, and
who had given Florence the best form of republican
government it had ever possessed, should almost boast
of hearing voices in the air, of seeing the sword of the
Almighty, of being the ambassador of Florence to the
Virgin! It behoves the historian to deal plainly with
this fact, showing it in its true light and true proportions,
for it may thus afford the philosopher a lofty theme
of meditation. It is undoubtedly a solemn thing to see
how inexorably Providence humbles even the greatest
men, and reminds us that they were mere mortals, by
counterbalancing their highest faculties by utterly human
weaknesses.

This singular contrast was very marked in Savonarola;
but still more so in the age that he inaugurated. It
seemed as though in that rejuvenescence of the human
race, men's faculties were strained to a higher pitch,
and as though life were almost a fever, in which none
could escape delirium. We have seen how the grave
Marsilio Ficino daily changed the jewels in his rings,
according to the mood of the moment; how he also
alternated his amulets, composed of the claws and teeth
of various animals, and gave lectures from the professorial
chair on the occult virtues contained in them. We have
told how Francesco Guicciardini declared himself *to have
had experience of aërial spirits*, and how Cristoforo Landino
drew the horoscope of the Christian religion. Hence
it may be concluded that the only difference between
Savonarola and his most celebrated contemporaries was
that he ascribed to religious and supernatural agencies the
same phenomena which other philosophers and thinkers
attributed to occult powers. But at the next step in this
period of the Renaissance, our wonder passes all bounds.

The dreams of Pomponaccio, Porta, and Cardano are far wilder than those of Savonarola. The daring spirits whose researches in the occult sciences hewed out a path for Galileo apparently lived in a state of continual delirium. No one at this day could credit Cardano's faith in dreams and superstitions but for the evidence of his autobiography, and on reading his account of these things, all belief in his intellect would vanish but for the real discoveries recorded in his works. Instead of devoting his whole life to science, he wasted half his time in visionary imaginations. If he had a singing in the ears, it was the voice of his familiar spirit; the sight of a wasp flying into his room inspired almost a volume of predictions, in which he had so firm a belief, that, according to some writers, he positively starved himself to death, in order that one of them might be fulfilled.[1]

These were the men, these the times destined to furnish so many martyrs to science! And, we must again repeat, that unless we place Savonarola at the head of this new epoch, it will be impossible to comprehend his character. In announcing his prophecies from the pulpit, he saw the future so clearly before him, that he seemed already across the threshold of the new century; he was so strongly imbued with its spirit, that he may be said to be its initiator. But whenever he tried to reason upon and explain the marvellous gift that was solely derived from his own greatness of soul, he fell back into the past, and, lost in the mazes of scholastic, could not even comprehend himself. In him, therefore, as in his age as a whole, we behold the past and future in mortal conflict. The past

[1] This statement is made by De Thou. *Vide* Libri, "Histoire des sciences mathematiques;" Cardani, "De vita propria." As to Porta, the reader may refer to Libri's account of him, and also to his own work upon "Magia." See also Carriere's "Die philosophisce Weltanschauung der Reformationszeit" (Stuttgart, 1847); and Ritter's "Geschichte der Philosophie."

seems still firmly established, but it is withered at the
root and losing its grasp of reality, while the future is
sending forth vigorous young shoots, and claiming the
world as its own.

CHAPTER VII.

VARIOUS FACTIONS ARE FORMED IN FLORENCE. SAVONAROLA TAKES HIS TEXTS FROM THE PSALMS ON FEAST DAYS; AND IN LENT, BY MEANS OF SERMONS ON JOB, INAUGURATES A GENERAL RE-FORMATION OF MANNERS WITH SIGNAL SUCCESS. CONVERSION OF FRÀ BENEDETTO.

(1495.)

RESUMING the thread of our history, we must now go back to the beginning of 1495, in order to trace the germs of civil discord, which, although as yet hidden from the eye, were soon to be developed and again divide Florence into factions. At this moment all seemed to be of one opinion, and of one party—*i.e.*, that of the Friar and the *Frateschi*. But on closer view it might have been discerned that there was considerable variety of opinion among the citizens. First of all there were some who, while devoted to popular government, had no sympathy for friars in general, nor for Savonarola in particular. These men were few, and disunited; they saw that the Friar's conduct of public affairs was favourable to the cause of liberty; and accordingly they always gave him and his followers the support of their votes in the Council Chamber. In consequence of their inoffensive attitude they were entitled the Whites (*Bianchi*), whereas a larger,

more compact and far more dangerous body of citizens
bore the name of the Greys (*Bigi*). The latter consisted of Medicean adherents, who, owing their pardon to
Savonarola, had apparently joined him and declared themselves in favour of the popular government. But in reality
they were engaged in secret intrigues and correspondence with Piero de' Medici, whose return they ardently
desired. And although it was not long before these
schemes came to light, they were carefully concealed at
first, and the Republic was long unaware of the treachery
lurking in its midst. It was precisely the secrecy of their
labours that rendered the Greys so dangerous, for Savonarola's magnanimous behaviour to them, and the over-
trustfulness of his followers, increased their facilities for
ruining the State. The honest inhabitants of Florence,
burning with enthusiasm for the Friar's doctrines, and fully
satisfied with the general amnesty and the liberty granted
to them, had no idea what sinister schemes and intrigues
were in progress ; and when Savonarola warned them
from the pulpit to be on the alert, " since there be some
that strive against liberty, and seek to play the tyrant,"
they were inclined to think that his zeal for the public
good betrayed him into exaggeration, and went about
declaring that the Medici had no longer any adherents in
Florence.

Meanwhile the popular party kept a strict watch on
other and more undisguised adversaries, *i.e.*, the partisans
of a limited government, who, as we have seen, had been
from the first most energetic opponents of the new *régime*.
These were men of wealth and experience whom the
Medici had often, though reluctantly, employed in State
affairs ; they had weighty influence at the Roman Court,
and were still more powerful in Milan, where Ludovico
the Moor, who was equally hostile to Piero de' Medici and
the Republic, gave them the utmost encouragement. The

aim of these men was to grasp the government in their
own hands and found a species of aristocratic republic as
in the days of the Albizzi. Consequently they felt a
fierce hatred for the Mediceans, and instead of pardoning
them as Savonarola had done, would have crushed them
by exile, confiscation, and death; they detested all
friends of the popular government, but were specially
virulent against the Friar as the main cause of their defeat,
and against his followers whom they sneeringly called
Piagnoni (Snivellers). Hence their title of *Arrabbiati*
(The Maddened).[1] They had, in fact, all the old, restless party spirit, seemingly indigenous to Florence, that
Savonarola alone could hold in check, and this was why
they so bitterly hated him. They were ready for any
risk, and eager to make some daring attempt, but were
still too weak a minority. For after the establishment
of the new constitution, the Arrabbiati were in a very
difficult position : they could make no assault on the
popular government without being opposed by the
Bianchi and Piagnoni, and still more decidedly by the
Bigi, who well knew that under a government formed
of Arrabbiati[2] they would be hopelessly excluded from
pardon. In this state of things even the Arrabbiati saw
fit to feign friendliness, or at least tolerance, to the
popular government, while concentrating all their hatred

[1] In after years, *i.e.*, during the siege of Florence (1529-30), these
names had a different meaning. Both *Piagnoni* and *Arrabbiati* then
signified adherents of the popular government, and the latter name was
more specially applied to the hottest champions of the popular cause.

[2] " And all well disposed to the universal government, desired that it
should be introduced and favoured by the Friar. In the which the
friends of the past Medicean rule very willingly concurred, in order to
escape the vengeance of their adversaries ; inasmuch as they would
have been exposed to much greater danger from them under the govern
ment of a particular (restricted) State, if by ill fortune of our city a
new restricted government should have been established" (Nardi,
" Istorie di Firenze," vol. i. p. 66). See, too, Violi, " Giornate ;" and
Parenti, "Storie." It would be a great blunder to infer from this that any
real friendship ever existed between Savonarola and the Medicean party.

upon Savonarola, who was plainly its leading spirit and mainstay. Therefore they persistently jeered at his visions and prophecies, declared that no friar had any call to meddle with politics, and that his charges against the Court of Rome were monstrous scandals. By this means they hoped to alienate the Bianchi and Bigi from Savonarola and his followers, and by attacking him as an individual to find a way of overthrowing his party.[1]

Accordingly they began hostilities in the early part of 1495 ; and when the Twenty Accoppiatori, after hot dispute, elected as Gonfalonier Messer Filippo Corbizzi, a man without administrative ability, indifferent to the people, and decidedly adverse to Savonarola,[2] the Arrabbiati gathered about him and found him a useful instrument for their designs. One day he adopted the very unusual measure of assembling in the Palace a council of theologians and ecclesiastics, including Frà Domenico da Ponzo, a noted enemy of the Friar. Marsilio Ficino was also of the number, for although already an admirer of Savonarola's doctrines, he still belonged to the Medicean party.[3]

---

[1] Nardi, vol. i. pp. 64 and 88.   See also Violi.

[2] Nardi, vol. i. p. 82 ; Ammirato, " Storia di Firenze," bk. xxvi.

[3] " Vita Latina," sheet 18^t ; Burlamacchi, 69 and fol.   Regarding Savonarola and his predictions Ficino expressed himself as follows : " Nonne, propter multa delicta, postremum huic urbi, hoc autumno (September and October, 1494), exitium imminebat, nullâ prorsus hominum virtute vitandum ?   Nonne divina elementia, Florentinis indulgentissima, integro ante hunc autumnum quadriennio, nobis istud pronuntiavit per virum sanctimonia sapientiaque præstantem Hieronymum ex ordine prædicatorum, *divinitus* ad hoc electum ?   Nonne *præsagiis monitisque divinis* per hunc impletis, certissimum iam iam supra nostrum caput imminens exitium nulla prorsus virtute nostra, sed præter spem opinionemque nostra mirabiliter vitavimus ?   *A Domino factum est istud, et est mirabile in oculis nostris.*   Reliquum est, optime mi Johannes, ut deinceps salutaribus tanti viri consiliis obsequentes, non solum ego atque tu, sed omnes etiam Florentini Deo nobis clementissimo grati simus, et publica voce clamemus : Confirma opus hoc, Deus, quod operatus es in nobis." (Letter to Giovanni Cavalcanti, 12th December, 1494. *Vide* Marsilii Ficini, " Opera," vol. ii. p. 963. Basileæ, 1576.) But later, in the days of Savonarola's adversity, Ficino basely turned against him.

Directly the members were assembled, the Gonfalonier
stated that he intended to proceed against the Friar for his
interference in the affairs of the State, and caused him to
be summoned. Savonarola presently appeared, accompanied by his faithful Frà Domenico of Pescia and quite
unaware of the purpose of the meeting. But scarcely had
he crossed the threshold than the mob of theologians
began to attack him with a furious storm of invectives.
The fiercest of his assailants was Tommaso da Rieti, a
Dominican friar, reputed to be a skilled theologian, and
who, by reason of his diminutive stature, daring temper
and subtlety in argument, was nicknamed the Garofanino
(spicy little clove). Taking for his text the apostle's
words, *Nemo militans Deo, implicat se negotiis sæcularibus,*
this man delivered a diatribe against Savonarola, who,
waiting until all the others had finished speaking, then
quietly rose and said in reply : " Now the Lord's words
are fulfilled : *Filii matris meæ pugnaverunt contra me ;*
yet it saddeneth me to see that my fiercest foe is likewise
clad in the robe of St. Dominic. That robe should remind
him that our founder took no small part in worldly affairs ;
and that our order hath produced a multitude of saints and
holy men who have been engaged in the affairs of the
State. The Florentine Republic must surely remember
Cardinal Latino, St. Peter Martyr, St. Catherine of Siena,
and St. Antonine, all members of the order of St. Dominic.
To be concerned with the affairs of this world in which
God Himself hath placed us, is no crime in a monk, unless
he should mix in them without any higher aim, and without
seeking to promote the cause of religion." He therefore
challenged all present to cite a single passage of the Bible
forbidding men to give their support to a free government in
order to ensure the triumph of morality and religion. And
he said in conclusion : " Far easier will it be to find it forbidden to discuss religion in profane places, or theology in

the Palace." The divines were so confounded by this address, that no one knew what to reply. One of them, however, started to his feet and cried in a fury : " Come, then, tell us plainly : are thy words truly inspired by God, or are they not?" "That which I have said was said plainly," rejoined Savonarola ; "I have nothing more to add now." And thereupon this strange meeting was dissolved.[1]

Having thus routed and confounded his foes, Savonarola continued his labours in the pulpit, seeking to soothe men's minds, quiet their passions, and extinguish party strife. At one time he would inculcate universal peace, at another the advantages of the Greater Council ; then we find him enthusiastically comparing the different steps in the formation of the government he had instituted with the seven days of the Creation ; [2] while on another occasion he compares them with the hierarchy of the angels.[3] " Carry on your reforms," was his unceasing cry ; " continue in the way ye have begun, and the blessing of the Lord will be with ye." In the course of his last sermon on Haggai he announced that it was the Lord's will to give a new head to the city of Florence ; and after keeping his audience long in suspense, finally declared : " This new head is Jesus Christ; He seeks to become your King !" He then dilated on the supreme felicity of having no ruler, no guide save Christ, and the overflowing prosperity that would thus be vouchsafed to all. " O Florence, then wilt thou be rich with spiritual and temporal wealth ; thou wilt achieve the reformation of Rome, of Italy, and of all countries ; the wings of thy greatness shall spread over the world."[4]

[1] " Vita Latina," sheet 19 ; Burlamacchi, p. 69 and fol.
[2] Predica xviii., "sopra Aggeo."
[3] Predica i., " sopra i Salmi."
[4] Predica xxii., " sopra Aggeo."

With this proclamation of Jesus Christ as King of Florence, his Advent sermons on Haggai came to an end amid tremendous outbursts of popular enthusiasm. Politics and religion are so closely and strangely commingled in these discourses, that they form a true record of the times and of the diverse passions stirring the souls of the people and their Friar. He then bade his congregation farewell on the score of needing repose ; but he did not allow himself much rest, for in January, 1495, we find him again in the pulpit, delivering sermons from the Psalms on the Sundays before Lent. Thus we have seven more lengthy sermons, resembling those on Haggai both in matter and form,[1] but likewise containing many indications of the civil discord, and the contest with the Arrabbiati, by which the preacher was now harassed. " O ungrateful Florence, ungrateful people ! For thee have I done that which I would not do for my own brethren, in whose behalf I have ever refused to offer so much as a single prayer to any prince of this world. And now that which I have done for thee hath stirred ecclesiastics and laymen to all this hatred against me." [2]

One of these sermons on the Psalms demands special mention, namely, that delivered on the 13th of January, and known as the " Renovation Sermon." Taking for his text the celebrated words heard by him in his visions, *Ecce*

---

[1] " Prediche del. Rev. P. Frate Hieronimo fatte sopra diversi Salmi e Scripture in S. M. del Fiore, cominciando il giorno dell' Epifania e seguitando gli altri giorni festivi, raccolte per ser Lorenzo Violi," Florence, 1496. As we have already stated, the first seven of this series forms a sequel to that on Haggai ; the eighth, addressed to certain nuns, treats of conventual vows ; then come seventeen others delivered after the Lenten series on Job. Later, Savonarola added a few more on the same theme. These sermons are all long and fill a bulky volume, with the addition of a few of Frà Domenico's discourses, to which we shall allude further on. Several of the later editions of this book are mutilated, and particularly those published at Venice in 1517 and 1543.

[2] Predica ii., " sopra i Salmi," delivered on the 11th of January, 1495 (common style).

gladius Domini super terram cito et velociter, Savonarola expounded all his own theories on the coming renovation. He began by saying that future and contingent events are known to God alone ; hence astrology, which pretends to ascertain the future from the stars, is fallacious, inasmuch as it is contrary to the rules of faith and the principles of science. After refuting at length the assumptions of astrology, he proceeded to treat of the light of prophecy, " which by Divine participation reveals the future, without any special grace in the seer, even as Balaam, for instance, was a sinner though a prophet." He then explained the various ways in which the future may be revealed, and finally touched on his own visions : " They came to me," he said, " even in my earliest youth, but it was only at Brescia that I began to proclaim them. Thence was I sent by the Lord to Florence, which is the heart of Italy, in order that the reform of all Italy might begin."

After these general remarks, he spoke on the need of chastisement and renovation. He first enumerated the natural reasons for this need, namely, the oppression of the elect, the obstinacy of sinners, the desire of the righteous, and so on to the last reason—*i.e.,* the universal conviction. " Thou seest ! all seem to look forward to chastisement and tribulation. Thou seest ! all hold it to be just that our many iniquities should be punished." He reminded his hearers of Abate Gioacchino, " who likewise foretold renovation at this period ; " he cited a great number of parables,[1] in order to prove the probability of the scourge ; he drew a thousand distinctions as to the diverse nature of visions, and finally recounted those vouchsafed to himself. But his minutest descriptions were of the vision

---

[1] It was true that, according to Abate Gioacchino, the world's renovation should have been accomplished in 1260. But, the prediction not being fulfilled at that time, his followers transferred the date to a later period.

of the sword bent towards the earth, and that of the two
different crosses he had seen arise from Rome and Jerusalem. It is impossible to describe the fervour with
which he related these dreams, and his perfect conviction that they were heavenly revelations. He repeated
the words he had heard uttered by invisible beings in
heaven ; [1] the solemn tones of his voice rang through the
vault of the temple, were received as Divine manifestations by the spell-bound people, and thrilled them with
mingled emotions of wonder, delight, and terror. In
that age all men, and especially the more incredulous,
revelled in supernatural visions such as these ; hence
there was an almost magnetic sympathy between the
preacher and his audience ; and it would be hard to say
which dominated the other, which was the exciting force.
Both were strung to a pitch of feverish exaltation,
scarcely to be described, much less realized at the present
day.

But, to prove the necessity of chastisement, Savonarola
did not confine himself to arguments of this kind ; on the
contrary, he recapitulated his theme in order to prove it by the
authority of the Scriptures. " Daniel the Prophet hath said
that Antichrist shall come to persecute the Christians in
Jerusalem : therefore it is necessary to convert the Turks.
And how shall they be converted unless the Church be
renewed ? St. Matthew hath told us that the Gospel shall
be preached throughout the world ; but who now is fitted
to preach it ? Where are good pastors and preachers to
be found ? " Continuing in this strain, he concluded as
follows : " Wherefore thou mayest see that the Scriptures
and revelation, natural reason and universal consent, an-

---

[1] Here are some of these utterances : "Audite omnes habitatores
terræ, haec dicit Dominus : Ego Dominus loquor in zelo sancto meo :
ecce dies veniet et gladium meum evaginabo super vos. Convertimini
ergo ad me antequam compleatur furor meus. Tunc enim, angustia
superveniente, requiretis pacem et non invenietis."

nounce the coming of the scourge. O Italy ! O princes !
O prelates of the Church ! the wrath of God is upon ye,
neither is there any hope for ye, unless ye be converted to
the Lord. O Florence ! O Italy ! these adversities have
befallen ye for your sins. Repent ye before the sword be
unsheathed, while it be yet unstained with blood ; otherwise neither wisdom, power, nor force will avail. . . .
Wherefore these are my last words : I have revealed all
things to thee with reasons, both human and Divine ;
I have prayed thee, made supplications unto thee ;
command thee I may not, being thy father, not thy lord.
Do thy part, O Florence ; mine is but to pray the Lord
to enlighten thine understanding." [1]

This sermon was immediately printed and circulated
throughout Italy, Savonarola's enemies being as active
in its dissemination as his friends. It was useful to the
latter as a proof of their master's eloquence and to
increase the diffusion of his doctrines; to the former, as
a specimen of his audacity and a means of inflaming
the Pope and princes against him. And, in the hands
of the Arrabbiati, it proved a valuable document with
which to rouse the smouldering wrath of Alexander
VI. Already, at the close of 1494, the Arrabbiati had
contrived to obtain from Rome a mandate for Savonarola's removal to Lucca ; and they now urged the Pope
to turn a deaf ear to the Signory's request to be
allowed to retain him in Florence.[2] Accordingly, more
stringent orders arrived from Rome, and even the pressing
solicitations of the Ten failed to reverse the decree.[3]

[1] "Predica della Rinnovazione." It is the third sermon on the
Psalms, and was also published separately. There is an undated copy
of it in the Guicciardini Collection.

[2] Nardi, Pitti, Violi, and other writers repeatedly state that the first
orders from Rome were sent at the suggestion of the Arrabbiati and of
Ludovico, of Milan.

[3] The Sig: y sent a despatch on the 28th of December, 1494, to beg
that Savonar a might remain in Florence : " Hoc nobis populoque nostro

Hence the Arrabbiati, having now won the Gonfalonier to their side, hoped that affairs would turn in their favour and the Friar be dismissed. Savonarola, in fact, being determined to cause no scandal, was already preparing to leave at the appointed time. Meanwhile, however, he gave four more sermons, and in the first exhorted the people to be steadfast in seeking to perfect their new government, and inculcated the duties of charity, peace, and concord. In the second he treated of simplicity and the moral life ; urged his hearers to bestow their super-fluities on the poor, and suggested that the convents should be the first to set the example. And should the requisite permission be obtained from Rome, St. Mark's, he added, would be one of the first to begin. " Nowhere in the Gospel have I found a text recommending golden crosses and precious stones ; rather have I found : I was athirst and ye gave me not to drink ; I was a hungered, and ye gave me no meat. Should ye obtain the consent of Rome, I, for my own part, will give everything away, beginning with my own mantle." [1] In the two concluding sermons [2] he bade farewell to the people, saying that he must yield to the wrath of his foes. " I must go to Lucca, and thence perhaps elsewhere, as I may be ordered ; pray the Lord to aid me in teaching his Word. There be many in this city who would fain make an end of me ; but know that my hour hath not yet come. I depart, because it behoveth me to obey orders, and I would generate no

universo ita gratum erit, ut nihil gratius acceptiusque ac salutarius, ets omnia gratissime expectemus, hoc tempore accidere possit." (*Vide* " Il Savonarola e i Lucchesi, nuovi documenti," Florence : Cellini, 1862.) The letter of the Ten was sent to Rome with another addressed to their am-bassador, the 8th of January, 1495, containing these words : " Present it (the letter) without delay, and endeavour to obtain a Brief addressed to Frate Hieronymo, authorizing him to preach here this year, as has been already said." Meier gives this document at page 80, note 2.

[1] Predica v., " sopra i Salmi."

[2] Predica vi. (January 20th) ; Predica vii. (January 25th).

scandal in your city. As for ye, the chosen of the Lord, be steadfast in prayer and charity ; be not afeared of the scourges and tribulations which ever befall the righteous ; but be ye firm in holy deeds." Having pronounced these words, he left the pulpit amid the agitation and grief of all his friends.

But although the Gonfalonier Corbizzi was adverse to the Friar, and the Signory then in power readier to help him by words than deeds, the Ten were now counted among his warmest adherents. Assured of the support of the whole people, they again wrote to Rome, urgently beseeching the Holy Father to permit Savonarola to remain in Florence as Lenten preacher, notwithstanding the orders transferring him to Lucca. The whole city was in commotion at the announcement of the Friar's departure ; many regarded the popular government as already overthrown ; and epistles of all kinds were despatched to Rome, praying that the order might be revoked. So far, in fact, Alexander had no serious reasons to hate Savonarola, for he knew little and cared less concerning his visions and prophecies. Besides, King Charles, the friend of the Florentines and their Friar, was now in Naples at the height of his prosperity, and the Pope was unwilling to arouse his enmity. Therefore he was easily persuaded to yield to the request of the Ten, and revoking his decree, permitted Savonarola to preach during Lent in Florence.[1]

But, although apparently of little moment in itself,

[1] " Concerning the which thing (namely, the Friar's departure) the majority of the citizens were greatly moved, inasmuch as all the magistrates and men of honest disposition held his sermons to be very beneficial to morals, and very necessary for the pacification of the discordant minds of ill-disposed citizens at the beginning of the new government. Wherefore by the endeavours and messages of many devoted followers, especially of the Ten of liberty and peace, a revocation of the above-mentioned Brief was sought from the Pope, and was thus easily obtained " (Nardi, vol. i. p. 65).

this act made a powerful impression on the Friar's mind. He could never forget it, and it turned his ideas into a new channel.[1] The order to leave Florence and preach elsewhere was undoubtedly painful to him; nevertheless, regarding obedience as a sacred duty, nothing would have led him to violate the command. But what was he to think, when the Head of the Church showed so little respect for his own Briefs as to issue and recall them, at the pleasure of the last supplicant? It was now certain that the Decree had only been issued to please those enemies of the Friar who had already begun to lay all kinds of snares for him. How then could he, Savonarola, attach any weight to a command to which none was given by the Pope himself? Ought he to have obeyed it, supposing he had known all this at first? For the moment, however, Savonarola banished these thoughts as harassing temptations. He sent Frà Domenico to Lucca, and being solicited by that city to promise at least to go there in 1496, replied that, unless compelled by unforeseen events to remain in Florence, he would certainly come.[2] Meanwhile he immediately began his Lenten sermons. As if to show his need of patience, he took his texts from the Book of Job, and refrained as much as possible from touching on politics, so that his enemies might have no fresh excuse for attacking him. There was another reform to effect, no less useful and imperative than the change of government had been, namely, the *reformation of manners*; and to this his whole energy was given in his sermons on Job. These discourses, however, have come down to us in almost as mutilated a form as the series on Noah's Ark. Reported

---

[1] Savonarola afterwards alluded to these impressions in his sermons.

[2] In his letter to the Lucchese dated 18th of March, 1494 (common style, 1495), he made this reply to their request. *Vide* the beforementioned pamphlet, "Il Savonarola e i Lucchesi."

in a very incomplete and fragmentary fashion, by one who continually explains that he is too much shaken by emotion to transcribe the preacher's words, they were first rendered into Latin, then back into Italian, and first published at Venice in this shape in the year 1545.

The godly life, union, and concord of the citizens form the principal subject of these sermons. From the beginning he laid down the rule that all may be saved if they honestly endeavour to live a godly life: "Nought can excuse us, O my brethren ; rectitude draws us near to the Lord, and the Gospel is the staff of our weakness." [1] In these sermons the godly life is the all in all. He treats of friendship ; and after discussing its differences of degree and quality, concludes by saying that the only friendship worthy of the name, and really firm and enduring, is that which is founded upon goodness, honesty, and virtue. [2] He treats of the essence of freedom, and arrives at the same conclusion : "God is essentially free, and the just man is free after the likeness of God. The only true liberty consists in the desire for righteousness. It seemeth to thee that a good monk hath no liberty, because he hath submitted his will to that of others ; but his freedom is greater than that of laymen, exactly because he willeth to do that which is commanded him by others. What liberty is there in being dominated by our own passions ? Now, in our own case, dost thou, Florence, desire liberty ? Citizens, would ye be free ? First of all love God, love your neighbour, love one another, love the general welfare ; and if ye have this love and union among ye, true liberty will be yours." [3] He continually urged the necessity of concord. "Florence ! I tell thee thou must be united, if thou wouldst be freed from thy woes. For if thou sayest: oh ! union is ours, thou dost lie. I repeat that if thou sayest union is thine,

---

[1] Predica ii., "sopra Giobbe."   [2] Predica iii.   [3] Predica xiv.

thou dost lie ; a second and a third time, thou dost lie.
. . . Wert thou united thou wouldst have already won
that which I promised thee. . . . Wherefore, be ye united.
If ye desire to have strength and virtue from God, let
the flesh be prepared to receive them, and the preparation
needed is union, the which, O Florence, thou hast not.
Where is union, there is God ; and where is God, there
is all strength and all virtue." [1]

He continually declared these to be the commands
of God and addressed by Him to the Florentines. It
would seem that, while prudently abstaining from politics, he indulged more freely in visionary flights. He
gave an entire sermon on the light of prophecy ; [2] in
another he stated that the world was divided into two
hosts ; *i.e.*, the host of evildoers led by the Devil, and
of the virtuous led by Jesus Christ ; he suggested that
the chosen should make alliance with Christ, and offered
to go to Him as their ambassador. Then, in subsequent
sermons he recounted his dialogues with Christ and the
Virgin during this strange mission, and these also chiefly
turned on union and goodly living. Jesus Christ had said to
him : " Behold how all natural things are gradually fused
into one more perfect than the rest. Every movement
of material things is subject to the movement of the
heavens ; every movement of our body to that of the
heart ; every movement of the soul to reason ; all rules
and governments to God, the prime ruler of the universe.
Consider how, when the elements of a thing are dispersed,
that thing is said to no longer exist, and only by some
force reconstituting its unity can it be restored to existence. Had it been possible to display all My power and
goodness in a single creature, I would have so displayed
it ; and only because no one creature could be capable
of containing it all, have I created a multitude, which

[1] Predica xiii., "sopra Giobbe."   [2] Predica xii.

represent together a greater and vaster unity. Observe nature as a whole, and thou wilt perceive that every individual being craves unity ; all creation seeks it save this Florentine people that would rather be separate and divided." In the course of the same sermon, Savonarola again touches on the theme of holy living. " Goodness " —the Lord is still supposed to be speaking—" is diffusive in its nature, wherefore I, who am supreme goodness, inform the whole created world, and have given life to all creatures ; and all that is good in them is a share of My goodness. By goodness I came down among men, in the likeness of man, and was fastened on the Cross. Behold, therefore, the sign by which the good man shall be made known : namely, when one shall infuse his goodness into others, and make them share the good that is in him, verily that man is good and a sharer of My goodness. But when the contrary is seen, and men neither infuse nor spread the talent I have given to their charge, this is a manifest token that they have no share in My goodness. The Christian life consisteth not in ceremonies, but in the practice of goodness, *i.e.,* of compassion and mercy. Wherefore declare thou unto all, that thus is the goodness of man made known ; namely, by seeing whether he be pitiful, whether he share that which he hath with others, and especially with the poor. And in this consisteth the Christian religion, which is founded on love and charity." [1]

Thus the chief theme of these sermons is always the reformation of manners, a more pressing need at that time than the political reform, which was in full progress. It is true that the discourses are overladen with visions, allegories, and fantastic interpretations of the Bible, rendered still more fantastic by the superstitious ignorance of their agitated and unskilled compiler. But in fact the

[1] Predica xvi., " sopra Giobbe."

preacher's fancies were only, as it were, the outer husk of
reasonings intended to enforce holy living and union upon
the citizens. Here, for instance, is an example of the
moral conveyed by his visions, and by the scriptural allegories which he always interpreted on the same plan :—
" It is recounted by St. Mark that early in the morning
after the Sabbath day (Holy Saturday) the three Marys
came to the Lord's sepulchre, with fragrant ointments to
anoint the body of our Saviour. The three Marys represent the perfect, the proficient, and the incipient who are
in search of Christ. As I have before told ye, regarding this Gospel, they bear aromatic and fragrant drugs—
id est, virtues which are pleasing to Jesus. They reach the
sepulchre, *orto jam sole*—*i.e.,* when the sun was already
risen." . . . " If thou dost seek Jesus, the sun of justice
will arise in thee, thou shalt be enlightened, and thy desire
shall be fulfilled. But thou must walk in righteousness and
labour, since by labour shalt thou be made perfect. Behold
the three Marys! they walked in righteousness, seeking their
Lord, and thou seest, they were comforted at last. And
they thought to themselves by the way, Who will be able
to lift the stone ? Thus saying, they reached the temple,
and lo, the stone was already lifted. The which signifieth,
that if thou goeth by the path of good life seeking the
Lord, even if thou knoweth Him not, He abideth in thee,
and lifteth the stone of thy ignorance ; and the light revealed shall say unto thee, as said the Angel unto the
Marys, *Jesum quæritis Nazarenum ? Surrexit, non est
hic.*" " I know that ye seek Christ ; He is risen, He is
not here. That is to say, seek Christ in heaven ; seek
Him not in the things of this life, neither in the things
of this world ; seek Him in celestial, divine, and spiritual
things ; renounce the love of temporal things. He is in
heaven, and lo, He awaiteth ye. O Christians ! what do
ye here ? Seek to go where is thy head, for there shall ye

be blessed. *Venite et videte*, said the Angel to the
Marys; that is, come and see that Christ lieth not in the
sepulchre, for He is arisen. *Sed ite*, but go, walk from
virtue to virtue in the present life, if ye would find
Christ in the next." [1] Thus ended the Lenten course on
the Book of Job, the concluding sermon, as well as many
of the others, being interrupted by the emotion of the
scribe who was noting it down.[2]

Immediately after Lent Savonarola seemed broken down
by fatigue. His old energy still flashed from his eyes,
but he was terribly emaciated, looked thoroughly worn
out, and was increasingly weakened by an intestinal complaint. The incessant struggle and over-excitement of the
last few years were too great a strain to be long endured
by any mortal constitution; and political life had tried his
strength more than he was himself aware. The direction
of the revolution and reform of the State had not only
cost him ceaseless thought, speech, and counsel; but had
also loaded him with the immense responsibility of
practically deciding the destinies of a nation whose sole
trust was in him. He had felt the necessity of preserving
his moral ascendency, of animating, as it were, the whole
multitude with his own spirit, ruling it by his own will,
and had therefore lived in a perpetual state of tension
and feverish excitement. Yet so great was this Friar's
earnestness, that when the political strife had abated,
instead of taking any rest, he immediately began another
reform of equal magnitude by means of his sermons
on Job. And into this, as into all his other undertak-
ings, he had thrown his whole strength, with an indescribable devotion and tenacity of purpose. The words in
themselves are probably the least part of these sermons;

[1] Predica xlv., "sopra Giobbe."
[2] "So greatly was I overcome by emotion and tears, that I could not
go on writing." The amanuensis subjoined this note to many of these
sermons, including the last.

at all events in the incomplete form in which they have reached us. The subject treated in them was the one dearest to the Friar's heart; his mental excitement was increased by physical weakness, and his words were emphasized by fiery glances and energetic gesticulations. And although he gave too much importance to the visions of his brain, so great was the force of his sincerity, goodness, and benevolence as to have unprecedented effect upon his hearers. Never was a multitude so entirely dominated by pious emotion, so easily plunged in tears! By the end of Lent, Savonarola had won almost a greater victory than the political triumph achieved by his sermons on Haggai.

The aspect of the city was completely changed. The women threw aside their jewels and finery, dressed plainly, bore themselves demurely ; licentious young Florentines were transformed, as by magic, into sober, religious men ; pious hymns took the place of Lorenzo's Carnival songs. The townsfolk passed their leisure hours seated quietly in their shops reading either the Bible or Savonarola's works. All prayed frequently, flocked to the churches, and gave largely to the poor. Most wonderful of all, bankers and tradesmen were impelled by scruples of conscience to restore ill-gotten gains, amounting to many thousand florins.[1] All men were wonderstruck by this singular and almost miraculous change; and notwithstanding the shattered state of his health, Savonarola must have been deeply rejoiced to see his people converted to so Christian a mode of life. Now indeed he might have died content! But his hour had not yet come ; he was called by God to a higher fate.

---

[1] Besides the evidence on this point furnished by the " Vita Latina," Burlamacchi, Pico, Barsanti, Frà Benedetto, and other biographers, the reader may refer to all contemporary historians, as, for instance, to Nardi, Guicciardini (" Storia Fiorentina "), and the correspondence of the Ten with the Court of Rome, edited by Padre Marchese.

This new state of things was naturally turned to ridicule by the Arrabbiati, who grew more and more furious, and vented their feelings by jeering at the Friar and his followers, and nicknaming them Piagnoni (Snivellers), Collitorti (Wrynecks), Stropiccioni (Toadies), and Masticapaternostri (Prayer-mumblers). Nevertheless, the Piagnoni were the only determined defenders of the people's rights; the readiest to fly to arms when Florence was threatened by the French; the most generous in giving money to the State, and in tenderly succouring the poor who were suffering from the high price of food and scarcity of work. For their devotion to the Republic was all the more tenacious, because liberty and religion were as one in their hearts; and in all public emergencies it was only on these followers of the Friar that the country could really depend.

Accordingly, to the great disgust of the Arrabbiati, the enthusiasm for Savonarola and St. Mark's became more and more general. Peasants and nobles from all the country round journeyed to Florence by night to be in time for the morning's discourse; some came even from distant Bologna to spend the Lenten season in Florence;[1] and the vast Duomo itself was too small to contain the throng. Many new converts asked leave to join the Tuscan congregation, and the number of brethren wearing the robe of St. Mark was incredibly multiplied. Instead of fifty, as at first, the community now counted two hundred and thirty souls; hence it was necessary to obtain from the Government the adjacent buildings of La Sapienza, which were accordingly connected with the convent by a passage tunnelled under the Via del Maglio. Many of the new monks were scions of the leading houses of Florence, such as six brothers of the Strozzi family; several of the Gondi, Salviati, and Acciaiuoli; others were

[1] " Vita Latina," Burlamacchi and the Florentine historians.

men of mature age and of high standing in literature, science, and statesmanship, such as Pandolfo Rucellai, Giorgio Vespucci, uncle of the celebrated navigator, Zanobi Acciaiuoli, Blemmet, the Jewish teacher of Pico della Mirandola, the physician, Pietro Paolo da Urbino, and many more.[1]

The mode of these men's conversion is likewise worthy of special remark, since it proves that Savonarola, instead of encouraging sudden resolves and fits of enthusiasm, always proceeded with the utmost caution. We find an example of this in the account given by the Florentine Bettuccio, more generally known as Frà Benedetto, of his own conversion. He was the son of a goldsmith, exercising the then profitable art of miniature painting, was in the prime of youth, of a joyous temperament, full of dash and courage, prompt to quarrel, a singer, musician, and poet, fond of good living, and entirely devoted to pleasure. Consequently he was a favourite guest in the gayest society, and led a life of frivolous gallantry.

> " Tanto musco e profumo allor portavo,
> Con tante pompe e leggiadrie e gale,
> Che col cervel senza penne volavo." [2]

But these, he tells us, were evil days; in the time of Pope Alexander, days rife with avarice, sensuality, and unbelief:

> " Nè quasi si credea dal tetto in su." [3]

Such was the life led by Bettuccio, the miniature painter, when Savonarola began to be renowned, and all Florence

---

[1] *Vide* Padre Marchese, " Scritti," p. 141 and fol., for which work the author consulted the ancient annals of his own convent of St. Mark.

[2] (So much musk and perfume I wore, so many gauds and finery and frippery, that my head flew without wings.) *Vide* Frà Benedetto, " Cedrus Libani," a little poem published by Padre Marchese in the " Archivio Storico Italiano," Appendix vii.

[3] When one scarce believed in aught above one's roof.

flocked to his sermons. Bettuccio, however, refused to follow the herd; for he was on the side of the Arrabbiati, and joined in their scoffs against the Piagnoni. But one day, when in the house of a noble and beautiful matron, the latter spoke of Savonarola's sermons in the warmest terms. He laughed at the time; but on another day he was induced by the lady's persuasions to accompany her to the Duomo. He describes his deep confusion on entering the church and finding himself among so great a company of believers, who stared at him with astonishment. At first he longed to escape, but somewhat reluctantly decided to remain. And as soon as Savonarola mounted the pulpit everything seemed changed to him. Having once fixed his eyes on the preacher he was unable to withdraw them; his attention was powerfully arrested, his mind impressed; and then, he says, "At last I knew myself to be as one dead rather than living." When the sermon was over, he wandered forth into lonely places, "and for the first time I turned my mind to my inner self." After long meditation he went home, and became a changed man. He threw aside his songs and musical instruments, forsook his companions, and discarded his scented attire :

> "Come un vento
> Spoglia 'mi al tutto d'ogni leggiadria." [1]

From that day he was one of the most assiduous of Savonarola's hearers, frequented the convent of St. Mark, repeated prayers and litanies, and even beheld strange visions and heard heavenly voices in the air." [2] "I had a hard struggle with my companions," he tells us, "who

---

[1] "Cedrus Libani." With the speed of the wind, I stripped off every dornment.

[2] He mentions these visions in bk. iii. of his "Vulnera Diligentis," MS. 2,985 of the Riccardi Library. See particularly chap. xx. and chap. xxiii., in which he describes a vision beheld by Michelangiolo Buonarotti in Rome. *Vide* Appendix to the Italian edition, doc. xix.

went about making mock of me ; and a still harder
struggle with my own passions, which, breaking loose again
from time to time, assailed me very fiercely." At last,
when he felt sure of himself, he sought the austere Prior
of St. Mark's and cast himself at his feet. His voice
trembled, he could scarcely utter a word in the presence
of him to whom he owed his regeneration ; nevertheless he
stammered forth his desire to join the brotherhood.
Savonarola reasoned with him on the danger of precipitate
resolves, the difficulties of the monastic life, and concluded
by counselling him to make a better trial of himself by
leading a Christian life in the world, before crossing the
convent threshold. The advice proved to be needed, for
Bettuccio had again to fight against the violence of his
passions, and was not always victorious in the struggle.
After doing severe penance for these fresh lapses, and
when assured by long trial of having really mastered the
flesh, he returned to Savonarola in a calmer frame of mind.
But the latter, who had kept him carefully in sight, would
not yet allow him to assume the monastic robe, sending
him instead to minister to the sick and bury the dead :

> " Cosi più mesi, in un santo ospitale,
> A vivi e morti carità facevo." [1]

From time to time he was summoned to the Friar's cell,
to receive advice and hear lectures on the monastic life ;
finally, on the 7th of November, 1495, he put on the robe,
and on the 13th of November of the following year took
the full vows, and assumed the name of Frà Benedetto.[2]

---

[1] Thus, in a holy hospital, for many months, I did charity to the quick
and the dead.

[2] The whole account of this conversion is taken from Frà Benedetto's
own poem. For further particulars of his career, the reader may refer
to the preface to the poem, written by Padre Marchese, and reprinted in
a revised form in the latter's " Scritti varii."

The Florentine libraries contain many works by Frà Benedetto. Except-

This was how Savonarola gained one of the most faithful of his followers, one of the most steadfast in the hour
of peril, and who preserved to the last an increasing
admiration and almost worship for his master. The Friar
was equally cautious in his advice to others, and never
pressed any one to join the brotherhood. His only con-

ing the above-mentioned poem, "Cedrus Libani," all are inedited, and
nearly all treat of Savonarola. The Codices xxxiv. 7, and xxxvii. 318, of
the National Library (the former being, as the author says, the last copy
revised and corrected by himself), contain the first two books of the
"Vulnera Diligentis," which gives, in the form of a dialogue, many
biographical details of the highest value concerning Savonarola. Book
iii. of the same work, discovered by the present writer, contains numerous
particulars of the trials and execution of Savonarola and his fellow-
martyrs, with narratives, explanations, and commentaries of his visions and
prophecies. As before said, it is comprised in Codex 2,985 of the Riccardi
Library. The Rinuccini Codex in the National Library, ii. 8, 123, contains the *secunda parte delle prophetie dello inclito martire del Signore
Hieronymo Savonarola*. The first letter is illuminated, and has a miniature
portrait of Savonarola, said by Padre Marchese to be the only known
specimen of Frà Benedetto's work. Chap. xiii. also begins with an illuminated capital letter, representing the vision of the hand brandishing a
sword over Florence. This, too, may be attributed to Frà Benedetto.
Codex xxxv. 90, of the National Library, is a collection of several minor
works of the same author :—1st, "Fons Vitæ," finished at sheet 88, is in
three books and written in Latin. Book i. is a dialogue between
Homicida and *Dominus*, and gives details of Frà Benedetto's life. Book
ii. is on visions ; book iii. consists of religious meditations, hymns, and
chants. The Homicida of bk. i. is Frà Benedetto himself, for after
Savonarola's death he killed a man in a riot, though, according to Padre
Marchese, in self-defence. He expiated this crime by prolonged
penance and many years' imprisonment, during which period most of his
works were composed. Accordingly he often refers to himself in these as *Frà
Benedetto the homicide*, and is sometimes designated in old catalogues by
the same appellation. This was why his works remained unknown for
some time. 2nd, "Fasciculus Mirræ," from sheet 95 to 224, is a collection of sonnets, canticles, and religious hymns. 3rd, The little poem,
"Cedrus Libani," from sheet 231 to sheet 257. 4th, A *most faithful* copy,
in Frà Benedetto's hand, of all Savonarola's best poems. It also contains
a few prayers and other items of slighter importance. At sheet 280 is a
psalm by Savonarola. The lauds contained in the "Fasciculus Mirræ"
includes one upon Savonarola (sheet 214), God's prophet and martyr.
   We should note, in conclusion, that Frà Benedetto, while zealously
defending his master in these works, and attacking his detractors and
persecutors with equal vigour, repeatedly declares his own submission to
the Catholic Church.

cern was for the improvement of manners, the diffusion of morality, and the regeneration of the true doctrines of Christ, to which men's souls appeared dead. It was to this end that he now specially dedicated his whole time and strength, his entire heart and soul. When preaching on the holy life and Christian virtue his soul almost seemed to shine forth from his eyes, and his spiritual energy to be transfused by his voice into the people, who daily and visibly improved under his beneficent influence. Contemporary writers never cease expressing their wonder at this quasi-miracle; some are edified by the triumph thus achieved by religion, others regret the days of joyous ballads and carnival songs; but all are equally emphatic as to the change in public manners, and acknowledge that it was solely the work of Frà Girolamo Savonarola.

71
72
74
75
76
79
80
83
87
88